Dengguo Feng, Yu Qin, Xiaobo Chu, Shijun Zhao
Trusted Computing

Advances in Computer Science

Volume 2

Dengguo Feng, Yu Qin,
Xiaobo Chu, Shijun Zhao

Trusted Computing

Principles and Applications

DE GRUYTER

清華大學出版社
TSINGHUA UNIVERSITY PRESS

This work is co-published by Tsinghua University Press and Walter de Gruyter GmbH.

Authors

Dengguo Feng
Yu Qin
Xiaobo Chu
Shijun Zhao
Institute of Software, Chinese Academy of Science.

ISBN 978-3-11-047604-0
e-ISBN (PDF) 978-3-11-047759-7
e-ISBN (EPUB) 978-3-11-047609-5
Set-ISBN 978-3-11-047760-3
ISSN 2509-7253

Library of Congress Cataloging-in-Publication Data
A CIP catalog record for this book has been applied for at the Library of Congress.

Bibliographic information published by the Deutsche Nationalbibliothek
The Deutsche Nationalbibliothek lists this publication in the Deutsche Nationalbibliografie; detailed bibliographic data are available on the Internet at http://dnb.dnb.de.

Typesetting: Integra Software Services Pvt. Ltd.
Printing and binding: CPI books GmbH, Leck
♾ Printed on acid-free paper
Printed in Germany

www.degruyter.com

Preface

With further development of computer network, the three most prominent threats are gradually highlighted, including attacks from malicious code, illegal stealing of information and illegal corruption of data and system. Within these threats, attacks from malicious code have surpassed traditional computer virus to be the predominant threat to private information of computer users. These threats originate from the situation that computer architecture lacks an immune system against malicious code. Thus, it is a core issue to accommodate immune system in computer architecture and ensure a computer platform to run securely and trustworthily.

Trusted computing is a kind of technique proposed under this background. By establishing a mechanism of integrity measurement, trusted computing enables computing platforms to distinguish between trusted programs and untrusted programs. In this way, computing platforms employ reliable countermeasures to prevent untrusted programs from disrupting.

I led a team starting research in trusted computing technique as early as 2003. Since 2006, I have been the chairman of TCMU (Trusted Cryptography Module Union) of China. I actively promote research, development and industrialization of trusted computing in China, and have achieved satisfactory results. Our team has taken a number of national research projects, including projects from Chinese 863 Program, industrialization projects of high technique from National Development and Reform Committee and major programs from National Natural Science Foundation. We have made breakthrough in several key aspects of trusted computing, including establishing and repairing technique of chain of trust, remote attestation protocol based on TCM and automatic generation method of test use cases based on reduction. We have also proposed a series of products, including advanced security supporting platform of trusted computing with self-owned intellectual property and test and evaluation system of trusted computing that supports compliance test, security test and performance test of trusted computing. These products have obtained good social and economic benefits now. Our research result "Research and Application on the Security Supporting Platform and Key Technique for Trusted Computing" achieved the first prize of Information Science Technique awarded by Chinese Institute of Electronics in 2010. In the future, we will continue our work and strive for better achievements and greater honor.

This book includes eight chapters. Chapter 1 is introduction. We introduce the research background, development status of technique and our contributions. Chapter 2 introduces trusted platform module, including TPM, TCM and MTM (Mobile Trusted Module). Chapter 3 focuses on establishing techniques of chain of trust, including root of trust, systems based on static and dynamic chain of trust and chain of trust in virtualization platforms. Chapter 4 discusses trusted software stack, including TSS (TCG Software Stack), TSM (TCM Service Module) and development of trusted application.

DOI 10.1515/9783110477597-202

Chapter 5 describes trusted computing platform, such as PC, server, trusted mobile platform, trusted virtualized platform and applications of trusted computing platform. Chapter 6 introduces test and evaluation of trusted computing, including test and evaluation of trusted platform module, analysis of trusted computing security mechanism, certification and evaluation of trusted computing and comprehensive test and analysis system of trusted computing platform. Chapter 7 introduces remote attestation, and Chapter 8 proposes trusted network connection.

The main content of this book comes from my formal monograph "Trusted Computing – Theory and Practice" (ISBN:9787302314226), which is written in Chinese and published by Tsinghua University Press in 2013. We've made our effort to translate the monograph,make corrections on its contents which are outdated and add a few new technologies, so as to present the highest quality collection of trusted computing technology. A group of my colleagues and doctor candidates have participated in writing and proofreading this book, including Yu Qin, Xiaobo Chu, Shijun Zhao, Jing Xu, Dexian Chang, Jianxiong Shao, Weijin Wang, Bo Yang, Bianxia Du and Wei Feng. We have also got great help from many researchers and editors. We want to express my sincere thanks to them here.

Dengguo Feng
March 17, 2017.

Contents

1 Introduction

With rapid development of cloud computing, Internet of Things and mobile Internet, information technology has changed society management and public life profoundly, and ubiquitous information has already been treated as important digital assets of a nation, an enterprise or a person. Considering widespread computer virus, malicious software and enhanced hacker technique, these important assets are facing more and more practical threats. It is no doubt a preferential security requirement from nation, enterprise and person that a trustworthy computing environment should be built to maintain confidentiality, integrity, authenticity and reliability of information. Traditional security technologies like firewall, IDS and virus defense usually focus on server-side computing platforms, thus relatively vulnerable client-side terminals are gradually becoming the weak link of an information system. Against these requirements and threats, trusted computing (TC) technology aims at establishing a trust transfer system by improving the security of computer architecture, so as to ensure the security of platform and solve the trust problem of man-to-program, man-to-computer and man-to-man.

Trusted computing is an emerging technology under this background. Up to now, there exist many different ways of understanding of "trusted." Several authoritative organizations, such as ISO/IEC, IEEE and TCG (Trusted Computing Group), have made efforts to establish their own explicit definitions [1–3]. TCG has further proposed a novel and widely accepted solution for enhancing security of computer system by embedding TPM (Trusted Platform Module) into hardware platform. In this book, our point of view is similar to that of TCG. We argue that a "trusted" computer system should always act in an expected way, and this property could be achieved by a trusted computing environment established upon a dedicated security chip.

Early in the middle of 1990s, some computer manufacturers began to research security solutions based on trusted computing technology. By adding a security chip into computer hardware, these solutions implement a series of mechanisms, such as the root of trust, secure storage and chain of trust, and achieve the secure goal of trusted computing environment. This kind of technical schemes was widely accepted by the IT industry, and as a result TCPA (Trusted Computing Platform Alliance, a mainstream industry alliance of trusted computing technique) was founded in 1999. After TCPA proposed TPM1.1 specifications in 2001, trusted computing products proposed by some mainstream IT manufacturers were gradually accepted by market and industry society. In 2003, TCPA was renamed to TCG and owned about 200 members, including nearly all international mainstream IT manufacturers. Technical specifications proposed by TCG had already formed a systematic architecture, which involves major IT areas like security chip, PC, server and network, and four core specifications were accepted as ISO standards in 2009. By 2010, TPM had already been a standard component of laptop and desktop, and mainstream PC-related manufacturers such as Microsoft and Intel also had adopted trusted computing in their core products.

DOI 10.1515/9783110477597-001

As a country with special security requirements and supervision rules, China has made achievement on both products and specifications of trusted computing. TCM, referred to as DNA of Chinese information security, is the most important contribution of China in trusted computing area. Upon its own cryptographic algorithm, China has established TCM-centered specification architecture of its trusted computing technology. Broadly speaking, development of Chinese trusted computing technology has undergone the following three phases.

From 2001 to 2005, China concentrated on tracking and absorbing concepts of TCG technology. Manufacturers like Lenovo and SinoSun published TCG-compliant products, and Work Group 1 of National Information Security Standardization Technical Committee (TC260) founded a special trusted computing workgroup that greatly impulsed trusted computing standard research.

From 2006 to 2007, China established architecture of its own trusted computing theory, technology and standards. In these years, China carried out research on trusted computing technical solution based on its own cryptography algorithms and proposed "cryptographic application scheme for trusted computing." China also set up a special workgroup on researching application of trusted computing technology. Later, this group changed its name to China TCM Union (TCMU). TCMU published TCM-centered specification "Technical Specification of Cryptographic Support Platform for Trusted Computing" [4] and "Functionality and Interface Specification of Cryptographic Support Platform for Trusted Computing" in December 2007.

After 2008, China focused on promoting its trusted computing industry. A series of TCM products have been put on the market and well accepted by governments, military troops and civilian areas. TCMU has nearly 30 members now, including Lenovo, Tongfang and NationZ, and has greatly given impulse to Chinese trusted computing industry with the support of Chinese government. Until 2010, TCMU established a comprehensive trusted computing industry system, including security chip, trusted computer, trusted network, trusted application and test/evaluation of trusted computing products. To promote industrialization of trusted computing, special committee of information security of China Information Industry Association has founded China Trusted Computing Union (CTCU) in 2008.

1.1 Related Work

The purpose of trusted computing technology is to improve computer architecture by introducing trusted computing security chip so as to enhance trustworthiness of common computing platform and network. TCG embeds TPM into PC or server's motherboard and provides several novel security mechanisms [5]. Microsoft has started NGSCB [6] plan. In NGSCB, a trusted execution environment based on microkernel is built to enhance Windows security and privacy. Meanwhile, Intel dedicates to TXT [7] hardware security technology to implement trusted computing through a series of hardware, including CPU, chipset and IO devices. China also manages to release its own security chip TCM, and establishes architecture of cryptographic supporting platform for trusted computing.

To sum up, trusted computing technology, driven by related industrial community, is undergoing a rapid development process. Meanwhile, academic community also carries out trusted computing research and makes achievements related to trust of platform, trust of network, test/evaluation of trusted computing and so on. Basic idea of related work is to establish trust in a single terminal platform, then to establish trust between platforms by remote attestation and finally to extend trust to network.

1.1.1 Security Chip

Current mainstream architecture of trusted computing technology and specification is proposed by TCG whose history can be traced back to 1990s. As the core of TCG trusted computing technology, TPM specifications, first published in 2001, have been modified and upgraded iteratively. TPM mainly acts as the root of trust in computing platform, provides key cryptographic functions and shielded storage locations and then builds a reliable computing platform with the help of other software/hardware. Currently, TPM specifications have already been accepted by most IT giants. TPM products, usually acting as the core component of trusted applications and services, have already been widely deployed in various laptops, desktops, servers and other kinds of computing platforms.

Chinese trusted computing specifications were published in 2007, and corresponding products have appeared on market since then. In general, TCM absorbs concept and architecture of international trusted computing technology, but there are great differences in the concrete design principle between these two kinds of products. On one hand, TCM adopts more secure and efficient elliptic curve cryptography (ECC) algorithms instead of RSA. On the other hand, TCM initiates several aspects of key technology for meeting Chinese local security and market requirements.

Recently, new trends in technology of security chip have emerged. In 2006, the specification of "Mobile Trusted Module" (MTM) was published by TCG mobile workgroup. Compared with TPM and TCM, MTM is more flexible in implementation and deployment and concerns more stakeholders. Obviously, it has been attached much importance that new security chip should be verifiable, upgradable and customizable. Furthermore, mainstream IT vendors propose several influential TC-related security technologies, including Intel TXT and ARM TrustZone. By complementing and coordinating each other, these new achievements constitute comprehensive technology architecture for establishing a reliable trusted execution environment.

1.1.2 Trust within a Terminal Platform

The main method to establish trust within a terminal platform is building a chain of trust. From the perspective of building time, building a chain of trust consists of two phases: trust boot and OS measurement. From the perspective of building method, the chain of trust can be categorized into static and dynamic ones. Up to now, most works in this aspect focus on OS measurement. Representatives of the early works include Copilot [8] and Pioneer [9], both relying on special peripherals to complete measurement. TCG proposes a method to build measurement system by using TPM as root of trust for common terminal platforms. Under the TCG architecture, IBM T.J. Watson research center proposes Integrity Measurement Architecture (IMA) [10] and Policy-Reduced IMA (PRIMA) [11]. CMU further gives BIND system [12], which is a fine-grained measurement architecture for distributed environment. Chinese researchers have also proposed their solutions [13, 14] based on IMA.

Another research area about trust of terminal is Trusted Software Stack (TSS). TSS is a kind of software that packs and abstracts TPM functionalities. It is one of the most important components in trust platform, and can be regarded as extension of trust functions from hardware to application layer. TCG has published TSS specifications, which define architecture and interfaces that TSS developers should follow. In 2005, IBM gave the first TCG-compliant TSS product – Trousers, which is regarded as fundamental open-source software in trusted computing area. Similar to IBM, IAIK in Austria and Sirrix AG in Germany developed jTSS and μuTSS for Java applications and mobile devices.

Based on the above technology, industrial community gradually releases products of trusted PC and server. Recently, two kinds of new trusted computing platforms have drawn more and more attention. On one hand, in the mobile trusted platform, researchers follow basic idea of MTM and present mobile terminals with trusted computing functions and characteristics. As an example, Samsung publishes TrustZone-based KNOX system in their mobile phone. On the other hand, in the virtualization trusted platform, researchers take full advantage of isolation to prevent critical software from being interfered, and present a batch of advanced technology schemes, such as LKIM [15], HIMA [16], HyperSentry [17] and vTPM [18]. LKIM and HIMA both leverage isolation mechanism in virtualization platform and implement integrity measurement by supervising memories of virtual machines (VM). HyperSentry further uses hardware mechanisms to implement measurement in a transparent manner. VTPM, presented by IBM, provides every virtual machine with a dedicated virtual TPM, which can be used to solve problem of resource conflict when sharing TPMs between virtual machines. Ruhr University enhances availability of vTPM by promoting vTPM to property-based TPM virtualization scheme [19]. The limitation of these two schemes is lack of effective binding between vTPM and TPM.

1.1.3 Trust between Platforms

Based on chain of trust for terminal, remote attestation is used to extend trust of local terminal platforms to remote terminal platforms. It can be divided into platform identity attestation and platform state attestation.

In the aspect of platform identity attestation, TPM v1.1 specification adopts a scheme based on Privacy CA, which authenticates platform through attestation identity key (AIK). Its limit lies in that anonymity cannot be perfectly achieved. To achieve anonymity, TPM v1.2 adopts Direct Anonymous Attestation (DAA) scheme based on CL signature [20, 21]. Ge and Tate further propose a more efficient DAA scheme for embedded device [22]. Researchers start to make DAA protocol research with ECC instead of RSA cryptography, so as to overcome shortcomings in literals [21, 22] like over length signature and massive computation. Brickel et al. propose the first DAA based on bilinear maps under LRSW assumption [23, 24], which greatly improves computation and communication performance. Chen and Feng make a step forward by designing a scheme under q-SDH assumption [25, 26]. Brickell and Chen alternate fundamental cryptography assumptions of existing DAA schemes, and thus significantly reduce TPM's computation in DAA [27, 28]. Performance of their schemes is simulated and analyzed on ARM CPUs [29].

In the aspect of platform state attestation, TCG recommends binary attestation method, and IBM implements a prototype system following this method [30]. This method is easy and reliable, but incurs poor scalability and configuration privacy. To counter these shortcomings, property-based attestation (PBA) alternates to attest security properties that are obtained by evaluating binary measurement values. IBM and Rulr University successfully propose their own PBA architectures [31, 32], and Chen then presents the first concrete PBA protocol [33], which achieves provable security in random oracle model and supports revocable property certificate and blinded verification. Chen also presents a PBA protocol without the trusted third party, which uses ring signature technology to hide configuration of platform into property sets [34]. Kühn et al. introduce an implementation method of PBA, which does not require any software/hardware modification [35]. Besides, Haldar et al. give semantic-based attestation [36]. This scheme attests semantic security of Java programs through using trusted virtual machine. CMU proposes software-based attestation [37] for embedded device. Li et al. convert platform configuration into history behavior sequence, and propose system behavior-based attestation [38].

1.1.4 Trust in Network

Considering popularization of Internet application, just establishing trust for terminals is not satisfiable. It is desirable to extend trust to network, and make the whole network into a trusted execution environment.

Cisco and Microsoft proposed their Network Access Control (NAC) [39] and Network Access Protection (NAP) [40] solutions. NAC advantages in connection control and supervision of network equipment, while NAP is good at terminal state evaluation and supervision. In 2005, TCG proposed Trusted Network Connection (TNC) architecture specification v1.0 [41], the main feature of which is introducing integrity of terminal into the decision of network connection access control. After 2005, TNC specifications have been updated continuously. In recent version, TNC incorporates Meta Access Point (MAP) and MAP client such that it can dynamically control network access according to change of metadata. Meanwhile, TNC also supports interoperation with NAP. Chinese researchers have also carried out research on trusted network based on TCG TNC [42].

Besides TNC, NAP and NAC, security protocols have also been improved. Current protocols such as SSL/TLS and IPSec only authenticate users' identities and ensure integrity and confidentiality of network data, but cannot authenticate terminals' integrity. Against this issue, IBM extends terminal integrity attestation to SSL [43]. In [43], terminal negotiates security parameters with trusted network, attests the integrity of platform configuration under SSL protocol with terminal integrity extension and finally establishes trusted channel between terminal and trusted network. Rulr University finds scheme in [43] may suffer man-in-the-middle attack. To solve the problem [44], researchers in Rulr University provide platform property certificate to bind SSL identity and AIK. Rulr University also implements TLS-compatible trust channel based on OpenSSL [45].

1.1.5 Test and Evaluation of Trusted Computing

In aspect of test and evaluation of trusted computing technology, research work appears in the fields of compliance test for TPM specifications, security mechanism analysis and products security evaluation.

As the name implies, compliance test aims at examining the compliance degree between concrete TPM products and specifications. It is one of the most important research directions in the trusted computing test and evaluation. In this aspect, Rulr University proposes the first TPM test solution [46]. Their scheme describes details of manual test, which is nonautomated and lacks quality analysis of test results. Chinese researchers are dedicated to automation of compliance test for TPM specifications [47, 48]. Based on the model of extended finite state machine (EFSM) of TPM/TCM, Institute of Software, Chinese Academy of Sciences (ISCAS) introduces a set of comprehensive methods, including test model, automatic generation method of test case and analysis method of test case quality. Effect and performance of these methods have been justified in practical test work upon real TPM/TCM products.

Analysis of trusted computing mechanism embodies traditional method of security protocol analysis in trusted computing area. Analysis objects of this research area are relatively abstract and theoretical part of trusted computing technology, mainly including protocols and critical mechanisms, such as authorization protocols (AP) in TPM/TCM, DAA, extending of PCR and establishing of chain of trust. Target of this kind of work is to theoretically detect defects in the protocols and mechanisms or to prove their security properties. Most work adopts formal method, which can be further divided into model checking and theorem proving. Up to now, Milan University, Rulr University, Carnegie Mellon University (CMU) and Institute of Software, Chinese Academy of Science have successfully found defects in TPM/TCM authorization protocols, DAA, chain of trust and key migration [49–54].

Evaluation of trusted computing products embodies importance of security engineering in the international information security area. According to the basic idea of security engineering, to ensure security of product, it is necessary that whole life cycle of products, including requirement analysis, designing, production and deployment, is under strict control and evaluation. TCG has already started evaluation projects of TPM [55] and TNC. According to the result of these projects, Infineon's SLB9635TT1.2 is the first TPM product passing the evaluation based on TPM protection profile [56, 57]. Meanwhile, seven TNC-related products from Juniper and Hochschule Hannover, including IC4500 access control suites, EX4200 switch and StrongSwan, have been certified by TCG.

Above all, current research achievements on trusted computing test and evaluation are relatively rare, and it needs to be improved in both coverage and deepness of trusted computing test and evaluation. First, in the aspect of test target, current works have only verified and analyzed small part of trusted computing products and security mechanisms. Most of trusted computing mechanisms, protocols and products, especially those emerging TC-related technologies mentioned below, are not concerned yet. Second, in the aspect of test level, current works reside in independent components of a computing platform, namely, research on overall security of computing platform is still scarce. Third, in the aspect of specification, only a few products like TPM can be tested according to test and function specifications. Most trusted computing products can only be tested and evaluated without any formal guidance. Some mechanisms, like chain of trust, even lack detailed function specifications.

1.2 Our Work

Research team led by author of this book has carried out in-depth and systematic research on key technologies of trusted computing. Our contributions can be concluded as follows.

First, in the aspect of trust model and chain of trust, we mainly focus on overcoming shortcomings of previous integrity measurement schemes, such as poor scalability and dynamics. We establish a trust model based on trust degree, and introduce methods of dynamic measurement on OS and recoverable trusted boot. We further implement these methods and manage to build a complete chain of trust prototype system, which covers the whole running process of a computer from terminal boot to application.

Second, in the aspect of remote attestation, we construct a novel pairing-based PBA and the first pairing-based DAA under q-SDH assumption. These important achievements significantly promote the research level of China on remote attestation protocol. Adoption of pairing has broadened the way of remote attestation research, and laid theory foundation for application of key technology of remote attestation.

Third, in the aspect of test/evaluation of trusted computing, we propose a reduction-based automatic test case generation method from the extended finite state machine. Based on this method, we further implement a test/evaluation system for trusted computing platform that supports compliance test for TPM/TCM specifications. It has already been used by test and evaluation authority in China. We also carry out work on formal analysis of TCM authorization protocol, and successfully find a replay attack against this protocol. These works have played an important role in improving security and quality of Chinese trusted computing products and standardizing Chinese trusted computing industry.

1.2.1 Chain of Trust

Establishing trust within a terminal platform is fundamental for building trust between platforms and in network, and has always been an active research field. For trust model, we comprehensively take into account influence of each boot-time component on overall trust, and propose a terminal trust model based on trust degree. For building methods of chains of trust, we propose efficient and secure measurement schemes for bootloader and OS, respectively. These schemes completely cover the whole computer running timeline from terminal boot to application running.

1.2.1.1 Trust Model Based on Trust Degree

To establish a trust on terminal platform, a trust model must be built to describe the way in which trustworthiness of any software, firmware and hardware can be ensured at both boot and running time. In TCG's architecture, computer boots from security hardware and authenticates each entity in boot process step by step so as to ensure trustworthiness at boot time. After that, computer could use access control method following BLP or BiBa model to ensure trustworthiness at running time. However, TCG is not fully concerned about environment that platform resides in, and trusted boot of any entities may be influenced by previously booted entities. Furthermore, ensuring trustworthiness by access control model may face some difficulties such as lacking reliable method to judge trust degree and lacking adaptability to change of trust degree; thus, TCG's method may be hard to implement and use. Given the above consideration, we propose a trust model [58, 59] based on trust degree. To figure out process to establish trust at boot time, we leverage the concept of trust degree to describe influence of booted entities on booting entities. Meanwhile, in order to figure out process to establish trust at runtime, we give out rules to dynamically adjust trust degree of entities at runtime and implement access control based on trust degree of entities.

1.2.1.2 Recoverable Trusted Boot

Chains of trust can hardly be recovered once corrupted at boot time, thus we propose a recoverable trusted boot scheme. The basic idea of this method is to verify the chain of trust established at boot time, check integrity of critical parts of OS such as kernel and key files and recover the OS by another secure system if the chain of trust is corrupted.

We implement a trusted boot subsystem based on this scheme. The system uses TPM/TCM as the root of trust, and extends common boot system with functions like system components measurement, verification, configuration and recovering. Once running, the system successfully measures all components running before OS using TPM/TCM, verifies established chain of trust before OS and checks integrity of critical system file and kernel of OS. If all checks pass, OS will be booted successfully. Otherwise, corrupted files will be recovered and the chain of trust will be rebuilt.

Trusted boot subsystem significantly enhances robustness of chain of trust in boot phase. Meanwhile, the recovery function only imposes a little influence on system performance, thus extra delay caused by the system is acceptable.

1.2.1.3 Chain of Trust within OS

The chain of trust within OS is much more complex than trusted boot. The main challenge is to design and implement an efficient measurement architecture. Existing architectures, such as IMA, suffer from coarse-grained measurement and TOCTOU (time of check, time of use) attacks. Against these problems, we propose component measurement [60] and dynamic measurement [61] for building the chain of trust on Windows/Linux. These methods could provide fine-grained and dynamic measurement functions on kernel modules, components and applications, so as to ensure load-time and runtime trustworthiness of these codes.

According to the above methods, we implement boot-time and runtime chain of trust on Windows/Linux [62]. We make OS measurement grain finer and verify system's security by several popular attacking experiments. The experiments show that our system could detect common attacks on integrity of system process at an affordable cost on system performance.

1.2.2 Remote Attestation

Remote attestation is an important security mechanism aiming at solving problems of trust between trusted computing platforms or nodes in trusted network. Remote attestation can be divided into platform identity attestation and platform state attestation. These two basic attestation models are similar. Participants in attestation include a trusted platform P with TPM/TCM as prover, a remote platform V as verifier and a trusted third party (TTP) T as supporting role. TPM/TCM and trusted third party act as trust anchor in this model: TPM/TCM guarantees platform's authenticity and trusted third party guarantees correctness of protocol.

Attestation protocol is the hotspot of current research on remote attestation. Main attestation protocols include DAA and PBA.

1.2.2.1 Direct Anonymous Attestation

Next Generation of DAA. Since RSA cryptography-based BCL DAA [21] appeared in 2004, groups of researchers dedicate to DAA protocol improvement. Elliptic curve cryptography is much more efficient than RSA and owns shorter private key and signature (at the same security level), thus ECC and pairing is more suitable for next generation of DAA. In 2008, we first adopted ECC to improve DAA and proposed next generation of DAA protocol [26, 63], which promoted performance of DAA and related research greatly.

Our scheme is based on q-SDH and DDH assumptions, and is one of the earliest q-SDH and pairing-based schemes. It is provable secure under idea-real system model. Compared with original DAA, its signature length is shortened by 10 % and its computation is also reduced significantly. We further propose a DAA protocol [64] based on improved BB signature [25], which nearly doubles computation efficiency of "join phase" of DAA. These works guide the direction of adopting q-SDH assumption to improve DAA protocol. Based on our work, a lot of following works have made continuous improvements on DAA protocol.

A Forward-Secure DAA. While designing DAA protocol, researchers mainly focus on user-controlled anonymity and user-controlled traceability, but pay little attention to the situation of leak of TPM internal secret, say f. Once f leaks, it not only corrupts all security properties of current DAA protocol instance but also influences previous DAA signatures. To solve this problem, we carry out extension research on DAA security and propose a forward-secure DAA [65]. This scheme not only satisfies all basic security requirements but also enhances platform anonymity when DAA secret leaks. This work is only the first step of extension research on DAA security research, and lots of problems still need to be solved.

Besides the above-mentioned improvements, we have also addressed other issues of DAA. We have researched on DAA that has anonymous authentication problem across several security domains, and proposed a cross-domain DAA scheme [66]. This scheme is expected to solve the problem across different security domains or TPMs from different vendors. We have also made continuous efforts in applying DAA in various special scenarios, including wireless terminals, mobile phones and other embedded devices, and designing of DAA protocols in these scenarios still needs further study.

1.2.2.2 Property-Based Attestation

Attestation of platform's integrity is one of the most important issues in trusted computing research. Within various solutions, property-based attestation (PBA) is the most promising and practical one. We carry out research on PBA systematically, and related works mainly lie in three aspects: attestation granularity, attestation performance and DAA-PBA-joint attestation [67, 68].

Fine-Grained Component-Based PBA. Traditional PBA [35] attests the property of whole platform. This kind of scheme is coarse-grained and faces some difficulties in practical application. For example, it is hard to issue and update property certificates for the whole platform if not impossible. To solve these problems, we propose a component-based PBA and implement a prototype [68]. The basic idea of this scheme is to convert requirements on platform property attestation into logic expressions about properties of related components, then prover only needs to attest property of each independent component. Through zero-knowledge proof method, attestation of component property proves that cryptographic commitments on components measurement meet requirements in components' property certificate.

The scheme is provable secure under random oracle model, and enjoys the following features: first, it is fine-grained, scalable and verifiable; second, no temporarily issued certificate is needed, and revocation and verification is efficient; third, privacy of platform configuration is well protected. This scheme moves a step forward on improving traditional PBA, and solves basic problems of PBA application in both aspects of protocol design and system implementation.

Paring-Based Efficient PBA. Traditional RSA-based PBA suffers from heavy computation of zero-knowledge proof and low performance. Thus, in [67], we construct an efficient PBA for TCM. This protocol shares the same security model with traditional protocols, and they all aim at proving unforgeability and configuration privacy. In the scheme, each platform configuration-property pair(cs, ps) has been issued with a property certificate $\sigma = (a, A, b, B, c)$ based on CL-LRSW and pairing. Through signature proof of knowledge method, a platform can prove that commitment on configuration value stored in TCM meets specific requests of platform's property.

The scheme leverages pairing to simplify PBA, and is provably secure in signature unforgeability and privacy of configuration. Compared with RSA-based PBA, the scheme also reduces computation by nearly 32 % and shortens signature length by about 63 %.

DAA-PBA-Joint Attestation Protocol. DAA and PBA concern platform anonymity and configuration privacy, respectively, and they can be combined in practical application to achieve better result. That is, both DAA and PBA can be conducted in a single attestation process. Literature [69] gives a joint attestation scheme. Its basic idea is embedding anonymous authentication into property attestation process. In detail, trusted third party first verifies platform's anonymous identity, and then issues a compound certificate (f, cs, ps)about anonymous identity and configuration-property pair. In this way, a single attestation process achieves the goals of both DAA and PBA, which no doubt enjoys a better performance.

1.2.3 Trusted Network Connection

Most current research on trusted network is based on TCG TNC architecture. Through verifying integrity and authenticity of terminals, TNC architecture ensures trustworthiness of identity and running state of terminals, and further ensures trustworthiness of the whole network. However, TNC still has some disadvantages. First, privacy of terminal is not well protected. Second, interaction between TNC entities has not been protected by secure protocols. Third, a terminal is not continuously supervised after connected. For the terminal privacy protection on connecting time, we propose a TNC-based anonymous access scheme [70] for network connection. The scheme is implemented in two concrete forms in our prototype: an IpTables-based system in IP layer, and an 802.1x-based system in data link layer. Both kinds of implementation share the same architecture, which consists of access connecting terminal, network access control server and enforcement point of network access control, as is shown in Figure 1.1. In this architecture, enforcement point transmits authentication

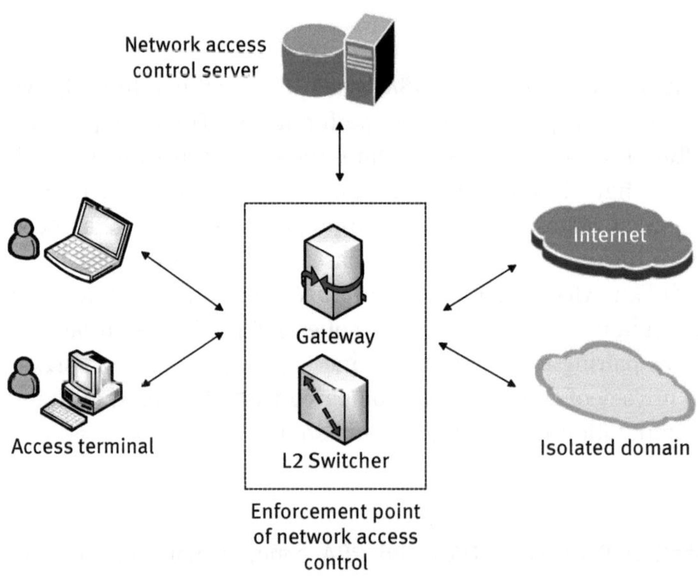

Figure 1.1: Architecture of TNC.

messages between connecting terminal and network access control server, and enforces the access policy given by network access control server. Enforcement point is implemented as a secure gateway in IP layer of TNC architecture, or as a switch supporting VLAN isolation in data link layer of TNC architecture. According to AR's identity and integrity, PDP gives the decision result of network access control. When an AR conforms to access control policy, it is allowed to connect to network. Otherwise, it is only allowed to connect to an isolated domain. In this way, network access control is realized based on identity and integrity.

For terminal privacy protection, we propose an anonymous TNC scheme based on TCG TNC and DAA. Before connecting to network, terminal should apply for an anonymous credential DAA Cert from platform identity issuer. We extend the fourth and sixth steps of current TCG TNC work flow (platform certificate verification phase) [41], so as to implement network connection in an anonymous style. In the fourth step, terminal computes signature of knowledge according to DAACert, and sends this signature to platform identity issuer for an authentication credential of anonymous identity key. In the sixth step, terminal uses the authenticated identity key to sign the measurement value of platform, and then platform identity issuer will verify authenticity of anonymous identity and correctness of integrity measurement.

In general, TNC extends terminal trust to network but does not concern about protection of terminal identity privacy. Our TNC system combines TNC and DAA, so as to effectively supervise terminals while protecting their privacy. It meets the security requirement of network connection in open environment.

1.2.4 Application of Trusted Computing

Trusted computing is now widely applied in many areas such as secure PC, trusted network, trusted storage and DRM. We mainly focus on trusted storage and trusted usage control for ensuring data confidentiality and freshness and implementing access control administration of data in a trusted style.

1.2.4.1 Trusted Storage

In TCG architecture, trusted storage is mainly implemented by sealing function of TPM. When TPM seals data, it encrypts the data and binds data with system configuration (in PCR), so as to ensure confidentiality of data. Due to the frequent change of software/hardware in PC and server, sealed data are easily inclined to be unavailable in practical application, and TCG sealing scheme often suffers from poor scalability. To handle this situation, we propose a property-based sealing scheme for virtualization platform [71]. In this scheme, a TPM is multiplexed by several virtual machines to protect their data security, and properties are organized in hierarchical and graded manner to enhance operational flexibility of sealed data. Every VM has a set of virtual PCRs (vPCR) to store its system configuration. While sealing data, sealing proxy first transforms VM configuration into properties and extends these properties into PCRs, and then TPM seals the data with the properties. While unsealing data, sealing proxy compares security level of current VM's property with that of sealed property. Only when security level of VM's property is relatively higher, proxy extends the properties into resetTab.PCR and invokes TPM to unseal data. That is to say, sealed data can only be accessed when security level of VM's property does not degrade.

Another feature at hardware level of TCG trusted storage is that data can be bound with TPM's monotonic counter, which is critical for ensuring data's freshness and preventing replay attack. But due to limited production cost, very few counters are provided to meet freshness requirement of massive data storage. Thus, we propose a novel virtual monotonic counter scheme [72]. In this scheme, virtual monotonic counters are constructed based on physical counters in TPM, and security properties of virtual counters like monotonic growth and tamper resistance are guaranteed by hardware TPM. In detail, creation and increment operations of virtual counters will trigger real increment operations on physical counters, and these real operations are protected by TPM transport session. Because log of transport session records all operations on TPM counters and corresponding virtual ones, virtual and physical counters are strictly bound.

1.2.4.2 Trusted Usage Control

In distributed applications, data can be accessed both locally and remotely; thus, it is desired that data should be mused according to its owner's policy, no matter where data actually locate. Thus we implement a trusted usage control system [73, 74], which concerns not only local access control but also data and policy's security after they are distributed. Through enhancing expressiveness of policy language and introducing policy enforcer into remote data user's platform, we guarantee that remote data user could only use the data according to policy designated by data owner.

In our system, integrity of user's platform needs to be verified when data are distributed to the user. During the distribution process, the security of data and policy as well as configuration privacy of data user's platform should be protected. We leverage TLS to guarantee confidentiality and authenticity of data and policy. We further adopt key authentication method to verify configuration of data user's platform, without corrupting privacy of platform's configuration [73]. In detail, data owner will designate a trusted configuration set S, and any configuration in this set is considered to conform to owner's security policy. Then data user sends an encryption key K to owner and attests that this key is bound to certain configuration C in S. The attestation method is carefully designed so as to not reveal any concrete information about configuration. Finally, data user gets the data encrypted by K, and are forced to decrypt the data in condition that system's configuration is C.

Against concrete application, we also make effort on solving technical problems of trusted usage control in practice, and utilize our trusted usage control system to further propose a TPM-based DRM scheme [75] and a layer usage control scheme of digital content [76].

1.2.5 Test and Evaluation of Trusted Computing

Test and evaluation is now a hotspot in trusted computing research field. Our work includes three aspects. First, we carry out research on automatic compliance test for TPM/TCM specification. Compared with traditional manual method, automatic scheme advantages in low cost and high performance. Furthermore, this scheme supports good analysis of test result (such as statistics on test coverage) and facilitates quantification of trustworthiness of test results. Second, we carry out research on analysis and evaluation of trusted computing protocols, especially model checking-based analysis of TCM authorization protocols, and successfully find their defects. Third, we implement a comprehensive test system of trusted computing platform, and it is the first practical trusted computing test system in China. This section will summarize key points in these works, and further contents could be found in Section 1.1.5.

1.2.5.1 Automatic Compliance Test for TPM/TCM Specification

In compliance test for TPM/TCM specification, main difficulty lies in automation and quality analysis of test result. Against this situation, we make breakthrough in the following three points [77, 78].

First, in the aspect of TPM test model, we use standard specification language to describe TPM v1.2 so as to avoid ambiguity and error in specification. We further give an EFSM-based test model through analyzing TPM functions and lay the foundation of automation test.

Second, in the aspect of automatic compliance test method, we use a two-phase test case generation method. Through splitting test phase, we significantly reduce test complexity and promote degree of automation of test. Furthermore, test workload and the interferences of artificial factor on test result are reduced.

Third, in the aspect of quality analysis of test cases, we use reachability tree to accurately evaluate test quality. Through clarifying relationship between quantity and coverage of test cases, we can choose appropriate test case generation policy, and thus provide sufficient evidence of trustworthiness of test result.

1.2.5.2 Analysis of TCM Authorization Protocol

TCM authorization protocol is critical for protecting TCM internal secrets. Because Chinese specifications of trusted computing are published at a relatively late time, works on analysis of this protocol are just starting out. We propose the first work on security analysis of AP protocol using model choking, and successfully find replay attacks on this protocol.

We first use symbolic model to describe AP, which eliminates ambiguity. Then, we set assumptions about cryptography and attackers, and use PROMELA to describe participants' behaviors and protocol properties, that is, honest participants' sessions must match. Finally, we input description of protocol and properties into SPIN and find a theoretical replay attack against AP. By taking certain security countermeasures, this attack can be well prevented.

1.2.5.3 Comprehensive Test/Evaluation System of Trusted Computing Platform

Comprehensive test/evaluation system of trusted computing platform is a suite of systems for testing, analyzing and emulating security chip, cryptography algorithms and protocols. Main functions of the system include compliance test on security chip and trusted software, correctness and performance test on cryptography algorithms and simulation of trusted computing protocols. The system is scalable and effective in testing work, and as the first comprehensive test system of trusted computing in China, it has already been put into practice in Chinese authority of test and evolution on information security product. In practical testing works on Chinese trusted computing products, this system has successfully detected defects of TCM products, such as noncompliance with specifications and poor interoperability. The system also finds incompleteness and ambiguity of Chinese specifications in the aspects of key management, key authentication, command audit, counter and locality. We argue that all defects should be carefully considered for future specification updating.

1.3 Problems and Challenges

As an emerging security technology, trusted computing has already been a research hotspot. Mainstream desktop and laptop products in both China and international area have all been equipped with TPM or TCM. Though trusted computing industry has made great progress, there are still many problems to be solved in both theoretical and technical aspects [79]. As pointed out by Chinese experts in 2007, there are still barriers in five aspects for trusted computing development [80]. As research of trusted computing deepens in recent years [81, 82], breakthrough has already been made in theoretical and key technical aspects of some of these problems.

There is no doubt that trusted computing is a kind of technology with broad prospects, but in practice, it is not "catholicon" to solve all IT security problems. There are still challenges and barriers for pervasive applications. First, research on theoretical model for trusted computing is still rare, and nearly no progress has been made in recent years. Second, trusted computing chip is too complex, and its compatibility and specification compliance need to be improved. Third, the key technology of trusted computing such as integrity measurement suffers from poor scalability and complexity for administration. Fourth, trusted computing has not been deeply merged with other security mechanisms of OS, network and application.

We believe that bottleneck of trusted computing will eventually be broken through with the deepening of related research and developing of information security technology. In other words, we regard trusted computing as a breakthrough direction for future information security technology.

1.4 Structure of This Book

This book includes eight chapters and one appendix. The first chapter is the introduction of background, state-of-the-art and our work on trusted computing. Chapter 2 introduces security chips, including TPM, TCM and mobile modules. Chapter 3 explains technology for establishing chains of trust, such as root of trust, static chain of trust, dynamic chain of trust and chains of trust for virtualization platform. Chapter 4 presents trusted software stack, including TSS, TSM and development of trusted application. Chapter 5 introduces various trusted computing platforms, such as PC, server, mobile platform, virtualization platform and application of trusted computing platform. Content of test and evaluations that is mentioned above, such as TPM/TCM test, analysis of critical trusted computing mechanisms, evaluation of trusted computing product and comprehensive test system, will be further explained in Chapter 6. Chapter 7 presents remote attestation, and finally in Chapter 8 TNC is detailed. Last but not least, algorithms and preliminaries used in trusted computing will be illustrated in appendix.

2 Trusted Platform Module

In today's society, various types of computing platforms have been applied to the social, economic and military fields. The increasing complexity of computing platforms and sharp increase in the number of their defects and vulnerabilities lead to frequent attacking and tampering with computing platforms. It can be said that the security of computing platforms has great relationship with all aspects of the individual privacy to national interests.

Traditional security solutions are realized either in pure software form or by using the dedicated hardware devices. The former can be easily affected by network communication or other software running on the computing platforms. It is unable to defend the platforms against existing security threats [83]. Although the latter is more secure, it has disadvantages such as high costs and heterogeneity of the different products. In addition, the traditional security solutions rarely consider attestation to be trustworthy. However, the platform attestations to remote verifiers are essential to new applications such as the e-commerce.

In summary, it is necessary to introduce a new type of security hardware in the computing platforms. Based on this hardware, the trusted computing platforms can be built and their trustworthiness can be attested to remote verifiers. In order to popularize this technology, the introduced hardware must meet the following two requirements. First, it should be economical and not alter the existing computer architecture to balance the security, usability and economical factor. Second, the authoritative industry organizations or governments should define a set of unified technical specifications, so as to ensure the interoperability of products from different manufacturers.

Since 2001, Trusted Computing Group (TCG) [3] has released a series of trusted computing specifications, especially the Trusted Platform Module (TPM) specifications version 1.1 (2001) and version 1.2 (2003) [5], mainly for the PCs and servers. The specifications specify the functionalities, interfaces, security features and implementations of the hardware-based security module. TCG also has launched the Mobile Trusted Module (MTM) specifications [84] for the new application environments such as mobile platforms, which enriches and improves the trusted computing standard architecture.

Trusted Cryptography Module Union (TCMU) [85] is an organization of the Chinese IT industry manufacturers under the leadership of the Chinese government agencies such as Office of Security Commercial Code Administration. TCMU has proposed a series of trusted computing specifications that take the Trusted Cryptography Module (TCM) as the core of the cryptographic support platform for trusted computing. In 2007, TCMU developed the Functionality and Interface Specification of Cryptographic Support Platform for Trusted Computing [86].

DOI 10.1515/9783110477597-002

In this chapter we first describe the design goals of the trusted platform module[1] according to the TCG specifications, TCM specifications and the latest academic research. Then we describe in detail the main functionalities and security features of several typical trusted platform modules, such as TPM, TCM and MTM, according to the different application environments and specific requirements. Finally, we give a brief description of several new security technologies and their impacts on the trusted platform module.

2.1 Design Goals

Trusted platform module is the foundation of the trusted computing platforms. Its design goals can be divided into two aspects. First, the trusted platform module itself must be secure, which is the basis of its effective working. Second, the trusted platform module must have all kinds of functionalities for trusted computing platforms and remote attestations. These functionalities are the core of the trusted platform module.

The trusted platform module itself must be secure. That is, it should provide reliable security protection for storage and computing. First, it should protect the confidentiality and integrity of the critical data such as the keys, and prevent external tampering. Second, it should ensure the effective execution of functions to avoid external interference. In order to reduce the costs and then to improve the popularity, the trusted platform module degrades the security level to resist hardware attack, and only requires the ability of detecting software attacks and retaining the attack evidence. Therefore, the trusted platform module provides neither tamper resistance nor tamper response, but tamper evidence. This level of security is enough to deal with the vast majority of the security threats in reality, especially the security threats in cyberspace.

The trusted platform module should have all kinds of functionalities required for the trusted computing platforms and remote attestations. The trusted platform module is based on key management and data encryption and decryption, takes the core concept of characterizing security and trust by integrity and provides the functionalities to establish the chain of trusty of the platforms and to do remote attestations. If the measurement value of binary program code is identical to the standard value and it is executed without interference, the program is trusted. Furthermore, if all programs have run or are running on the computing platform with legitimate integrity, the computing platform is trusted. In summary, the functionalities of the trusted platform module should include the following:

- Platform data protection: It includes the basic cryptographic functions, such as the key management and data encryption and decryption, and the data sealing function that combines the encryption and integrity protection.

1 In the following, the term "Trusted Platform Module" not only covers the TCG-TPM security chips but also includes the TCM and the MTM.

- Integrity storage and reporting: The integrity measurement value indicates the important information that represents the security and trust of the program and the platform. Thus, it should be stored in the trusted platform module. In addition, the trusted platform module should be able to attest and report the authenticity of the integrity measurement value by using the digital signature.
- Identification: The identity key of the trusted platform module should be used to sign the integrity measurement value in the integrity reporting. The identity key should be certified by the trusted third party before use. The trusted platform module should be able to apply for and manage this kind of key.

Note that it is not possible to achieve the goal of establishing the trusted computing environment and remote attestation by just relying on the trusted platform module itself. In a complete trusted computing architecture, the trusted platform module only acts as the root of trust for storage and reporting. The functionalities that are closely related to the applications or might lead to high cost and bad usability should be implemented by other entities on the platform. For example, integrity collection of the platform is implemented by hardware and software in platforms such as BIOS or CPU. Without affecting the security of the platform, this design can reduce the cost of the trusted platform module and the impact on the existing computer architecture as much as possible.

2.2 TPM Security Chip

2.2.1 Introduction

In this section, we first introduce the TCG specifications to explain the role of the TPM security chip and the relationships between the TPM and the other components in the platform. Next, we explain the internal logic functionalities and the detailed hardware composition of the TPM. The part of the logic functionalities can be regarded as an outline of Sections 2.2.2–2.2.6. Finally, we describe the external hardware and software interfaces of TPM, including the TPM commands and the integrated method between the TPM and the motherboard.

2.2.1.1 TCG Specification Architecture

In 1999, the international IT industry giants set up the Trusted Computing Platform Alliance (TCPA), and in 2003, it was succeeded by the TCG. Approximately 200 companies have joined TCG, including almost all IT industry giants. It has a dominant position in the industry. Since 2001, TCG (TCPA) has published a series of trusted computing specifications. After years of development, TCG trusted computing specifications have formed a complete architecture:

- PC Client Specification [87] and Generic Server Specification [88]: define the functionalities and the security features of the computing platform from a hardware perspective.
- TPM Specification [5]: defines the functionalities and the features of the security chip.
- TIS Specification [87]: defines the integrated method between TPM and host platform.
- TSS Specification [89]: defines the software stack from the TPM driver to the application layer interface, providing users with easily accessible interfaces.
- TNC Specification [90]: defines the system architecture, operational principles and standard interfaces of the trusted network connection.
- MTM Specification [84]: defines the functionalities, security features and the interfaces of the root of trust for the mobile platforms, but do not restrict the form of implementation. TSS and TNC specifications can also be applied to the mobile platforms.

As the core of TCG specifications, the TPM specification versions 1.2 and 2.0 were released in 2003 and 2014, respectively. In 2009, version 1.2 was adopted as an international standard [91] by the International Organization for Standardization (ISO) and it was updated to version 2.0 [92] in 2015. TPM 2.0 specification has some significant adjustments to the previous version, such as the addition of support for the elliptic curve cryptography and some higher security levels.

2.2.1.2 TPM Internal Components

The logic functionalities of the TPM are described in Figure 2.1. According to the TPM specifications, the TPM functionalities can be divided into the following categories:

- Cryptographic system: It implements cryptographic engine with algorithms such as encryption, digital signature, hash function and random number generator. It is an internal functional module that does not provide external interfaces. Most TPM functionalities are built upon the cryptographic system.

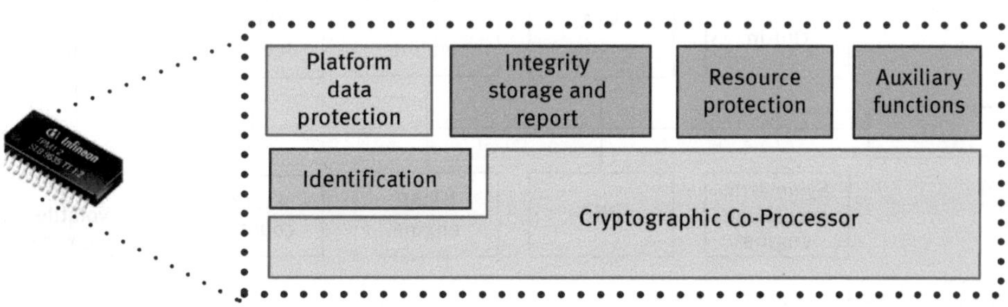

Figure 2.1: TPM functionalities.

- Platform data protection: It provides key management and the protection of confidentiality and integrity of all kinds of data. It is directly based on the cryptographic engine. The computing platform can use it to build cryptographic service provider. It is the basic application of the TPM security chip.
- Identification: It provides the application and management of the identity key certificate, which is the basis of remote attestation (integrity reporting to the remote verifier).
- Integrity storage and reporting: It provides the storage and signing (reporting) of the integrity measurement value, which directly embodies the "trust." The computing platform can use it to establish a chain of trust for the platform and to do the remote attestation. It is the main application of the TPM security chip.
- Resource protection: It provides the access control to the TPM internal resources.
- Auxiliary functions: It provides the support for TPM functions. The computing platform can use these functions to set the way TPM boots and runs and improve convenience of TPM operations. They can also be used to protect the communications between the applications and the TPM and obtain the trusted timestamps and counters.

The major TPM component architecture is described in Figure 2.2. The internal components include the cryptographic functional module, nonvolatile and volatile memory, I/O, power detection, clock, counters and opt-in:

- Opt-in: It provides the storage and maintenance of the state of flags (including owned/unowned, enabled/disabled and activated/deactivated) that are closely related to the TPM routine works.
- RSA Cryptographic Engine: According to the standard PKCS#1, it provides the RSA cryptographic algorithms for data encryption and decryption, digital signature and verification. It supports three security levels: 2048 bits (recommended), 1024 bits and 512 bits.

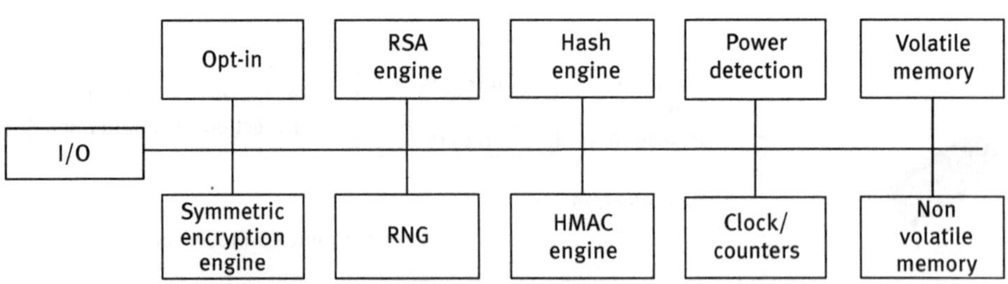

Figure 2.2: TPM hardware architecture.

- Symmetric encryption engine: The mandatory mechanism is a Vernam one-time pad that is generated by MGF1 key derivation algorithm. Advanced Encryption Standard (AES) may be supported as an alternative symmetric key encryption algorithm.
- Random number generator (RNG): According to IEEE P1363, it generates the nonce in the protocol and the keys of the symmetric encryptions.
- Hash engine: According to the standard FIPS-180-1, it adopts the SHA1 algorithm as the hash function.
- Nonvolatile memory: It provides the storage of the TPM persistent keys such as the Endorsement Key (EK) and the Storage Root Key (SRK), integrity information, the owner's authorization value and a few important application data.
- Volatile memory: It provides the storage of the temporary data in the computation.
- Power detection: It provides the management of the TPM power states, and supports physical presence assertions. The latter is essential to the techniques depending on physical signal such as the DRTM.
- I/O: It manages the communications between the TPM and the external entities, and between the TPM internal components. The I/O component can encode, decode and forward messages and enforce access control on modules.

2.2.1.3 TPM External Interfaces

TPM provides the interfaces to the upper level of the software. They are TPM commands in the TPM specifications. Although the TPM commands are different at logic level, the sequence of their parameters follows a unified rule, which simplifies the process of the TPM. In the following, we give an example to explain the unified structure.

As described in Table 2.1, the input parameters of all the TPM commands can be divided into three parts: the command header, the command-specific parameters and the authorization data. The structure of output parameters is similar to that of input parameters, so we do not repeat it.

- Command header: It is used to indicate whether the parameters are input or output, type of the authorization protocol, length and command type. The metadata of all the commands is composed of command tag, size of parameters (*paramSize*) and ordinal.
- Command-specific parameter: It is used to pass the external data required for TPM computation, or to indicate the TPM internal resources used by the TPM command. It includes the specific parameters used by the logic of the TPM command. The following example contains three command-specific parameters: *keyHandle*,

Table 2.1: The example of command parameters.

Parameter		HMAC		Type	Name
#	**Size**	**#**	**Size**		
1	2			TPM_TAG	tag
2	4			UINT32	paramSize
3	4	1S	4	TPM_COMMAND_CODE	ordinal
4	4			TPM_KEY_HANDLE	keyHandle
5	1	2S	1	BOOL	inArgOne
6	<>	3S	<>	BYTE[]	inArgTwo
7	4			TPM_AUTHHANDLE	authHandle
		2H	20	TPM_NONCE	authLastNonceEven
8	20	3H	20	TPM_NONCE	nonceOdd
9	1	4H	1	BOOL	continueAuhSession
10	20			TPM_AUTHDATA	inAuth

inArgOne of type BOOL with length 1 and *inArgTwo* of type BYTE[] with a variable length.

- Authorization Data[2]: It is used to prove to the TPM that the user has the permission to use the TPM internal resources (*keyHandle* in the example) specified in the input parameters. The authorization data of all the commands are composed of five parameters: the handle of the authorization session *authHandle*, two nonces*authLashNonceEven*[3] and *nonceOdd*, the session continuous flag *continueAuthSession* and the authdata value *inAuth*[4].

TCG does not specify the implementation form of the TPM integration interfaces. It only requires that the TPM must be strictly bound with the root of trust for measurement (RTM). (In fact, it requires TPM should be bound with the computing platform.) Manufacturers are able to implement this binding in physical way (e.g., embedding the TPM into the motherboard) or in cryptographic way (e.g., communicating by a pre-shared key between the TPM and BIOS). When the TPM is successfully embedded into the computing platform, the platform vendor or the trusted third party can issue a "platform certificate" for the computing platform. This certificate asserts that the

2 In order to simplify the internal structure and reduce the cost of the chip, the TPM specification restricts that at most two authorization sessions can be used in the same command. It might use no authorization.

3 *authLastNonceEven* is not the input (empty in the column Parameter). It is only used in the computation of *inAuth*.

4 *inAuth* is compute by using other authorization parameters. The computing method is described in the following sections. The column HMAC labels whether or not the corresponding parameter is used to compute *inAuth* and indicates the ordinal.

computing platform is a genuine one with certain hardware TPM and stratifies some specific features.

In recent years, researchers have found that the binding of the TPM and the computing platform has no benefit for some usage (such as key storage and management). They began to study the portable mobile TPM. For these results, their application scenarios are scarce and they cannot form an influential research trend. Thus, we omit them here.

2.2.2 Platform Data Protection

The functions of platform data protection include key management, data storage and data migration. For the key management, the limitation of TPM internal memory is the main problem. TCG designs the protected storage hierarchy to solve this problem. For the data storage, the TPM provides the traditional encryption and the sealing operation that bind the platform integrity. For data migration, TCG developed a mechanism that allows the data to migrate between different platforms. This mechanism establishes links between protected storage hierarchies in different platforms.

2.2.2.1 Key Management

Key Type. In order to facilitate the key management and enhance the security, TPM provides the following key types:

- Identity key: It identifies the TPM and the computing platform. It is mainly used to quote the platform integrity measurement value, that is, the integrity reporting.
- Binding key: It is used for data encryption and decryption.
- Signing key: It is used to sign the user-selected data. It can also be used to quote the platform integrity measurement value. It is different from the identity keys because the ordinary signing keys do not have the identity key certificate and its security can only be certified by another key.
- Storage key: It is used to protect other keys, or to seal data into the computing platform.
- Legacy key: It has the features of both binding key and signing key. In general, it is not recommended to use this key, unless the cryptographic scheme requires that a key must be used for both signing and encrypting.
- Migrate key: When the TPM plays the role of the Migration Authority (MA), this kind of key is used to protect the migrated key. Note that this kind of key is different from the Migratable Key.

Protected Storage Hierarchy. As shown in Figure 2.3, TCG utilizes the protected storage hierarchy for key management to protect the security of the TPM key,

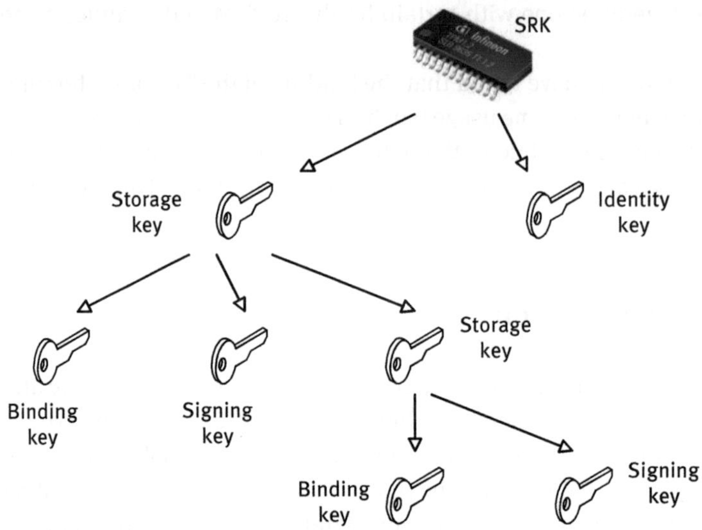

Figure 2.3: TPM protected storage hierarchy.

especially the key stored outside TPM. The protected storage hierarchy is a logic tree structure implying the protection relationship. It is composed of the storage key and the protected key objects. The root of the tree is the Storage Root Key (SRK), which is stored in the TPM nonvolatile memory and never used outside the TPM. The leaf nodes are protected objects, including keys, sealed data, nonvolatile memory and counters. The non-leaf nodes except the SRK are all storage keys. For any storage key or protected objects to be created in the TPM, an existing storage key (in the protected storage hierarchy) must be designated as the protection key. If the TPM does not load any key, the SRK can be used as the protection key. If the TPM has created a storage key, it can be loaded and used as the protection key.

The TPM commands for key creating, loading and clearing are as follows:

- *TPM_CreateWrapKey*: This command is used to generate a TPM key.[5] Its input mainly includes the parent key of the new key and the key authorization data. Its output mainly includes the public key in plaintext form and the encrypted key blob (including the private key, the key type and algorithm).
- *TPM_LoadKey*: This command is used to load the key into the TPM. Its input mainly includes the parent key handle. Its output is the loaded key handle.
- *TPM_FlushSpecific*: This command is used to clear the key out of the TPM. Its input mainly includes the key handle and the key type. In the TPM 1.1

5 The creating and loading of the identity key and the certified migration key are special. We describe it in the following sections.

specification, the command *TPM_EvictKey* achieves the similar functionality. It has been deprecated.

2.2.2.2 Encryption and Sealing

Encryption and decryption are basic functionalities for data storage. In order to reduce the cost, the TPM only provides functionalities of asymmetric decryption and the access to public keys. The corresponding commands include the following:

- *TPM_UnBind*: Its input includes the key handle and the encrypted data blob. Its output is the plaintext.
- *TPM_GetPubKey*: Its input includes the key handle. The TPM outputs the public key. If the user needs to perform encryption, it can use this command to get the public key, and then use the software (such as trusted software stack) to encrypt the data.[6]

In addition to the data decryption function, the TPM also provides the function to seal data. It is a special kind of encryption function to bind the secret data to a certain platform configuration. The sealed data are kept secret during the storage. It can be unsealed only on a platform with the specific configuration. The data sealing function embodies the integrity and trust in the aspect of data protection. It is also one of the most characteristic functions of TCG technological hierarchy. It is of great significance to build the trusted computing environment. The corresponding commands include the following:

- *TPM_Seal*: Its input includes the handle of the storage key, the PCR value[7] (identifies the platform configuration), data to be sealed and the authorization data for usage. The TPM outputs the sealed data blob.
- *TPM_Sealx*: It has the same function as the command *TPM_Seal*, but with the new data structure introduced by the TPM 1.2 specification.
- *TPM_UnSeal*: Its input includes the handle of the storage key and the sealed data blob. TPM checks whether the current PCR value matches the one specified in the sealed blob. Only if they are the same, the TPM can perform the decryption operation and output the data. Note that *TPM_UnSeal* is one of the few commands in the TPM specification that need two authorization data. It needs the authorization for both the storage key and the sealed data blob.

Similar to the data sealing, there is another mechanism that can restrict the data decryption operation under the specific platform configuration. When the key is created by using the command *TPM_CreateWrapKey*, it requires that the key can be used only if the platform is in a specified configuration. Thus, if the data are encrypted

---

6 The user can record the public key, when the key is created.

7 PCR is the simplification of the Platform Configuration Register.

by a key bound with a specific configuration, they can only be used under this specified platform configuration. It can be said that this mechanism is a kind of "implicit sealing."

2.2.2.3 Key Migration

Key migration is used for migrating a key generated by a TPM (the source TPM) to the protected storage hierarchy of another TPM (the target TPM). The main application of the function is the key duplication and backup. In the key migration, TPM requires the user to provide the migration authorization value of the key, which is set in the creation of the key. If the key is created as a migratable key, its migration authorization value should be specified. If it is non-migratable, a TPM random number is specified as the "migration authorization value," which users cannot know. Thus, when a user tries to migrate a non-migratable key, the migration aborts because the authorization value is incorrect. The key migration has two ways: REWRAP and MIGRATE.

REWARP. The REWRAP way is used when the key is to be migrated to a deterministic target TPM. It has two steps (the migration key is denoted by MK). (1) Creation of the migration blob: The source TPM obtains the public key (denoted by PK) of the key in the target TPM, which is used to protect the migration key. Then it uses PK to encrypt MK. (2) Conversion of the migration blob: The target TPM uses the corresponding private key of PK to decrypt and obtains MK. TPM provides the commands *TPM_AuthorizeMigrationkey* and *TPM_CreateMigrationBlob* for step 1. The former is used by the owner[8] of the source TPM to select PK, and the latter is used to re-encrypt MK with PK as the input. Logically, the two commands in step 1 can be merged. However, the command after the merging needs three authorizations (the owner authorization of the source TPM for selecting the PK, the migration authorization of MK and the authorization of the parent key of MK for decrypting the blob), which violates the design principle that any TPM command needs at most two authorizations. TPM provides the command *TPM_ConvertMigrationBlob* for step 2.

MIGRATE. In the scenarios where the target TPM has not been determined, such as the key backup scenario, it needs to introduce the so-called MA as the third party to temporarily escrow keys, such that in the future it can be migrated to the target TPM. This migration is called the MIGRATE way. It needs the following three steps:

(1) Creation of the migration blob: The source TPM obtains a public key (denoted by PK_{MA}) from MA, and uses PK_{MA} to encrypt MK. In order to prevent the prying of a malicious MA, the source TPM can use the one-time pad way to encrypt MK before it uses PK_{MA} to encrypt it. The key for one-time pad can be stored and passed to the target TPM in an out-of-band way.

8 Namely, the administrator of the TPM. We explain it in the following sections.

(2) Delivery of the migration blob: MA decrypts the blob to get MK. It obtains the public key (denoted by PK_{DT}) from the target TPM, and then uses PK_{DT} to encrypt MK.
(3) Conversion of the migration blob: The target TPM uses PK_{DT} and the one-time pad key to decrypt the blob to obtain MK.

In order to support the MIGRATE way, the command *TPM_CreateMigrationBlob* needs to support the dual encryption, and adds a one-time pad key as the output. Accordingly, the command *TPM_ConvertMigrationBlob* needs to support the dual decryption, and adds the one-time pad key as the input.

2.2.3 Identification

In order to certify the data sent out, the TPM must have the identity certified by the trusted third party. The identity has a twofold role: (1) confirm that the TPM is authentic (thus, the TPM has sufficient security and functionality); (2) confirm that the TPM is "a specific TPM."

The authenticity of the TPM can only be certified by the manufacturer or some specific professional institutions; thus, if the third party has issued a certificate for the identity key, the key cannot be easily changed. At the same time, due to the frequent use of the identity key or the requirement of keeping anonymous, the identity key must regularly be updated to ensure its security and privacy. For the two contrary needs, the TCG designs two different kinds of identity keys for the TPM: (1) Endorsement Key (EK), which generally cannot be updated, and only participates in a few necessary operations. (2) Attestation Identity Key (AIK), which can be used for frequent signing operations. The user can generate new keys and apply for the corresponding certificates at any time. In order to solve the problem of the anonymous authentication, TCG also introduces the mechanism of anonymous identity.

According to the TPM specifications, the TPM security chip must be strictly bound with the computing platform. Thus, the identity of TPM is actually the hardware identity of platform. We will not distinguish these two identities below.

2.2.3.1 Endorsement Key

Endorsement Key is typically a 2048-bit RSA key pair. One TPM has only one EK. The private key of EK is permanently stored in the TPM internal memory (EK and SRK are the only two persistent keys stored in the TPM internal memory), and is only used to perform decryption in a few critical operations such as taking TPM ownership and the certificate application of the Attestation Identity Key. Thus, EK enjoys long-term protection and low frequent usage, and its computing results by the private key are never exposed to the external (EK cannot be used to sign). EK is considered to achieve a rather high security level.

In order to ensure security and privacy, in principle, EK should be generated by the TPM, and its certificate should be applied for from the trusted third party under user's control. However, for the facility of the production and use in practice, EK can be loaded into the TPM from outside and its certificate can be issued by the TPM manufacturer. The manufacturers can also optionally support the revocable EK. The related commands of EK mainly include the following:

- *TPM_CreateEndorsementKeyPair*: It creates the EK. If EK already exists, the command execution will fail.
- *TPM_CreateRevocableEK*: It is newly added to the TPM 1.2 specification. It can be used to create the revocable EK. If EK already exists, the command execution will fail.
- *TPM_ReadPubek* and *TPM_OwnerReadInternalPub*: The former is used to read the public portion of the EK and the latter is used to read that of the EK or the SRK with the owner authorization.
- *TPM_DisablePubekRead*: It is used to prohibit the reading of the EK public key. The command has actually been deprecated by the TPM 1.2 specification.

2.2.3.2 Attestation Identity Key

The Attestation Identity Key is non-migratable identity key generated by TPM, which is a 2048-bit RSA key pair. AIK is distinguished from the EK as follows:

- Creation: Usually AIK is created by the user. The TPM user can apply for the AIK certificate by showing the EK certificate, the platform certificate and the compliance certificate.
- Usage: AIK can only be used to sign. It is mainly used to report the integrity (by using the command *TPM_Quote*) or to certify other keys created by the TPM (by using the command *TPM_CertifyKey*). It has a relatively higher frequent usage.
- Storage: It is the same as the common key that the AIK is loaded into the TPM only when needed.
- Quantity: The TPM can apply for multiple AIKs at the same time.
- The corresponding commands include the following:
- *TPM_MakeIdentity*: It is used to generate identity application blob for AIK.
- *TPM_ActivateIdentity*: It is used to check the format of the identity key certificate from the trusted third party, and then obtain the session key to decrypt the certificate.

2.2.3.3 Anonymous Identity

In the TCG technical architecture, the main purpose of the TPM identity is to guarantee the authenticity of the data sent by it. For this purpose, essentially the data receiver only needs to ensure that the TPM and the platform are trusted, but does not need to identify their specific identity. Thus, the anonymity is an important requirement for the identification in trusted computing. Here the anonymity contains twofold meanings: first is the confidentiality of the identity, namely, the data receiver cannot know the identity of the sender; second is the unlinkability, namely, the data receiver cannot determine whether any two signatures are from the same sender.

Although the TCG adopts the Privacy-CA scheme (Section 7.3.1), which can achieve the anonymity of the AIK identification, the Privacy-CA scheme has some serious defects. In order to obtain the unlinkability, the TPM must apply for a new AIK for each signature to be sent. It brings a heavy cost to the TPM, the computing platform and the Privacy-CA. Moreover, once the Privacy-CA and the data receiver collude, the TPM identity will be exposed.

For the above reasons, TCG has added the Direct Anonymous Attestation (DAA) in the TPM 1.2 specification. The DAA function can be regarded as specific application of traditional anonymous credential systems in trusted computing field. With DAA, the TPM only needs to apply for the certificate from the issuer once, and it can attest the identity for any times. Even in the scenario that the issuer and the data receiver collude, the anonymity of the TPM can still be kept. The computing steps of the DAA scheme in the TPM 1.2 specification are very complex. We will show its design principles and the latest researches in other section. The DAA-related commands in TPM include the following:

- *TPM_DAA_Join*: It is used to apply for the anonymous credential, and requires authorization of the TPM owner. This is a very special TPM command as it needs 24 stages to complete the execution, and each stage requests the user to input different parameters. This is because the DAA protocol is complex and TPM resources are limited.
- *TPM_DAA_Sign*: It uses the anonymous credential to certify the data or another AIK, and needs the owner authorization. Similar to the above command, the computation of the command is very complex.

2.2.4 Integrity Storage and Reporting

Integrity measurement, storage and reporting are core functionalities of the trusted computing technical architecture. Measurement is performed by the software based on the root of trust for measurement. Integrity storage and reporting are realized by the TPM. It means the external software does the measurement and stores the result in the TPM, and the TPM performs the integrity reporting when needed.

2.2.4.1 Integrity Measurement and Storage

When the computing platform powers on, the first booted entity (namely, the RTM, such as the trusted BIOS) computes the hash of the code of the next entity (such as the bootloader of the operating system), and stores the result in the TPM. Similarly, the bootloader measures the operating system kernel and stores the integrity measurement values. The above bootstrap forms the chain of trust in the way that each entity measures and loads the next entity, and completes the measurement and storage of the platform integrity.

In order to securely store measurement values, the TPM has a dedicated internal memory for their storage, namely, the Platform Configuration Register (PCR). In the TCG technical architecture, TPM uses a hash value to characterize the integrity. Thus, the length of the PCR is 160-bit, the same with the output length of the SHA1 algorithm. The TPM specification requires that at least 16 PCRs and at most 230 PCRs are provided. Most of the current products actually provide 24 PCRs.

In order to protect the security during the updating of the PCR, TCG designs the following protection and updating mechanisms:

- PCR should be located in the TPM-shielded location.
- When the platform boots, the value of the PCR should be reset to the default value.
- After the platform boots, PCR is updated in an "extension" way. The so-called PCR extension is the following computation: PCR New = HASH (PCR Old value || value to add). The extension way helps PCRs store infinite integrity measurement values without erasing. At the same time, the extension way has the properties of sequentiality (the results are not equal when extending the same values in a different order) and one-wayness (unless reset, the PCR value cannot roll back to the value at a previous time).

In order to support some specific programs (such as the security code based on the dynamic root of trust for measurement (DRTM), which will be introduced below), TPM can also provide a number of resettable PCRs. Through the mechanism of locality, TPM can implement access control by determining the source of the PCR reset operations.

The TPM commands of the PCR operations include the following:

- *TPM_PcrExtend*: It is used to extend the measurement values into the PCR.
- *TPM_PCR_Reset*: It is used to reset PCR to the state of the TPM initialization. If the PCR cannot be reset, command execution will fail.
- *TPM_PcrRead*: It is used to read the PCR values.

2.2.4.2 Integrity Reporting

TPM can report the integrity by using the quote function. The process of reporting generally contains the following steps:

(1) The remote challenger sends the request of integrity report with the challenging nonce.
(2) The prover platform software sends the request of integrity reporting to the TPM.
(3) The TPM uses the identity key or the signing key to sign the integrity of the platform with the challenging nonce.

(4) The prover's platform obtains the signature, and sends the signature and the information list of all the measured software and hardware to the challenger.
(5) According to the information list of the measured software and hardware provided by the prover, the challenger can obtain the standard integrity values of the measured hardware and software, then compute the result of the PCR extension and finally verify the correctness of the signature.

The commands of the integrity reporting are as follows:
- *TPM_Quote*: It is used to quote the PCR value, namely, it uses the AIK to sign the PCR value and returns the signature. It is one of the core TPM commands. The TPM specification also allows using the signing key to quote, but this key cannot get an identity certificate. As a result, it is needed to use the command *TPM_CertifyKey* and another AIK to certify the signing key.
- *TPM_Quote2*: It is used to quote the PCR value, but it requires the data structure that includes the locality information to characterize the PCR.

2.2.5 Resource Protection

In order to prevent TPM from being controlled by an illegal user and to protect the TPM internal resources, the access control mechanism is required to check the authorizations of the TPM commands. In this section, we describe four kinds of resource protection mechanisms in the TPM: TPM ownership, authorization protocols, physical presence, and locality. The TPM ownership mechanism mainly checks the caller's ownership rights in the critical operations such as the application of the AIK certificate. Authorization protocols are used to check whether the caller has the rights to use the TPM internal resources (keys, nonvolatile memory, etc.). Physical presence mechanism is mainly used to check whether the caller can physically manipulate TPM in the operations that are related to the management of the TPM internal flags and the ownership. Locality mechanism checks the trust level of the caller. It is closely related to some new security technologies such as the dynamic root of trust for measurement and the trusted operating system. The secure storage, key operation, nonvolatile memory and transport protection all depend on the locality control.

2.2.5.1 TPM Ownership

The TPM owner is the TPM manager who has the exclusive control of the TPM. The main purpose to set the TPM ownership is to prevent TPM from being controlled by an illegal user (especially an illegal network user). Only the TPM owner has the right to apply for the AIK certificate, migrate the key and set the TPM internal flags or to perform other critical operations.

Generally, TPM products do not have the owners when leaving the factory. Only when the privileged commands are to be executed, the user can take the ownership.

After that, some important keys or internal variables are generated, such as the SRK and the TPM Proof (the specific migration authorization of the non-migratable key).

TCG sets strict restrictions on taking the TPM ownership. First, if the TPM ownership has been taken, it cannot be set again unless the current owner is cleared. Second, the operator must know the public key of EK to be able to take the ownership, which can not only prevent the network attacks to some extent but also make it possible to remotely take the ownership. Third, only if the TPM internal flag *ownership* is true, the user can take the ownership. It needs the physical presence[9] to set this flag. This restriction indicates that although the TPM allows taking ownership remotely, essentially it needs the person with the physical manipulation of TPM to participate. For security and economic considerations, currently the TPM supports only one owner.

The TPM commands related to the ownership include the following:

- *TPM_TakeOwnership*: It is used to specify the owner authorization, the SRK authorization and some options for SRK parameters.
- *TPM_OwnerClear*: It is called by the owner to clear its privileges, and all the secrets will be discarded. All the discarded secrets cannot be recovered.
- *TPM_Forceclear*: It is used to clear the owner mandatorily. It needs the physical presence.

2.2.5.2 Authorization Protocols

Except for a small number of computing resources (e.g., hash function), most of the TPM resources may affect the security of the computing platform or the trustworthiness of storage and integrity reporting. Therefore, TCG designs the authorization protocols for the access control of these resources. The authorization value is a secret shared between the TPM and the caller. Thus, the design principles of the authorization protocols are similar to that of the authentication protocols based on secret sharing and Message Authentication Code (MAC). However, if we design the authorization protocols fully following these protocol methods, each time a caller uses the TPM resource, the TPM must send a nonce to the caller to prevent replay attacks. It seriously reduces efficiency of TPM. In order to avoid this problem, TPM gives out the authorization protocols by adding the unique nonces management, which is based on the authentication protocols with shared secret and MAC computation.

- Before the execution of any TPM commands that require authorization, the caller should call the command *TPM_OIAP* or *TPM_OSAP* to establish the authorization session. In *TPM_OIAP*, TPM sends the first nonce to the caller. In *TPM_OSAP*, the TPM and the caller not only exchange nonces but also negotiate a session key according to the nonces and key authorization value. After the session

9 We will explain the TPM internal flags and physical presence in the following sections.

setup, the two sides share the nonce or a session key, and an authorization session handle (the index of the session-related data for the caller and the TPM to manage the nonces).

- When the caller first calls the TPM command, it can compute the MAC according to the above nonces or the session key. In response, based on the MAC, the TPM can verify the right of the caller and return the fresh nonce for the next interaction.

OIAP. The command *TPM_OIAP* is used to establish the OIAP authorization session. The invocation of the command is shown in Figure 2.4. The caller invokes the *TPM_OIAP* command. The TPM initializes the resources required by the authorization session and generates the session handle *authHandle* and a nonce *authLastNonceEven*. It associates *authLastNonceEven* and *authHandle* with session, and finally sends *authLastNonceEven* and *authHandle* to the caller.

After the establishment of an authorization session, the caller can invoke the TPM command. The invocation of the command in OIAP protocol is shown in Figure 2.5 (assuming that the caller invokes the command *TPM_Example* and specifies the resource as key and the authorization session handle as *authHandle*):

(1) After the establishment of the authorization session, the caller first invokes the command *TPM_Example*. In addition to the necessary command metadata (*tag*,

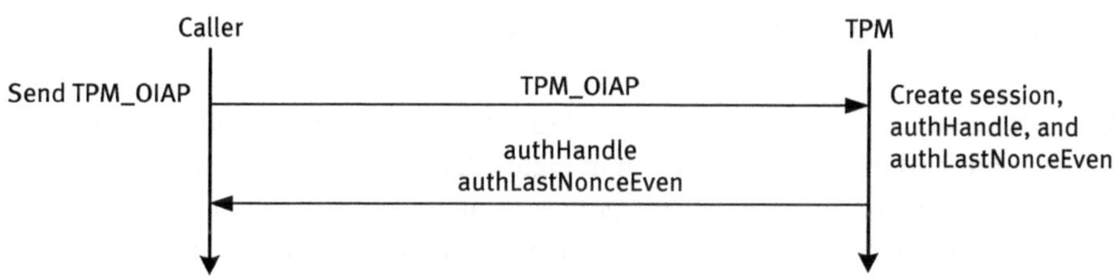

Figure 2.4: Establishment of an OIAP authorization session.

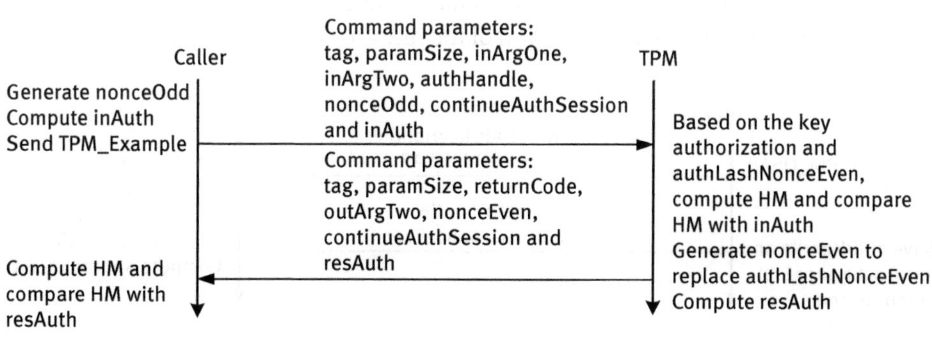

Figure 2.5: First invocation of TPM_Example with OIAP.

paramSize, ordinal) and command parameters (*keyHandle, inArgOne and inArgTwo*), the caller also sends the *authHandle* to the TPM, the fresh nonce *nonceOdd, continueAuthSession* and the HMAC value *inAuth*, where *continueAuthSession* identifies whether the caller decides to close the session. The computation of *inAuth* is as follows:

inParamDigest = SHA1(*ordinal, inArgOne, inArgTwo*),

inAuthSetupParams = (*authLastNonceEven, nonceOdd, continueAuthSession*)

inAuth=HMAC(*key.usageAuth, inParamDigest, inAuthSetupParams*).

(2) Based on *authHandle* sent by the caller, the TPM retrieves the corresponding *authLastNonceEven'*. Based on *keyHandle*, it retrieves the corresponding *key.usageAuth*. Then the TPM computes HM following step (1). By comparing HM and *inAuth*, the TPM checks whether the caller has the right to access the resource and whether the parameters are tampered. If all parameter checks pass, the TPM replaces *authLastNonceEven* in the session with the fresh nonce *nonceEven*. Then it returns to the caller the parameters tag, *paramSize, returnCode, outArgOne, nonceEven, continueAuthSession* and *resAuth*, where the computing method of *resAuth* is similar to that of *inAuth*. It is used to prove that the result is indeed computed and returned by the TPM.

When the caller wants to access another resource *newKey*, it can use the same authorization session. Except replacing *key.usageAuth* with *newKey.usageAuth*, there is no change in the authorization. The nonce *authLastNonceEven* used at this time is *nonceEven* returned from the TPM in the previous command.

OSAP. The command *TPM_OSAP*()is used to establish the OSAP authorization session. The command invocation is shown in Figure 2.6. The establishment of the OSAP session no longer just exchanges the nonces, but negotiates the session key (denoted by *sharedSecret*) through the exchange of the nonces. It binds *sharedSecret* and *authLastNonceEven* to the specified resource (identified by *keyHandle*).

After the establishment of an authorization session, the caller can invoke the TPM command. The invocation of the command in the OSAP protocol is shown in Figure 2.7. As shown in the figure, the OSAP is very similar to the OIAP. It uses the shared secret to replace the corresponding authorization of the resource. Because the secret sharing is

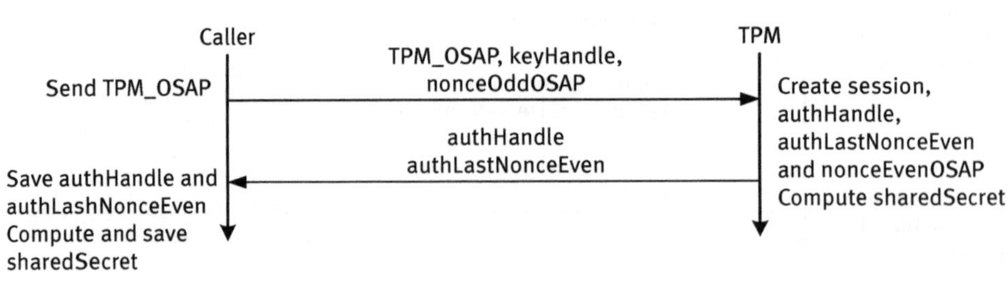

Figure 2.6: Establishment of an OSAP authorization session.

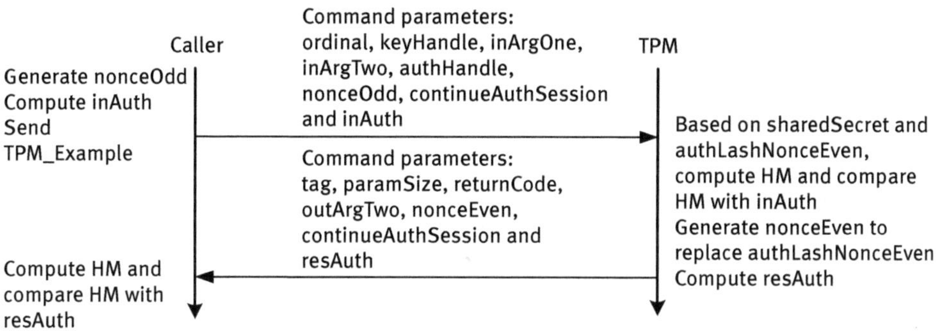

Figure 2.7: First invocation of *TPM_Example* with OSAP.

bound to the session, the disadvantage of OSAP is that one authorization session can only access one resource. The advantage is that it reduces the chance of exposure of the authorization value. It improves the security of the protocol, and the caller prefers to entrust the shared secret to the software for storage so that the caller convenience is enhanced.

For most TPM commands, the caller can arbitrarily select OIAP or OSAP. Callers should consider the following three factors when choosing OIAP or OSAP:

- Trade-off between security and the efficiency: When a caller program needs to frequently access different resources, OIAP is recommended to reduce the number of establishments of the authorization sessions. When the caller needs a higher security level, or wants to access the TPM resource repeatedly by inputting the authorization value only once, OSAP is recommended.
- The scenarios where OIAP must be used: OIAP should be used where there is no specified entity or the entity does not have handle, such as the commands for taking ownership, creating key migration blob and changing of the authorizations.[10]
- The scenarios where OSAP must be used: OSAP should be used in commands setting or changing the object authorization value (actually for the following ADIP\ADCP\AACP). These commands serve for creating ordinary key/identity key/certified migratable key, sealing data, defining the nonvolatile memory, creating the counters and changing the authorization values.

---

10 The command *TPM_ChangeAuth()* for change of the authorization is a special case, where it needs the authorizations for both the entity and the parent key. These two authorizations should be provided, respectively, by an OIAP session and an OSAP session.

ADIP. The role of the ADIP is to set the authorization values for the objects during their creation (ordinary keys, identity keys, certified migratable keys, data sealing blobs, nonvolatile memory and counters). Essentially, ADIP is a special usage of the OSAP: Before the creation of the object, the caller should first establish an OSAP session for the parent key, which is used to protect the newly created object. When the object is being created, the shared secret in the OSAP session is used not only to protect the parent key but also to encrypt the authorization values of the newly created object (namely, the execution of ADIP).[11] After the object is created, the OSAP session should be closed.

One of the important features of the ADIP is that only the owner of the parent key can access the newly created object. It is because the caller should load the parent key before the use of new objects. The owner of the parent key can deduce the authorization value of newly created key from the *sharedSecret*.

ADCP. The role of the ADCP is to change the authorization value of the existing TPM resource. It can only be used in the commands *TPM_ChangeAuth()* and *TPM_ChangeAuthOwn()*. Similar to the ADIP, ADCP is a special usage of the OSAP. It also uses the shared secret in the OSAP session for the parent key of the resource to encrypt the new authorization value.

AACP. As mentioned above, in ADIP and ADCP, the owner of the parent key knows the authorization value of the new object, which actually means the TPM owner knows the authorization values for each object in the protected storage hierarchy. In order to allow the caller to obtain the exclusive access to a certain object, TPM provides the AACP, which uses a specific key (only known by the creator of the object) to protect the authorization value of the new object. Thus, the caller can use the ADIP to create the authorization value of the object, and then use the AACP to modify it. In the TPM 1.1 specification, AACP is achieved by the two commands *TPM_ChangeAuthAsymStart()* and *TPM_ChangeAuthAsymFinish()*, and in the TPM 1.2 specification, these two commands are replaced by the transport protection mechanism.

2.2.5.3 Physical Presence

The physical presence is a kind of access control mechanisms at the physical level. Its main functionality is to confirm that in the execution of some instructions that require

11 Setting of the authorization data of the identity key is special. In order to ensure that only the owner is able to create an identity key, the user needs to create the OSAP session for the owner rather than the SRK in the creation of the identity key. Therefore, the shared secret used in ADIP is based on the owner authorization rather than the SRK (the parent key of the identity key) authorization.

special privileges, the instruction comes from the operator of TPM and platform rather than the malicious software or remote operators. “Special privileges” are mainly related to the management of the owner and TPM start-up, including the mandatory clearing of the TPM owner and deactivating or disabling the TPM. The TPM specification does not specify the implementation of the physical presence mechanism. It allows the manufacturers of the TPM and the computing platforms to implement it on their own. It only requires that the implementation of the physical presence mechanism is able to resist malicious software. Hardware switches and circuit modes are recommended. For example, some Lenovo Thinkpads use Fn key as a physical presence.

2.2.5.4 Locality

The invocation of the TPM commands might come from multiple sources whose trustworthiness is different. The typical sources include DRTM processor, trusted system software, ordinary system software and applications, and their trustworthiness declines in turn. In order to distinguish these different sources to achieve the corresponding access control (mainly for the access control for PCRs), TPM introduces the locality mechanism. It requires the TPM manufacturers to introduce special pins or bus circuits, so that the TPM can know about the source of the signal instruction at the hardware level.

At present, TPM defines six locality levels (Localities 0–4 and Locality None) in total. Locality 4 exclusively belongs to the trusted hardware. Locality 3 exclusively belongs to the auxiliary components and it is defined by the manufacturers. Locality 2 exclusively belongs to the runtime environment of the dynamically launched operating system. Locality 1 exclusively belongs to the environment used by the dynamically launched operating system. Locality 0 exclusively belongs to dynamic chain of trust, the static root of trust for measurement and environment for static root of trust. Locality None is used for compatibility with the TPM version 1.1.

2.2.6 Auxiliary Functions

2.2.6.1 Start, Self-Test and Operational Mode

From the start, TPM will go through four stages: start, self-test, operations of commands and shutdown.

The TPM starts in two phases. In the first phase, the TPM is powered on and waits for the user to input the start-up options. In the second phase, the TPM completes the start-up according to the options of the user. The two phases depend on the commands*TPM_Init()* and *TPM_Startup()*, respectively, which are the first two commands of the entire TPM life cycle. *TPM_Init()* is a symbolic hardware-based command. *TPM_Startup()* can start the TPM by using the default start-up state (*ST_CLEAR*), or recover the state preserved in the previous life cycle (*ST_STATE*, which needs the execution of the command *TPM_SaveState()*), or directly go into the deactivated state (details will be explained in the following).

The TPM must complete all self-tests before using its functionalities. It does not enforce the user to complete the self-tests of all functionalities after the start. In fact, the TPM only performs a small amount of the necessary self-tests after the initialization, so that the TPM can execute a few commands. After that, the user can use the command *TPM_ContinueSelfTest()* or *TPM_SelfTestFull()* to complete all the self-tests.

When the auto self-tests are completed, the TPM enters the stage of the operations of commands (although the functionalities that have not been tested still need to be self-tested). Three internal boolean flags define the operation modes. They are *disabled*, *ownership* and *deactivated*.

- Only if *ownership* is true, the user can take the TPM ownership. When the ownership is taken, this flag can be set to prevent the malicious user from taking the ownership again. Because of the importance of this flag, the command *TPM_SetOwnerInstall()* that can set the flag must use the physical presence for access control.
- Only if *disabled* is false, the user can use the TPM internal resources. In the *disabled* state, the TPM can perform the computing operations such as the hash function, but cannot use the TPM internal resources. The significance of the *disabled* state is that it allows disabling all commands that might change the TPM internal state without shutdown of the TPM. The commands to set this flag (such as *TPM_PhysicalEnable()*) require the physical presence or owner authorization.
- The flag *deactivated* is nearly the same to the *disabled* flag. The main difference is that the user can take the ownership in the former. The significance of *deactivated* is that in the deactivated state, the user can take the ownership and confirm it is successfully set up, and then set the TPM into the activated state to begin to execute the commands. It can preemptively prevent the malicious software or remote user from taking the ownership and immediately using the owner privileges to execute commands. The command that sets this flag requires the physical presence or an operator's authorization.

2.2.6.2 Context Management

Context management, namely, the context storage and loading, allows the TPM to encrypt and save the internal resources at some time, and in the future reload the context into the TPM. The resource types include keys, authorization sessions, nonexclusive transport sessions and DAA sessions. The purpose of designing the context management is to set aside some "direct channel" in TPM access control. This makes it possible to temporarily interrupt some session occupying internal resources for a long time, and avoid unnecessary access control rules when recovering them in the future. It enhances the flexibility and availability of the TPM.

In the following, we use an example from the TPM specification to further explain the context management. If the use of key3 requires PCR3 to be in a certain state, changes of the PCRs other than the PCR3 should not affect the use of key3. However, according to the existing TPM specification, loading key3 might require loading its ancestor key key1, which requires PCR1 to be in a certain state. Thus, the change of PCR1 indirectly affects the use of key3. In this case, if the TPM has previously saved the context of loaded key3, it can directly use the context management to reload the context. Thus, it avoids the unnecessary effects of PCR1 on key3.

Any saved or reloadable state itself is considered to be trusted. Thus, the context management does not need privilege control. The security of the recoverable resource depends on the access control mechanism of the resource itself. In other words, any user can restore the TPM internal resource (such as a key), but the use of this resource needs the corresponding authorization. Note that the differences between the saved context (*TPM_SaveContext()*) and the saved state (*TPM_SaveState()*) are as follows:

- The target is different: As mentioned above, the context management mainly aims to avoid the unnecessary access control mechanism and to restore the saved resources quickly and conveniently. Saving state mainly aims to remind the TPM to save some internal states to avoid the loss of information because of the power off.
- The time to save and restore is different: In the context management, the time to save and restore the context is determined by the user. For the state, the time to save states is often before special states of TPM, such as the shutdown or power-off state. The time to restore is during TPM initialization (execution of the command *TPM_Startup()*).
- The contents to be saved are different: The context management mainly involves keys and three kinds of sessions (authorization sessions, DAA sessions and transport sessions). The user can specify the contents to be saved. The states to be saved and restored include keys and three kinds of sessions. It must also contain the internal information such as *TPM_STCLEAR_DATA*. The user is not able to specify the states to be saved.

2.2.6.3 Maintenance

The maintenance mechanism is designed to migrate the TPM internal secret information, which mainly contains the SRK, to another platform. The fundamental need comes from the fact that when the computer system containing a TPM is damaged or replaced, operators hope to retain the storage hierarchy protected by TPM. In the view of the technical implementation, both the maintenance and the key migration are operations on the protected storage hierarchy. Thus, many documents introduce them together. However, in the view of the goal, maintenance mechanism is dedicated to providing management mechanism at a platform level. Its influence scope and harm degree are wider and deeper, respectively, than those of the key migration while exploiting vulnerabilities.

The risk of the maintenance mechanism is that it can migrate all keys, no matter whether the key is migratable or non-migratable. It might undermine the uniqueness of the non-migratable key, which is essential for the TPM-related confidentiality and nonrepudiation. Accordingly, TCG requires the following rules: (1) The maintenance mechanism is optional. (2) If the maintenance mechanism is realized, the user can use this mechanism only with the help of manufacturer. (3) The manufacturers have the obligation to ensure the uniqueness of the non-migratable key. (4) The maintenance mechanism of the TPM products from different manufacturers cannot be interoperable in principles (which further restrict the spread of the key). (5) The maintenance mechanism can be disabled by the owner through the command *TPM_KillMaintenance()*, and the disabled maintenance mechanism cannot be restored until the next ownership is taken. Although these rules weaken the availability, flexibility and interoperability of the maintenance mechanism, it is reasonable considering the scenarios and the frequency of its uses.

Due to the requirement of noninteroperability, the TCG specification only defines the interfaces of the maintenance mechanism. The implementation is manufacturer specific. The principle of the maintenance mechanism is similar to that of the *MIGRATE* way, but they have the following differences:

- The "migration key" used in the maintenance (the so-called *ManuMaintPub*, corresponding to the asymmetric key used to encrypt the migration blob) is embedded into the TPM by the manufacturer in the chip production stage. It cannot be created or specified by the user.
- Only chip manufacturers can be the trusted medium entity to migrate the key in the maintenance.
- When the maintenance blob (corresponding to the migration blob) is generated, the information contained in the migration blob contains not only the SRK but also the owner authorization, *TPMproof*.

2.2.6.4 Counter

Counter is a common mechanism used in security protocols. TPM provides the secure counter mechanism for the high-level applications based on the internally maintained main counter (internal base). The TPM secure counter mechanism must provide at least four external counters, and the increases in these four counters will not affect each other. In every TPM life cycle (from the command *TPM_Startup()* to power-off), only one counter can be used. The TPM specification requires that for any counter, it allows for seven years of increments every 5 seconds without duplication.

The specific implementation of the TPM counters is as follows:

(1) In the start of a new TPM life cycle, it first creates (through the command *TPM_CreateCounter*()) or activates (through the command *TPM_IncrementCounter()*) a counter C. Then it sets an internal variable *startup*

to be the current value of the internal base. Finally, it sets the internal variable (related to C) *diff_C* to be the current value of the internal base (for the newly created counter) or *diff_C* to be the previous value of C + 1 (for the activated counter).

(2) The increment of any one of the external counter (through the command *TPM_IncrementCounter*()) causes the increment of the internal base.

(3) When the user requests to read the counter C (through the command *TPM_ReadCounter*()), the TPM returns its value (the internal base value – *startup* + *diff_C*).

2.2.6.5 Time Stamp

Time stamp is a common mechanism used in security protocols. TPM provides a reliable time stamp for high-level applications. Time stamp of the TPM is not a real time, but the total number of time ticks from the start of the current time session to now. The user calls the command *TPM_GetTicks()* to obtain current time ticks and calls the command *TPM_TickStampBlob()* to add time stamp to the message and sign it.

2.2.6.6 Transport Protection

The transport protection (or transport session) mechanism provides the confidentiality and audit for the TPM commands. Users can generate a secret and transport it to the TPM to obtain the shared secret between the two sides. Based on the shared secret and the nonces aiming to resist replay attacks, the TPM and the user can generate a symmetric encryption key, and use this key to provide confidentiality for the execution of the command. The process of the transport protection mechanism is as follows:

(1) The user first invokes the command *TPM_EstablishTransport()* and uses an encryption key to transport the shared secret to the TPM. Both sides take the shared secret, *nonceEven* and *nonceOdd* as the inputs and call MGF1 function to generate the stream cipher encryption key. In this step, the user can set the three attributes of the transport session, which contains encryption, audit and exclusion.

(2) The user invokes the command *TPM_ExecuteTransport()*. The actually executed functional command is transported to the TPM as the parameters of the command *TPM_ExecuteTransport()*. If the user has set the encryption property, a part of the parameters of the functional command will be in an encrypted form. The TPM returns the result in a similar form.

(3) When the user needs to audit the result of the command, it invokes the command *TPM_ReleaseTransportSign()*. This command returns the digest, which is the hash of some parameters of all commands in the session. There is a contradiction between the goal of the audit (to restore the parameters of the commands for checking) and the encryption (to prevent the restoring of execution parameters). Thus, if the user sets both the encryption and the audit, the audited contents only include the ordinals of executed command, and the execution results.

(4) Another kind of special session is the exclusive transport session. The so-called exclusive means that execution of any commands other than *TPM_ExecuteTransport()* and *TPM_ReleaseTransportSign()* causes the invalidation of the exclusive transport session. The goal of the exclusive transport session is to ensure the atomicity of the session.

2.3 TCM Security Chip

TCM is the trusted computing security chip developed by China. In its development, TCM refers to concept and architecture of international trusted computing technology. Its development also takes into consideration the Chinese national regulations of information security. Its design principles and the technical ideas are quite different from those of the TPM. On the one hand, based on the Chinese cryptographic algorithms, the security and efficiency of TCM are greatly enhanced rather than those of the TPM. On the other hand, combined with the security needs and the market demand, TCM has made innovations in several key technologies.

The successful development of TCM and related products marks the maturity of Chinese independent trusted computing technology and industry. China has made great progress in the development and innovation of the trusted computing technology. China has established a complete and large-scale trusted computing industry. It has promoted the development of some related information technology industry such as the integrated circuit, computer, application software and network equipment. TCM also provides a strong support for the construction of information security system in China, and provides practical technical means for the protection of the critical agencies such as the governments, militaries and information infrastructures. TCM also enhances the position of China in the fields of trusted computing and information security. It enables China to take part in the development and upgrade of the international trusted computing specifications and standards, and further influences the design and development of the security chips, trusted software and other related products.

In this section, we focus on the functional features of TCM and several important TCM commands.

2.3.1 Main Functionalities

Although the development of TCM refers to the concept and architecture of international trusted computing technology, there is a big difference between the ideas in TCM and TPM. Besides the differences in the use of cryptographic algorithms, the security features of TCM also have their own characteristics. First, it adjusts some design principles of the TPM that contradict the security requirements in China. For example,

TPM only implements the AIK certificate for the signing key. In China, the public key infrastructure requires the certificates for both the signing key and encryption key. Thus, TCM adopts the dual-certificate system. Second, as TPM is unable to meet some specific security application requirements, TCM has made some innovations in the key management and the basic cryptographic service. For example, TCM has introduced the functionalities of data symmetric encryption and key agreement. Third, TCM has eliminated the vulnerabilities of the TPM. For example, TCM enhances the ability to resist replay attacks on authorization protocols.

In order to facilitate readers' reading and comparison, in this section we describe the TCM functionalities in a way similar to that of the TPM. We divide them into platform data protection, identification and integrity storage and reporting. Since TCM and TPM are similar in their functionalities, in this section we focus on the features of the TCM, especially on the comparison between the TPM and TCM.

2.3.1.1 Platform Data Protection

For the platform data protection, the TCM and the TPM follow the same design principle. It adopts the way of protected storage hierarchy to protect key and data. The interfaces of the key management, data encryption and data sealing are similar. However, the platform data protection of TCM has its own features. On the one hand, the difference in the basic cryptographic algorithms directly affects the key types and other functionalities such as data encryptions. On the other hand, in China TCM is more often used in secure key management and as a cryptographic computing engine. Thus, the TCM provides a richer functionality for data storage.

Key Type. The TCM key types and their descriptions are listed in Table 2.2. It includes the storage keys and binding keys that adopt SM2-3 and SMS4 algorithms, signing keys and identity keys that adopt SM2-1 algorithm and platform encryption keys that adopt SM2-3 algorithm. Compared with the TPM, the main feature of the TCM is to support symmetric encryption algorithm for storage keys and binding keys. Moreover, it adds the new key type for platform encryption, which is compatible with the dual-certificate system in China.

Data Encryption and Sealing. TCM provides the functionalities of data encryption, decryption, sealing and unsealing. The differences between these functionalities in TCM and TPM are as follows. In TCM, all storage keys and encryption keys support the symmetric encryption algorithms[12] as well as the asymmetric encryption algorithms, but in TPM, they only support the asymmetric algorithms. In other words,

12 It only supports the symmetric encryption algorithm for the SMK.

Table 2.2: TCM key type.

Key type	Description
TCM_SM2KEY_STORAGE	It is an SM2 key to protect other keys in the protected storage hierarchy, often used in key creation and data sealing
TCM_SM2KEY_SIGNING	It is an SM2 key used to sign ordinary data as well as to quote platform integrity. Users cannot apply the platform identity certificate for it
TCM_SM2KEY_BIND	It is an SM2 key used to encrypt and decrypt data. Note that it cannot be used in data sealing
TCM_SM2KEY_IDENTITY	It is an SM2 key used to identify TCM and do remote attestation. Users can apply the platform identity certificate for it
TCM_SM2KEY_PEK	It is an SM2 platform encryption key. It is introduced by TCM for the dual-certificate system in China
TCM_SMS4KEY_STORAGE	It is similar to *TCM_SM2KEY_STORAGE*, but adopts the SMS4 algorithm, which has a higher efficiency in storage
TCM_SMS4KEY_BIND	It is similar to *TCM_SM2KEY_BIND*, but it adopts the SMS4 algorithm, which has a higher efficiency in data encryption and decryption

TCM supports a complete system of the cryptographic algorithms, which takes into account the different application requirements, such that it can be independently used as the key management module and cryptographic engine with high security level. For the most common computations for enormous data encryption, decryption or sealing and unsealing in local platform, the TCM can perform them by using the symmetric key algorithm, which is more efficient. For the situations that require external participants (e.g., the external encryption needs to be decrypted by the TCM), the user can adopt the asymmetric algorithm. Compared with TCM, TPM does not provide functions for symmetric encryption and decryption. Although it helps to simplify the TPM internal logic, it enforces the user either to use asymmetric algorithm to do all encryption and decryption or manage the symmetric key by himself. Therefore, the user cannot achieve both the security and usability of key management and cryptographic computation.

Key Migration. Similar to the TPM, TCM provides two migration ways: Rewrap and Migrate. Meanwhile, the key migration of the TCM has the following features:

(1) As the Storage Master Key (SMK) is a symmetric key, it cannot be used as the parent key of the migrated key, otherwise the SMK will be exposed in the migration. In other words, the migratable key cannot use the SMK as the parent key, or be used as the SMK. Thus, in target TCM, the migrated key must be located in the third level of the protected storage hierarchy or in a lower level. In contrast, only the SRK in the TPM cannot be migrated.

(2) In TCM, the Migrate way adopts the digital envelope, namely, the key migration blob is in the form of $\{(KEY)_{SK}, (SK)_{MK}\}$, where KEY is the key to be migrated, SK

is the symmetric key and MK is the asymmetric key to protect the migration. In contrast, the Migrate way in TPM adopts the dual-encryption method, namely, the resulting key migration blob is in the form of $\{((KEY)_{SK})_{MK}\}$. Obviously, the Migrate way in TCM avoids a part of the time-consuming asymmetric encryption. It has an advantage of high computational efficiency. In the TPM Migrate way, it is convenient for the migration authority to convert the migration key blob to the form $\{((KEY)_{SK})_{MK2}\}$, where MK2 is a storage key in the target TPM. Thus, in TPM, it is convenient for the migration authority to work as a re-encryption proxy.

Key Agreement. The key agreement is one of the important cryptographic services provided by the cryptographic devices. It is of great importance for communications between the computing platforms. TCM provides the key agreement protocol. By using the TCM, two computing platforms can agree on a session key, which is under the protection of security chips. It enhances the security of the session. In contrast, TPM does not provide the key agreement protocol, which is a disadvantage when it is used as the key management module and cryptographic engine. The TCM key agreement process can be divided into two steps:

(1) Key agreement preparation: In this step, the TCM of each party generates an asymmetric key pair with a short life cycle. Then they both initialize the resources required by the key agreement. These resources and the ephemeral key pair should be bound to the session handle generated randomly.
(2) Key agreement computation: The two parties compute the shared new key by using the other's public key, identity and their own long-term and ephemeral key pairs.

2.3.1.2 Identification

Cryptography Module Key. The TCM cryptography module key is similar to the TPM endorsement key. They both are used to identify the security chip and the computing platform. For TCM, the cryptography module key is an SM2 key pair. The private key is permanently stored in the internal memory. It is used only in a few cases, such as applying for the platform identity certificate and taking the platform ownership.

The trustworthiness of the cryptography module key is certified by the third party in the form of a certificate, which must conform to the X.509V3 standard. It mainly includes the following fields:

- The names of the entity and the issuer, the public key of the entity and the expiration of the certificate.
- The identification of the certificate algorithm.
- The digital signature of the above information.

Platform Identity Key. The TCM Platform Identity Key (PIK) is similar to the TPM AIK. They both are used to sign the integrity measurement value and other keys. The PIK is an SM2 key pair, whose creation must be authorized by the owner. The platform identity key certificate must conform to the X.509V3 standard. The steps of the creation of PIK are as follows:

(1) The TCM creates the PIK, whose private key is protected by the SMK.
(2) Using the private key of PIK, TCM obtains the PIK signature by signing the public key of the PIK and the public key digest of the trusted party.
(3) The TCM sends the public key of the PIK, the public key of the cryptography module key and the PIK signature to the trusted party.
(4) The trusted party verifies the PIK signature. If valid, it uses the SM2 signature algorithm to issue the platform identity certificate.
(5) The trusted party uses the digital envelope to encrypt the identity certificate and the digest of the public key of PIK. The inner key of the digital envelope is SK. The outer key is the public key of the TCM cryptography module key EK.
(6) The TCM opens the digital envelope, and checks that whether the digest obtained is the same as the digest of the public key of the PIK in the platform. If it is true, the TCM returns the SK and the platform identity certificate can be obtained by further decryption.

Platform Encryption Key. In addition to the platform identity key, TCM also introduces the Platform Encryption Key (PEK) that plays the role of identification. The PEK is an SM2 key pair dedicated to data encryption and is associated with the PIK. It is different from the encryption key in the fact that PEK is first created and activated by the trusted entity (CA), and then loaded into the TCM. The main goal of the PEK is to make TCM be compatible with the dual-certificate system in the Chinese public key infrastructure. Based on the PEK mechanism, the key can be escrowed to the trusted third party, which is convenient for the data recovery after loss. It also facilitates the regulation of critical information for nations.

The process for applying for the PEK is as follows:

(1) TCM specifies the parameters of the PEK, and sends them to the CA.
(2) The CA creates PEK and the corresponding certificate PEKCert according to parameters given by the TCM. Then it generates the symmetric keys SK1 and SK2 (SK1 and SK2 may equal) and encrypts PEK by using SK1, encrypts PEKCert by using SK2. It also encrypts SK1 and SK2 by using EK of the TCM. Finally, the encryption blobs $\{PEK\}_{SK1}$, $\{SK1\}_{EK}$, $\{PEKCert\}_{SK2}$ and $\{SK2\}_{EK}$ are returned to the TCM.
(3) TCM opens the two digital envelopes to obtain PEK and PEKCert.

TPM does not provide the PEK mechanism. However, some applications need to use the encryption key that is certified by the trusted party and is similar to the PEK. In this case, TPM can use the key certification mechanism to achieve a similar functionality.

The TPM first generates an encryption key BK, and then uses the AIK to sign the information containing public key of BK, algorithm and so on. Remote users can verify the signature to check the authenticity of BK, and then use BK to transfer data to the TPM and its computing platform. Although this key certification mechanism does not make the encryption key be escrowed to the trusted party, BK still gets an indirect certification from the trusted party.

2.3.1.3 Integrity Storage and Reporting

Integrity Storage. Similar to the TPM, TCM utilizes PCRs to store the integrity measurement values. These PCRs are located within the shielded memory. TCM uses the "extended" way to update them. They will be reset when the platform is restarted. Due to the use of SM3 hash algorithm, the length of the TCM PCR is 256 bit. The TCM specification does not explicitly define the number of PCRs. Most of the existing products support 24 PCRs.

Integrity Reporting. TCM can use the quote function to complete the integrity reporting when needed. The integrity reporting should meet the following requirements: (1) TCM should be able to provide the quote results of the PCR values (i.e., the signatures by PIK) according to the PCR indexes and nonces provided by the verifier. (2) The platform that hosts the TCM should be able to provide to the verifier the event log for the integrity measurement and extension. (3) Through the analysis of the event log, the verifier can judge whether the PCR value is from the correct measurement procedure and verify the signature by using PIK public key. Finally, it can determine the trustworthiness of the attestation platform.

2.3.1.4 Resource Protection

For the resource protection mechanism, the TCM also provides mechanisms for ownership management, authorization protocols, physical presence and locality. The functionalities and interfaces of ownership management, physical presence and locality are very similar to those of the TPM. For the authorization protocols, the TCM improves the TPM OSAP and OIAP. In this section, we focus on these contents.

TCM uses the command *TCM_APCreate()* to start an Authorization Protocol (AP) session. According to different parameters, the command sets up two types of sessions corresponding to the TPM OIAP and OSAP, respectively. The output of *TCM_APCreate()* does not include the nonce (*authLastNonceEven* in TPM) used for the next protocol interaction. It outputs a randomly selected sequence number *seq*. In the next execution of commands that requires the authorization session, both the sides rely on *seq* to prevent replay attacks. Each interaction causes the increment of *seq* by 1 to keep freshness. Since the TCM no longer needs to generate and output the nonces for each interaction, the I/O efficiency is improved. The main goal of this design is to make use of the predictability of the TCM commands. Namely, the freshness of the messages is kept by a sequence value (*seq*) agreed on both sides rather than simply using randomness of nonces. The procedure for the authorization protocol is as follows:

(1) The user invokes the command *TCM_APCreate()*. He can choose from two kinds of authorizations: the type-dependent (similar to the OSAP) or the type-independent (similar to the OIAP).
(2) The TCM receives the request of *TCM_APCreate()*. If the user chooses the type-independent authorization, the TCM directly initializes the resources of the authorization session, generates the authorization session handle and creates the nonce to resist replay attacks. If the user chooses the type-dependent authorization, in addition to above operations, the TCM generates the shared secret according to the nonce provided by the user. This secret will be used as the authorization value for future use.
(3) When the user invokes the TCM commands that need to be authorized, he needs to compute the message authentication code according to the input parameters (command ordinal and the specific parameters), the sequence number and the shared secret.
(4) The TCM receives the command parameters and the message authentication code. Then it performs the verification.

TCM provides the command *TCM_APTerminate()* to explicitly terminate the authorization session. It helps users to detect the replay attacks in time. The TPM 1.2 specification abandons the counterpart command *TPM_Terminate_Handle()*, where the user can only terminate the session by setting the *continueAuthSession* to false. When the TPM user has established an authorization session, the potential attacker who can control the communications between the TPM and the host can intercept the parameters and the authorizations of the command sent by the user. This kind of attack has the same phenomenon caused by communication failures of the network or host. Thus, the TPM user cannot detect such an attack. If the user ignores this authorization session, the attacker can replay the intercepted messages in the future and thereby change the states of the TPM internal resources. In contrast, the TCM provides an explicit command to terminate the authorization session. The user can terminate the session at any time. He does not need to execute a functional command to terminate the session. If the session is terminated successfully, the user considers the danger has been cleared. If the session cannot be terminated, the user can also choose some other means to keep security, such as restarting the platform.

2.3.2 Main Command Interfaces

The functionalities of the TCM security chip are embodied by all the TCM command interfaces, and the user also invokes the TCM commands by using the application program to realize its security functionalities. Since TCM and TPM have the similar technical framework and concept, their command interfaces are similar except for only a few differences. In this section, we introduce several important TCM commands. We focus on the description of how these commands achieve the functionalities and features of the security chips. For some critical or commonly used commands, we give out the application instances in the form of pseudo code. We do not detail their parameter settings and execution procedures in those commands that are explicitly specified by the TCM specification or are similar to the corresponding TPM commands.

2.3.2.1 Platform Data Protection Commands

Key Management Commands. The TCM commands for key management are the same to those of the TPM, including the commands for creating key (*TCM_CreateWrapKey*), loading key (*TCM_LoadKey*), reading EK public key (*TCM_GetPubEK*) and certifying key (*TCM_CertifyKey*). Note that due to the differences between the TCM key types and the TPM key types, the specific parameters of the above commands are not the same.

Key Migration Commands. The TCM commands for key migration include the authorization migration command: *TCM_AuthorizeMigrationKey*, the command for creating the migration blob: *TCM_CreateMigrateBlob* and the command for importing the migrate blob: *TCM_ConvertMigrateBlob*. Although the name and the function of the command are the same as those of the TPM, the command *TCM_CreateMigrateBlob* is different from the counterpart of the TPM in Migrate way. Since digital envelope is used to protect the migration information, the TCM command *TCM_CreateMigrateBlob* outputs two single encryption blobs. The TPM command *TPM_CreateMigratieBlob* outputs one dual-encryption blob and the inner-layer encryption key in plaintext.

The following pseudo code takes the Rewrap mode as an example to describe the key migration procedure. The source platform creates the key to be migrated key2 and its parent key parKey. The target platform creates the key to protect the migration migrateKey. The source platform performs the authorization of migrateKey, and then uses parKey and migrateKey to complete the creation of the migration blob of key2. The target platform loads migrateKey and finally imports it by converting the migration blob. In order to simplify the description of commands, we attach the command authorization session information after the name of the command and indicate the entity type, the entity handle and the authorization data of the authorization session.
(1) Create the key to protect the migration in the target platform:

```
//on the target platform
TCM_CreateWrapKey[AP=(0x0001,0x40000000,"parentAuth")]
INPUT
        TCM_COMMAND_CODE ordinal=(0x0000801F);
        TCM_KEY_HANDLE parentHandle=(0x40000000);
```

```
        TCM_ENCAUTH dataUsage =("newAuth");
        TCM_KEY key = (TCM_ECCKEY_STORAGE, 0x00000000,
TCM_AUTH_NEVER, TCM_ALG_ECC, TCM_ES_ECC, TCM_SS_ECCNONE,
4,256, null);
OUTPUT
 TCM_RESULT returnCode1=(0);
 TCM_KEY migrateKey;
```

(2) Create the key to be migrated and its parent key in the source platform:

```
//on the source platform
TCM_CreateWrapKey[AP=(0x0001,0x40000000,"parentAuth")]
INPUT
      TCM_COMMAND_CODE ordinal=(0x0000801F);
      TCM_KEY_HANDLE parentHandle=(0x40000000);
      TCM_ENCAUTH dataUsage =("newAuth");
      TCM_ENCAUTH migUsage =("newAuth");
TCM_KEY key = (TCM_ECCKEY_STORAGE, 0x00000002,
TCM_AUTH_NEVER, TCM_ALG_ECC,
TCM_ES_ECC, TCM_SS_ECCNONE, 4,256, null);
OUTPUT
      TCM_RESULT parentReturnCode=(0);
      TCM_KEY parkey;
      TCM_LoadKey[AP=(0x0001,0x40000000,"parentAuth")]
INPUT
      TCM_COMMAND_CODE ordinal=(0x000080EF);
      TCM_KEY_HANDLE parentHandle=(0x40000000);
      TCM_KEY key=(ref_parkey);
OUTPUT
      TCM_RESULT retCode;
      TCM_KEY_HANDLE loadedKeyHandle;
      TCM_CreateWrapKey[AP=(0x0001,ref_loadedKeyHandle,
              "newAuth")]
INPUT
      TCM_COMMAND_CODE ordinal=(0x0000801F);
```

```
        TCM_KEY_HANDLE parentHandle=(ref_loadedKeyHandle);
        TCM_ENCAUTH dataUsage =("newAuth");
        TCM_ENCAUTH migUsage =("newAuth");
TCM_KEY key = (TCM_ECCKEY_STORAGE, 0x00000002,
TCM_AUTH_NEVER, TCM_ALG_ECC,
TCM_ES_ECC, TCM_SS_ECCNONE, 4,256, null);
OUTPUT
        TCM_RESULT returnCode2=(0);
        TCM_KEY key2;
```

(3) Perform the migration authorization in the source platform and create the migration blob:

```
//on the source platform
TCM_AuthorizeMigrationKey[AP=(0x0002,0x40000001,"parentAuth")]
INPUT
        TCM_COMMAND_CODE ordinal=(0x000080C3);
  UINT16 migrationScheme=(0x0001);
        TCM_PUBKEY migrationKey=("fromKey",migrateKey);
OUTPUT
        TCM_RESULT returnCode3=(0);
        TCM_MIGRATIONKEYAUTH outData;
TCM_CreateMigratedBlob[AP2=(0x0001,ref_loadedKeyHandle,
"newAuth", 0x0012,0x00000000,"newAuth")]
INPUT
        TCM_COMMAND_CODE ordinal=(0x000080C1);
        TCM_KEY_HANDLE parentHandle=(ref_loadedKeyHandle);
        UINT16 migrationScheme=(0x0001);
        TCM_MIGRATIONKEYAUTH inData=(ref_outData);
        BYTELIST encData=(refKey_key2);
OUTPUT
        TCM_RESULT returnCode5=(0);
        BYTELIST random;
        BYTELIST encryptedData;
```

(4) Import the migration blob into the target platform:

```
//on the target platform
TCM_LoadKey[AP=(0x0001,0x40000000,"parentAuth")]
INPUT
      TCM_COMMAND_CODE ordinal=(0x000080EF);
      TCM_KEY_HANDLE parentHandle=(0x40000000);
      TCM_KEY key=(ref_migrateKey);
OUTPUT
      TCM_RESULT returnCode11;
      TCM_KEY_HANDLE migrateKeyHandle;
TCM_ConvertMigratedBlob[AP2=(0x0001, ref_migrateKeyHandle,
"newAuth", 0x0001,ref_loadedKeyHandle,"newAuth")]
INPUT
      TCM_COMMAND_CODE ordinal=(0x000080C2);
      TCM_KEY_HANDLE keyHandle=(ref_loadedKeyHandle);
      TCM_KEY_HANDLE handle=(ref_migrateKeyHandle);
      BYTELIST random=(ref_random);
      BYTELIST encryptedData=(ref_encryptedData);
OUTPUT
      TCM_RESULT resutfinal = (0);
      BYTELIST data;
```

Key Agreement Commands. Key agreement protocol is an important cryptographic service, which is used to agree on the session key between the two TCM The TCM commands for key agreement protocol include the command *TCM_CreateKeyExchange*, which is used to create the key agreement sessions, the command *TCM_GetKeyExchange* to obtain the session key and the command *TCM_ReleaseExchangeSession* to clear the key agreement sessions. *TCM_CreateKeyExchange* is used to complete the first step of the above key agreement protocol, namely, to create the ephemeral key used in the key agreement protocol, and to initialize the computational resources. *TCM_GetKeyExchange* is used to complete the second step, namely, to finish the computation of the shared key. *TCM_ReleaseExchangeSession* is used to release the established session. Note that since TCM allows for only one key agreement protocol session, a new session cannot be started until the old session has been cleared.

Data Encryption and Sealing Commands. The TCM commands for data encryption include the command *TCM_SMS4Encrypt* for SMS4 encryption, the command *TCM_SMS4Decrypt* for SMS4 decryption, and the command *TCM_SM2Decrypt* for SM2 decryption. The TCM commands include the command *TCM_Seal* for data sealing and the command *TCM_UnSeal* for data unsealing. In these commands, the main feature of the TCM is that it supports both symmetric and asymmetric encryption algorithms.[13] The following pseudo codes take the SMS4 symmetric encryption and decryption commands as an example to explain the TCM encryption and decryption procedures.

(1) Create SMS4 encryption key by using the SMK as the parent key: The SMK type value is 0 × 0001, the SMK handle is 0 × 40000000 and the SMK authorization value is "parentAuth". Taking these three parameters as the inputs, the user can establish the authorization session. The type of key1 is the SMS4 binding key. The authorization data of key1 are "keyAuth". After loading, the handle of key1 is *loadedKeyHandle*.

```
TCM_CreateWrapKey[AP=(0x0001,0x40000000,"parentAuth")]
INPUT
        TCM_COMMAND_CODE ordinal=(0x0000801F);
        TCM_KEY_HANDLE parentHandle=(0x40000000);
        TCM_ENCAUTH dataUsage =("keyAuth");
        TCM_ENCAUTH migUsage =("keyAuth");
        TCM_KEY key = (TCM_SMS4KEY_BIND, 0x00000002,
TCM_AUTH_ALWAYS, TCM_ALG_SMS4, TCM_ES_SMS4_CBC,
TCM_SS_ECCNONE, 28, 0x80,
0x80,0x00000000000000000000000000000000, null);
OUTPUT
        TCM_RESULT returnCode1=(0);
TCM_KEY key1;
```

(2) Load key1

```
TCM_LoadKey[AP=(0x0001,0x40000000,"parentAuth")]
INPUT
        TCM_COMMAND_CODE ordinal=(0x000080EF);
        TCM_KEY_HANDLE parentHandle=(0x40000000);
        TCM_KEY key=(ref_key1);
```

13 The storage key and encryption key support both symmetric and asymmetric algorithms, but the SMK only supports the symmetric algorithm.

```
OUTPUT
        TCM_RESULT returnCode2=(0);
        TCM_KEY_HANDLE loadedKeyHandle;
```

(3) Use this key to encrypt data *encryptedData*:

```
TCM_SMS4Encrypt[AP=(0x0001,ref_loadedKeyHandle,"keyAuth")]
INPUT
        TCM_COMMAND_CODE ordinal=(0x000080C5);
        TCM_KEY_HANDLE handle=(ref_loadedKeyHandle);
        IV iv=(0x00000000000000000000000000000000);
        BYTELIST
toBeEncrypted=(0x00909090909090909090908787878787);
OUTPUT
TCM_RESULT returnCode3=(0);
        BYTELIST encryptedData;
```

(4) Use this key to decrypt the data. The data *decryptedData* obtained should be the same as the plaintext *toBeEncrypted*.

```
TCM_SMS4Decrypt[AP=(0x0001,ref_loadedKeyHandle,"keyAuth")]
INPUT
     TCM_COMMAND_CODE ordinal=(0x000080C6);
     TCM_KEY_HANDLE handle=(ref_loadedKeyHandle);
     IV iv=(0x00000000000000000000000000000000);
     BYTELIST encryptData=(ref_encryptedData);
OUTPUT
     TCM_RESULT returnCode4=(0);
     BYTELIST
decryptedData=(0x00909090909090909090908787878787);
```

Data Signing and Other Cryptographic Services. In addition to data encryption and decryption, TCM also provides some other commands to protect the integrity and freshness of the platform data, such as the command *TCM_Sign* for signature, the command *TCM_SCHStart* for the initialization of the hash function, the command *TCM_SCHUpdate* for the computation of the hash function, the command *TCM_SCHComplete\TCM_SCHCompleteExtend* to complete the computation of the hash function and the command *TCM_GetRandom* to get the random number. Uses of these commands are similar to those of the TPM.

2.3.2.2 Identification Commands

The TCM identity-related mechanisms are mainly used to set up identity for the TCM itself, namely, to create the identity key, and obtain its certificate from the trusted party. Its functions include the creation and reading of the cryptography module key and the creation and activation of the platform identity key and the platform encryption key. The commands are as follows:

- Cryptography module key management:
  (1) *TCM_CreateEndorsementKeyPair* is used to create the EK. If the TCM already has an EK, the command will fail.

  (2) *TCM_CreateRevocableEK* is used to create a revocable EK. If the TCM already has an EK, the command will fail.

  (3) *TCM_ReadPubEK* is used to read the public key of EK, which does not require authorization.

  (4) *TCM_OwnerReadInternalPub* is used to read the public key of EK or SRK, which requires the owner authorization.

- Platform identity key management:
  (1) *TCM_MakeIdentity* is used to create PIK, and to build an application blob for the PIK certificate. In its execution, the command first verifies the authorization of the ownership and the SMK. Then it creates the PIK and sets the corresponding authorization value, and then uses the private key of the PIK to sign the hash value of the public key of the trusted party and the public key of the PIK. Finally, it outputs the public key of the PIK, the public key of the cryptography module key and the PIK signature.

  (2) *TCM_ActivateIdentity* is used to activate the PIK. In its execution, the TCM first opens the digital envelope and decides whether or not the obtained hash value equals the hash value of the public key of PIK in the platform. If they are same, it returns the session key and the platform identity certificate can be obtained by further decryption.

- Platform encryption key management:
  The PEK is generated by a trusted third party (key escrow authority), and is sent to the TPM in the way of digital envelope. Therefore, PEK management commands are mainly used to open the digital envelope.
  (1) *TCM_ActivatePEK* is used to get the PEK. In its execution, the TCM will use EK to decrypt the symmetric key blob, and use the symmetric key to decrypt and obtain the PEK. This command requires the authorizations of the ownership and the SMK.

  (2) *TCM_ActiviatePEKCert* is used to obtain the PEK certificate. In its execution, the TCM will use EK to decrypt and obtain the symmetric key. The external software can use this key to decrypt and obtain the certificate. This command also requires the owner authorization, but not the SMK authorization.

2.3.2.3 Integrity Storage and Reporting Commands

The TCM commands for integrity storage and reporting are similar to corresponding TPM commands. A typical integrity reporting example is described by the following pseudo codes. It includes the identity creation, PCR extension and PCR quote. In this example, the PIK is used to quote. If it uses assigning key to quote, the command *TCM_CertifyKey* is needed to certify the signing key. It guarantees that the integrity reporting is indeed generated by the TCM chip.

(1) Create and load the identity key. Here we omit the external creation of the platform identity (namely, the application for the platform identity key certificate).

```
TCM_MakeIdentity[AP2 = (0x01, 0x40000000, "smkAuth", 0x02,
0x40000001, "ownerAuth")]
INPUT
        TCM_COMMAND_CODE ordinal=(0x00008079);
        TCM_ENCAUTH encAuth=("newAuth");
        BYTELIST hash=
(0x1234567812345678123456781234567812345678123456781234567 8);
        TCM_KEY pik= (TCM_ECCKEY_IDENTITY, 0, 1,
TCM_ALG_ECC, TCM_ES_ECCNONE, TCM_SS_ECC, 4,256, null);
OUTPUT
        TCM_RESULT returnCode1=(0);
        TCM_KEY PIK;
        BYTELIST sig;
        TCM_LoadKey[AP=(0x0001,0x40000000,"smkAuth")]
INPUT
        TCM_COMMAND_CODE ordinal=(0x000080EF);
        TCM_KEY_HANDLE parentHandle=(0x40000000);
        TCM_KEY key=(ref_PIK);
OUTPUT
        TCM_RESULT returnCode2;
        TCM_KEY_HANDLE loadedKeyHandle;
```

(2) Invoke the command *TCM_PcrExtend* to extend the integrity measurement value into the PCR. In practice, it usually includes many times of extensions to multiple PCRs.

```
TCM_Extend
INPUT
        TCM_COMMAND_CODE ordinal=(TCM_ORD_Extend);
        UINT32 index=(2);
OUTPUT
        TCM_RESULT result=(0);
        TCM_DIGEST newDigest;
```

(3) Quote the extended PCR.

```
TCM_Quote[AP=(0x0001,ref_loadedKeyHandle,"newAuth")]
INPUT
        TCM_COMMAND_CODE ordinal=(TCM_ORD_Quote);
        TCM_KEY_HANDLE keyHandle=(ref_loadedKeyHandle);
        TCM_AUTHDATA antiReplay=("antiReplay");
        TCM_PCR_SELECTION pcrSelection=(2,0x0011);
OUTPUT
        TCM_RESULT returnCode3=(0);
        TCM_PCR_COMPOSITE pcrComposite;
    BYTELIST signature;
```

2.4 Mobile Trusted Module

With the emergence and development of some new computing platforms, the trusted platform modules (TPM and TCM), which are designed to serve for traditional computing platforms such as PC and server, cannot adapt to the requirements of these new platforms. Problems, that it is difficult to customize, verify and update devices, are gradually exposed. Therefore, both industrial and academic communities have launched the researches of a new kind of trusted platform module to meet the actual needs of the new platforms such as mobile platforms and embedded platforms. These works highlight customizability, verifiability and updatability of the new modules.

In 2006, TCG mobile platform working group published the MTM specification for the first time, aiming to promote the trusted computing technology in the mobile fields and guide the future works on technical specifications. Since then, TCG has successively published a series of specifications related to the MTM, involving specifications for the MTM data structures and interfaces (Mobile Trusted Module Specification), the use case and analysis (MTM Use Case Specification and MTM Selected Use Case Analysis Specification) and the architecture of the mobile platform with MTM and the usage (Mobile Reference Architecture Specification).

2.4.1 Main Features of MTM

Although the design principles and the architecture of the MTM are similar to those of the TPM, the new features of the mobile platform environments have put forward some special requirements for the design and implementation of the MTM. To sum up, the features of the MTM mainly include the following four aspects:

- There might be more than one MTM embedded in one mobile platform. As the stakeholders of the mobile platform are more complex, one mobile platform uses multiple MTMs to represent different stakeholders. There are two types of MTM: the MLTM (Mobile Local Trusted Module) and the MRTM (Mobile Remote Trusted Module). The former's stakeholders are the local owners (such as the users). It supports functionalities similar to that of existing TPM. The latter's stakeholders are the remote owners such as device manufacturers or Internet service providers. They do not have physical access to devices.
- It requires a secure boot process based on the MRTM. Since mobile platforms are generally under the regulation, it is necessary to ensure the correctness of the software and hardware running on it. Secure boot not only measures the boot sequence of the mobile platforms but also needs to halt any unexpected state transitions, which is very important for security services.
- The manufacturer can determine the implementation way according to the design principles of the specification. Because of limited resources and diversiform platforms, the MTM cannot be limited to a unified implementation way. In general, MTM can be implemented as a dedicated MTM chip, by using the TPM and the software layer (for the implementation of additional commands), based on the secure computation of the mobile platform, based on the CPU chip in the mobile platform and in the virtualized engine under the protection of the underlying hardware.
- The features of the functionalities and commands are different from those of the TPM. MTM only needs to implement a part of the TPM 1.2 specification commands, and the requirements of the same command in the MTM and the TPM might be different.

2.4.2 MTM Functionalities and Commands

Inheriting the TPM architecture, the MTM especially emphasizes the simplification of the functionality and the satisfaction of the application requirements in mobile environments. Thus, there are great differences between the functionalities of the MTM and the TPM.

For the functionalities and the commands specified in the TPM specification, the inheritance principles of MTM can be summarized as follows: reserve the necessity, simplify the alternative and eliminate the conflicts.

- Reserve the necessity: MTM must reserve the functionalities and commands that maintain the basic trust relationship and the functional principles of the TPM, including platform data protection, identification and integrity measurement and reporting.
- Simplify the alternative: For the TPM functionalities and commands of auxiliary and application classes specified by specifications, the MTM manufacturers can simplify them according to the practical needs to enhance the flexibility. These commands include direct anonymous attestation, time stamp, transport protection, key migration and maintenance. They do not affect the trust relationship and the functional principles of the TPM.
- Eliminate the conflicts: For the functionalities and commands of the TPM that conflict with the MTM demands, the MTM specification directly discards them. For example, the TPM physical presence is to prevent remote malicious users but the MRTM owners are all remote users. Thus, it is not necessary to reserve the physical presence for the MRTM.

In addition to the inheritance of TPM, MTM (MRTM) also especially highlights the secure boot function. TCG has considered the secure boot in the TPM design. However, the specification did not explicitly support the storage, protection and update management of the reference integrity value. TCG did not consider how to ensure the authenticity, freshness and validity of the reference integrity value. In contrast, the TCG defines that the reference integrity value in the MTM architecture should be provided by trusted third parties in the form of reference integrity certificate (a signature on the reference integrity value, denoted by RIMCert). In order to authenticate the reference integrity value, the computing platform must have an asymmetric key to verify the certificate RIMCert. The key is usually imported into the computing platform during the production and is protected by the MTM. Based on this root key, the user can import into the MTM a new verification key of RIMCert. MTM defines the commands *MTM_LoadVerificationKey* and *MTM_LoadVerificationRootKeyDisable* to complete above functionality. The manufacturer can use the former command to load the verification root key into the TPM. Users can also use this command to load new verification keys by using the verification root key or the owner authorization value. Once the manufacturer has loaded the verification root key, the latter command can be used to prohibit the reloading of the verification root key.

When the key is loaded, the computing platform can use it to verify the reference integrity value. MTM defines the command *MTM_VerifyRIMCertAndExtend* to merge the procedures of the verification and extension of the integrity value. The merging of the two procedures improves the efficiency. Note that MTM also defines a similar command called *MTM_VerifyRIMCert*, which is used only for debugging and diagnostics. In order to improve the efficiency and security, in MTM it is recommended to convert the certificate based on digital signature (external certificate) into the certificate based on message authentication code (internal certificate). Given an external certificate, MTM can use the command *MTM_InstallRIM* to extract its information, and use an internal secret key to compute an HMAC value as the new internal certificate.

With the functionality for the verification of reference integrity value, MTM can use the internal certificate to launch the secure boot, which is the so-called standard boot or normal boot. When the internal certificate is not available in MTM producing or completing firmware update, the user can only boot using an external certificate, which is the so-called initial boot.

In order to ensure the freshness (a newly loaded certificate cannot be older than the original certificate) and the validity (a newly loaded certificate has not been revoked) of the loaded certificate, the MTM has two internal monotonic counters: *counterBootstrap* and *counterRIMProtect*.

- *counterBootstrap* is used to record the security version number of the external certificate. When the external certificate is verified in the boot, MTM will use this counter to check whether the certificate has been revoked. Since an external certificate might be used for a number of platforms and the version numbers of components in these computing platforms should be the same, the trusted third party can release the value in the form of an external certificate. The counter is permanently stored in the shielded memory of the MTM. Given an external certificate, the computing platform can use the command *MTM_IncrementBootstrapCounter* to set its value. Note that only when some specific external certificate has security risks, the trusted third party will update the value. The change of the version of components does not necessarily cause the change of the value.
- *counterRIMProtect* is used to record the version number of the internal certificate. When the internal certificate is verified in the boot, MTM will use this counter to check the freshness of the certificate to prevent version rollback attacks. Since each internal certificate is unique, the *counterRIMProtect* values of different computing platforms are not necessarily the same. This counter can be implemented by an ordinary monotonic counter. The user can set its value at any time in need. In principle, any upgrade of components should cause the change of the counter.

2.5 Developments of Related New Technologies

In recent years, the international information industrial giants have launched a number of system security technologies, including the Intel TXT, Intel VT, AMD-V and ARM TrustZone. These technologies have a significant impact on the industrial development and academic research, which are closely related to the trusted platform module. In this section, we briefly introduce their developments in two aspects: dynamic root of trust for measurement and the virtualization technologies. The DRTM technologies, such as the Intel TXT and the AMD-V, can bind the RTM to a special security CPU instruction to make it possible for the dynamic establishment of the trusted environment. Furthermore, it has a direct impact on the functional design of the trusted platform module. The virtualization technologies, such as the Intel VT, provide a hardware-based isolation environment to solve the problem of mutual isolation between software. It is a good complementary to the trusted platform module in building a trusted computing environment.

2.5.1 Dynamic Root of Trust for Measurement

According to the design principles given by the TPM specification, from the power-on of the platform, the chain of trust[14] must check and report all the programs that have run or are running in the system. This idea essentially originates from the requirements of constructing system-level trusted environment, and it cannot meet the requirements of constructing application-level dynamic trusted environment.

To solve this problem, the international microprocessor manufacturer giants Intel and AMD introduced their own DRTM technologies, namely, Intel TXT (Intel Trusted Execution Technology) [93, 94] and AMD Presidio, respectively. The two technologies extend CPU and motherboard chipsets, which enables the system to enter into the trusted execution environment at any time and enjoy a minimum trusted computing base. The working principles of the DRTM are as follows: (1) The system software loads the codes to be executed into the trusted environment and then triggers the DRTM launch instruction provided by the CPU. (2) The instruction is broadcasted to the whole hardware platform, and then all the environmental contexts are saved. The components that can directly access the memory, such as DMA, are disabled. The interrupts are disabled. The dynamic PCR[15] in TPM is reset. (3) TPM begins to execute the codes set in step one. All executed codes are extended into the dynamic PCR step by step. (4) The DRTM termination instruction is executed, and then the system restores the saved contexts. The platform can do remote attestation by quoting the dynamic PCR. Since only the DRTM launch instruction can reset the dynamic PCR and the reset initial value is different from the initial value set in the restart of the system, the remote challenger can verify that the system has really entered the trusted execution environment launched by DRTM.

DRTM relies on the TPM locality mechanism to perform access control for hardware instructions. It also relies on the TPM integrity storage and reporting

---

14 The concept of trust chain will be explained in the following sections. Here it means the logical chain structure formed by programs in their launching order whose integrity should be measured and reported.

15 It can also be reset in the running of the TPM.

mechanisms. Thus, it can be said that DRTM has enriched existing technology architecture of chain of trust, which is originally designed to protect the operating system. It still follows the basic design principles of the trusted computing technology.

2.5.2 Virtualization Technology

The virtualization technology uses a single hardware platform to simulate a number of homogeneous devices, so as to improve equipment utilization, reduce energy consumption, and support the parallel execution of multiple operating systems or applications. From the viewpoint of system security, virtualization technology can provide the runtime isolation mechanism for operating systems or application programs and can effectively prevent the intrusion on systems or programs.

In order to improve the running efficiency of the virtualized system platforms and enhance the compatibility of the virtualization technology to existing operating systems, it should seek solutions at the hardware level, such as the processors and the motherboard chipset. Intel and AMD have introduced the Intel VT and AMD-V processor enhancement technologies, respectively. We take the VT-x as an example. Under the traditional CPU 0-3 privilege levels, it adds a dedicated "−1" level for monitor. The virtual machine monitor that is responsible for monitoring the virtual domains can run in this special privilege. It facilitates both the protection of the virtual machine monitor and the monitoring of the virtual domains. Thus, it has solved the contradiction in the above system-level virtualization. In addition to the virtualization of processors, Intel also released the VT-d technology. Through adding the address mapping mechanism controlled by the VMM to the motherboard chipset, it strongly supports the virtualization of the direct IO components such as DMA, and guarantees the isolation of the information transfer between virtual domains.

Combining the trusted computing technology and virtualization technology is conducive to take advantage of their feature to build secure execution environments: The trusted computing technology can build chains of trust in the system boot and provide the protected storage, integrity storage and integrity reporting mechanisms; the virtualization technology can provide the isolation of the protected system components while the system is running. It refines the protection granularity of trusted environments and enhances the dynamicity and extensibility of trusted computing environments. It can be said that the virtualization technology makes up some deficiencies of current trusted technical architecture.

2.6 Summary

Trusted platform module is the core of the trusted computing technology and standard architecture. The typical trusted platform modules include the TCG TPM security chip and Chinese TCM security chip. They follow a similar design principle but also have many differences. Based on Chinese cryptographic algorithm, the security and efficiency of TCM are greatly enhanced compared with those of the TPM. Combined with the security needs and the market demand, TCM has experienced the innovations in the several key technologies. TCM has fixed the vulnerabilities exposed in the use of the TPM.

As the core technical component of the trusted computing technology, researches on the trusted platform module develop rapidly with the changing application requirements. All kinds of theoretical and technical progresses emerge, mainly in the following two development trends.

First, the implementation forms of the trusted platform module are diversified, and the functionalities will be further enriched. The existing trusted computing technical architecture originates from the desktop computing era, when the mainstream computing platforms are PCs and servers. The depth and breadth of the application of computer network are not the same today. The current computing platforms are comparatively more and more diversified. The applications based on the network have more requirements for the trustworthiness of the computing platforms. Therefore, the trusted computing technical architecture should be adjusted. As the core of the trusted computing technical architecture, the implementation form of the trusted platform module should be diversified. Its functionality should be customizable and its cost should be adjustable, so as to provide elasticity and flexibility for today's complex trusted computing environments.

Second, the combination of the trusted platform module and other system security technologies will be more close. Like the other security technologies, trusted computing is not a panacea. The design idea of the trusted computing is great, but in fact existing trusted computing technology can only support a specific part of it. In this case, it is necessary to enrich the whole technical architecture in condition of keeping the essence of existing trusted computing technology. Through the introduction of other advanced system security technologies and taking advantages of all kinds of technologies, they can complement each other, and finally propose complete solutions for system security and trustworthiness.

3 Building Chain of Trust

Corrupting critical components of computer systems, tampering system running codes and modifying configuration files of computer systems have become the most popular attack methods used by hackers. These attacks change original trusted execution environment (TEE) of systems via modifying running code and critical configuration files, and then use this untrusted execution environment to launch attacks. So building TEEs for computer systems is a critical security problem in current computer security area.

To build a trusted execution environment, we first need to clarify the definition of trust. There are many different definitions for trust in trusted computing. The international standard ISO/IEC [95] defines trust as follows: "A trusted component, operation, or process is one whose behavior is predictable under almost any operating condition and which is highly resistant to subversion by application software, virus, and a given level of physical interference." IEEE [96] defines trust as follows: "the ability to deliver service that can justifiably be trusted." TCG defines trust as follows [3]: something is trusted "if it always behaves in the expected manner for the intended purpose." All these definitions have one common point: they all emphasize the expectable behavior of one entity and the security and reliability of the system. TCG's definition centers on the characteristic of entity's behavior, and it is more suitable to describe users' requirements for trust. This trust framework requires to research the method to implement trust. TCG gives a method to build trusted execution environment for computer systems: chain of trust.

Chain of trust based on trusted computing is a technology introduced in above background. By measuring every layer of computer systems and transferring trust between entities, TCG establishes trustworthiness from the hardware to the application layer and uses the security chip embedded in the platform to protect the measured data. In this way, chains of trust build TEE for computer systems. This kind of chains of trust not only provides TEE for users but also provides evidence of program's running in TEE. It can also be combined with traditional network technology to extend trustworthiness to network environment.

In this chapter, we first introduce trust anchor: root of trust, including the root of trust for measurement (RTM), the root of trust for storage (RTS) and the root of trust for reporting (RTR). Next, we will introduce principles of building chains of trust. Then we will introduce popular system of static chains of trust and dynamic chains of trust. Finally, we will introduce the method of building chains of trust for virtualization platforms.

DOI 10.1515/9783110477597-003

3.1 Root of Trust

3.1.1 Introduction of Root of Trust

Consider a common scenario where an entity called A launches an entity called B, and then B launches an entity called C. The user must first trust B, then he/she can trust C and so on. The user should finally trust entity A. To build such a chain of trust, we should perform as follows:

(1) Entity A launches entity B, then transfers control to entity B.
(2) Entity B launches entity C, then transfers control to entity C.

Then here the question arises: Who will launch entity A? As there is no entity that runs earlier than A, A is such an entity that must be trusted. To build a trustworthy chain of trust, entities such as A should be implemented by certified manufacturers, and their trustworthiness is guaranteed by the manufacturers. Entities like A are called root of trust (RoT) in chains of trust.

RoTs for platforms should satisfy the minimal functionality requirements that used to describe the platform's trust. Generally, trusted computing platform has three kinds of RoTs: RTM, RTS and RTR. In the following, we will first introduce RTM that has the most close relationship with building chains of trust and then we will introduce RTS and RTR.

3.1.2 Root of Trust for Measurement

During the development of trusted computing technology, two kinds of RTMs appear successively. The static RTM (SRTM) technology appears first. SRTM, the first entity that runs on the hardware since power on, is used to establish a chain of trust from the hardware to the OS even to the application, and the chain of trust established by static RTM is called static chain of trust. There is a new technology called dynamic RTM (DRTM), which can establish a chain of trust when the system is running. DRTM can establish a chain of trust whose TCB requires very small amount of hardware and software by invoking a special CPU instruction, and this kind of chain of trust is called dynamic chain of trust. In the following, we will introduce these two kinds of RTM.

3.1.2.1 Static Root of Trust for Measurement

SRTM, which first controls the platform since the system powers on, is used to establish a chain of trust from the platform's hardware to the upper application, and the SRTM plays the role of trust anchor in the chain of trust. Since SRTM must run first in the platform, it is usually implemented as the first running codes or the whole codes in the BIOS and also called as core root of trust for measurement (CRTM). There exist two kinds of CRTM in current PC architecture:

(1) CRTM is the first running code in the BIOS. In this kind of architecture, the BIOS consists of two independent block: BIOS boot block and post BIOS. The BIOS boot block plays the role of CRTM.
(2) CRTM is the whole BIOS. In this kind of architecture, the BIOS is indivisible, so the whole BIOS is the CRTM.

CRTM runs first since the platform powers on, and is responsible for measuring the following codes that run on the platform. If CRTM is the BIOS boot block, then it will first measure all the firmwares of the platform's mainboard, and then transfer the control to the post BIOS, which will boot the following components. If the CRTM is the whole BIOS, it will directly measure the following components, such as bootloader, and then transfer the control to bootloader, which is responsible for establishing the following chain of trust.

3.1.2.2 Dynamic Root of Trust for Measurement

SRTM suffers from several drawbacks, for example, it cannot establish a chain of trust dynamically in the running time and its trusted computing base (TCB) is too big. To deal with these drawbacks, the DRTM technology is proposed, and has been adopted by TPM 1.2 specifications. DRTM relies on a special CPU instruction, which can be triggered at any time when the platform runs, and then establish an isolated execution environment whose TCB contains only a few hardware and software codes. DRTM has an advantage of flexible trigger timing, and that's why it is called dynamic RTM. The CPU giants, Intel and AMD, propose CPU architectures supporting DRTM, respectively, Trusted Execution Technology (TXT) and Secure Virtual Machine (SVM). In the following, we will introduce SVM and TXT.

AMD DRTM Technology. The SVM architecture proposed by AMD consists of virtualization and security extensions, and the security extension is mainly used for establishing isolated execution environment based on DRTM.

SVM DRTM technology uses the SKINIT instruction as the dynamic root of trust for measurement, which can be triggered at any time when the CPU runs. When the SKINIT instruction is triggered, it runs the Secure Loader Block (SLB[1]) code, which requires protection. Besides the flexibility of the trigger time, the AMD DRTM technology provides protection against DMA attacks for the SLB memory region: It provides an address register SL_DEV_BASE pointing to a continuous 64K memory space, and peripheral is prohibited to issue DMA access to this memory. However, the SVM DRTM technology doesn't clear the sensitive data in the SLB, so the SLB should do this itself when it exits.

1 SLB is used to store the code block running in the isolated environment, and its total size is 60 KB.

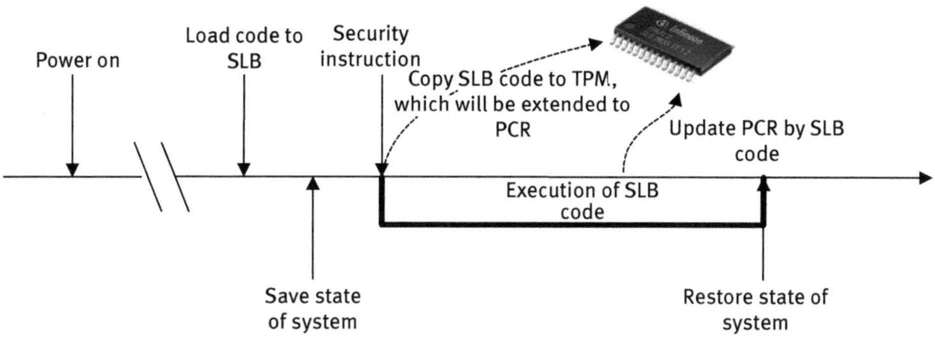

Figure 3.1: SKINIT timeline.

The SKINIT instruction takes the physical address as its own input operator, and it will build an isolated TEE when it is triggered as described in Figure 3.1:

(1) Re-initialize all the processors, then enter the 32-bit protected mode and disable the page table mechanism.

(2) Clear bits 15–0 of EAX to 0 (which is the SLB base address) enable the SL_DEV protection mechanism to protect SLB's 64K bytes region of physical memory and prohibit any peripheral from accessing this memory using DMA.

(3) Multiple processors perform an inter-processor handshake (all other CPU processors are suspended).

(4) Read the SL image from memory and transmit it to the TPM, and ensure that the SL image cannot be corrupted by software.

(5) Signal the TPM to complete the hash and verify the signature. If any failures occur, the TPM will conclude that illegal SL code was executed.

(6) Clear the Global Interrupt Flag (GIF) to disable all interrupts, including NMI, SMI and INIT, and ensure that the execution of subsequent code cannot be interrupted.

(7) Set the ESP register to be the first address beyond the end of SLB (SLB base + 10000H), so that the data pushed onto the stack by SL will be at the top of SLB.

(8) Add the 16-bit entry point offset of SL to the SLB base address to form the SL entry point address, jump to it and execute it.

Intel TXT Technology. Intel proposed the TXT technology, which is similar to the SVM architecture in 2006. TXT technology consists of VT-x technology and Safer Mode Extensions (SMX), and SMX is mainly used to build the TEE. TXT technology involves the processors, chipset, IO bus, TPM and other components.

The SMX of TXT provides an instruction set called GETSEC, which can be used to build a TEE. The SENTER instruction of GETSEC set is used as the dynamic root of trust for measurement, and can be triggered at any time when CPU runs. Just like AMD SVM,

TXT also provides DMA protection for the user codes running in the TEE (including the SINIT AC module[2] and MLE code[3]), and currently TXT can isolate 3M memory address space for sensitive codes.

TXT also provides a mechanism called launch control policy (LCP) that can be used to check the platform's hardware configuration. LCP mechanism is a part of the SINIT AC module, and is used to check whether the chipset and processor's configuration meets current security policy. The LCP consists of three parts:

(1) LCP policy engine: Part of the SINIT ACM and enforces the policies stored on the platform.
(2) LCP policies: Stored in the TPM, they specify the policies that SINIT ACM will enforce.
(3) LCP policy data objects: Referenced by the policy structures in the TPM; each contains a list of valid policy elements, such as measurement values of MLEs or platform configurations.

Figure 3.2 describes the relationships between the LCP components. The LCP policy engine of the SINIT AC module reads the index of policy engine stored in TPM NV memory, decides which policy file will be used and checks whether the platform's configuration and MLE satisfy the LCP policy. If yes, the LCP policy engine will transfer the control to the MLE.

Before building an isolated TEE for MLE, TXT first needs to load the SINIT AC module and MLE to memory and then trigger GETSEC instruction. GETSEC builds a secure environment for MLE by the following steps (for more details, please refer to Figure 3.3):

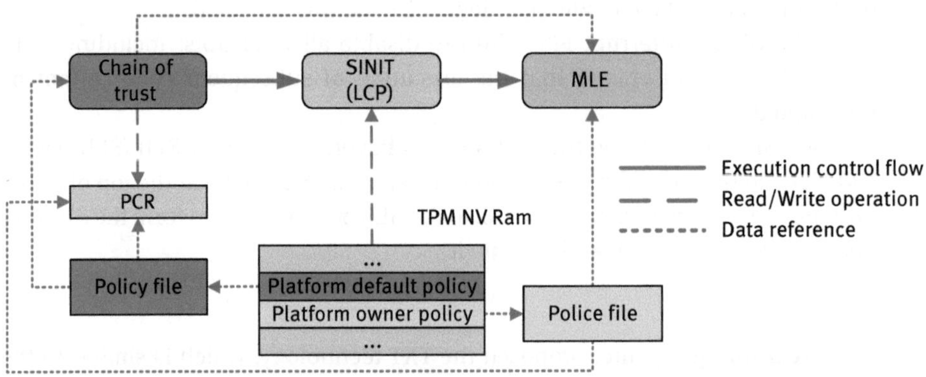

Figure 3.2: LCP components.

2 SINIT AC module is used to check hardware configuration in the TXT technology.

3 MLE is the code running in the isolated environment, and this and the SINIT AC module need to be loaded into the memory before the establishment of isolated environment.

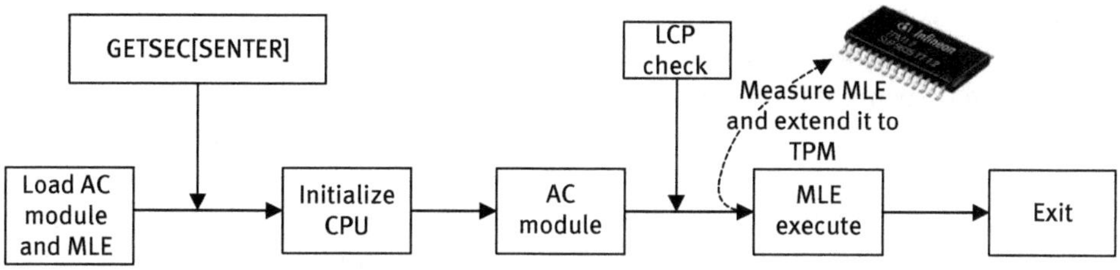

Figure 3.3: The process of building TEE using Intel TXT technology.

(1) The GETSEC[SENTER] instruction can only run in the Initial Logical Processor (ILP), and other processors are called Responding Logical Processor (RLP). ILP broadcasts GETSEC[SENTER] instruction messages to other processors in the platform. In response, other logical processors disable their interrupts (by setting interrupt mask), and inform ILP that they have disabled their interrupts, entered SENTER hibernate state and waited for joining the TEE build by ILP. By now, RLP can only waken up by WAKEUP instruction in the GETSEC set.

(2) After ILP receives the RLPs' readiness signal, it loads, authenticates and executes the AC module. The AC module checks whether the configuration of the chipset and processors satisfy the security requirements, including the LCP check concerned above.

(3) AC module measures MLE and stores the measurement result to the TPM, and leverages the DMA protection mechanism to protect the memory region where MLE resides.

(4) After the execution of AC module, CPU launches the GETSEC[EXITAC] instruction to perform the initial code of MLE, which is the code first run in the isolated environment. The initial code of MLE builds an execution environment for the following code of MLE, and at this time it can trigger WAKEUP instruction to invite other RLPs to join in MLE.

(5) When MLE decides to destroy the secure execution environment it builds, ILPs can trigger SEXIT instruction to exit TXT.

3.1.3 Root of Trust for Storage and Reporting

3.1.3.1 Root of Trust for Storage

The TCG defines the RTS as a computation engine that maintains the integrity measurement value and sequence of the measurement value. RTS stores the measurement value in the log, and stores the hash value of the measurement to the PCR. Besides, RTS is responsible for protecting all the data and cryptographic keys delegated to the security chip. We will introduce RTS of security chips in this section.

In order to reduce the cost, security chips are usually equipped with a little volatile memory. However, security chips need to protect lots of cryptographic keys and delegated secure data. In order to ensure the normal usage of security chips, a special storage architecture is designed for RTS: A key cache management (KCM) module locates between the external storage device and RTS in the security chip. KCM is used to transfer cryptographic keys between the security chip and external storage device: It transfers the cryptographic keys that are not required any more or not activated outside of the security chip, and transfers the cryptographic key that will be used into the security chip. This kind of design not only reduces the memory resources of the security chip but also guarantees the normal usage of the RTS.

3.1.3.2 Root of Trust for Reporting

The RTR is a computing engine that guarantees the integrity attestation function. RTR has two functions: First, it displays the integrity measurement values stored in the security chip; second, it proves to the remote platform its integrity measurement values based on the platform identity attestation. The integrity reporting function leverages the attestation identity key (AIK) to sign the PCRs that store the platform's integrity measurement values. The remote verifier uses the signature to verify the platform's state. The typical platform's integrity measurement reporting protocol is as follows: The verifier requests for the platform's configuration of the attester with a random nonce that is used to resist replay attacks and also for the PCR values stored in the security chip, and then the security chip signs the PCR values with the nonce using the AIK; the attester transfers the signature to the verifier, who will verify the signature using the public key of the verifier's AIK to check the integrity state of the attester.

3.2 Chain of Trust

3.2.1 The Proposal of Chain of Trust

The Internet is the main way to communicate, while it is also the main way for the malicious codes such as Trojan horse and virus to spread. All the malicious codes come from some terminal, so protecting the security of the terminal is always a focused research point in the field of computer security. Currently, there are many technologies that protect the computer system, such as antivirus tools, intrusion detection systems and system access control. Although these technologies can improve the security of the system, all of them use the principle of putting patches on the system, which cannot improve the system's security thoroughly. In this background, trusted computing proposes the technology of chain of trust, which can ensure that all the codes running on the system are trustworthy by measuring the running components and the transitive trust. So the chain of trust can solve the security problems of computer system from the source.

Trusted computing technology gives us a way to build chains of trust by embedding the RTM in the computer system. We transfer the trust from the RTM to the whole computer system by measuring and verifying hardware/software layers of the system one by one, and thus guarantee that the whole system is trustworthy. In the earlier works, the representative measurement system is the Copliot system [8] proposed by University of Maryland and the Pioneer system [9] proposed by CMU Cylab. These two systems perform the measurement leveraging a customized PCI card and an external trusted entity, respectively. The disadvantage of the two systems is that they cannot be deployed on general terminal platforms. Taking the TPM as the root of trust, TCG proposes a way of building chain of trust for general terminal platforms by measuring the hardware, operating system and applications step by step.

Chains of trust are categorized as the static chain of trust and the dynamic chain of trust by the kind of RTM they are based on. The static chain of trust takes the static RTM as the RoT, and can ensure the whole platform's trustworthiness. The static chain of trust was proposed in early days and now it is a mature technology. TCG specifies its procedure in some specifications. With the development of technology, the dynamic chain of trust has been proposed. It can establish a dynamic chain of trust at any system running time by leveraging the flexibility of the dynamic RTM.

3.2.2 Categories of Chain of Trust

3.2.2.1 Static Chain of Trust

The static chain of trust starts from the SRTM and establishes a chain of trust from the platform's hardware to the applications by measuring and verifying the hardware/software layers one by one. It transfers the trust from the RTM to the code of applications, and thus guarantees the trustworthiness of the whole platform. The static chain of trust is based on two technologies: integrity measurement and transitive trust. We first introduce these two technologies and then introduce the procedure of establishing the static chain of trust specified in TCG's specifications.

Basic Principles of the Static Chain of Trust. TCG calls the measurement of an entity performed by one trusted entity as measurement events. A measurement event refers to two classes of data: (1) data to be measured – a representation of codes or data to be measured and (2) measurement digests – a hash of those data to be measured. Entity that is responsible for performing measurement obtains the measurement digest by hashing the data to be measured, and the measurement digest is a snapshot and the integrity mark of the data to be measured.

Measurement digest marks the integrity information of the data to be measured, and the integrity report also requires the measurement digest; so the measurement digest needs to be protected, which is done by the RTS of security chip. The data to be measured do not require to be protected by security chip, but should be remeasured during the integrity attestation. So the computation platform needs to store the data.

TCG uses the Storage Measurement Log (SML) to store the list of software involved in the static chain of trust, and SML mainly stores the data to be measured and measurement digests. TCG does not define data encoding rules for SML contents but usually recommends following appropriate standards such as Extensible Markup Language (XML).

The TPM uses a set of registers, called Platform Configuration Registers (PCR), to store measurement digests. TPM provides an operation called Extend for PCRs. Updates to a PCR follows as PCR[n] = SHA1 (PCR[n] || data to be measured). The Extend operation produces a 160-bits hash value, which can be used as the measurement digest of the measured software, and the later measured data will be extended based on the old PCR value and will produce a new PCR value after the Extend operation. In this way, PCR records the extended data list. For example, PCR[i] is extended by a list data of m1, ..., mi, and finally PCR[i]= SHA1(..SHA1(SHA1(0||m1)||m2)...||mi), and the digest in PCR[i] represents the execution sequence of m1,..., mi.

Transitive Trust. Transitive trust follows the method below: First measure and then verify and finally execute (denoted by measure-verify-execute method). From the RTM, every running component should first measure the next components and then check its integrity according to its measurement digest. If the integrity check passes, the running component will transfer the execution control to the measured component; else, the chain of trust will abort as it indicates that the measured component is not the target we expect. By this process, we can transfer trust from the RTM to the application layer. Figure 3.4 describes the procedure how the trust is transferred from the static RTM to the upper application layer.

Establishment of the Static Chain of Trust. Conventional computer system consists of hardware, bootloader, operating system and applications, and boots as follows: When the system is powered on, BIOS first runs the Power On Self Test (POST) procedure and then invokes the INT 19H interrupt to launch the subsequent program (normally the bootloader stored in the MBR of hard disk) according to the boot sequence set by BIOS, and then the bootloader launches the operating system and finally the applications.

By the idea of transitive trust, TCG defines the procedure of how to establish the chain of trust from RTM to the bootloader:

(1) After the system is powered on, CRTM extends itself and POST BIOS (if exists) and motherboard's firmware on the platform to PCR[0].
(2) After BIOS gets control, it extends PCRs in the following way: First, extend the configuration of platform motherboard and hardware components to PCR [95]; second, extend the optional ROM controlled by BIOS to PCR [96]; third, extend

Table 3.1: PCR usage.

PCR index	PCR usage
0	Store measurement values of CRTM, BIOS and Platform Extensions
1	Store measurement values of platform configuration
2	Store measurement values of option ROM code
3	Store measurement values of option ROM configuration and data
4	Store measurement values of IPL code (usually the MBR)
5	Store measurement values of IPL code configuration and data (used by the IPL code)
6	Store measurement values of state transition and wake event information
7	Reserved for future usage

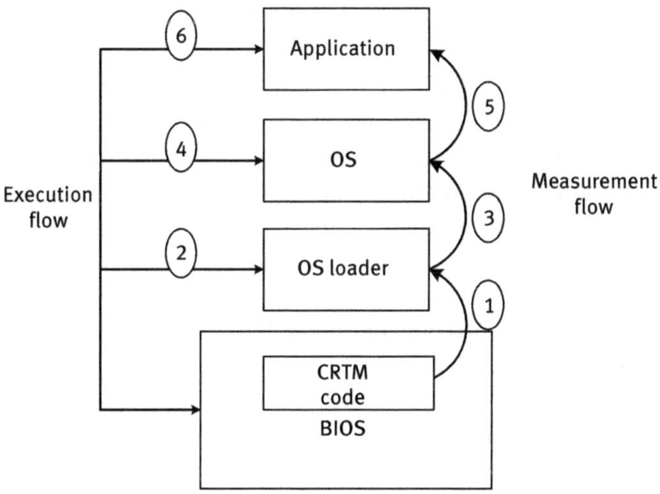

Figure 3.4: The static chain of trust.

the configuration of optional ROM and related data to PCR [3]; fourth, extend the IPL, which reads MBR code and finds the loadable image from the MBR to PCR [97]; fifth, extend the configuration of IPL and other data used by IPL to PCR [98]. The details of PCR usage is listed in Table 3.1;

(3) Invoke INT 19H to transfer the execution control to MBR code (usually bootloader). At this time, the chain of trust is extended to bootloader.

After the chain of trust is established to the bootloader, the bootloader and the OS must obey the measure-verify-execute method if they want to extend the chain of trust. The establishment of the whole static chain of trust is described in Figure 3.4.

3.2.2.2 Dynamic Chain of Trust

The static chain of trust introduced earlier takes SRTM as RoT, and can only be established when the system is powered on. This inflexibility brings inconvenience to users. To deal with this problem, AMD and Intel propose CPU security extensions supporting special instructions that can be used as DRTM. Combined with TPM version 1.2, these instructions can establish dynamic chain of trust based on DRTM. First, this kind of chain of trust is based on CPU's special security instructions, and can be established at any time; second, the dynamic chain of trust greatly reduces TCB of the platform by making the chain of trust not rely on the whole platform system.

Because of its flexibility, the application scenario of dynamic chain of trust is not confined. Current dynamic chain of trust can not only provide functions like static chain of trust, such as trusted boot and TEE building for general computation platforms and virtual machine platforms, but can also be used to build chain of trust for any code running on system.

Although dynamic chains of trust can be applied in many kinds of scenarios, the establishment procedure is alike. Except for some slight differences in technical details, the DRTM technologies provided by AMD and Intel have the same principle. In the following, taking the virtual machine platforms based on hypervisor as an example, we will describe how to build a dynamic chain of trust for a piece of code (which is called SL in SVM architecture and MLE in TXT technology). The details are depicted in Figure 3.5.

(1) Load the code of hypervisor and check-code for the platform (such as AC module in TXT technology).
(2) Invoke security instruction, which does the following work:
    (a) Initialize all processors in the platform.
    (b) Disable interrupts.
    (c) Perform DMA protection for hypervisor code.
    (d) Reset PCR 17 to 20.

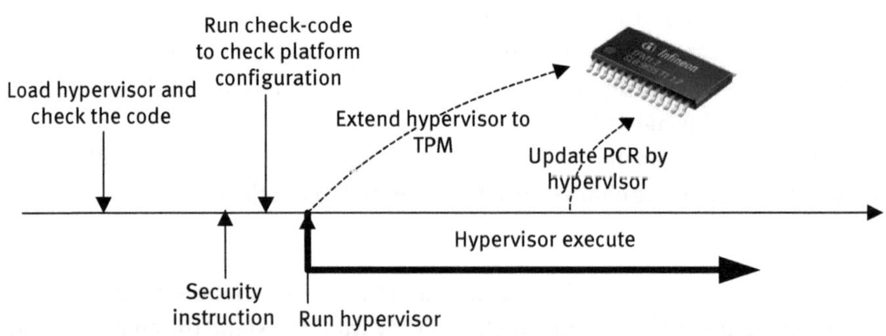

Figure 3.5: The establishment process of dynamic chain of trust.

(3) The main processor loads the check-code for the platform, guarantees its legality by checking its signature and then extends this code to PCR 17.
(4) Run the check-code for the platform to ensure that platform's hardware satisfies the security requirements and then measure hypervisor and extend it to PCR 18.
(5) Run hypervisor in the isolated TEE and wake other processors to join in this isolated environment according to its requirement.

Please note that when the security instruction is invoked, PCR 17 to 20 will be reset, and the reset value is different from the initial value set when the system is powered on. The difference makes the remote verifier believe that the system indeed enters into the isolated TEE established by DRTM. To guarantee the correctness of remote attestation, system designers must guarantee that only the security instruction can reset dynamic PCRs. To achieve this goal, TPM version 1.2 specifications present the locality mechanism, aiming to deploy access control when platform components access TPM resources (such as PCRs). There are six localities defined (Localities 0–4 and Locality None). The following text describes each locality and its associated components:

- Locality 4: Trusted hardware components. It is used by the DRTM to establish the dynamic chain of trust.
- Locality 3: Auxiliary components. This is an optional locality. If used, it is defined upon implementation.
- Locality 2: Runtime environment of OS launched dynamically (dynamic OS).
- Locality 1: Environment used by the dynamic OS.
- Locality 0: The Static RTM, dynamic chain of trust and environment for SRTM.
- Locality None: This locality is defined for TPM version 1.1 and is used for downward compatibility.

To adapt DRTM, TPM v1.2 adds 8 PCRs compared to TPM v1.1, and the added PCRs are PCR 16 to 23. These PCRs are also called dynamic PCRs, and PCR 0 to 15 defined in TPM v1.1 are called static PCRs. TPM v1.2 also adds PCR reset (pcrReset), locality reset (pcrResetLocal), locality extend (pcrExtendLocal) attributes for DRTM technology, and the locality mechanism supports usage control on these dynamic PCRs. Table 3.2 lists PCR attributes and the usage control on PCR of each locality: 0 in the table indicates that the PCR has no such attribute and 1 indicates that the PCR has such an attribute. The 0/1 value in the locality reset and locality extend columns indicates whether the components with localities 0–4 have this attribute.

Locality level represents the physical binding relationship between the platform's components and TPM. For more details, please refer to Table 3.3. For example, locality 4 is bound to DRTM, so only DRTM possesses the control of TPM resources, particularly the control of PCR.

Table 3.2: PCR attributes.

PCR index	Alias	PCRRest	LocalityReset	LocalityExtend
0–15	Static RTM	0	0, 0, 0, 0, 0	1, 1, 1, 1, 1
16	Debug	1	1, 1, 1, 1, 1	1, 1, 1, 1, 1
17	Locality 4	1	1, 0, 0, 0, 0	1, 1, 1, 0, 0
18	Locality 3	1	1, 0, 0, 0, 0	1, 1, 1, 0, 0
19	Locality 2	1	1, 0, 0, 0, 0	0, 1, 1, 0, 0
20	Locality 1	1	1, 0, 1, 0, 0	0, 1, 1, 1, 0
21	Controlled by dynamic OS	1	0, 0, 1, 0, 0	0, 0, 1, 0, 0
22	Controlled by dynamic OS	1	0, 0, 1, 0, 0	0, 0, 1, 0, 0
23	Application specific	1	1, 1, 1, 1, 1	1, 1, 1, 1, 1

Table 3.3: Locality usage.

Locality	Control entity	PCRs that can be reset	PCRs that can be extended
All	All software	16, 23	16, 23
0	Static CRTM and Static operating system	None	0–15
1	Dynamic operating system	None	20
2	Dynamic operating system	20, 21, 22	17, 18, 19, 20, 21, 22
3	Auxiliary trusted components	None	17, 18, 19, 20
4	Dynamic RTM	17, 18, 19, 20	18

3.2.3 Comparisons between Chains of Trust

The chain of trust aims to build isolated TEE from the root of trust. Table 3.4 gives a detailed comparison of static chain of trust and dynamic chain of trust from the aspects of hardware requirements, time of establishment, TCB, hardware protection, development difficulty, user experience and so on.

Table 3.4 shows that the static chain of trust has lower requirements on hardware, so we can establish the chain of trust for the whole system by adding some corresponding functionalities that are transparent to users and have less effect on user experience. However, due to the effect of CRTM, the static chain of trust can only be established at the time of system start, so we need to reboot the platform if we want to reestablish the chain of trust. In addition, the static chain of trust can only start from the hardware level of the platform and extend to the application level one by one, so its TCB contains the whole system. Meanwhile, the bigger the TCB, the more possibilities of security problems, and the lower the security level of the system. Kauer [98] overviews all kinds of attacks on static chain of trust, including TPM reset attack,

Table 3.4: Comparisons between static chain of trust and dynamic chain of trust.

	Static chain of trust	Dynamic chain of trust
Hardware requirements	General PC architecture equipped with security chips	Security chip and the CPU need to support security instructions
Time of establishment	Only at the time of system start	At any time
TCB	The whole computer system	Small amount of hardware and software
Hardware protection	No	DMA protection for isolated environment
Development difficulty	Easy, don't require special program	Difficult to develop, program must be self-contained
User experience	Have little effect on user experience	Have poor user experience, can only run isolated code
Known attacks	TPM reset attack, BIOS replacement attack, TCB bug attack	None

BIOS replacement attack and attacks exploiting bugs in the code. TPM reset attack finds a way that resets TPM v1.1 without resetting platform and leverages it to break the static chain of trust. Current BIOS is stored on the motherboard's flash, which can be replaced. As the foundation of static chain of trust, the CRTM stored in the BIOS can be replaced. This makes the static chain of trust not to be trustworthy. The TCB of the static chain of trust is big, and Kauer [98] finds a bug in the bootloader, which can be used to attack the static chain of trust.

Compared to the static chain of trust, the dynamic chain of trust has its advantages in the aspects of establishment time, size of TCB and protection on the isolated environment. However, this new technology is not mature on usage and user experience. First, it is difficult to use, because all the codes should be self-contained as the execution environment built by DRTM is totally isolated from the system. For the code that has dependence on the other libraries, it needs to build a running environment itself, which increases the difficulty of development. Second, DRTM might bring poor experiences for users, because the isolated environment provided by DRTM only runs sensitive code requiring protection, and all the other programs will be suspended.

3.3 Systems Based on Static Chain of Trust

The establishment of the static chain of trust consists of phases of BIOS, bootloader and Operating System. All the phases of static chain of trust have the same principle: measure and extend the next running code to the corresponding PCR of security chips after getting execution control. The phase of BIOS is based on the CRTM stored on the computers' motherboard, and the TCG PC specification gives a detailed description of the establishment of the chain of trust in this phase. Computer vendors adopt this specification to build the chain of trust for their products.

The chain of trust in bootloader layer aims to check the security of the bootloader based on the trusted BIOS, and builds trusted execution environment for the OS. There are lots of research on chain of trust of this layer, such as the open-source project Trusted GRUB [99] and IBM's Tpod System [100]. According to the procedure of establishing a chain of trust defined by TCG's specifications, these trusted boot systems establish chains of trust by the principle of measuring first and then executing based on the open-source bootloader GRUB. Besides the basic functionalities of chains of trust, Trusted GRUB provides GRUB commands with the extension of trusted computing functionalities to facilitate users. The Institute of Software Chinese Academy of Sciences (ISCAS) proposes a trusted bootloader subsystem supporting OS recovery. The subsystem checks the measurement values of the OS kernel and important configuration files before launching the OS. If the check shows that they do not meet the integrity requirement, the system will enter into a recovery subsystem, which can repair the OS by recovering the tampered files.

The chain of trust in operating system layer is somewhat complex. Modern operating systems provide many kinds of services and applications, which run without fixed order. This brings a great challenge for extending the chain of trust to OS layer or application layer. To confront this challenge, IBM T. J. Watson research center proposes the IMA system [10] and MicroSoft research center proposes Palladium/NGSCB [101] system. IMA and Palladium/NGSCB adopt the principle that all the executable components loaded to the system are measured before execution. This principle follows the idea of the establishment of chains of trust that performing measurement before execution guarantees the integrity status of the program when it is loaded to the system. The researchers of IMA then propose a successive scheme that combines the measurement and mandatory access control and develops a prototype called PRIMA [11]. PRIMA measures the components that have relationship with mandatory access control model and uses mandatory access control to ensure the integrity of critical components' information flows. This kind of design reduces overload of measurement and guarantees the integrity of the system at running time. We have designed a chain of trust by combining measurement at loading time and measurement at running time, which supports two kinds of measurement methods: components measurement and dynamic measurement. Our chain of trust has the following advantages: first, we refine our measurement granularity to system components level; second, we can measure the running program in the system on time, which guarantees the integrity of the system at running time.

We will introduce principles and technologies used to establish chains of trust to bootloader and OS, respectively, and take our chain of trust as an example to elaborate the system and method to establish the static chain of trust from hardware to operating system, to applications and finally to the network access.

3.3.1 Chain of Trust at Bootloader

The chain of trust at bootloader is a kind of chain of trust taking TPM/TCM as the root of trust. It starts from the hardware layer of the system and then extends the chain of trust to BIOS, bootloader, which builds trusted execution environment for the operating system. It is the first phase and foundation for the computer system to establish a whole chain of trust.

As the hardware and BIOS have strong tamper-resistance ability, most researches on trusted boot focus on the bootloader layer, which is much more vulnerable. Establishing the chain of trust in bootloader layer requires checking the security of the code, configuration and related files of the bootloader, and the most typical trusted boot system is Trusted GRUB. To ensure the security of execution environment before OS starts, Trusted GRUB takes advantage of TPM measurement mechanism to check every stage of GRUB, the configuration of GRUB and the OS kernel image and extends the measurement values of the software to PCRs. The main steps that Trusted GRUB performs to build a chain of trust are as follows:

(1) When the system runs to the BIOS phase, BIOS measures the MBR in the hard disk, that is, the code of GRUB Stage1, stores the measurement values to the PCR 4 of TPM and then loads and runs Stage1.
(2) GRUB Stage1 loads and measures the first sector of GRUB Stage1.5, extends the measurement values to PCR 4 and then executes Stage1.5.
(3) After getting execution control, GRUB Stage1.5 loads and measures GRUB Stage2, extends GRUB Stage2 to PCR4 and then transfers the execution control to GRUB Stage2. At this time, the bootloader has finished starting up, and can load the OS to memory.
(4) GRUB measures its configuration file grub.conf, extends the measurement values to PCR 5, measures the OS kernel and checks its integrity.

Trusted boot ensures the security of the OS loader, and can prevent attackers from injecting malicious code before OS running, which sets up the security foundation for OS boot. All trusted boot systems use the similar method to build chain of trust, and their main goal is to guarantee the integrity of the bootloader, configuration files of bootloader and the OS kernel image.

3.3.2 Chain of Trust in OS

Chains of trust in OS layer aim to provide trusted execution environment for applications and platform integrity attestation services for remote verifiers. After bootloader transfers execution control to OS kernel, the chain of trust in this layer should protect the security of all kinds of executable programs, such as kernel modules, OS services and applications, which might affect the integrity of the whole system. There are many kinds of methods to establish a chain of trust for OS: From the viewpoint of the time performing measurement, some systems perform measurement when software is loaded into the system to guarantee the system loading-time integrity, and some systems perform measurement while software is running to guarantee the system running-time integrity; from the viewpoint of granularity of measured software, some systems measure the whole OS kernel image and some systems measure components running in the OS one by one, such as kernel modules, important configuration files and critical data structures of OS; from the viewpoint of security policies, some systems perform measurement following the mandatory access control policy deployed in the system to ensure that mandatory access control security policies are correctly enforced. The IMA and NGSCB systems start from the point of time and strictly follow the principle of performing measurement when the executable software is loaded, and can ensure the integrity of the software before it gets execution control. However, this kind of chain of trust has some potential security risks especially when modern operating systems are more and more complex and cannot guarantee program's running-time integrity. The PRIMA system starts from the point of mandatory access control policy and proposes the method of guaranteeing the running-time integrity of information flows. We design a chain of trust from the point of measurement granularity and measurement time. By proposing technologies of component measurement and dynamic measurement, our system not only refines the granularity of measured components but can also guarantee the running-time integrity of the system. In the following, we will first introduce methods of establishing chains of trust based on loading-time measurement and information flow control, respectively, and then introduce our chain of trust.

3.3.2.1 Establishing Chain of Trust by Loading-Time Measurement

The chain of trust at OS layer aims to extend the chain of trust from trusted bootloader to OS, and to applications. To ensure the security of the chain of trust, the measurement agent is usually implemented in the OS kernel. As the trusted bootloader has checked the integrity of the OS kernel, the measurement agent in the OS kernel is assumed to be trustworthy. After the bootloader decompresses the kernel image, according to the execution flow of OS, the OS measurement agent measures the OS modules and kernel services when they are loaded into the kernel by invoking TPM, so that the OS chain of trust subsystem is established. After the OS starts, to ensure the security of running applications, every loaded program should be measured by the OS measurement agent before it executes. This kind of chain of trust can combine the black/white-list mechanism for applications to enhance the runtime security of the system.

The necessarily considered issues when designing and implementing the chain of trust in OS layer are: measurement content, the measurement timing and the storage of the measurement data. As any program loaded to the OS kernel might contain security vulnerabilities that can be exploited by attackers to break the integrity of the system, the chain of trust measures all the executable programs loaded to the kernel, including the applications, dynamic link libraries, static link libraries and even the executable shell scripts. When they are loaded into the kernel, we leverage the hook functions to obtain the content and then perform the measurement, and finally store the measurement values in the OS kernel and protect them using the security chip. In this section, taking the Linux as example, we will describe the principle and method of establishing a chain of trust based on loading-time measurement.

Architecture. Figure 3.6 depicts the architecture of the chain of trust in OS layer, whose core modules consist of measurement agent, attestation service and measurement lists for storing measurement values. All of these modules reside in OS kernel. The measurement agent runs first after OS kernel is decompressed, measures all the executable programs loaded into the OS, extends the measurement values into corresponding PCRs and stores the measurement log in the kernel's measurement lists. Measurement lists store the measurement values measured during the OS running, and these measurement values are actually logs that record the sequence of software extended to PCRs. These measurement values play an important role in integrity verification for platform. The attestation service is used to prove the security of the OS chain of trust subsystem, and usually adopts the binary attestation scheme defined by TCG.

Implementation. The core module of the system of chain of trust in OS layer is the measurement agent. For Linux, the measurement agent is a Linux Security Module (LSM), and for Windows it is a virtual kernel driver module whose launch privilege is relatively high. The measurement agent needs to measure OS-related programs and files and the executable programs in application layer when they are loaded into the

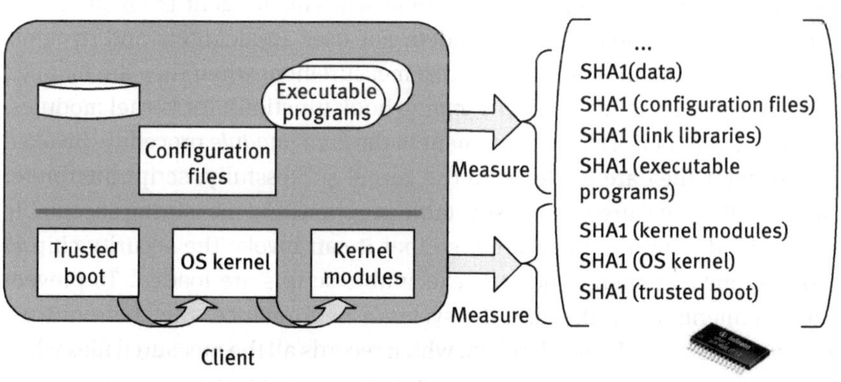

Figure 3.6: Architecture of chain of trust at operating system layer.

kernel, and the measurement contents include kernel modules, executable programs in user space, dynamic link libraries and executable scripts.

(1) Kernel modules: These are kernel extensions that can be loaded into the kernel dynamically. There are two ways of loading kernel module: the explicitly loading and the implicitly loading. The explicitly loading way needs users to load Linux kernel modules actively using the insmod or modprobe commands; and the implicitly loading way requires the kernel itself to automatically invoke modprobe to load the required kernel module in the user processes context. In Linux version 2.6, both ways will invoke the load_module system call to inform the kernel that the kernel modules have been loaded successfully.

(2) Executable programs in user space: All executable programs in user space are executed through the execve system call, which resolves the binary codes of executable programs and then invokes the file_mmap hook function to map the codes into the memory space. Measurement agent performs the measurement of the executable programs during the mapping. Finally, OS creates context for user process, and then jumps to the main function to execute the user process.

(3) Dynamic link libraries: Dynamic link libraries are shared code libraries that are required by system programs and user applications. When executable programs run, OS will load the necessary dynamic link libraries. Dynamic link libraries are also loaded into the OS through the file_mmap hook function, so that the measurement method of dynamic link libraries is the same with applications in user space.

(4) Executable scripts: Running executable scripts depends on script interpreter (such as bash), which is measured as an executable program by the OS when it is loaded by OS. Executable scripts might have a great effect on the integrity of the system, so measuring executable scripts is an important part in establishing the chain of trust in OS layer.

Usually the integrity measurement work of the measurement agent is finished after programs requiring to be measured are loaded. For user applications and dynamic link libraries, the measurement agent performs measurement when they are mapped into the memory space (namely, in the *file_mmap* hook function); for kernel modules, the measurement agent performs measurement in the *load_module* procedure invoked by the modules after they are loaded into the kernel successfully; script interpreter (such as bash) itself is measured as an executable program, and measuring executable scripts requires modifying the interpreter, so that it can invoke the security chip to perform integrity measurement when the executable scripts are loaded. To prevent frequent measurements from affecting the system's performance, the chain of trust adopts the measurement cache mechanism, which records all the measured files when performing measurement for the first time. When new measurement request occurs, the measurement agent measures only the programs that have never been measured or only the programs that have been modified. The measurement cache mechanism can greatly improve the performance of the chain of trust system without reducing the security level of the system.

The above chain of trust follows TCG's static measurement idea and establishes a chain of trust from the trusted bootloader to OS and to applications, which provides trusted execution environment for applications. This kind of chain of trust leverages hook functions of OS to implement the measurement of kernel modules, dynamic link libraries, static link libraries, applications and executable scripts when they are loaded, and in this way it almost measures all the executable programs that can affect the execution environment of OS, so this kind of chain of trust to some extent can detect loading-time attacks on all programs. Another feature of this kind of trust is that it requires very small modification on OS, especially for Linux: It only needs to have a little modification on the source codes of Linux and then can achieve a relatively high security level.

As it does not have protection mechanism at runtime, the chain of trust above cannot guarantee the security of the execution environment when system is running, and cannot prevent attacks at runtime, which makes the system vulnerable in practice. Besides, this kind of chain of trust measures all the programs loaded into the system, including some programs having no effect on system's security, so that it brings some unnecessary overload on the system.

3.3.2.2 Chains of Trust Based on Information Flows

Loading-time OS measurement has two issues: runtime integrity is not concerned and the measured content is too large. To solve these two issues, research institutions propose the method of establishing chains of trust based on information flows [11]. This kind of chain of trust is based on mandatory access control models, and it measures the integrity of information flows to ensure that the system meets the preset mandatory access control policy. Another good feature of this kind of chain of trust is that it only measures the components that have effect on the system's information flow and overcomes the disadvantage of loading-time measurement system.

Chain of trust based on information flows requires that the OS kernel supports mandatory access control function (such as SELinux). Its main idea is to leverage the mandatory access control model to ensure the integrity of the OS's information flows and also to leverage the measurement function to ensure that the mandatory access control model is correctly enforced. The mandatory access control model labels the subjects and objects that affect the information flows of OS and defines policies that restrict the information flow between subjects and objects. In this way, mandatory access control model ensures that the information between subjects and objects can flow only as the policies have defined them. However, current mandatory access control models prohibit all information flows from entities with low integrity level to entities with high integrity level, which makes them not applicable to practical systems. So chains of trust adopt mandatory access control models like CW-Lite [102], which allow receiving data from entities with low integrity level by adding interfaces filtering data with low integrity level. The interfaces allow only data that do not affect the execution environment of the system passing through. The measurement agent measures two aspects of data: (1) policy files of the mandatory access control models; (2) the subjects and objects defined in the policy files. The measurement agent makes a decision about the executable processes loaded into the OS; if they belong to subjects and objects defined in the policy files, then measure them, otherwise, ignore them.

The integrity verification of this kind of chains of trust follows the idea of checking whether the mandatory access control models are correctly enforced. First, check whether the subjects, objects and policy files satisfy the integrity requirement, then check whether information flows between subjects and objects meet the rules defined in the policy files. If all checks pass, it can be concluded that the information flows at runtime meet the integrity requirements.

Chains of trust based on information flow control implement the integrity measurement and control of information flows of the system at runtime. It measures the subjects and objects that affect the system's integrity according to the mandatory access control policy and restricts the access behaviors of subjects and objects by measurement results. This kind of chains of trust ignores the subjects that do not affect the system's integrity. In one word, by combining the mandatory access control mechanism and chains of trust, we can greatly reduce the measurement content and improve the performance of establishing the chain of trust.

3.3.3 The ISCAS Chain of Trust

After researching the methods used to build static chain of trust, we design and implement the ISCAS chain of trust system, which includes trusted boot, OS measurement, application measurement and the trusted network connection (TNC). The ISCAS chain of trust system consists of the trusted boot subsystem, the OS chain of trust subsystem, the TNC subsystem and realizes the trust establishment of the platform initialization environment, trusted execution environment and the network access environment. Based on the trusted BIOS, the trusted boot subsystem establishes a chain of trust with BIOS and bootloader by measuring and checking bootloader and corresponding configuration files. Based on the trusted boot subsystem, the OS chain of trust subsystem extends trust to the OS layer and application layer by leveraging the dynamic measurement method and component measurement method. These two methods can not only implement the chain of trust to OS at loading time but also implement the dynamic establishment of chain of trust for applications and their dependent programs.

Figure 3.7 depicts the whole architecture of the ISCAS chain of trust system, which consists of trusted boot subsystem, the OS chain of trust subsystem and the TNC

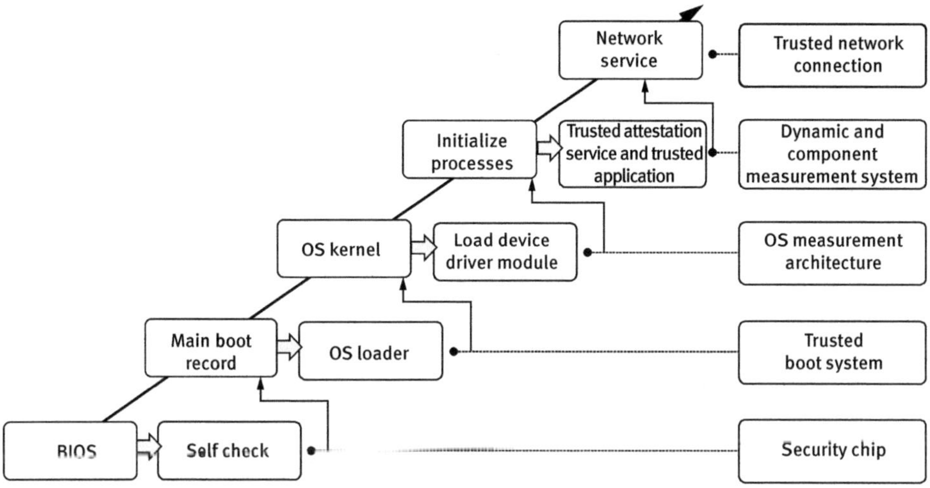

Figure 3.7: The architecture of ISCAS chain of trust system.

subsystem. The trusted boot subsystem establishes a chain of trust following TCG's specifications: First, it measures configuration files of bootloader and OS kernel files; second, it extends the measurement results to the security chip; third, it transfers the execution control to OS kernel. The OS chain of trust subsystem establishes a chain of trust to the OS layer and application layer by leveraging the component measurement and dynamic measurement. The component measurement refines the granularity of measured data to components of the OS and uses hook functions to measure them when they are loaded into the OS. Dynamic measurement can measure programs in real time according to user's measurement request, which ensures the security status of the system during its runtime. These two kinds of measurement methods establish the chain of trust in the OS layer. Based on ISCAS chain of trust system, the platform can provide attestation services, which can prove the integrity status of the platform to remote verifiers, and can also provide system's integrity information for network services such as the TNC, which extends the trust of the system to the network. In the following sections, we will introduce the technical implementation of trusted boot subsystem, the OS chain of trust subsystem and TNC subsystem.

3.3.3.1 Trusted Boot Subsystem

The trusted boot subsystem starts from power on of computer and establishes a chain of trust from trusted BIOS to bootloader based on current boot sequence. This subsystem follows TCG's specifications on the procedure of establishing a chain of trust and usage of security chips and builds a trustworthy execution environment for OS. The detailed boot sequence of the trusted boot subsystem is depicted in Figure 3.8. This

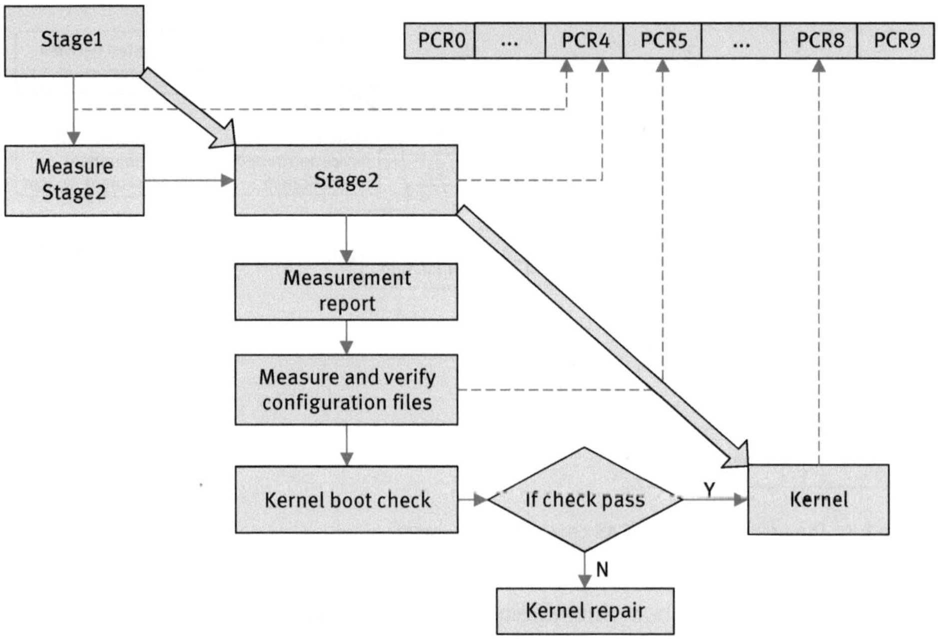

Figure 3.8: The boot sequence of the trusted boot subsystem.

subsystem also provides the demonstration functionality, which can show the trusted boot sequence as an experiment platform.

Besides the basic function of establishing a chain of trust, the trusted boot subsystem provides the functions of report and verification of chain of trust, integrity report and verification of files, configuration of trusted boot, kernel repair and control of the secure boot.

(1) Report and verification of chain of trust: Report the measurement results of trusted boot and verify this trusted boot.
(2) Report and verification of files: Before the start-up of OS, display the measurement and verification results of important files during the establishment of the chain of trust.
(3) Configuration of trusted boot: Configure the parameters of trusted boot, for example, system files needed to be measured during boot phase, and the choice of trusted boot or secure boot.
(4) Kernel repair: Guarantee that the system enters the repair system to repair the OS kernel files that do not meet the integrity requirements if the measurement results of OS kernel and configuration files do not meet the integrity requirement.
(5) Control of secure boot: Provide GRUB commands with trusted computing functions, and users can control the boot sequence of the system.

Trusted boot subsystem is compatible with the open-source project GRUB. Its main feature is that by introducing the security chip, it ensures that the booted system is trustworthy. First, before the start-up of the OS, every boot stage and important boot files can be reported and verified in the trusted boot subsystem. Second, the OS kernel and important system files must be measured and verified before being loaded, which guarantees the trustworthy of the OS start-up. The trusted boot subsystem can not only ensure the normal boot of OS but also repair the OS using the kernel repair function when important files of OS are abnormal, for example, the kernel is corrupted or broken.

3.3.3.2 The OS Chain of Trust Subsystem

The OS chain of trust subsystem is based on the trusted boot subsystem, extends the chain of trust from trusted bootloader to application by leveraging the OS measurement technology and provides trusted execution environment for user applications. It also provides attestation services through which verifiers can obtain the integrity verification proof. On the aspect of measurement, the OS chain of trust subsystem ensures the system's integrity status when the OS is loaded into the memory by measuring all executable programs loaded into the OS, such as kernel modules, dynamic link libraries and user applications. Moreover, it also measures the processes and kernel modules in the OS to ensure the integrity status of the system at runtime. The attestation service not only provides platform's integrity data for remote verifiers but also supports the TNC to build trusted network environment.

By combing the trusted boot subsystem, the OS chain of trust subsystem supports the establishment of a whole chain of trust for trusted computation platform and also Windows and Linux. As Windows is not open source, the chain of trust only guarantees the integrity of the whole kernel image and the processes running on the OS. For Linux, the OS chain of trust subsystem provides measurement with finer granularity: Besides measuring the whole OS image, it measures critical data structures and components. The measurement technology that combines component measurement and dynamic measurement can resist loading-time attacks on programs and can measure running programs of the system in real time, which can overcome the issues of TCG's static measurement.

The OS chain of trust subsystem builds trust for the platform by leveraging the OS measurement technology, which can enhance the security of the system, and can be used to implement trustworthy OS. This kind of chain of trust also provides system attestation service of proving system's security status, which proves the integrity status of the system to remote platforms, and can be used to establish trusted channel based on platform's status. This kind of chain of trust can also provide trusted network authentication service based on user and platform identities, which guarantees that all the endpoints connected to the network satisfy the specific security policy, and by this way we can extend the trust to the whole network.

Component Measurement. A system usually consists of some interrelated program codes, and we define an executable program of the system and its directly dependent codes as a component. The component measurement measures the programs and their directly dependent codes. When components are loaded into the OS, the measurement agent measures the executable program and its directly dependent codes (such as static and dynamic link libraries). We implement the component measurement by adding measurement functions on the path where the executable program and its dependent codes are loaded and the measurement functions measure the integrity of executable program and its directly dependent codes. This kind of measurement ensures the integrity of components in the application layer when they are loaded and can also ensure the integrity of their dependent program codes. So it has wider measurement scope and finer measurement granularity than loading-time measurement.

The ISCAS chain of trust system implements the integrity measurement of OS components and application components. When these components are loaded, they will trigger the measurement functions embedded into the system hook functions, which perform integrity measurement on them. The steps of the component measurement are as follows:

(1) When executable programs are loaded into the OS or the measurement agent receives users' measurement requests, the measurement agent finds all of the directly dependent codes of this program, such as static and dynamic link libraries and kernel modules, and all of these programs make up a component.
(2) The measurement agent checks whether the programs contained in the component exist in the measurement log one by one. If a program does not exist in the log, it must be loaded into the OS for the first time, and the measurement agent will compute the integrity measurement value of the program and add it to the measurement log. For the programs that exist in the log, the measurement agent checks whether the dirty bit is set. If the dirty bit is not set, then it returns directly.
(3) If the dirty bit is set in step (2), the program must have been modified in the memory, and it should be re-measured. The measurement agent remeasures the program and adds it to the measurement log.

Dynamic Measurement. Components measurement can measure the dependent code that has relationship with the executable code, but it still performs measurement when the code is loaded, and thus cannot perform integrity verification after the code is loaded. For attacks happening when programs are running, such as self-modifying code attack, the component measurement cannot verify the integrity of the programs after they are loaded. To verify the integrity of programs after they are loaded, we propose a method for establishing a chain of trust that can measure the integrity status of programs at anytime (we call it dynamic measurement) and can verify the integrity of programs after they are loaded.

Dynamic chains of trust aim to check and report the integrity of running programs in real time and systems built by dynamic chains of trust must consider the following two factors: measurement objects and measurement timing. The scope and granularity of measurement objects are determined by system security goals and the general principle is that the measurement objects must contain programs capable of affecting the system's runtime integrity, such as kernel modules, system services and related user processes. From the view of timing, the real-time measurement is the best, but this method will seriously affect the running performance of the system. So we require that the measurement agent can perform measurement at any time during the running of processes, which can prevent the integrity of processes from being tampered with a large probability.

(1) System architecture

The architecture of dynamic measurement contains three layers: hardware layer, kernel layer, and user application layer. The security chip is in the hardware layer, and the measurement agent is divided into two parts, which are in the kernel layer and the user application layer, respectively. The measurement agent in the user application layer receives measurement requests from users and then sends the requests to the measurement agent in the kernel layer, which measures processes and kernel modules running in the system and returns the measurement results to the agent in the user application layer. In order to ensure the continuity of the chains of trust, the measurement agent in the kernel layer must be measured by the trusted boot system. Figure 3.9 depicts the architecture of the ISCAS chains of trust system.

(2) Process measurement

Process measurement actually describes characteristic information of process integrity in the system. The Linux OS contains a data structure in the memory

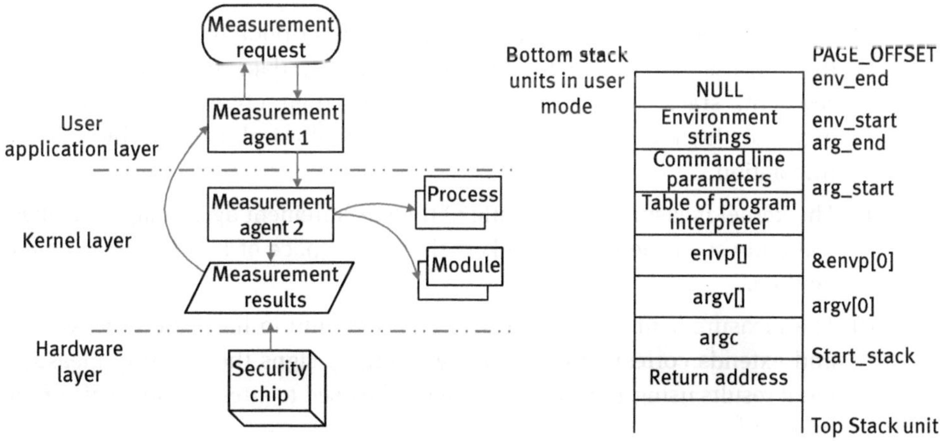

Figure 3.9: Dynamic measurement architecture (left) and stack of process image (right).

used to describe process's state and parameters for every process and we can find this data structure for some specific process by searching the process link list. The data structure for process is depicted in Figure 3.9, and some important parameters are as follows:

- start_code, end_code: the start and end linear addresses of process's code segment;
- start_data, end_data: the start and end linear addresses of process's data segment;
- arg_start, arg_end: the start and end linear addresses of arguments of commands in the stack.

The start_code labels the start address of the code segment. For attacks tampering the codes, they modify the content of this segment. So this is also the primary part for dynamic measurement to verify the process integrity. Arg_start is the start address of the process's stack for command arguments. The security strength of the running process is closely related to command input arguments, and the dynamic measurement also requires verifying the integrity of this part. Start_data is the memory field for data generated by running process, but as the content of this field has little relationship with the security of the process, and the content is always changing in the process's life cycle, we do not include this field in the scope of the dynamic measurement.

When the integrity of the process needs to be verified, the user requests the measurement agent to measure the current state of the process. Its measurement steps are as follows:

(a) The measurement agent resolves the process name (or process ID) in the request, and obtains the process handle by searching the process description data structure in the process link list, which is maintained by the kernel.
(b) The measurement agent obtains all process description information through the process handle, including code segment, data segment, argument segment, stack segment and so on, and then obtains the linear address of the measurement object and the physical address by address translation.
(c) The kernel measurement module of the measurement agent maps the physical address of the process to kernel process space of kernel measurement module.
(d) The measurement agent requests TPM/TCM chip to hash the process data and extends corresponding PCRs, and finally signs the integrity measurement results using TPM/TCM, which can be used to attest the integrity of the process.

(3) Kernel module measurement
In Linux, the dynamic measurement of kernel modules is similar to process measurement. Linux maintains a data structure called *struct module* for each kernel module. The communication between the kernel module and other modules can be achieved by accessing the *struct module*. The link of all the *struct module* of kernel module makes up a *module-link list*. The *struct module* describes address, size and information of the kernel module. The dynamic measurement of kernel module is achieved by measuring these critical data structures.

After the kernel measurement, module of the measurement agent receives the measurement request; if the request is for kernel module and the module has been loaded into Linux kernel, the measurement agent first resolves the kernel module name and then searches the kernel module in the *module-link list* maintained by kernel to obtain module handle. The kernel measurement agent obtains the address and size of the executable code in the module by the handle, and finally dynamically measures the kernel module according to the method of dynamic measurement on process.

3.3.3.3 The Trusted Network Connection Subsystem

With the rapid development of Internet and cloud computing, terminal security has more and more influence on the security and trustworthiness of network computation environment. The trusted computing technology proposes the idea of extending the trustworthiness from terminals to network, and this idea has been one of the important ways to improve the network environment trustworthiness. TCG proposes the TNC technology by combining chains of trust for terminals and traditional network access technology. TNC requires the network access server to verify the integrity of the terminal before it accesses the network, and only terminals meeting the system integrity requirements specified by the access policy are allowed to access the network. TNC ensures that the terminal platforms in the network are trustworthy, and prevents malicious terminals from accessing the network, which prevents the spreading of malicious code in the network from the origin.

The TNC subsystem extends the chain of trust of terminal to the network. The TNC server gives access decisions based on the integrity status of terminal platforms, which is collected by component measurement and dynamic measurement on terminal, and the integrity status provides fine-grained and dynamic integrity evidence for the terminal to access the network. First, component measurement provides component-level integrity information, which makes the TNC access server assess the integrity of terminals more precisely based on access policy set by network administrator. Second, dynamic measurement provides the newest integrity measurement information of terminal platforms and to some extent overcomes the TOCTOU problem. It can also provide technical support for dynamic integrity verification of terminals after connecting the network, and further ensure the security of the network.

3.4 Systems Based on Dynamic Chain of Trust

As the static chain of trust does not concern the runtime integrity status and the building procedure is complex, the industrial field proposes the technology of dynamic chain of trust based on DRTM. Compared with the static chain of trust, the dynamic chain of trust can be established at any time and is suitable for many simple and constrained computing environment. The dynamic chain of trust is established by triggering a special CPU instruction. Its security does not rely on trusted components such as hardware and BIOS that are needed when system is booted, so it can be used to solve some security problems of trusted boot system. The dynamic chain of trust can be established at any time after OS is launched. It is usually used for user-specific applications to establish a trusted execution environment.

Many research institutions proposed various schemes for establishing dynamic chain of trust based on DRTM technology. OSLO [98] performs a comprehensive security analysis on trusted boot systems based on static chain of trust, and points out some security risks due to some inherent defects and the big TCB of the static chain of trust. OSLO also reviews a variety of attacks on this kind of systems: TPM reset attacks, BIOS replacement attacks and attacks based on bugs of the trusted GRUB itself. The first two attacks are caused by the break of the chain of trust when the RTM and TPM starts asynchronously, and the third attack is due to bugs in the TCB. OSLO proposes the idea of solving above problems based on dynamic chain of trust, which uses security extensions of AMD CPU to transfer the RoT from the BIOS to DRTM and also TPM's dynamic PCRs to store measurement results. In this way, OSLO solves the problem of breaking static chain of trust. OSLO also prevents attacks caused by bugs in the TCB by removing the BIOS and bootloader from TCB. Intel develops a similar system called *tboot*, which uses Intel's TXT technology as DRTM to establish the trusted boot, and its principles are similar to those of OSLO.

The typical system based on dynamic chain of trust in the OS layer is Flicker [103] designed by CMU Cylab, which establishes an isolated trusted execution environment based on AMD's CPU security extensions, and it can be used to protect user security-sensitive code (called PAL[4]). Flicker can establish a security execution environment for PALs based on hardware isolation and extend PALs to dynamic PCRs to provide execution evidence of PALs' running in the isolated environment for remote verifiers, thus achieving the remote attestation function. Compared with the static chain of trust, the typical feature of Flicker is its flexible establishment time and the small size of the TCB. As Flicker can establish a dynamic chain of trust at any time, it can build trusted execution environment for multiple user codes without rebooting system. The Flicker system adopts DRTM technology to establish chain of trust, which greatly reduces its TCB to only a little hardware and software, and thus reduces security risks caused by TCB.

---

4 Flicker calls the protected user code as PAL (Piece of Application Logic).

Although Flicker provides fine-grained trusted execution environment and its TCB is small, it has great impact on system's efficiency as it requires launching CPU's security instruction to build isolated environment every time. For codes whose workload is small, the burden used to establish the isolated environment even accounts for half of the overall costs. To solve this problem, researchers in Cylab propose TrustVisor [104] system that is more convenient to use and more efficient. To reduce the size of TCB, TrustVisor is implemented as a simple hypervisor above the hardware layer, and only provides memory isolation, DMA protection and a micro-TPM (μTPM) with necessary interfaces such as Seal/Unseal, Extend and Quote. TrustVisor itself is protected by DRTM, and leverages memory isolation mechanism to ensure that each PAL can only be invoked by TrustVisor and creates a μTPM instance for each PAL. Any invocation or access to a PAL will be trapped into TrustVisor, which will control these accesses, and only correct invoking address is allowed to run the PAL. For illegal PAL invocations, TrustVisor will return error to calling applications. The memory isolation mechanism and μTPM provided by TrustVisor not only protect users' sensitive code but also reduce burden on the system caused by DRTM, which makes it have good application prospect.

3.4.1 Chain of Trust at Bootloader

Compared with static chain of trust, the trusted boot systems based on DRTM have smaller TCB and can avoid a lot of attacks on static chain of trust, thus providing a more secure environment for the launch of OS. Trusted boot is usually implemented as a kernel start-up entry, and it measures OS kernel in the secure environment established by DRTM after booting. In this way, the establishment of chain of trust will not contain BIOS and bootloader, so it prevents attacks leveraging bugs existing in BIOS and bootloader. As the RoT is based on DRTM, it prevents TPM reset attacks and BIOS replacement attack. It boots the OS following the below steps:

(1) The user selects trusted boot in the bootloader, which would trigger CPU's security instruction. The security instruction will reset dynamic PCRs of TPM and perform security check mechanism of DRTM, such as TXT's launch control policy, which is used to check whether components configuration meets security requirements.
(2) If the hardware configuration satisfies security requirements, the trusted execution environment has been built. The trusted boot system will run in this environment, and be extended to PCR17.
(3) The trusted boot system loads and measures the OS kernel and extends the measurement results to dynamic PCRs, and finally transfers execution control to the OS kernel.

3.4.2 Chain of Trust in OS

The dynamic chain of trust in OS is mainly used to build trusted execution environment for user security-sensitive codes. As the TCB of trusted execution environment built by DRTM only consists of a little hardware and some initialization codes, and the OS is excluded from the TCB, the potential vulnerabilities of OS will not affect the security of user applications. Dynamic chain of trust will prohibit DMA access of external devices during its establishment, which provides hardware protection for user applications and avoids DMA attacks on system.

The architecture of dynamic chain of trust in OS layer is very simple, which is usually implemented as a kernel module that encapsulates user's security-sensitive codes (PAL) to executable codes directly running in the isolated environment built by DRTM. As establishing isolated environment requires suspending OS and resuming OS at the ending of the isolated environment every time, the chain of trust system needs to add codes protecting OS states and resuming OS. The construction of the chain of trust in OS is as follows (for details, please refer to Figure 3.10):

(1) Acceptation of PAL: The establishment of dynamic chain of trust is triggered by a kernel module in the OS. The user sends execution request to the kernel module, and the request contains application code and its parameters.
(2) Initialization of PAL: After the kernel module receives the user's request, it assembles the PAL, input parameters and other system function code and then generates the executable code block (PAL block) directly running in the isolated environment.
(3) Suspension of the OS: The execution of the DRTM security instruction will not save the context of current running environment. In order to return to context of current OS after the execution of the isolated environment built by DRTM, we need to save the context of OS, such as the kernel page tables, before executing the security instruction.
(4) Execution of security instruction: First, establish DMA protection mechanism to prevent DMA attacks on the isolated environment; second, disable interrupts to prevent the OS from regaining the control of current execution environment; third, reset dynamic PCRs, check hardware configuration following the default security policy and then execute the assembled PAL.
(5) Execution of the PAL: The security instruction will measure the PAL block in the end, extend the measurement results to TPM dynamic PCRs and then execute the PAL. In order to protect user's privacy, PAL must clear private information generated during its execution.
(6) Extension of PCR: When the PAL completes its execution, a preset value will be extended to the PCR. This value indicates the end of execution of the isolated environment.

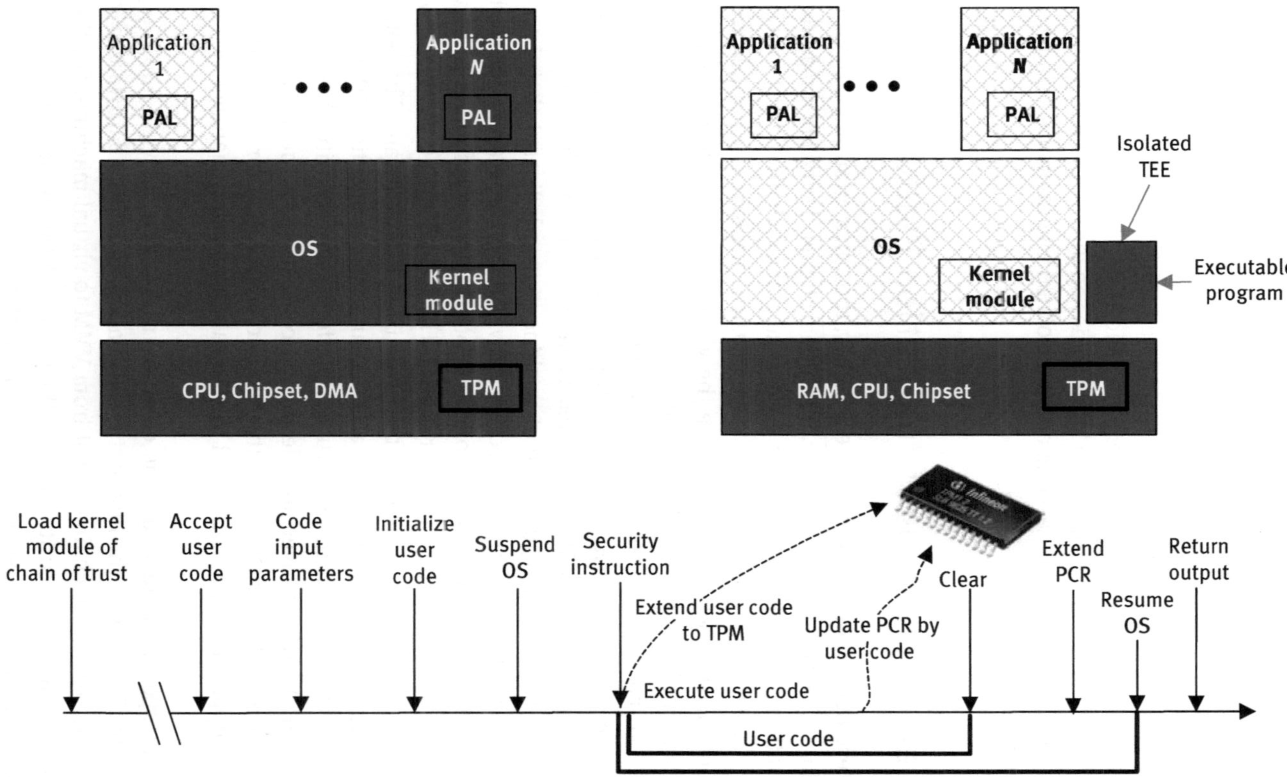

Figure 3.10: Building procedure of chain of trust in OS layer based on DRTM.

(7) Recovery of the OS: When the PAL completes its execution, the CPU will restore the context of OS and transfer the execution control to the kernel module that triggers the establishing procedure of chain of trust. The kernel module obtains the PAL's output generated in the isolated environment and returns it to the user.

Although the dynamic chain of trust can achieve a relatively high-level security, the OS will be suspended while the user's security code runs and the OS is always in the suspended state during the running of the isolated trusted execution environment, which makes the user unable to run other applications simultaneously. Since the code in the trusted execution environment no longer relies on the OS, the PAL must be self-contained and cannot rely on any code outside isolated environment. This increases the development difficulty of PALs.

3.5 Chain of Trust for Virtualization Platforms

With the development of virtualization technology, the application scope of virtualization platforms becomes wider. However, traditional chains of trust are not applicable to virtualization platforms, so there is a need to customize chain of trust for virtualization platforms. On general platforms, each physical machine is equipped with an independent physical security chip, while the virtualization platform has only one security chip for all of the virtual machines. So there is no one-to-one relationship between the virtual machine and the security chip like general platforms.

In order to solve the above problem, TCG proposes Virtualized Trusted Platform Architecture Specification [105], which gives a common virtualization platform architecture that ensures that each guest virtual machine owns a dedicated virtual security chip. The virtualization platform architecture is divided into three layers: the top layer is virtual machines that are isolated from each other under the support of services provided by the virtual machine monitor (VMM). The second layer is the VMM, which provides services for virtual machines by virtualizing the hardware. The bottom is the hardware layer. Based on the above architecture, the specification [105] proposes a general architecture of virtualized trusted platform: The security chip and physical RTM on the hardware layer provide trusted computing for the VMM layer, and the VMM layer provides a virtual security chip and virtual RTM for every virtual machine in the upper layer by its internal virtualization platform manager (vPlatform Manager).

Due to its special architecture, the chain of trust system for virtualization platforms consists of two parts: the first part is the chain of trust from hardware to VMM, and the second part is the chain of trust from VMM to virtual machine. For the first part, we can leverage the security chip and the physical RTM on the hardware layer to establish a static chain of trust or a dynamic chain of trust from hardware to VMM.

In virtualization platforms, security chips and RTMs on the hardware layer establish the chain of trust from the hardware to VMM, which can guarantee the security of VMM. After VMM starts, it measures every instance of virtual security chip and virtual RTM; we can then extend the chain of trust to virtual machines. Every virtual machine does not know that it is in a virtualization platform, and it can establish its own chain of trust by leveraging the virtual security chip and virtual RTM just like the general platform. The above operations establish the whole chain of trust from the hardware layer to the virtual machine.

3.6 Summary

This chapter introduces principles and methods proposed by the trusted computing technology, which aim to protect computer systems by establishing chain of trust on computer architecture. The trusted computing builds trusted execution environment for applications by measurement and transitive trust technologies and provides a fundamental solution for the security problems of computer system. The chain of trust protects the execution environment of terminals, and it can extend trustworthiness to network or remote verifiers by combining remote attestation technology.

The chain of trust can be categorized into static and dynamic chains of trust by the type of root of trust. The static chain of trust takes the first running code (CRTM) as the root of trust when the platform powers on and then establishes the whole chain of trust by measurement and transitive trust layer by layer. The dynamic chain of trust takes the DRTM technology provided by AMD or Intel's security CPU and builds secure isolated execution environment with hardware protection mechanisms. The above two types of chains of trust have both advantages and disadvantages in usage: The static chain of trust can guarantee security of the whole system, but it can only be established when the platform powers on and it also has defects of big computation cost on measurement and complex integrity management. The dynamic chain of trust is much better than the static chain of trust in the aspects of establishment timing and size of TCB, but it still has some problems in the aspects of user experience and development difficulty. Overall, the trends of the technology of chain of trust are reducing TCB and protecting security of system at running time. With the popularization of virtualization technology and smartphones, chain of trust will have a wide application prospect in these new computation platforms.

4 Trusted Software Stack

In order to use physical security chips (including TPM and TCM), users require a software module to interact with them. This module is called Trusted Software Stack (TSS).[1] As the entry of using a security chip, TSS usually locates between the security chip and user applications. It facilitates user applications to invoke security chip interfaces, and provides functions such as security chip access, security authentication, cryptographic services and resource management. Different security chips need appropriate software stacks such as TCG Software Stack corresponding to TPM and TCM Service Module (TSM) corresponding to TCM.

TSS is the bridge of interaction between user applications and security chip. A security chip provides core functions for building trust environment such as key generation, key storage and signature verification. Meanwhile, TSS provides auxiliary functions for building trust environment such as key usage, integrity measurement and communication between applications and security chips. In summary, the main goals of TSS are as follows [89]:

(1) To provide a set of APIs for user applications to synchronously access security chip.
(2) To manage requests from multiple applications and provide synchronous access to security chip.
(3) To shield processing procedure of internal commands for user applications in the manner of appropriate byte stream order and parameter assignment.
(4) To manage limited resources of security chip.

TSS simplifies the use of security chip. To code a security chip-based application, a programmer only needs to know basic concepts of security chip and upper interfaces provided by TSS, and is not required to concern about complexity of internal structure of security chip.

In this chapter, we introduce the overall architecture and functions of TSS, and then take the TSM as a TSS example to illustrate the definitions of interfaces at different layers and their invoking relationship. We will further introduce basic instances of TSS-based development and outline implementation and application of some existing open-source TSSs.

1 Without specification, TSS in this chapter means a general software stack using a security chip, not specially indicating TCG Software Stack in TPM or TSM in TCM.

DOI 10.1515/9783110477597-004

4.1 TSS Architecture and Functions

4.1.1 TSS Architecture

Trusted software stack serves as a standardized interface for security chips. The design of its architecture should take into full consideration the feature of cross-platform and shield the details of different hardware systems. Even though the implementation of each function module varies in each platform and operating system, the relationship of these modules' interactions and communication should be all the same. The architecture is presented in Figure 4.1.

Trusted software stack provides interfaces for an upper user, so it needs to run in user system and match the running mode of user system. In general, there are two definitions of platform modes in the user system:

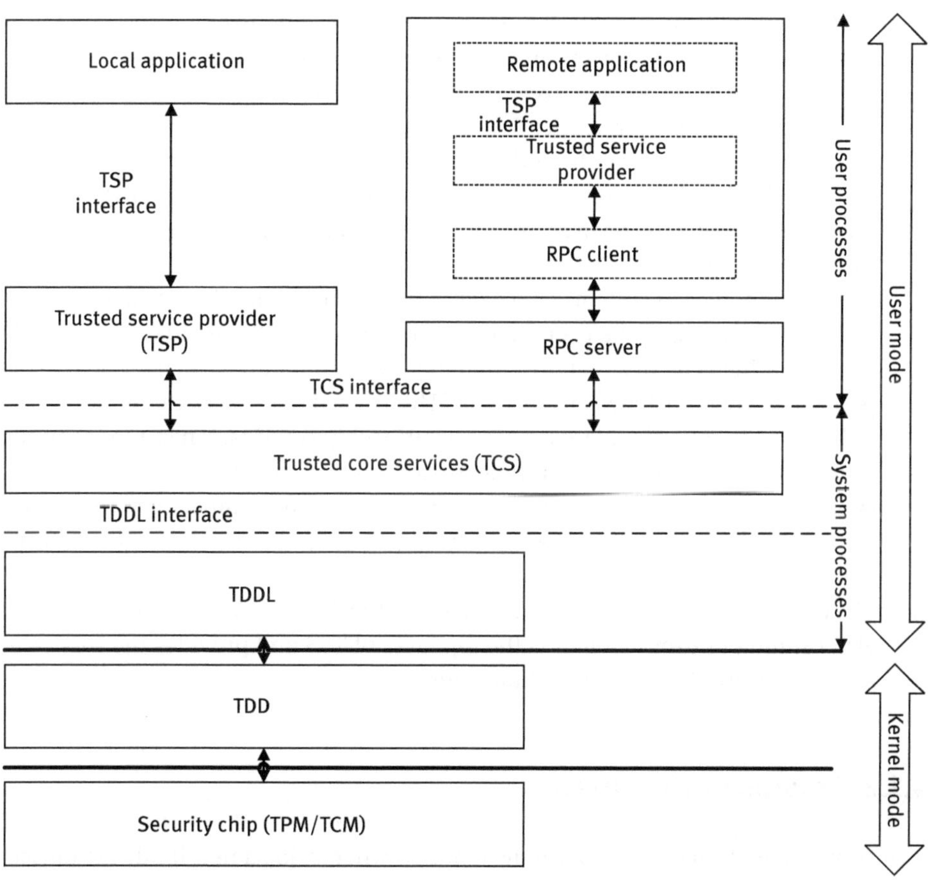

Figure 4.1: TSS architecture.

(1) Kernel mode: This is where the device drivers and the core components of the operating system execute. Code in this area(mode) maintains and protects the applications running in user mode and usually requires some type of administrator permission to modify and update.
(2) User mode: This is where user applications and system services execute. A user application is an executable code provided by the user. Only when the application is used, the corresponding code is initialized by the user. Therefore, it is less trustworthy on the platform. The code for system services is generally started during initialization of the operating system. Since this code executes in the form of system service process that differs from user application process, it is considered more trusted than user applications.

Based on the definition of platform modes in the above user system, TSS running in user system needs to match its functions with the corresponding user platform mode. TSS mainly includes three layers (as shown in Figure 4.1): kernel layer, system service layer and user application layer. Main function modules and the corresponding user platform modes of the three layers are specified as follows:
(1) The core module of kernel layer is the Trusted Device Driver (TDD) running in the Kernel Mode of user application. TDD is mainly responsible for transmitting the incoming byte stream from the Trusted Device Driver Library (TDDL) to the security chip, and then returning the data from the security chip to TDDL. TDD is also responsible for saving or restoring the security chip state when the power exception occurs.
(2) The core modules of system service layer are the TDDL and the Trusted Core Service (TCS) running in the user mode. Among them, TDDL provides a user mode interface which ensures that the different trusted computing core services can be ported conveniently between platforms. The Trusted Core Service interface (TCSi) is designed to control and request the security chip services. It has a set of public services that can be used for multiple trusted applications. The public services set is mainly responsible for parameter packing, parameter unpacking, log, audit, certificate management for the security chip interface and coordinates multiple applications to synchronously access security chip.
(3) The core module of user application layer is the Trusted Service Provider (TSP), also running in user mode. It is the top layer of TSS and provides the service to access security chip for applications directly.

4.1.2 Trusted Device Driver

A corresponding device driver is usually required when using a new hardware device. While using security chips, there is also need of the corresponding device drivers, such as tpm device driver provided by different chip manufacturers based on TPM's functional specifications. As a basic component to use security chip, TDD is located in the kernel layer of the operating system. It passes the byte streams received from TDDL to security chip and then returns the responses from security chip back to TDDL. It is also responsible for saving or restoring the security chip state when the power exception occurs. Generally, the TDD is loaded when the system is initialized to ensure that security chip interfaces can be invoked by the user applications in the upper layer.

The upper user applications need to invoke relevant software interfaces so that they can get access to the bottom hardware devices. Therefore, when using the trusted computing services based on security chip, the upper user applications in user mode must make use of the TSS that is also located in the user mode and call the TDD loaded in kernel mode to access the security chip. Since the security chip can handle only one request at a time in design, its driver only allows a process to exclusive access. For the multiple requests from the upper user applications, we need the TSS's relevant functions (such as TCSi) to manage the queuing and synchronizing of requests.

As a hardware device, the design of security chip driver involves the chip manufacturers and operating systems. In order to port applications across the TPM chips made by different manufacturers, IBM developed a standard interface for Linux. It makes the data communication independent of the TPM chips and facilitates the development of trusted applications. In the Linux where TPM driver is loaded, the device file corresponding to TPM chip is /dev/tpm0. The device number increases sequentially if there are multiple TPM chips. The kernel modules of device driver mainly include tpm_atmel, tpm_nsc, tpm_infineon and tpm_tis. These kernel modules provide required hardware drivers for the applications using TPM. The first three modules are TPM drivers manufactured by Atmel, NSC and Infineon, and tpm_tis is a universal TPM device driver meeting the TCG TIS (TPM Interface Specification). This specification provides a universal interface accessing TPM chips, and the interface is independent of various manufacturers.

4.1.3 Trusted Device Driver Library

TDDL is a component of TSS communicating with the underlying security chip and is also the first functional component of TSS running in the user space. TDDL mainly converts trusted computing commands and data between the kernel mode and the user mode. The main objectives of the TDDL are as follows:

(1) To ensure that different implementations of TSS can communicate with the security chip.

(2) To provide the interfaces independent of the operating system for the security chip applications.

TDDL provided by the security chip manufacturers is located between the TCS layer and the kernel device driver layer and is able to provide invocation interfaces for the upper-layer TCS in user mode. Because the underlying security chip driver allows only one accessing process, the corresponding driver library interface is designed as a single-threaded synchronous interface. Normally, this interface is a standard interface in C language so that multiple and different TCS can be ported across platforms.

The security chip manufacturers define the interfaces between TDDL and the physical security chips, and choose the communication and resource allocation mechanisms between TDDL and TDD. In most of platform implementations, TDDL needs to be loaded when operating system starts up.

4.1.4 Trusted Core Services

Due to the limited hardware resources, a security chip should take into consideration its data-handling capability when designing its functions. Taking TPM as an example, it can only perform one operation once and has the limited number of key slots and the authorization session handles, hence it can only conduct serial communication with the driver. The design leads to low operating efficiency when the upper applications use the security chips. Therefore, there requires a mechanism to manage the multiple calling requests from the upper layer concurrently.

The TCS is designed to address such problems. The processing efficiency of the requests to trusted computing services can be improved by implementing the resource management of security chips simply and efficiently. For this purpose, TCS layer adopts the following methods [106]:

(1) Implementing queue management for multiple operating requests to a security chip.
(2) Making its own response for the operating request that does not require processing by a security chip.
(3) Providing virtually unlimited resources by optimizing the management of limited resources of a security chip.
(4) Offering a variety of access ways such as local or remote invocation for a security chip.

The TCS layer provides a direct and simple way to use a security chip. To the upper applications, it is a public service set that can be used by all the TSP layers on the same platform. The main functions in the TCS layer include the context management, key and certificate management, event management and parameter block generator management. These functions are briefly described as follows:

(1) TSS Core Service interface (TCSi): TCSi allows multithreaded access to the TCS; each operation must be atomic. In most environments it exists as a system process, different from the application and service provider processes. If the TCS

resides in a system process, communication between the service providers and the TCS would be via a remote procedure call (RPC) and needs to use TCSi.

(2) TCS context manager: The TCS context manager provides dynamic handles that allow for efficient usage of both the TSP's and TCS's resources. Prior to sending command to the TCS, the upper service provider needs to open a context. The TCS context manager provides management functions for multiple contexts, allocates required memory and creates object handle for each context. Different threads within the service provider may share the same context or may acquire an independent context for service provider.

(3) TCS key and credential manager: Keys and credentials may be associated with the platform, the user or individual applications. Hence, it may be more convenient for an application to use a common authorization component to store and manage the keys and credentials. The key and credential manager stores and manages keys and credentials associated with the platform (e.g., the endorsement, platform and conformance credentials) and it allows multiple applications access to them. It should be noted that the persistent storage (PS) provided by the TCS is different from that provided by TSP mentioned later. There is only one storage area in TCS, while there are different storage areas for different users in TSP.

(4) TCS event manager: This component manages the event-related data structures (such as TSS_PCR_EVENT in TPM or TSM_PCR_EVENT in TCM) and their associations with their respective PCR. Meanwhile, this component provides the required event records for external entities. Since they are associated with the platform but not with the application, applications and service providers should obtain only copies of these structures. The TCS must provide the functions to store, manage and report these data structures and their associated PCR indexes. The event-recording data are stored in the corresponding database instead of the persistent storage area, because it can detect whether an event record has been tampered by comparing the hash value of the event record with the value stored in the PCR.

(5) TCS security chip parameter block generator: All the commands such as C-style data structures should be converted into the byte streams that the underlying device driver can understand, while the byte streams from the responses of security chip are required to be converted into the data structures that the upper layer can recognize. Parameter block generator completes the conversion through the interaction with the modules inside the TCS.

4.1.5 Trusted Service Provider

TSP is located in the top layer of TSS. It provides interfaces for applications to use trusted computing services and provides protection for data transmission between applications and security chips. The TSP layer is implemented externally as TSP instances in practice. It is located in user layer and has same run level with the user applications. Each user application can run one or more TSP instances to use the trusted computing services. TSP instances provide the high-level trusted computing functions allowing applications to focus on their specific security functions while relying on the TSP instances to perform most of the trusted functions. In addition, TSP also provides a small number of auxiliary functions not provided in the security chips such as data binding and signature verification.

The TSP directly interacts with the applications and provides numerous trusted service modules. To ensure the interaction between different applications, the TSP provides standard C language interfaces. Meanwhile, in order to facilitate the developers to quickly understand and use these interfaces, each module's object type definition is given with anon-strict "object-oriented" concept when implementing TSS. According to the different data types and usages, the main objects in TSP include context objects, policy objects, security chip (TPM/TCM) objects, key objects, encrypted data objects, PCR objects, nonvolatile memory (NVRAM) objects, hash objects and so on.

The TSP mainly provides the appropriate application interfaces, context manager and cryptographic functions, which are briefly described as follows:

(1) TSP interface: This is an object-oriented interface. It resides within the same process as the application. The application gathers the object's authorization data from the user, passes it to the TSP for processing by using the interfaces and finally forms the command's authorization data.
(2) TSP context manager: The TSP context manager provides efficient usage of the TSP's resources for applications in a dynamic management way. Each request provides the context related to TSP instance. Different threads within the application may share the same context or may acquire a separate context per thread.
(3) TSP cryptographic functions: To take full advantages of the protection functions of a security chip, the TSP must provide cryptographic support functions and interfaces, such as hashing algorithm and byte-stream generator.

4.2 TSS Interface

The TSS is mainly designed to provide necessary interfaces for upper applications to use trusted computing functions; therefore, it is necessary to design and implement the corresponding interface function for each functional layer of the TSS mentioned above [106], such as the TSP interface in application layer, the TCS interface and TDDL interface in system service layer and the TDD interface in kernel layer.

The following description takes TSM as an example. We briefly introduce the functional interfaces provided by the TSM [86]. These interfaces correspond to the functional layers mentioned in Section 4.1. The naming conventions of TSM interface functions are described in the Table 4.1.

Table 4.1: Naming conventions of TSM interface functions.

Layer	Prefix	Description
TSP	Tspi_	TSP interface called by user applications
TCS	Tcsi_	The interface used by TSP layer
TDDL	Tddli_	TDDL interface
TDD	Tddi_	Standard interface of OS

4.2.1 Object Type in TSM

TSM provides object-oriented Application Program Interface (API), each of which is associated with one object type. For this reason, we need to explain the object types defined in TSM before the introduction of specific interface functions.

There are ten different object types in the TSM specification: context object, policy object, TCM object, key object, encrypted data object, PCR composite object, hash object, NVRAM data object, migration data handling object and key agreement object. The definitions are shown in Table 4.2.

Each API is named according to its corresponding object type in the TSS, such that developers can know which object type they are operating. To take the context object handling in the TSM as an example, the function Tspi_Context_Create() informs the TSM service provider to generate a new context handle and return it to the applications. According to the differences of operating objects, the prefixes of APIs' names are different, for instance, the API for data object begins with "Tspi_Data_" while the API for key object starts with "Tspi_Key_".

Each TSM object type has its corresponding functional operating function. Developers should know the role and usage of each object type well so that they can write relevant applications.

Table 4.2: TSM data object type.

Type	Definition	Description
TSM_HCONTEXT	TSM_HOBJECT	Context object handle
TSM_HPOLICY	TSM_HOBJECT	Policy object handle
TSM_HTCM	TSM_HOBJECT	TCMobject handle
TSM_HKEY	TSM_HOBJECT	Key object handle
TSM_HENCDATA	TSM_HOBJECT	Encrypted data object handle
TSM_HPCRS	TSM_HOBJECT	PCR composite object handle
TSM_HHASH	TSM_HOBJECT	Hash object handle
TSM_HNVSTORE	TSM_HOBJECT	NVRAM data object handle
TSM_HMIGDATA	TSM_HOBJECT	Migration data handling object handle
TSM_HEXCHANGE	TSM_HOBJECT	Key agreement object handle

4.2.2 TDDL Interface in TSM

The TDDL interface is a component used by TSM to communicate with a physical security chip. It is the bottom functional component running in the user space and provides the switch from kernel mode to user mode. In the TSM architecture, it is located between the TCS and TDD layers, and provides application interfaces for the TCS layer. The TDDL interface is a single-threaded synchronous interface, and the TCM commands sent to this interface must have been serially processed.

The TDDL interface mainly includes three types of functions:

(1) Ensuring the communication with the security chip driver and providing command interfaces such as Open, Close and GetStatus.
(2) Obtaining or setting the attributes of security chip, security chip driver or driver library and providing command interfaces GetCapability and SetCapability.
(3) Transmitting or cancelling the commands sent to the security chip.

4.2.2.1 Main Interfaces

The TDDLinterface provides the following nine interface functions to interact with the security chips, so that the program can directly access the hardware devices:

(1) Tddli_Open: This function establishes a connection with the TDD. A successful execution of this function means that the TDD has prepared to process TCM command requests from the upper application. If this call fails, it gives warnings that the TDD is not loaded, started or the TCM does not support any protected requests. This function must be called before calling Tddli_GetStatus, Tddli_GetCapability, Tddli_SetCapability or Tddli_TransmitData.
(2) Tddli_Close: This function closes a connection with the TDD. Following a successful response to this function, the TDD can clear up all the resources used to maintain a connection with the TDDL. If this call fails, it indicates that TDD is unable to clear up resources or may need to be restarted or reloaded.
(3) Tddli_Cancel: This function cancels a TCM command. In a corresponding context, an application can call this function to interrupt an uncompleted TCM command.
(4) Tddli_GetCapability: This function is used to query the attributes of TCM hardware, firmware and device driver such as firmware version and driver version.
(5) Tddli_SetCapability: This function is used to set the attributes of TCM hardware, firmware and device driver. An application can set the parameters of device driver and operation defined by the TCM vendor with this function.
(6) Tddli_GetStatus: This function queries the status of the TCM driver and device. An application can use this function to determine the running status of the TCM subsystem.
(7) Tddli_TransmitData: This function sends a TCM command to a TCM device driver directly, causing the TCM to perform the corresponding operation.

(8) Tddli_PowerManagement: This function sets and queries the TCM's power states, but there is no corresponding TSPI interface for this function.
(9) Tddli_PowerManagementControl: This function is used to determine and set which component receives and handles the platform's power state management signals. It should be called only during TSS initialization.

It should be noted that the TCM device driver library only provides the connection to the core service layer, and the core service layer is the unique component that can communicate with the TCM device driver.

4.2.2.2 Example

When the TCM driver is loaded successfully, a user can use the TCM commands to execute trusted computing services. There is detailed description of TCM commands in the TSM specification, and here is an example of returning relevant parameters using TDDLi commands.

Suppose the user wants to get the TCM device vendor information, he can use the TDDLi directly. The pseudo codes are shown as follows:

```
//Connect TDDLi
res = Tddli_Open();
//Pad the eligible data block on demands
res = Tddli_GetCapability(TDDL_CAP_PROPERTY,
TDDL_CAP_PROP_MANUFACTURER, buf,
&buf_size);
//Send a request to TCM and return the required information
res = Tddli_TransmitData(reset, sizeof(reset), buf,
&buf_size);
//Close TDDLi
res = Tddli_Close();
```

These commands can return current TCM version, the size of TCM loadable key space, the number of loaded key and PCR register.

4.2.3 TCS Interface in TSM

We use TCSi to denote TCS interface. This is a simple "C" style interface. (The real core service interfaces are defined in the .wsdl file released by the TSS/TSM.) While it may allow multithreaded access to the TCS layer, each operation is atomic. In most environments it resides as a system process, separating from the other upper applications running synchronously. Service providers can call the TCSi to communicate with the core TCS layer via a local procedure call (LPC) or an RPC.

4.2.3.1 Main Interfaces

The TCS layer mainly manages the resources, and includes context manager, key and credential manager, event manager and parameter block generator. They are briefly described below.

Context Manager. Before sending commands to the TCS layer, an upper application needs to open a TCS context. The TCS context manager manages multiple contexts, allocates the required memory for each context and sets the handle for each type of object, including the handle of the context itself. It also provides memory management for each context. The main relevant interfaces are: Tcsi_OpenContext for obtaining a new context handle, Tcsi_CloseContext for releasing the context and its resources, Tcsi_FreeMemory for releasing the memory allocated by the TCS and Tcsi_GetCapability for getting the TCS layer attribute values.

Key and Credential Manager. The key management mainly includes key cache and key storage management. Key cache means that a unique TCS key handle is assigned to a key that has been loaded. When there is no space in the key slot, a key is removed and then a new key will be loaded. It is necessary to establish a mapping table to get a quick query between the TCS and the TCM key handles. Key storage management defines a persistent key hierarchy to internally manage keys. All keys must be registered in it and a universally unique identifier (UUID) will be assigned to each key. The use of a subkey depends on its parent key. The main interfaces of key management include Tcsip_CreateWrapKey for key creation, Tcsi_RegisterKey for registration, Tcsip_LoadKeyByBlob and Tcsip_LoadKeyByUUID for loading and Tcsip_UnregisterKey for unregistration.

The TCS credential management is only responsible for managing the EK credential, platform credential and conformance credential. Only the owner can access credentials. The relevant interfaces include Tcsip_MakeIdentity for generating identities and Tcsi_GetCredentials for obtaining credentials.

Event Manager. It generates, manages and outputs the related event records PCR. The main event records such as runtime measurement IMA are managed by the TSM; other events that are not managed by the TSS are completed by other components, for example, BIOS measurement is completed by the CRTM and OS kernel module measurement is completed by the VMM or DRTM. Besides, event manager should provide event records for the external entities. The event records are stored in the corresponding database instead of the protected areas, because the tampering of event records can be detected by PCR checking.

The interfaces for event management mainly include Tcsi_LogPcrEvent for adding a new event record and Tcsi_GetPcrEvent for checking the event log.

Parameter Block Generator. All command data structures need to be converted to byte streams, which can be understood by the underlying device driver. The byte streams responded by TCM should be converted to the corresponding data structure. The generator needs to interact with each internal module in the TCS, so that the interfaces for the various modules have been defined, such as the authorization-related interfaces (Tcsip_TakeOwnership, Tcsip_OIAP, Tcsip_OSAP), transmission-related interfaces (Tcsip_EstablishTransport, Tcsip_ExecuteTransport) and key-related interfaces (Tcsip_CertifyKey, Tcsip_OwnerReadPubek).

4.2.3.2 Usage Method

Since the TSM core service is an underlying functional abstract, which implements the corresponding functions according to the upper commands and returns the results, it is seldom used to develop trusted applications directly. Here we just give an overview of their usage method.

Calling Methods. Usually, the TSM core services must provide interfaces for local procedure calls in order to ensure that local concurrent applications can use local TCM resources simultaneously. However, it also needs to provide the interfaces for remote procedure calls in practical use so that the services are available to the applications on other systems. The main reason for requiring such remote access is that the communication between software requires the authentication between the hosts to ensure security. And as a security chip, the TCM meets this authentication requirement (remote attestation). In addition to ensuring common security communication, the TCM can also provide the attestations of software's trusted states in different systems, which is impossible for the existing secure communication mechanisms. A brief description of the two calling methods is as follows:

(1) Local procedure calls. LPC means invoking other applications and components directly in the same process or address space. The calling and communication procedures are relatively simple, so we will not go into details.
(2) Remote procedure calls. RPC provides the interaction between processes, mainly including the following:
    (a) A rule set to marshal and unmarshal parameters and results.
    (b) A rule set to encode and decode information transmitted between two processes.
    (c) Some basic operations to trigger an individual call, to return its results and to cancel it.
    (d) A rule set to maintain and reference state shared by participating processes, which is specified by the operating system and process structure.

RPC requires a communication infrastructure to establish the path between the processes, and provide a framework for addressing and naming. Any procedure that provides these services has these features.

Using TCS. As mentioned in previous section, the TCS interface in TSM is defined in C language, but this in not always the case. C language definition is only for the convenient discussion. The real TCS interface definition is the *.wsdl* file released by the TSM, which is a Web Services Description Language (WSDL) format file. We will not describe its specification in detail, and please refer to other relevant contents (such as the relevant introductions of XML, SOAP and HTTP). This file is attempted to provide a high-level universal definition for the TCS interface, such that the different developers on different platforms can use compatible tools.

Ideally, developers can use the existing TSM application-layer codes in C language to interact with the C-like TCS interface in TSM without understanding the underlying details. The TSM application-layer codes do not concern the process in which data arrive at the TCS layer, and they just need call some C language functions looking like the TCS. For this reason, a tool resolving *.wsdl* file is needed so that the TSM application layer can call the resolved functions directly, including specific C/C++ header files and source files.

4.2.4 TSP Interface in TSM

The most commonly used interface when users access a security chip based on TSS is the TSP interface, which provides the corresponding functions for users to use the trusted computing functions. In the TSM, it defines the related interfaces of nine objects: context management, policy management, trusted cryptographic module (TCM) management, key management, data encryption and decryption, PCR management, NVRAM management, Hash operation and key agreement.

The following section describes the object relationship in the TSM, and then gives a brief description of the corresponding interface of each object.

4.2.4.1 Object Relationship in Application Layer

Working objects are subdivided into authorized and non-authorized working objects in TSM application layer. Non-authorized working objects include the hash objects and PCR objects. Authorized working objects include the TCM object, context objects, key objects, encrypted data objects, NV Objects, key agreement objects and policy objects.

Nonauthorized Working Object Relationship. The non-authorized working object relationship is shown in Figure 4.2. The context manager provided by the TCS creates

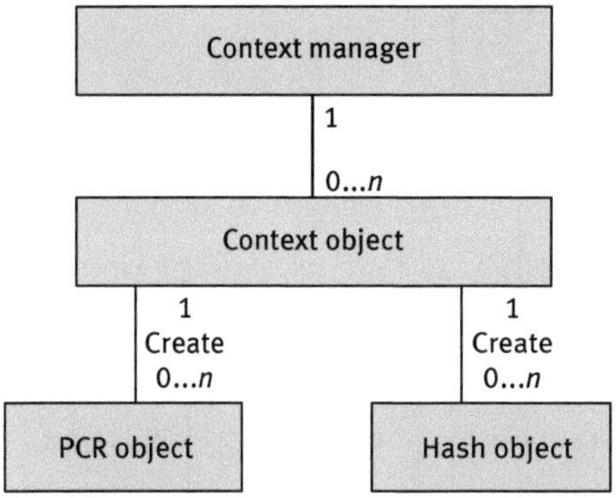

Figure 4.2: Non-authorized working object relationship.

multiple context objects, each of which can create multiple non-authorized PCR objects and non-authorized hash objects, thus showing a one-to-many relationship.

Authorized Working Object Relationship. The authorized working object relationship is shown in Figure 4.3. The user application may have to provide authorization data related to the policy objects when utilizing the authorized working objects via the TSP interface. A policy may be assigned to several working objects like key objects, encrypted data objects or TCM objects utilizing the Tspi_Policy_AssignToObject function. Each of these objects will utilize its assigned policy object to process TCM commands requiring authorization (based on internal functions of the policy object).

On creation of a context object, a default policy is created. This default policy is automatically assigned to each new created object. The default policy for each working object exists as long as no command assigns a new policy object to the working object.

For example, the relationship between policy objects and other objects in Figure 4.3 is shown as follows:

(1) When a context object is created, TSM will generate a default policy object. If an encrypted data object does not customize its own usage policy, the assigned policy will be the default policy. There is a one-to-one relationship between a TCM object and its policy object (operator policy).

(2) If a user needs to assign a new policy to a working object (such as a key object or a NV object), then the new policy should be generated using the context object. Here the relationship between context object and policy object is one-to-many (1:1 ... n), while the relationship between policy object and an ordinary working object is 1...2:0...1, where 1...2 represents that a certain working object generates one or two policies (usage policy or migration policy) and 0...1 indicates that the above policy may not be assigned after being generated or only be assigned to a certain object (this object can only be assigned to either usage policy or migration policy).

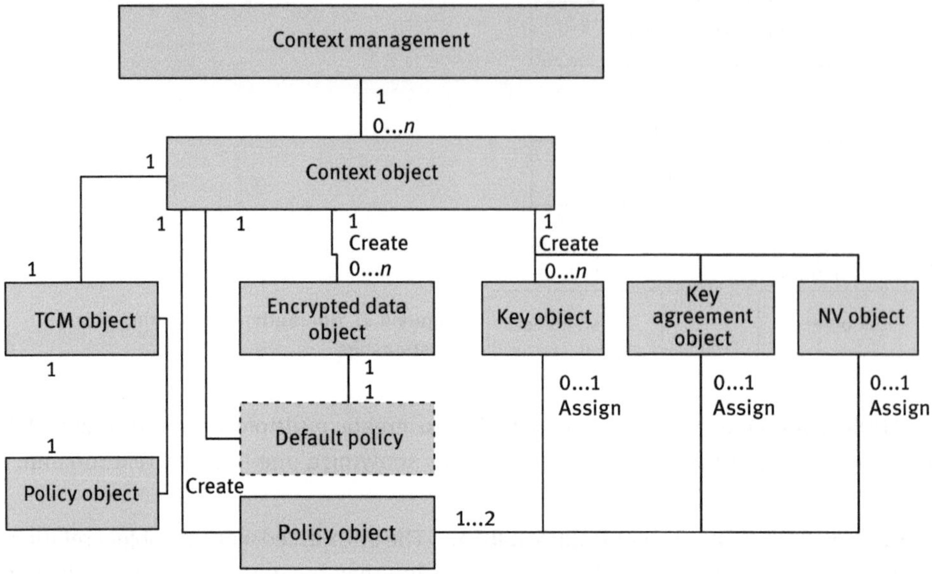

Figure 4.3: Authorized working object relationship.

4.2.4.2 Main Interfaces

The TSP includes context management, policy management, trusted cryptographic module management, key management, data encryption and decryption, PCR management, nonvolatile memory management (NVRAM management), Hash operation and key agreement. Their corresponding interface definitions will be described in the following sections.

Context Management. The context management object interface provides information about the TSP object's execution environment, such as the identity of the object, the transaction/communication with other TSM Software modules and memory management. According to the different functions, it can be divided into four specified categories: context management, object management, key management and information acquisition.

(1) Context management operation: It includes some specific functions such as Tspi_Context_Create for creating a context, Tspi_Context_Close for closing a context, Tspi_SetAttribUint32/SetAttribUintData for setting the context attributes (variable length or invariable length), Tspi_GetAttribUint32/GetAttribUintData for getting the context attributes (variable length or invariable length), Tspi_Context_Connect for connecting a context, Tspi_Context_FreeMemory for releasing a context, Tspi_Context_GetDefaultPolicy for getting default policy of a context, all of them are used to set and manage the context-related attributes.

(2) Object management operation: It includes two main interfaces: Tspi_Context_CreateObject for creating objects and Tspi_Context_CloseObject for closing

objects. Tspi_Context_CreateObject creates and initializes an empty object of specified type and returns the handle of this object. The empty object will be associated with an opened context object. Tspi_Context_CloseObject is used to destroy the object associated with a context and releases all related resources.

(3) Information acquisition operation: It includes two categories of operations: acquiring the platform capabilities and acquiring the TCM object handle. Tspi_Context_GetCapability for acquiring the platform capabilities is used to obtain the functionality/performance/attributes data of TSM service provider or core service; Tspi_Context_GetTcmObject for getting the TCM object handle is used to retrieve a context of the TCM object. Only one instance of this object exists for a given context and implicitly represents a TCM owner.

(4) Key management operation: It mainly refers to the interfaces provided by the TSM service provider, which facilitate users to call the underlying key management functions. The interfaces include the operations about the key loading, key generation and cancellation, key acquisition and others. For example, the interface for loading a key by its attributes is defined as Tspi_Context_LoadKeyByBlob, while the interface for getting a key by its ID is defined as Tspi_Context_GetKeyByUUID. For the interface definitions and usage of other operations, please refer to the specifications.

Policy Management Object. Policy management objects configure the corresponding security policies and behaviors for different applications. An application provides the specialized operation on authorization secret information for the authorization mechanism via the policy management. It includes the following operations:

(1) Setting policy authorization: Tspi_Policy_SetSecret sets the authorization data and mode for a policy object. The mode for policy to obtain authorization data is called secret mode, which includes the following cases in TSM:

TSM_SECRET_MODE_NONE: No authorization requests.

TSM_SECRET_MODE_SM3: Let *rgbsecret* point to a 32-byte hashed secret information.

TSM_SECRET_MODE-PLAIN: Let *rgbsecret* point to some plaintext, and *ulsecretLength* is the string length of *rgbsecret*.

TSM_SCRET_MODE_POPUP: TSM prompts a user to enter a password, which represents a TSM_UNICODE string and the string must be hash value.

(2) Flushing policy authorization: The function Tspi_Policy_FlushSecretis is used for flushing the cached policy authorization information, and it only requires an input parameter (the policy object handle *hPolicy*).

(3) Binding policy object: The function Tspi_Policy_AssignToObject assigns a certain policy to a working object (TCM object, key object, encrypted data object).

Each of these working objects will utilize its assigned policy object to process an authorized TCM command. By default, each new generated working object is assigned to the default policy. This function can bind a new policy to the working object, and meanwhile adds the policy to the policy list of the working object.

Trusted Cryptographic Module Management. TCM management object is usually used to represent TCM owner. TCM owner can be seen as the system administrator in a common PC environment. Therefore, there is only one TCM management object instance for each context, and this object is automatically associated with a policy object for handling the authorization data of TCM owner. In addition, it also provides some basic functions for controlling and reporting. Because the TCM management object is used most frequently, it provides the most functions and interfaces. According to its operation phases and functions, the functions and interfaces are divided into the following five categories:

(1) Request of creating platform identity and credential: This is mainly used to create a platform identity key (PIK), bind the user identity information and return a credential request packet.
(2) Activating platform identity and obtaining PIK credential: This is mainly used to verify the authenticity of a PIK credential and return the decrypted credential.
(3) PEK-related operations: Main operations include creating a PEK request, obtaining a PEK credential, importing a PEK key, creating an irrevocable EK, obtaining the public key of EK, creating a revocable EK, revoking an EK, creating a TCM owner, removing a TCM owner, setting operator authorization and setting TCM operation mode.
(4) Querying and obtaining TCM-related information: The main operations include querying and setting TCM state, obtaining TCM capability, full self-checking of TCM, obtaining self-checking result of TCM, obtaining the random number generated by TCM, obtaining a single event of TCM, obtaining a set of events of TCM and obtaining event log of TCM.
(5) PCR operations: The main operations include extending the PCR, reading the PCR value, resetting PCR, quoting PCR, reading TCM counter, reading the current TCM clock, obtaining the audit digest of TCM and setting the audit state of TCM command.

Key Management. The key management object interface is an entry for TSM to carry out key management functions. Each key object instance represents a specific key node in the TSM key storage hierarchy. Each key object requiring authorization should be assigned a policy object for managing authorization secret information. According to its functions, it can be divided into two categories:

(1) Functional interfaces for management: The interfaces mainly include the following functions: modifying the entity authorization data, getting policy object, setting key attributes (invariable or variable length parameter), getting key attributes (invariable or variable length parameter) and so on. They are defined by generic function interface.
(2) Functional interfaces related to key operations: This mainly includes the following interfaces: Tspi_Key_LoadKey for loading key, Tspi_Key_UnloadKey for unloading key, Tspi_Key_GetPubKey for getting public key, Tspi_Key_CertifyKey for certifying key, Tspi_Key_CreateKey for creating key, Tspi_Key_WrapKey for wrapping key, Tspi_Key_AuthorizeMigrationKey for creating migration authorization, Tspi_Key_CreateMigrationBlob for creating migration key data blob, and Tspi_Key_ConvertMigrationBlob for importing migration key data blob.

Data Encryption and Decryption. This object is used to associate the data generated by an external entity (such as a user or an application) with the system (binding to the platform or PCR), or to provide data encryption/decryption services for an external entity. In the authorizing process, this object can be assigned to another policy object. The object interface can be divided into two categories by function.
(1) Management operations: Management operations mainly include the following functions: modifying entity authorization, getting policy objects, getting data attributes (invariable-length parameter), setting data attributes (variable-length parameter), getting data attributes and other functions. They all utilize the general function interface definition.
(2) Data operations: They mainly include the following functions: data encryption, data decryption, data sealing, data unsealing, digital envelope sealing, digital envelope unsealing and other functions. They are described as follows:
   (a) Data encryption and decryption

   The main function is to encrypt plaintext and decrypt the corresponding cipertext. The corresponding interface functions are Tspi_Data_Encrypt for data encryption and Tspi_Data_Decrypt for data decryption. The cryptographic algorithm used by encryption and decryption depends on the key attributes.

   When an application calls the encryption command, if the symmetric encryption SMS4 is used, the encryption mode is CBC mode; if the asymmetric encryption SM2 is used, the input plaintext cannot exceed 256 bytes. When an application calls the decryption command, if symmetric decryption SMS4 is used, the decryption mode is CBC mode.

   (b) Data sealing and unsealing

   Data sealing is used to seal a data blob, whose corresponding interface is Tspi_Data_Seal, while data unsealing is used to unseal a specified data blob, whose corresponding interface is Tspi_Data_Unseal. If you want to unseal a sealed data, you must use Tspi_Data_Unseal on the same platform. Note that the sealing key used during data sealing should be a non-migratable key.

(c) Digital envelope sealing and unsealing

The main function is to seal digital envelope or unseal the sealed digital envelope. The corresponding interfaces are defined as Tspi_Data_Envelop for sealing data envelope and Tspi_Data_Unenvelop for unsealing data envelope. In the sealing process, the encrypted data get the data of digital envelope by Tspi_GetAttribData. In the unsealing process, the sealed data of digital envelope will be decrypted. Note that the interface function allocates memory for the plaintext data in the unsealing process, so the caller needs to release the memory explicitly.

PCR Management. PCR object interface is used to establish the trust level of system platform. The interface provides an easy way to select, read and write a PCR.

All the functions requiring PCR information use PCR object handle in their parameter list. The main interfaces include Tspi_PcrComposite_SetPcrLocality for setting PCR Locality attributes, Tspi_PcrComposite_GetPcrLocality for getting PCR Locality attributes, Tspi_PcrComposite_GetCompositeHash for getting PCR composite digest, Tspi_PcrComposite_SetPcrValue for setting PCR value, Tspi_PcrComposite_GetPcrValue for getting PCR value and Tspi_PcrComposite_SelectPcrIndex for selecting PCR index.

NVRAM Management. NVRAM management object is used to store the attribute information in nonvolatile memory area of TCM, which is used to define, read, write and release the NV area. This kind of commands establishes the size, index and various reading and writing authorization of NV memory area, and the authorization can be based on PCR value or authorization data.

In addition to the generic functions (setting or getting attributes), the interfaces of NVRAM management are mainly as follows: Tspi_NV_DefineSpace for creating a specified NV memory space, Tspi_NV_ReleaseSpace for releasing a NV memory space, Tspi_NV_WriteValue for writing data into a NV memory area and Tspi_NV_ReadValue for reading data from a specified NV memory area.

Hash Operations. Hash object provides a cryptographic security method for digital signature. In addition to the generic function interfaces to set and get the attributes, the main functional interfaces include Tspi_Hash_SetUserMessageData for carrying out the hash operation on user data, Tspi_Hash_SetHashValue for setting a hash value, Tspi_Hash_GetHashValue for getting the hash value of a hash object, Tspi_Hash_UpdateHashValue for updating a hash value, Tspi_Hash_Sign for signing a hash value, Tspi_Hash_VerifySignature for verifying the signature of a hash value and Tspi_Hash_TickStampBlob for adding time stamp to a hash object.

Key Agreement. Key agreement object is used to execute key exchange protocol operations. The main functional operations include creating a session, getting a session key and releasing a session. The corresponding interfaces are defined as follows:

(1) Creating a session: Tspi_Exchange_CreateKeyExchange creates a key agreement session handle with TCM and returns an ephemeral point on the elliptic curve. Two participants A and B generate their ephemeral points R_A and R_B, respectively, using this function. A transmits R_A to B, while B transmits R_B to A; then they complete the computation of key agreement with Tspi_Exchange_GetKeyExchange. When Tspi_Exchange_CreateKeyExchange has created a key agreement handle, it will return TSM_E_EXCHANGE_HANDLE_EXIST error code if you reuse it. You must release the key agreement handle by Tspi_Exchange_ReleaseExchangeSession, then Tspi_Exchange_CreateKeyExchange can be called again to establish key agreement handle with TCM.

(2) Getting a session key: The main function is to create a key agreement session handle with TCM and return an ephemeral curve point. An agreement session can only complete a key exchange.

    If a key agreement handle is not created by Tspi_Exchange_CreateKeyExchange, this function must return the error code TSM_E_EXCHANGE_HANDLE_NOT_EXIST.

    In case of a successful operation, the handle *hSessionKey* represents a symmetric key handle after a successful agreement. Assuming that the users A and B carry out a key agreement, after a successful operation using Tspi_Exchange_GetKeyExchange, the local verification data of A is S_A and the verification data sent to B is S_1; while the local verification data of B is S_B and the verification data sent to A is S_2. A needs to verify whether S_B and S_2 are equal and B needs to compare S_A and S_1. If validation fails, the encryption and decryption using the generated symmetric key will fail on both sides.

(3) Releasing a session: Tspi_Exchange_ReleaseKeyExchange releases a key agreement session handle established with TCM. The input parameter of this interface is key agreement handle *hKeyExchange*. If this handle is not created by Tspi_Exchange_CreateKeyExchange, this function must return the error code TSM_E_EXCHANGE_HANDLE_NOT_EXIST.

4.3 Trusted Application Development

As a bridge between user applications and a security chip, TSS provides bottom-up interfaces: TDDL interface, TCS interface and TSP interface. Developers can call appropriate interface to develop in different functional levels according to specific application requirements. This section will introduce specific trusted application development methods based on TSM. First, we introduce an interface's calling procedure and method. Then we take the usage of most common TSP interfaces as an example and give specific processes to call interface combined with practical application scenarios.

4.3.1 Calling Method of Interfaces

In order to use the underlying TCM chip, the TSM provides multiple functional interface layers to facilitate users to develop upper security applications based on trusted computing. When calling these interfaces, the basic calling procedure is shown in Figure 4.4 and a brief description is as follows:

(1) When a user application uses TSM to access TCM, the call between the user application and TSP layer adopts a dynamic link library (DLL) way. The corresponding header files and library files of dynamic link library are provided for developers to develop security applications.
(2) The communication between the TSP and the TCS adopts the way of LPC or RPC. It can automatically allocate memory in the communication procedure according to the definition of IDL (Interface Description Language).
(3) The interface between TCS and TDDL also adopts DLL method. Since the TDDL interface is standard, it also takes DLL method when using driver library in order to facilitate the port of TCS. In this way, TCS layer can use different driver libraries and run on the platforms with different security chips.
(4) The interfaces of driver library and device driver are standard interfaces that allow OS accessing driver.

In general, when trusted applications call the functions of a security chip, they only use the top TSPi interface rather than calling interfaces in each level of TSS. The underlying TCS interface, TDDL interface and TDD interface in TSM are only as abstract interfaces and not exposed to users explicitly. The commutation data between them are automatically implemented by TSS.

In the development process of a trusted application, the programmer first creates a context object using the TSP interface and then generates a corresponding target

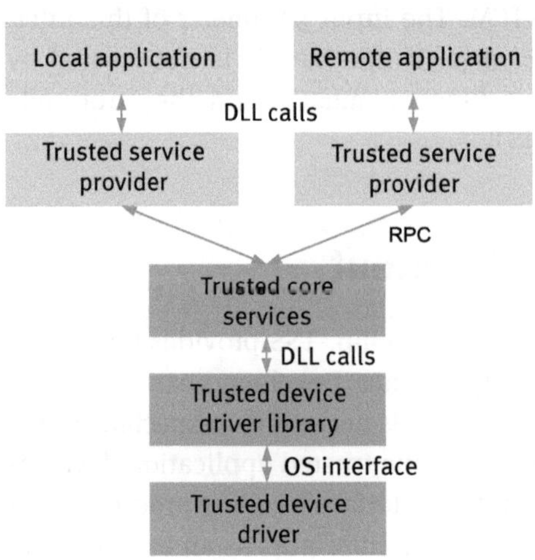

Figure 4.4: The calling method between TSM submodules.

object, such as a TPM object, a key object or a PCR object. After that, he should create or configure an authorization policy object for the above object, so as to conduct permission decision. Finally, he performs the specific trusted computing functional operations, such as key creation, digital signature and remote attestation.

Taking the file encryption and decryption and the signature verification in the DRM (Digital Right Management) as examples, we briefly describe the specific process of developing trusted computing applications based on TSM in the following sections.

4.3.2 Example 1: File Encryption and Decryption

Users need to protect their personal confidential files. Otherwise, sensitive data may be revealed because the files are copied or computers are lost. Compared to the traditional solution based on software encryption, a tamper-resistant security chip can protect keys in a more secure manner so that users' files can be protected better.

The main process of encrypting a user's file based on TCM chip is as follows: The user creates (he must input his own password) and loads a symmetric encryption key on the host embedded with a security chip TCM. The key is encrypted and protected by the TCM and can be bound to the current host configuration; then the user selects the file to be protected and calls the encryption interface to generate an encrypted file. When the user opens the file, he must enter the password to load the corresponding decryption key. In the following, we briefly describe the related encryption and decryption operations in the application development process, including initial setup, authorization policy setting, key operation, data encryption and decryption, resource release and so on.

4.3.2.1 Initial Setup

First, a basic context object should be created, which is the foundation of further operations of TSS and is used to establish the initial execution environment.

```
//Create and connect a context object
Tspi_Context_Create( &hContext );
Tspi_Context_Connect( hContext, get_server(GLOBALSERVER) );
```

4.3.2.2 Policy Setting

When TSM performs operations, it needs to create appropriate usage policies for the involved objects. First, it obtains the above created context object and then it gets a corresponding policy object *hOwnerPolicyObject* and sets the policy value for the policy object. Here we take policy mode TSM_SECRET_MODE_SM3 as an example. This mode takes a 32-byte array from external hash computation as authorization data. The input data won't be modified by TSM.

```
//Get a TCM object and set the corresponding usage policy
Tspi_Context_GetTCMObject(hContext, &hTCM);
Tspi_GetPolicyObject(hTCM,TSM_POLICY_USAGE,
  &hOwnerPolicyObject);
Tspi_Policy_SetSecret(hOwnerPolicyObject,
                      TSM_SECRET_MODE_SM3,
                      sizeof(rgbOwnerSecret),
                      rgbOwnerSecret);
```

4.3.2.3 Key Operation

The parent key *hSMK* must be loaded into the TCM before we use it to create a new key object whose usage policy will be set as the default policy *pDefaultPolicyObject*; then we can generate a new encryption key *hKey* based on the parent key handle and load it into the security chip. The code is presented as follows:

```
//Create Key Object
Tspi_Context_CreateObject(hContext,
                          TSM_OBJECT_TYPE_KEY,
                          TSM_KEY_TSP_SMK,
                          &hSMK);
//Parant key is the SMK storage master key
Tspi_GetPolicyObject(hSMK ,TSM_POLICY_USAGE,
  &pDefaultPolicyObject);
Tspi_Policy_SetSecret(pDefaultPolicyObject,
                      SMKSecretMode,
                      32,
                      TEST_SMK_AUTHDATA);
//Set the authorization policy
Tspi_Context_CreateObject(hContext,
                          TSM_OBJECT_TYPE_KEY,
                          TSM_SMS4KEY_TYPE_BIND,
                          &hKey);//Create bindingkey
//Create and load the local TCM key
Tspi_Key_CreateKey(hKey,hSMK,NULL);
Tspi_Key_LoadKey(hKey,hSMK);
```

4.3.2.4 Encryption and Decryption

To use a newly generated key object to encrypt and decrypt the files to be protected, we first create an encrypted data object *hEncData* (using the bound operation type TSM_ENCDATA_BIND) and then use the existing key *hKey* to perform encryption and corresponding decryption. The code is presented as follows:

```
//Encryption and decryption operations
Tspi_Context_CreateObject(hContext,
                         TSM_OBJECT_TYPE_ENCDATA,
                         TSM_ENCDATA_BIND,
                         &hEncData);
//Create data object used to perform encryption
Tspi_Data_Encrypt(hEncData,hKey,
                 TRUE,
                 (TCM_SMS4_IV*)IV, //Use symmetric
                   encryption algorithmSMS4
                 DATA, //The file data to be encrypted
                 strlen(DATA));
result = Tspi_Data_Decrypt(hEncData,hKey,
                          TRUE,
                          (TCM_SMS4_IV*)IV,
                          &ulDataLength,
                          rgbDataDecrypted);//Decrypt
                            using the corresponding key
```

4.3.2.5 Release the Resource

After the encryption and decryption operations are completed, the TSM resources related to this operation should be released, including evicting the key, closing the corresponding key object and releasing memory resources.

```
//Release the related resources and exit
Tspi_Key_UnLoadKey(hKey);
Tspi_Context_CloseObject(hContext,hSMK);
Tspi_Context_FreeMemory( hContext, NULL );
```

4.3.3 Example 2: Signature Verification in DRM

In order to protect the copyright of digital products, many digital service providers (such as the company providing online software downloading business) need to build their own DRM systems to prevent software from being copied and used without limit. The main way to implement DRM is to embed the copyright owner's signature into software while encrypting its digital contents. When a user starts the software, the service provider first verifies the signature. After a successful verification, the user can decrypt the contents and use the software. Compared with the existing software-based DRM schemes, the method with a tamper-resistant security chip can detect the authenticity and validity of software products, thereby providing a more secure DRM.

In the following example, we briefly describe the signature verification process based on security chip TCM in DRM, and we will further introduce the method of developing security applications based on TSM.

4.3.3.1 Initial Setup

First, we create data objects for the signature verification operation, including context object, hash object and key object, which establishes an initial environment for further TSM operations.

```
//Create and connect a context object
Tspi_Context_Create( &hContext );
Tspi_Context_Connect( hContext, get_server(GLOBALSERVER) );
Tspi_Context_CreateObject(hContext,
                          TSM_OBJECT_TYPE_HASH,
                          TSM_HASH_SCH,
                          &hHash); //Create a hash object
Tspi_Context_CreateObject(hContext,TSM_OBJECT_TYPE_KEY,
                          TSM_KEY_TSP_SMK,&hSMK);//SMK object
```

4.3.3.2 Policy Setup

We set the required authorization policy for this operation. Here we still take the policy mode TSM_SECRET_MODE_SM3 as an example. It takes a 32-byte array from external hash computation as the authorization data.

```
//Create and set the usage policy of SMK
Tspi_Context_CreateObject(hContext,TSM_OBJECT_TYPE_POLICY,
                          TSM_POLICY_USAGE, &hSMKPolicy);
Tspi_Policy_SetSecret(hSMKPolicy,
                      TSM_SECRET_MODE_ SM3,
                      32,
                      EST_SMK_AUTHDATA);
Tspi_Policy_AssignToObject(hSMKPolicy,hSMK);
```

4.3.3.3 Create a Signature Key

To sign a software product, we first need to create a signature key object whose type is TSM_ECCKEY_TYPE_SIGNING. Here we set its signature scheme as TCM_SS_ECCSIGN_SCH and its authorization mode as TSM_SECRET_MODE_SCH, and finally we create and load the signature key.

```
//Create a signature key object
Tspi_Context_CreateObject(hContext,
                          TSM_OBJECT_TYPE_KEY,
                          TSM_ECCKEY_TYPE_SIGNING,
                          &hSignKey);
Tspi_SetAttribUint32(hSignKey,TSM_TSPATTRIB_KEY_INFO,
                     TSM_TSPATTRIB_KEYINFO_SIGSCHEME,
                     TCM_SS_ECCSIGN_SCH ); //Set the
                       signature scheme
Tspi_Context_CreateObject(hContext,
                          TSM_OBJECT_TYPE_POLICY,
                          TSM_POLICY_USAGE, &hSignKeyPolicy);
Tspi_Policy_SetSecret(hSignKeyPolicy, TSM_SECRET_MODE_SCH,
                      sizeof(rgbSecret), rgbSecret);//Set
                        the usage policy
Tspi_Policy_AssignToObject(hSignKeyPolicy, hSignKey);
Tspi_Key_CreateKey(hSignKey, hSMK, NULL);//Create a
  signature key
Tspi_Key_LoadKey(hSignKey, hSMK);//Load the signature key
```

4.3.3.4 Sign and Verify

First, a service provider needs to generate/update a hash value for the software required to be protected (such as *rgbSecret*). Then the service provider signs this software with the existing signature key *hSignKey*. When the software product is released, the signature is bound to this product. When using the software, a user needs to submit the corresponding signature data. The service provider verifies the signature with the corresponding signature key. If the signature is verified successfully, it means that the software is authorized and the user can use it legally. If it fails, it indicates that the software is not authorized or the signature data have been tampered. For example, the correct signature value *prgbSignature* has been tampered into the wrong signature value *wrongSignature*.

```
//The process of signing and verifying
Tspi_Hash_UpdateHashValue(hHash,sizeof(rgbSecret),rgbSecret);
// Update the hash object
//Sign the above updated hash data via using the existing
  signature key hSingKey
Tspi_Hash_Sign(hHash,hSignKey,&pulSignatureLength,
  &prgbSignature);
//Verify the signature using the corresponding signature
  key hSignKey
Tspi_Hash_VerifySignature(hHash,hSignKey,pulSignatureLength,
  prgbSignature);
//If the verification fails, it indicates the software is
  not authorized or has been tampered.
Tspi_Hash_VerifySignature(hHash,hSignKey,pulSignatureLength,
  wrongSignature);
```

4.3.3.5 Release the Resource

After the operations are completed, the resources related to signing and verifying should be released, including signature key and SMK object.

```
Tspi_Key_UnLoadKey(hSignKey);
Tspi_Context_CloseObject(hContext,hSMK);
```

4.4 Open-Source TSS Implementation

This section describes the existing open-source TSS implementations, which are based on the TCG Software Stack Specification and provide most of the trusted computing functional interfaces for developers. Their specific implementations are mainly based on standard C language and Java language. C-based TrouSerS is the most popular TSS.

4.4.1 TrouSerS

TrouSerS is an open-source TSS software developed by IBM researchers, which is compatible with the TCG Software Stack Specification version 1.1 and version 1.2 and can provide interfaces accessing TPM for the user applications.

4.4.1.1 Basic Architecture

TSS consists of TSS Service Provider (TSP), TSS Core Services (TCS), TSS Device Driver Library (TDDL) and TSS Device Driver (TDD). TrouSerS realizes the TSP shared library, the TCS daemon *tcsd* and the TDDL library, and meanwhile provides the persistent storage of some resources like keys. The following are its main functional components:

(1) TSP shared library: Trousers implements TSP as a shared library libtspi.so, which enables applications to communicate with TCS daemon (or system service) *tcsd* locally or remotely. Meanwhile, TSP also manages various resources that are used to communicate with applications and *tcsd* and interacts with *tcsd* transparently when required.

(2) TCS daemon: TCS daemon *tcsd* is a daemon in user space. It is the unique entry to access TPM on demand of the TCG Software Stack Specification. When the system boots, TCS daemon is loaded and it will open TPM device driver. Since the system boots, all the operations that are used to connect TPM should be then based on TSS. The daemon *tcsd* manages TPM resources and processes the local and remote TSP requests.

(3) TDDL library: TrouSerS implements TDDL in the form of the static library *libtddl.a*, which is called by the upper-layer TCS and is the only bottom interface to interact with the hardware TPM.

(4) Persistent storage file: TSS provides two different types of persistent storage for the keys. PS can be regarded as a key database, in which each key is indexed by an UUID.

   (a) PS for users

   This kind of PS is maintained by the TSP library of applications. When writing the first key to the PS for users, TSP library creates a new file in *~/.trousers/user.data* and finds the working directory utilizing the effective user ID of the process. The environment variable TSS_USER_PS_FILE can also make the TSP library setting point to different locations of PS for users. This environment variable has the same life cycle with TSP context. So in order to store two keys to two files respectively, it needs to call Tspi_Context_Close, set the new location and open the context again.

   (b) PS for system

   This kind of PS is controlled by TCS and remains effective during the life cycle of all applications, *tcsd* reboot and system reset. The data registered in the PS for system remain effective until an application requests to delete it. The file of PS for system is located in the path */usr/local/var/lib/tpm/system.data* by default, which is usually created when the TPM takes ownership for the first time.

4.4.1.2 Run TrouSerS

By default, the TCS daemon cannot be accessed through the network; therefore, it can be executed as root role only in local access, and it should ensure that TPM device driver is loaded and started as root role. If Linux Kernel 2.6.12 and above are used and *udev* is started up, the following content should be added to the file *udev* (usually located in /etc/udev):

tpm[0-9]:tss:tss:0600

Then, itloads the corresponding device driver:

 # modprobetpm_atmel (the specific names are different according to different manufacturers)

Finally, it starts the TCS process, which is /usr/local/sbin/ tcsd by default:

 # /usr/local/sbin/tcsd

If you want to let TCS process communicate with software-based TPM via TCP network protocol, you need to use the option -e:

 # /usr/local/sbin/tcsd -e

The open-source TrouSerS has implemented the complete functional interfaces of TSS1.2, and it supports to run in the 32- and 64-bit platforms. Therefore, it is the most popular TSS currently. Most of the developments related to trusted computing products depend on this software.

4.4.2 jTSS

The interfaces of the published TCG TSS specification are defined in C language, which cannot be used in Java environment. Therefore, many institutions perform research on calling trusted computing functions in Java environment. Under the support of European openTC Project and Austria acTvSM Project, the researchers from IAIK institute (The Institute for Applied Information Processing and Communications) in Graz University of Technology in Austria developed a software stack named jTSS, which is also an open-source software interface.[2] It realizes all the TSS functions with Java language. At the same time, in order to support the local and remote access, jTSS also implements an RPC mechanism that is consistent with TSS1.2. This mechanism is based on the SOAP protocol and ensures that it can interact with various TSS of different vendors.

4.4.2.1 Basic Architecture

In order to implement functions required by the TCG Software Stack Specification, the jTSS interface mainly consists of three parts: TSP, TCS and TDDL. Its main function architecture is briefly described as follows.

2 At present, the latest version of jTSS is 0.7. For concrete installation and usage, you can refer to source-code instruction: http://trustedjava.sourceforge.net/index.php?item=jtss/about

TSS Service Provider. The TSP library provides APIs for developers to access all TPM functions. These APIs allow applications to use TPM via TSP. In jTSS, the APIs are defined as sets of interfaces located in the *iaik.tc.tss.api* package, while *iaik.tc.tss.impl* package is the actual implementation of API interface definition, and the *impl* package provides subpackages implemented by different types of TSP. The Java subpackage can include a complete Java implementation of TSP, while other subpackages may include some implementations such as a JNI implementation that supports to interact with a C-based TSP such as TrouSerS. The main advantage of separation of API implementation is that the applications above the top layer of TSP can easily switch between different TSP implementations in bottom layer by changing the library for creating TSP objects.

TSS Core Services. The TCS is the unique entity that can directly access TPM, so it is implemented as a system service or daemon that is responsible for TPM command stream generation, TPM command serialization, TPM resource management, event log management and persistent storage for system. In a typical TCS implementation, it is a daemon or system service supported by jTSS, and meanwhile jTSS provides the access to it in the form of libraries.

TDDL. The package *iaik.tc.tss.impl.java.tcs.tddl* contains a TDDL for different operating systems. The TDDL is a functional layer that can directly interact with TPM driver (e.g., through a device file or some specific mechanisms of operating system).

In addition, the code architecture of jTSS also provides the method to share files between TSP and TCS and the way of persistent storage. The multiple components shared by TSP and TCS are placed in the same directory. These components include the constants used in TPM and TCS, the data structures of TSS and TPM layers, the implementation of persistent storage and the common cryptography library. The jTSS provides two different types of PS.

The first type of PS uses the file system of operating system as the database. In the configuration file *.ini*, it needs to set different directories for two storage ways (system-level and user-level), where there must be only one for TCS system storage and one for each user (e.g., */home/<username>/.tpm/user_storage*). We must take care to set the access permission for the storage files. Since the directory structure is created automatically, it is recommended to create and set the file permissions before enabling jTSS.

The second type of PS uses the relational database. It provides some concrete implementation on demand; therefore, it can implement specific Java classes for persistent storage and configure it in the file. After TPM is executed, the SRK (storage root key) will be stored in the system storage area (not including the private key part). Note that in the TSS specification, the application developers are required to create and maintain a valid key structure.

4.4.2.2 Use jTSS

The jTSS source code gives some examples. Here we take context operation as an example to explain its invoking method. The following code illustrates the basic operations when using TPM:

```
import iaik.tc.tss.api.exceptions.common.TcTssException;
import iaik.tc.tss.api.tspi.TcIContext;
import iaik.tc.tss.api.tspi.TcTssContextFactory;
public class ShortestjTSSProgram {
    public static void shortestjTSSProgram() {
        try {
            TcIContext context = newTcTssContextFactory()
              .newContextObject();
            context.connect();
            // work with context here ...
            context.closeContext();
        }catch (TcTssException e) {
            e.printStackTrace();
        }
    }
}
```

In this example, *TcTssContextFactory* provides the context object *context* of *TcIContext* type and selects the local or SOAP binding automatically to implement the connection with TCS *context.connect()* based on the settings in the configuration file *jtss_tsp.ini*.

4.4.3 μTSS

The TCG Software Stack provides interfaces to use TPM for trusted computing application development. But the current TSS interface is very complex and is prone to errors in use. Besides, this complexity makes it unsuitable to the embedded devices with limited resource or security kernel; therefore, a simplified implementation of TSS interface is required. Aiming at the above requirements, Sirrix AG Company in Germany developed a software stack μTSS [107] that provides lightweight programming interfaces based on the TPM specification for developers. In the premise of ensuring correctness of μTSS, its design idea is to reduce the complexity of object wrapping and error handling and improve the usability in application development by further abstracting the interfaces. The μTSS also provides modular functional architecture, which enables it to provide corresponding subsets of functional interfaces for different requirements, for example, customizing different subsets of software stack for some environments such as embedded systems, mobile devices or systems based on security kernel. In addition, it can also be used for compliance test for the TPM specification and implementation of MTM.

The µTSS is developed by C++ language and supports object-oriented implementation. Compared with other high-level language such as Python, Java or C#, it requires a smaller runtime environment. Similar to TSS implementation, the basic architecture of µTSS includes oTSP, oTCS and oTDDL.

4.4.3.1 oTSP Layer

The oTSP layer provides an advanced abstract interface for application developers. It offers object-oriented abstract of TPM functions and defines the relevant objects in the TPM specification, such as TPM object and key object. But it hides the complexity of some functional interfaces as far as possible; for example, in the key object, it hides the complexity of key loading and key updating using the base class *PrivateKey*, so that the key is loaded automatically when used and is updated automatically when the application is closed.

4.4.3.2 oTCS Layer

The oTCS layer implements TCS interface. It provides TPM commands, sessions and interfaces to execute these commands. By defining each TPM command as a single C++ class, it supports a variety of different specifications and minimizes the interface. By implementing TPM command template, it becomes simple to modify (such as updating the TSS specification) or remove (such as the cases in embedded and mobile device environments) TPM commands.

4.4.3.3 oTDDL Layer

The oTDDL layer implements TDDL interface, including the interface connecting to TPM device driver. It provides various TDDLi back end interfaces. The *SocketTDDL* class sends TPM commands to the remote side using TCP/IP connection; the *DeviceTDDL* class provides access to TPM in local platform in different operating system environments.

The µTSS is mainly used in the following scenarios:

(1) MTM software stack and the software-based MTM implementation: The MTM is similar to TPM and is suitable for embedded and mobile devices. There are some differences between the command set of MTM and TPM; for example, some TPM commands are not available on MTM and MTM also adds a number of new commands, so a new TSS implementation is required. If there is no physical chip supporting MTM, the µTSS can be used to realize a software-based MTM.

(2) The development of compliance test set for the TPM specification: The test for TPM needs to cover most TPM commands. The oTCS layer of μTSS can be used to generate the input data for a test. Since the μTSS hides a lot of complex operations in TSS, it can generate test cases quickly and easily.
(3) The development of TPM manager: TPM manager is a graphical management tool for TPM. The early version took TrouSerS as back end. Afterward, μTSS was introduced as back end. The advantage is that *DeviceTDDL* implemented by μTSS enables the upper applications to get access to TPM driver directly without the daemon *tcsd*, which makes the *initrd* (containing TPM manager) very small.

Using the object-oriented design and implementation, μTSS provides convenient and efficient interfaces for developers. It effectively reduces the complexity of some functional interfaces in the TSS specification and provides for handling of runtime errors and compiling of time errors. The modular architecture design of μTSS makes it have a better application flexibility and can provide trusted service interfaces for various application environments such as embedded or mobile devices, so it will have a bright application prospect.

4.5 Summary

This chapter mainly describes the TSS-related contents. TSS is a support software to use a security chip. It can provide required interfaces for users to develop applications based on security chips. This chapter first describes the basic architecture, composition and functions of TSS. Then, taking the example of the software stack TSM, it illustrates the brief definitions and invoking relations of the interface of each layer in TSS. It also gives examples of developing trusted applications using TSS. Finally, it introduces the implementation and usage of popular open-source TSS.

In order to support wider application such as mobile applications and Java applications, TSS needs to provide flexible, multi-language and cross-platform implementation in the future. Moreover, since TSS is the most common way to communicate with secure chips, its security is directly related to the security of trusted applications. Therefore, formal modeling for the functional interfaces provided by the TSS is required, so that it can provide fine-grained and detailed analysis for the security properties of TSS and detect possible security vulnerabilities of the interfaces in use, thus enhancing the security of TSS.

5 Trusted Computing Platform

5.1 Introduction

To address the trust issues of software and their computing environments, Trusted Computing Group (TCG) first put forth the idea of trusted computing platform (TCP) [108], which can be concretized into a trusted personal computer, a trusted server and a trusted mobile device. The aim of TCP is to achieve the trustworthiness of system behaviors, that is, to ensure that behavior of software is consistent with the expectation in a given operating environment. The basic idea to build TCP is to introduce a security chip (TPM/TCM) as the root of trust on the hardware platform, then extend the trust boundary based on the security chip and finally change all or part of the general computing platforms into "trusted" computing platform. The security of TCP is rooted in the security chip (TPM/TCM) in possession of the security defense capability. Based on the services of security chips, such as isolated computation, integrity protection of computing environment and remote attestation, the trustworthiness of entities behavior in TCP can be guaranteed.

TCP is a security architecture built for a general-purpose computing platform using a security chip. In order to build a TCP, there must be two basic elements: First, it must be equipped with a hardware security chip, which is the basis and premise to protect the security functions of the target platform; second, it has to implement appropriate trusted computing technologies, including the security mechanisms such as chain of trust, trust measurement and remote attestation, which is the concrete way to achieve a trusted computing platform environment [5]. In general, the TCP provides the following trust insurances for user environment:

(1) Based on the mechanism of trust measurement, TCP can construct a chain of trust for the platform's start-up procedure, so as to establish the initial trust environment of platform. By verifying the integrity and trustworthiness of the runtime applications, TCP can ensure trusted execution of platform's local applications. Based on the key operation ability provided by security chips, TCP can provide hardware-based protection for platform's local data, thereby constructing platform's local trust.
(2) Based on the anonymous and remote attestation mechanisms, TCP provides correctness proof of platform's identity and software and hardware configuration. In this way, it constructs trust between platforms.
(3) Based on the integrity collection and remote attestation mechanisms of trusted computing platform, TCP verifies integrity status of the platform that will access to the network. It ensures trust of each node in the network and lays the foundation for constructing trust in the whole network.

DOI 10.1515/9783110477597-005

5.1.1 Development and Present Status

The demand of trusted computing platform stems from solving trust problems of terminal platform's behaviors. Hence, early work is mainly driven by the IT industry, including many members of the TCG such as Microsoft, IBM, HP and Intel. TCP makes use of the hardware security chip to solve the trust problems of platform at the architecture level, which has obvious advantages compared with traditional software-based security solutions. As a security-enhanced platform architecture, TCP still faces many challenges in data protection, computing environment protection, remote trust, system security architecture and so on. These challenges promote research on trusted computing platform at home and abroad.

Cambridge, Carnegie Mellon, Stanford, IBM Institute and other well-known universities and research institutions have launched research projects related to trusted computing platform, and made a series of research results. TCG developed the specifications for trusted PC, trusted server, trusted mobile phone, virtualized trusted platform and other related technologies and products, respectively, for different forms of trusted computing platforms, and these specifications provide standard support for further promotion and application of trusted computing technology. The industry field had developed a series of TCP products; for example, IBM, HP and other computer manufacturers had introduced a number of TCP products varying from the desktop and the laptop to the server. With the rapid application of mobile devices and mobile applications, Nokia, Samsung and other mobile phone manufacturers are working on appropriate products on trusted phones.

On the one hand, many research institutions in China, such as Institute of Software, Chinese Academy of Science (ISCAS), conducted in-depth research in the TCP technology and architecture and laid a solid foundation for the development of independent trusted computing technology and product. On the other hand, Chinese TCP had got the support and promotion from the chip and computer vendors to application service providers and end users: Lenovo, Great Wall, Tsinghua Tongfang and other computer manufacturers had launched their own TCP products, which are widely used in military, bank, government and other key national departments. In 2007, the Office of Security Commercial Code Administration (OSCCA) launched some independent technical specifications for TCP products, which provide standard support for further development and promotion of TCP.

The technology research and industry promotion of TCP has formed a good interaction, and comes into being as a cycle-forward momentum of development in the research, product, evaluation and standard. The rapid development of the Internet of Things, cloud computing and other new technologies further leads the users to concern the security of their computing environment. To this end, manufacturers are gradually introducing new TCPs, including trusted mobile platform (TMP) and embedded trusted platform (automotive device). We believe that TCP will be further promoted and applied with the rapid development of the trusted computing technology.

5.1.2 Basic Architecture

TCP is first proposed by TCG, which provides security enhancement for the general-purpose computing platform at the system architecture level. It takes the underlying security chip as the core and finally establishes a complete trusted running environment for the users' computing platform combined with the upper key mechanism for trusted computing. We divide the architecture of TCP into three layers from bottom to up, which is shown in Figure 5.1.

These three layers are the underlying hardware layer, the trusted service layer and the security application layer. TCP covers the entire computing platform system from the underlying hardware, the intermediate operating system kernel and trusted functional interfaces to the upper trusted applications.

(1) Underlying hardware layer: This layer mainly includes the physical security chip, combined with trusted BIOS, security CPU, security I/O and other structures that provide the root of trust for the entire computing system.

(2) Trusted service layer: This layer spans system kernel layer and user application layer, including operating system kernel and trusted software interface. Operating system kernel is the basis for running a computing system, and trusted software interface provides calling interfaces of trusted computing service for upper applications, for example, the trusted software stack TSS/TSM for different security chip TPM/TCM.

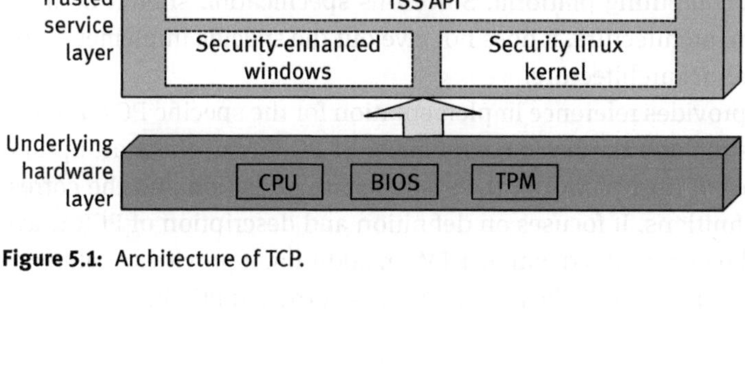

Figure 5.1: Architecture of TCP.

(3) Security application layer: This layer is located in the highest layer of TCP architecture. Based on the root of trust and foundational trusted operating environment, it implements security features for various security requirements and protects the trusted running environment for the users' applications by calling different trusted computing software interfaces.

Thus, it can be seen that, in the TCP architecture taking a security chip as the core, the underlying hardware layer provides the initial root of trust, which is a prerequisite for constructing TCP. The trusted service layer completes the establishment of chain of trust, integrity measurement and other key trusted mechanisms through the interaction with the hardware layer, and it provides a foundational trusted operating environment for the user applications. The security application layer implements the security user applications based on the trusted functions and calling interfaces provided by the hardware layer and service layer. The functions of each layer are complementary and indispensable, and eventually build a trusted computing platform meeting the security needs of the user.

5.2 Personal Computer

PC is the most widely used computing platform. Users need an assurance mechanism that can provide trusted execution for applications and systems. A trusted PC built on a security chip meets these needs. Trusted PC should not affect the execution and implementation of the existing system. Therefore, it must enhance the security of original system under the premise of being compatible with the original architecture. To this end, TCG gives the security technology specifications and standards for trusted PC to guide the implementation and application of the corresponding products.

5.2.1 Specification

For the PC Client architecture of general users' computing platform, TCG published PC Client Specific Implementation Specification [109], which has mainly been developed by HP, IBM, Intel and Microsoft. Its goal is to provide a reference implementation for the individual trusted computing platform. Since this specification should be independent of the platform architecture, it does not give out the specific implementation requirements in its abstract architecture.

The specification provides reference implementation for the specific PC platform, and its main contents include the basic components of PC Client, the start-up and configuration processes of host platform, the system state transition and the corresponding certificate definitions. It focuses on definition and description of PCR usage and the localities used by static and dynamic RTM. In addition, it provides a reference implementation architecture and application interfaces of trusted PC Client.

In order to provide better guidance for trusted PC Client, TCG also publishes other related auxiliary specifications:

(1) PC Client-Specific TPM Interface Specification [87]
TPM main specification defines a generic TPM interface used by a nonspecific platform, but it does not refer to special features of TPM (such as support for dynamic locality and resettable PCR) that relate to the specific platforms (such as personal PC or server). To this end, TCG develops this specification and defines the TPM interfaces supporting special features in a generic PC environment.

(2) PC Client Work Group Platform Reset Attack Mitigation Specification [110]
When a platform resets or turns off, the contents of the volatile memory RAM do not immediately disappear. Therefore, the attacker can reset the target platform and then rapidly activate an intrusion program to obtain the remaining memory contents, such as encryption keys and other secret information. In order to avoid this threat, this specification provides a solution that sets a bit called Memory Overwrite Request (MOR) for the resetting event of host platform. When the platform resets illegally, the existing contents of memory will be cleared before the platform loads the programs (e. g., rewriting the memory to zeros), which prevents an attacker from reading confidential information. For the case that the hosts are started by traditional BIOS and succeeding Unified Extensible Firmware Interface (UEFI), this specification gives the detailed interface definitions and methods of use for implementing the solution above.

(3) Two Specifications about EFI (Extensible Firmware Interface) [111, 112]
The TCG EFI Protocol Specification gives a standard interface definition for TPM usage on EFI platform in different scenarios. OS loader and relevant management components can measure and record the start-up events on EFI platform using these interfaces. TCG EFI platform specification gives detailed operational definitions for extending PCR for different types of events and adding new items to event log in the boot process of EFI platforms.

5.2.2 Products and Applications

Using the proposed specifications, different computer manufacturers can develop their own implementation architecture and manufacture different trusted computers. Currently, many manufacturers, such as IBM, HP, Lenovo and Tongfang, have launched a series of trusted computer products for different security needs.

In November 2001, IBM launched the first desktop computer whose motherboard is embedded with a TPM chip. In 2004, it also launched TPM-embedded laptops. In June 2003, HP launched TPM-embedded computers. Fujitsu and Acer also launched TPM-embedded computers in 2004. Popular desktop computers in the market mainly include HP/Compaq's dc7100, IBM's Netvista desktops and Dell's OptiPlex GX520; laptops include HP/Compaq's nw8000, IBM's T43 and Sony's VAIO®BX Series.

Many manufacturers have also launched trusted computers with independent intellectual properties, such as Lenovo, Reida, Tsinghua Tongfang, Inspur, Great Wall and Founder. Lenovo builds some trusted computing platforms with TCM that has own intellectual properties, including Lenovo KT M8000 and Zhaoyang K42A. It also provides Lenovo Data Shield Security Suite for trusted computers, which is application software developed based on the security chip. This software integrates a series of host security protection tools to provide many security functionalities such as local encryption and sharing with specified user, which can be used to protect the users' important files to prevent data leakage. Wuhan Ruida information security industry Co., Ltd. develops trusted computing platforms based on security chips with its own intellectual properties and launches the embedded cryptographic machines. Tongfang's trusted computing platform built on security chip TCM with own intellectual properties is able to provide full protection for the user's computer system and data, and support the functions such as security chip management, user file encryption and data recovery. It also provides a trusted network access services based on trusted computing platform. Westone company provides the security protection system that combines TCM and USB Key for PC operating system based on trusted computing platform, which provide security functions such as secure data storage and network access control.

In a word, the trusted computer merges multidisciplinary expertise, such as security chip, basic software, computer manufacturing, network equipment manufacturing and network application software. It integrates the corresponding trusted computing security chip, security middleware, security motherboard and platform software of chain of trust to meet military, finance, transportation and other specific industries' needs in data migration and security protection. Trusted computers have been widely applied in the traffic management, on-site rescue, data acquisition, equipment testing, communication supporting and so on. After trusted computers are launched, they rapidly win approval and praise from the industry-related users in a short time. With the increasing protection needs of privacy and data security from users, the trusted computers will be further applied and promoted.

5.3 Server

As a data control center, a server typically runs a number of key services and stores large amounts of data. Therefore, it leads to a large number of attacks against server systems. Like the personal computer, the server introduces the trusted computing technology to build a trusted execution environment in order to better protect the security of services and data located in the server.

5.3.1 Specification

Compared with trusted personal computers, trusted servers have many differences in aspects of the security chip TPM/TCM, chain of trust and TSS/TSM, including the following:

(1) Since the processing speed of a server is much more than of a normal PC, it requires the processing speed of the security chip, including the speed of cryptographic operation, to be fast enough. But the processing speed of existing security chips is quite slow.

(2) The security chip of a server should be able to support concurrency control. When multiple users simultaneously access a trusted server, security chip should be able to concurrently handle access requests, and to ensure the correctness of data and atomicity of operation. Servers often adopt multi-chip security mechanisms (physical security chip and virtual security chip). The change of a single security chip should not affect the security of other security chips. Moreover, security chips should also have the capabilities of migration, backup and recovery of confidential data.

(3) Now the connection between TPM and motherboard is through LPC bus, but the rate of LPC is not high, so it is not suitable for high-speed communication requirements of servers.

(4) Since a server typically has multiple processors and supports virtualization mechanism, its start-up mode is different from that of an ordinary PC. As a result, its chain of trust should also be different from ordinary PC.

(5) Because a server is not powered off in a long time after starting up, it requires the ability of performing trusted measurement multiple times.

To this end, TCG attempts to develop and publish the following series of server specifications that are independent of physical implementation architecture, which provide standard support for the development of trusted servers:

(1) Server Work Group Generic Server Specification [88]

Corresponding to the PC Client specification, this specification is developed according to the features of using TPMs in the servers, which is based on the main TPM specification. It gives the specific terms and function definitions based on the specific needs that servers use TPMs, such as server Trusted Building Block (TBB) and PCR usage. This specification is independent of specific server platform architecture. Therefore, each server vendor needs to define its own implementation architecture for a specific platform.

(2) Server Work Group Mandatory and Optional TPM Commands for Servers Specification [113]

For servers, the mandatory TPM commands that apply to the common PC platform can be optional, but the optional commands cannot be transformed into the mandatory commands. For this reason, this specification is developed to define server's mandatory and optional TPM commands explicitly.

(3) Other relevant specifications
Combining with TCG main specifications, TCG has developed Advanced Configuration and Power Management Interface (ACPI) specification [114]. It provides a framework that satisfies TCG specification for a variety of platforms (including server and client) that are desirable to use ACPI, including ACPI tables and basic method definition. TCG also provides Server Work Group Itanium Architecture Based Server Specification [115], which can be used as a reference to realize other system architectures.

5.3.2 Products and Applications

Driven by market demands, enterprises have begun to carry out the research and development of trusted servers. However, compared to the specification of trusted personal computers, the specifications related to servers lack definitions on implementation details. And the server is more complex than a personal computer and its technology performance requirements are much higher than a personal computer. Because of the characteristics of the server mentioned above, TSS for the server should also be different. Therefore, product development of trusted servers lags behind personal computers.

HP, IBM and many other well-known companies have also introduced some trusted server products. But these products mainly combine with the existing key mechanism of ordinary trusted platform and have not been widely used and promoted. For example, TPM chips are embedded into some products of HP ProLiant ML110 G6, HP ProLiant ML150 G6 series. In the applications, they are combined with BitLocker in Windows to provide security protection for servers' data.

In 2011, Lenovo introduced a mainstream tower server T168 G7. In terms of security design, it adopts trusted encryption protection technology based on TCM, whose purpose is to build a trusted computing environment for servers. This design has three main advantages. First, it builds the trust of a server platform. The security chip will monitor the loading of system programs in the boot time, alarm and even prohibit the execution once it detects a program on the exception state. Second is the authentication of users' identities in server. TCM stores a key to identify the platform and identifies itself with the outside world by signature or relevant digital certificate mechanisms. And the identification number is globally unique. The third advantage is encryption protection, the data encrypted by TCM can only be decrypted and processed on this server platform, and thereby confidential data are bound to this platform. Even if the encrypted data are stolen, they will not be identified since they are out of the corresponding platform and the attacker cannot access the decryption key, so that data protection is achieved. This product has been certified by the OSCCA and other authorities.

With the rapid development and application of server technology, the security requirements are also increasing. As the management center of data and services, servers are compelling to use trusted computing technology to provide security protection. Trusted servers meet these needs. On the one hand, they provide trusted execution environment for local services. On the other hand, they provide attestation of services and data for users, which allows users to verify the correctness and integrity of data located on a remote server.

5.4 Trusted Mobile Platform

With the rapid development of mobile communication technology, the utilization of mobile computing platform is more and more popular. Users install the programs of third-party service providers, such as applications and games, to extend the application function of mobile computing platform. So the mobile computing platform is not only a communication tool but is also used for operating (i. e., transmitting, receiving and storing) sensitive data, which leads to a big security risk of trusted mobile platforms. Security issues have become the focus of attention of mobile users. Particularly, users require mobile platforms to provide them with trusted assurance of high-quality services.

Due to differences between mobile computing platform and common computing platform in the hardware architecture, processing capability, storage space, communication bandwidth, production cost and other aspects, the way to build trusted execution environment using hardware security chip on a common computing platform is no longer suitable for mobile platform. Therefore, TCG and related mobile device manufacturers launch relevant specifications for trusted mobile computing platform together. At the same time, some research institutions also propose feasible implementation solutions of trusted mobile platform. The following section will briefly introduce trusted mobile platform in various aspects such as the specifications, system architecture, technology implementation and application.

5.4.1 Specification

Due to the special nature of mobile computing platform itself, we cannot directly use TPM/TCM to enhance the security of mobile platform. To this end, the relevant mobile device manufacturers and TCG have launched a series of specifications to meet the functional requirements of trusted mobile platform, while providing standard support for implementation of trusted mobile platform.

In October 2004, Intel, IBM, NTT DoCoMo and other companies developed the TMP specification for mobile platform based on trusted computing technology. In September 2006, TCG published Mobile Trusted Module (MTM) [84] specification by partially modifying the TPM specification according to the characteristics of mobile platform. This specification can be seen as the basis for building trusted mobile platform, and it has been updated recently [84]. Afterward, TCG also published the technology and implementation specifications related to trusted mobile platform and gave the following possible usage scenarios:

(1) TCG Mobile Reference Architecture Specification [116]
In order to provide the reference implementation for mobile trusted platform, TCG published Mobile Reference Architecture Specification. According to the initial start-up procedure and usage of functionality of trusted mobile platform, the specification provides a reference architecture for trusted mobile platform based on the main specification of trusted mobile platform. It mainly gives a scheme to realize the specific functionalities of trusted mobile platform such as architecture for functionalities, measurement and verification methods, establishment of chains of trust, trusted boot and lifecycle management.

(2) TCG Mobile Abstraction Layer Specification [117]
In order to provide the manufacturers and developers with specific application interfaces, TCG also published Mobile Abstraction Layer Specification. Based on the MTM specification and reference architecture specification, this specification gives the definitions for the abstraction layer of trusted components of trusted mobile platform. Its main contents cover various data types and structures, various specific TSS interfaces in the process of using the MTM. It is used for providing a standardized reference for manufacturers to produce trusted mobile products.

(3) TCG Mobile Trusted Module 2.0 Use Cases Specification [118]
For security threats to mobile platforms and embedded systems, MTM could be considered for enhancing their security. The specification takes the specific scenarios of trusted mobile platform as examples (such as e-payment and e-health), and then gives some technical requirements and user guides to use trusted mobile platform.

5.4.2 Generalized Architecture

According to the relevant mobile phone specifications of mobile platform and MTM specification, TCG proposed an abstract functional architecture for generalized trusted mobile platform, as shown in Figure 5.2. In this architecture, the trusted mobile platform is abstracted as a composite of trusted engines, and builds local or remote trusted mobile environment by mechanisms such as processing service requests, reporting current engine's state and providing trusted attestation. This architecture

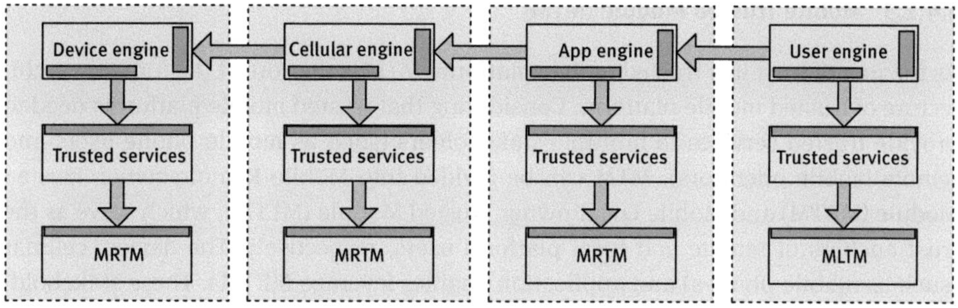

Figure 5.2: Generalized architecture of trusted mobile platform.

consists of three parts: various abstracted functionalities engines, trusted services and MTM.

5.4.2.1 Abstract Function Engines

The generalized architecture of trusted mobile platform contains multiple abstract function engines, each representing a different stakeholder in the mobile scenario and providing the relevant service. These engines are device engine, cellular engine, application engine and user engine, respectively. Each engine provides services to its user (i. e., stakeholder). The resources of each engine determine what services this engine can provide, and the owner of this engine determines how it provides services. The device engine provides basic platform resources, which include a user interface, debug connector, signal transmitter and receiver, random number generator, the International Mobile Equipment Identity (IMEI) and interfaces for a Subscriber Identity Module (SIM). The cellular engine takes charge of realizing data interaction interfaces, providing network connection and guaranteeing communication security. The application engine contains a number of extensible applications in a mobile platform, such as online game clients. The user engine directly provides services for users, and protects users' data using other function engines. In short, the device engine provides the necessary hardware to the cellular engine; the cellular engine provides basic data interaction services to application engine; the application engine provides specific data application services to the user engine; and the user engine is in charge of providing users with rich functionalities of mobile platform. In Figure 5.2, the solid rectangles indicate interfaces and the arrows indicate their dependency.

5.4.2.2 Trusted Services

Each abstract function engine corresponds to a trusted service, which measures each specific function module contained in the abstract engine, and extends those measurements to a MTM.

5.4.2.3 Mobile Trusted Module (MTM)

As the root of trust in a trusted mobile platform, MTM is the core of the function architecture of trusted mobile platform. Considering that trusted mobile platforms need to provide trusted services to multiple stakeholders (such as mobile phone users and remote mobile operators), MTM can be divided into Mobile Remote-owner Trusted Module (MRTM) and Mobile Local-owner Trusted Module (MLTM), which serve as the trust anchors of remote and local platform users, respectively. The device, cellular (such as mobile phones) and application engines leverage MRTMs. These stakeholders do not have physical access to the mobile device and need a secure boot process to ensure that their engines execute as per their expectations. The user engine leverages a MLTM. The local user has physical access to the mobile device, and can load the software he wishes to execute. The MTMs can be trusted to report the current state of their engines, and provide attestation on the current state of the engines to remote verifiers.

Taking the MRTM as an example, we briefly introduce how a MTM could be used, as shown in Figure 5.3. As the root of trust for storage (RTS) and root of trust for

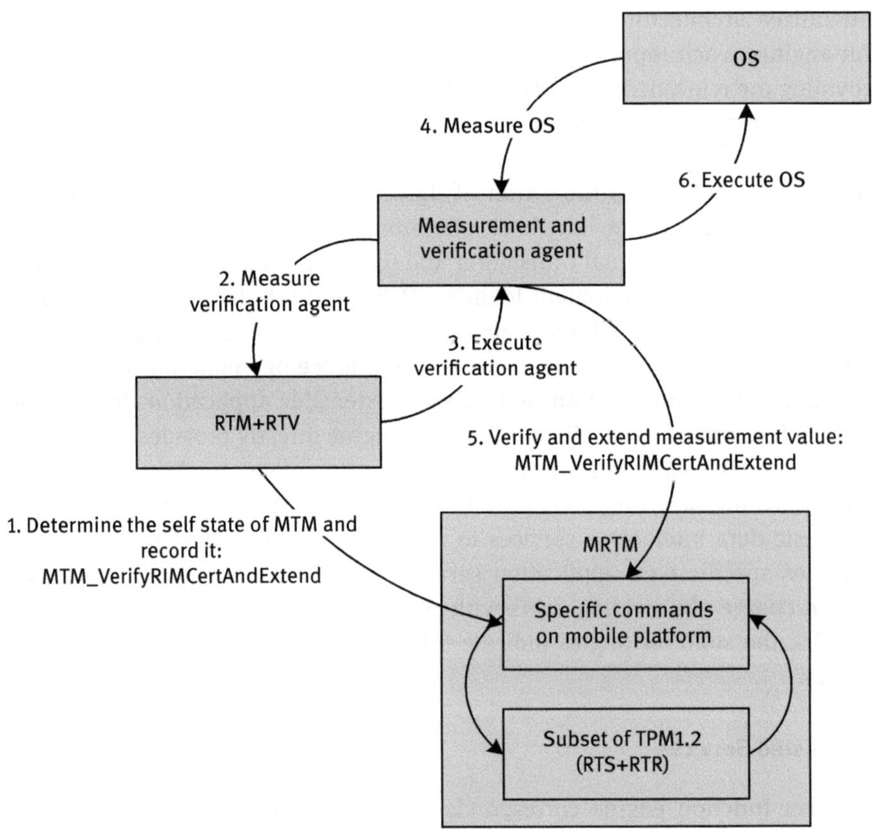

Figure 5.3: Overview of MRTM.

reporting (RTR) of a trusted mobile platform, the MRTM provides storage protection and the corresponding trusted resources for other system components (such as PCRs and signing keys). As the basic function components of a trusted mobile platform, the root of trust for measurement (RTM) and root of trust for verification (RTV) are outside of the MRTM. They implement the measurement and verification using the protection mechanism that MRTM provides. When building a trusted mobile environment using MRTM, the RTM and RTV modules are loaded first, then they perform a diagnostic measurement on their execution states. If the diagnostic measurement matches reference integrity metrics (RIM) value stored in the MRTM, it will be extended to MRTM (Step 1). Then the RTM would measure the measurement and verification agent (Steps 2 and 3). If the measurement matches the RIM value, it will be extended to MRTM. Then the control would be passed to the measurement and verification agent. Finally, the measurement and verification agent measures, verifies and stores the integrity of the OS image in the similar way before passing control to the OS (Steps 4–6). After verification, the operating system will run. Remote stakeholders (such as device providers or communication service provides) can verify the measurement values after receiving them to determine whether the execution of engines is trustworthy (such as the device engine and cellular engine).

5.4.3 Implementation of Trusted Mobile Platform

Due to the diversity of mobile platforms, TCG specifies neither the concrete implementation of MTM nor the definition of implementing the trusted mobile platform at the time of publishing the corresponding trusted mobile platform specifications. Thus, mobile device manufacturers can implement MTM in different ways and construct different trusted mobile platforms in accordance with the generalized architecture of the previous section.

The following section briefly describes two representative solutions for trusted mobile platform, in which the MTMs are implemented based on Java smart card and ARM TrustZone technology, respectively.

5.4.3.1 Trusted Mobile Platform Based on Java Smart Card

Common mobile platforms usually provide extra smart cards (such as expansion cards or SIM cards), which can support many common cryptographic algorithms and provide certain capabilities of data storage and processing. These smart cards are fit for being hardware security components that run MTMs. They can provide independent hardware firmware that are similar with TPM chips for MTMs, such that MTM can be used as an independent hardware root of trust and establish a trusted execution environment for the mobile platform. We take the Java smart card as an example and briefly introduce the MTM architecture that is implemented based on Java smart card [119, 120], then we describe a method to build a trusted mobile platform using this kind of MTM [121].

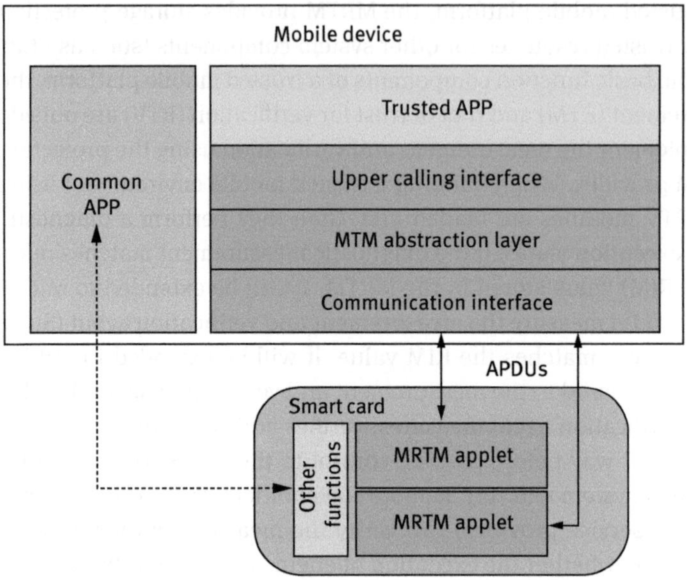

Figure 5.4: The software architecture of trusted mobile platform based on Java smart card.

MTM Based on Java Smart Card. The main idea behind taking Java smart card as security element to run MTM is to implement MTM as independent applications inside the smart card. These applications can support the commands in accordance with TCG specification. A mobile platform takes the smart card running the MTM as the root of trust and builds a required trusted mobile environment. The basic architecture is shown in Figure 5.4.

The functions of MTM are implemented inside the smart card, which can be divided into MRTM and MLTM that run in different Java applets of the smart card. It stores the endorsement key (EK) and authorization data (*authdata*) of MTM in the nonvolatile memory of the smart card, and implements cryptographic algorithms that MTM needs using the hardware cryptographic module. The MTM implemented based on Java smart card needs to provide calling interfaces for the upper users of a mobile platform, thus needs to provide relevant trusted software stack. Moreover, due to the limited resources of the mobile platform, it needs to redesign the communication protocols between MTM and the smart card. On the premise of ensuring data communication, these protocols should prevent the attacks on the MTM of the smart card.

Trusted Mobile Platform Built on a Java Smart Card. In a mobile platform using a Java smart card, the smart card can provide a variety of services for the mobile platform, and the MTM acting as the root of trust is just one important functionality of services. Therefore, when the above mobile platform uses trusted computing technology, it cannot affect the execution of other common applications. The trusted applications on a mobile device require the use of MTM's trusted software stack and corresponding abstract interfaces to invoke the underlying trusted computing services. These interfaces include the upper calling interfaces, MTM abstraction layer and the underlying communication interfaces. The MTM abstraction layer is similar to the Trusted Device Driver Library (TDDL), and provides a class library interface for access to the underlying implementation of MTM. It receives commands from upper applications and converts them to the format that MTM needs. It also takes charge of processing the sending and receiving of MTM commands. The underlying communication interfaces are used to ensure secure exchange of data between the smart card and user-trusted applications. The current data communication interface between the smart card and the outside world adopts the standard data communication protocol Application Protocol Data Units (APDU).

In order to build a trusted mobile platform, it must guarantee the security of MTM. The method implementing MTM based on a Java smart card can meet this security demand. The use of hardware protection mechanism of a smart card can prevent the MTM implementation from being tampered. At the same time, the two functions of MTM (MRTM and MLTM) concurrently run in the form of Java applets inside the virtual machines of the Java smart card and take advantage of the security mechanisms provided by virtual machines to ensure their isolated execution. In addition, the implementation of MTM based on a smart card also makes it inherit inherent security properties of the smart card. The mature methods of security assessment for a smart card also provide convenience to assess the security of the MTM based on a smart card.

5.4.3.2 Trusted Mobile Platform Based on TrustZone

Using ARM TrustZone to implement MTM is another common way to build the trusted mobile platform [120]. ARM TrustZone technology is proposed by ARM company for the embedded system field, which aims at providing a secure and trusted environment for the sensitive applications in a specific resource-constrained platform such as a mobile phone, a PDA, a set-top box. The platform's microprocessor (CPU) is added with domain isolation to provide isolated environment and security services for codes. This feature of the TrustZone can be used to provide security assurance for running an MTM, which could build a trusted mobile platform based on TrustZone. We will introduce the basic principles of protecting sensitive code execution by TrustZone technology, and then describe the basic process to build a trusted mobile platform based on MTM in the following section.

MTM Based on TrustZone. TrustZone technology carries out further security enhancement over a general ARM processor. The secure configuration register of the system control coprocessor inside an ARM processor adds an NS (non-secure) bit that is used to indicate the processor mode. The NS bit divides the processor into secure mode and non-secure mode (or normal mode), which correspond to the "secure area" and "non-secure area" of a platform, respectively. A processor in the secure mode can access all resources, while in non-secure mode it can access only the hardware and software resources of non-secure areas. The modes switch would be handled by a privilege code of CPU and must be executed under a special mode of the processor – "Monitor Mode." The processor may enter the monitor mode from the non-secure mode via a secure monitor call (SMC) executed by software or an interrupt caused by hardware.

When MTM is implemented by TrustZone, the software codes of its functions would be resided in the secure area. On the one hand, the hardware-based isolation ensures the security of MTM, on the other hand, the applications in a non-secure area can access MTM functions by switching the mode. In a specific implementation, because the secure area and non-secure area have their own privileged kernel layer and non-privileged layer, MTM can be used as a security application in the secure area, and the kernel of secure area ensures the trusted execution of the MTM.

Trusted Mobile Platform Built on TrustZone. The secure mode and non-secure mode established by TrustZone can be used to achieve hardware-based isolation between MTM and common applications. It provides a secure execution environment for MTM implemented by pure software. When an application needs to call the trusted services based on MTM, it applies to the monitor for switching to a secure area for processing. The basic architecture of trusted mobile platform based on TrustZone is shown in Figure 5.5.

In the two isolated areas called secure area and non-secure area, which are divided by TrustZone, there run two modified Linux kernels, respectively, for providing execution environment for MTM/user applications in the secure and non-secure areas. In the secure area, MTM relies on the features of process isolation and access control provided by the secure kernel to ensure its own security. This hardware-based isolation mechanism ensures that the malicious codes of non-secure area cannot tamper software of secure area. In the non-secure area, there run common user applications. If unauthorized, these applications cannot directly access the data and codes in the secure area. When a user application running in non-secure area requires the use of a trusted computing service running in secure area, it needs to first establish communication connection between the secure area and non-secure area by trusted API, and then applies for a session to the trusted service. After receiving the request, the trusted services establish a communication channel with the user application by the shared memory technology and realize data exchange between secure area and non-secure area, whose security is guaranteed by the TrustZone technology.

The above trusted mobile platform built on TrustZone-based MTM supports the following secure start-up process. First, it executes the secure bootloader program

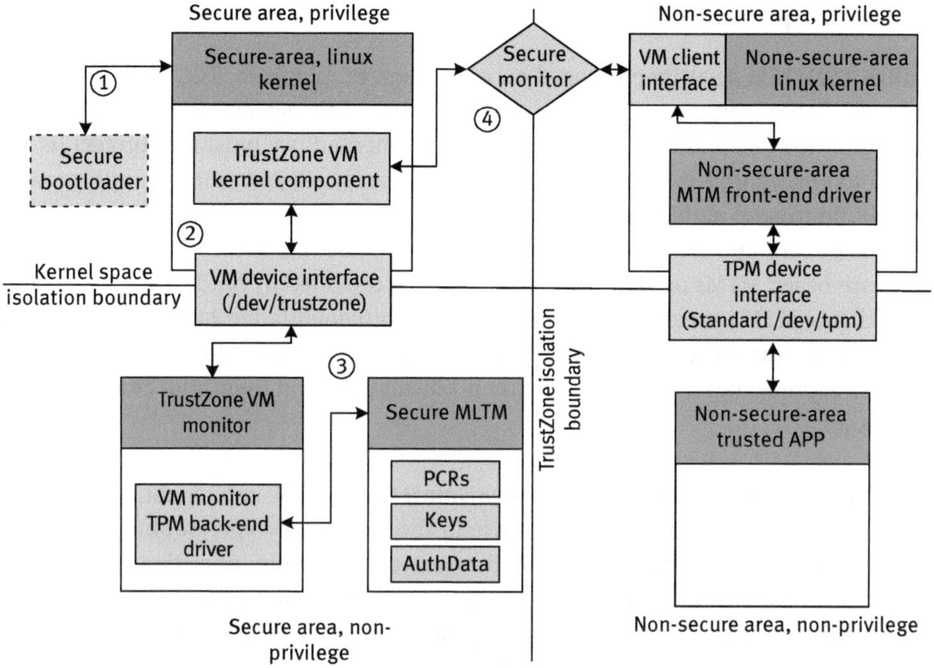

Figure 5.5: Software architecture of trusted mobile platform based on ARM TrustZone.

fused in the ROM after system is powered on. The ARM TrustZone technology prevents this program from being tampered. Next, the bootloader will pass control to MTM. Then, MTM performs the measurement on subsequent loaded program and passes control to it. Eventually, it builds a complete secure boot for mobile platform. We divide this start-up process into three phases:

(1) Bootloader first calculates the measurement value of the operating system kernel in the secure area, and then compares with the corresponding standard RIM value. If the verification succeeds, bootloader will load the operating system and transfer control to it, otherwise it hangs up. This is the operation carried out in the privileged kernel layer of the secure area (i.e., a)).
(2) Then it needs to verify the applications in the non-privileged layer (i. e. application layer) of secure area, including *Init* process, MTM main process and the relevant auxiliary process, whose verification processes are dependent on the respective standard RIM values. When these verifications succeed, execution control is passed to these processes, otherwise they hang up (i.e., b), c)).
(3) After the above programs of secure area are successfully loaded, it begins to initialize the programs of non-secure area, such as operating system and trusted applications, and compares the measurements of these programs with the standard RIM values to complete the platform start-up process (i. e. d)).

5.4.3.3 Comparative Analysis

Unlike TPM/TCM security chip used on a common PC platform, TCG does not give a concrete implementation of MTM in consideration of the special nature of a mobile platform. However, no matter how MTM is implemented, we must first protect its security to ensure that it can act as the root of trust for trusted mobile platform, and then build trusted mobile platform based on MTM. Both the MTM schemes based on Java smart card and TrustZone technology above protect the security execution of the software-based MTMs using security mechanisms provided by hardware. Throughout the existing MTM implementation methods, the implementation based on composite of hardware and software is the mainstream way of building trusted mobile platform. The two representative schemes have their advantages, and their brief comparison is as follows:

Implementation Scheme Based on Java Smart Card. The implementation scheme of MTM based on a smart card makes use of the hardware cryptographic algorithms and protection capability provided by the smart card. While inheriting the security features of smart card, it also provides customizable trusted computing functionalities for the mobile platform. The development technology based on smart card on mobile platforms develops rapidly at present, and it also provides technology foundation for this scheme. A significant feature of implementing trusted mobile platform based on a Java smart card is that it has a strong flexibility and a better application and prospect. The drawback is that the MTM on Java smart card is mainly implemented as multiple isolated small applications (applets) in a Java virtual machine, whose processing speed is influenced by the limited resources of mobile devices. It makes the effective use of resources in the mobile terminal more important. Moreover, we also need to consider using optimized bytecode on the Java smart card to improve performance.

Implementation Scheme Based on TrustZone. This implementation scheme is based on additional security features of the hardware processor such as memory management and process isolation; it leverages fine-grained control mechanisms over trust boundary and thus ensures the security execution of the MTM. A significant advantage of building trusted mobile platform based on this method is that it does not require any additional MTM hardware for implementing the trusted computing functions. The drawback is that this method should be implemented in a specific hardware architecture (such as TrustZone or M-Shield chip), so there are some application limitations.

5.4.4 Applications

At present, mobile computing platforms such as mobile phones, tablet computers, personal digital assistants (PDA) and embedded devices can deal with user-friendly business such as office work, communication and data publishing. But there also exit numerous attacks against mobile computing platforms. This situation has attracted users' attention and has become a huge obstacle in insensitive application fields. Using trusted computing technology to build trusted mobile platforms can enhance the security of the mobile computing platforms, so that the mobile platforms are further applied in the field of user privacy involved, such as banks, supervision and medical field. Unlike TPM/TCM security chips used in the common trusted computing platforms, current trusted computing specifications do not give a specific implementation of MTM. Therefore, manufacturers can produce their own MTM according to their own requirements, so as to realize different forms of trusted mobile platforms.

Based on different implementations of MTM, there are different application modes of trusted mobile platform. In 2007, Nokia company proposed a solution of software-based MTM [122]. This solution ensures the security of MTM based on a special hardware processor such as TI M-Shield, realizes the secure boot of smartphones, ensures the trustworthiness of the initial computing environment in mobile terminals and supports the mobile security applications at upper layer through the extended interfaces. This solution provides an important reference for the development of trusted mobile phones. Austria IAIK institute also studied the architecture of trusted mobile terminal based on Nokia 6131 development board [120]. On the one hand, they customized MTM module functions based on the existing mobile security extensions, on the other hand they designed and implemented MTM architecture of dynamic secure loading using ARM TrustZone technology, which provides effective trusted computing services to user applications of mobile devices. The solution further promotes the research and application of trusted mobile phones.

Like building trust in common computing platforms, it requires not only the theoretical and technical support in academic field but also the joint efforts of manufacturers, mobile operators and service providers to make use of trusted computing technology to build a trusted mobile environment, including hardware, operating systems, applications and network systems. We believe that trusted mobile platform and the Internet applications based on this platform will be rapidly promoted and developed with the increasing security requirements of applications in mobile platforms and the deepening studies of trusted mobile platform technology.

5.5 Virtualized Trusted Platform

Virtualization technology can effectively improve the utilization of system resources, lower application costs, reduce the complexity of configuration and management and provide an independent execution environment (guest virtual machine) for different users and applications. It is now widely used in many computing platforms such as servers, data centers and personal computers. Therefore, more and more enterprises and users store important data and deploy critical services on virtualization platforms, which lead to increasing attacks against virtualization platforms and great threats to users' data security. Thus, there is a need to provide security protection for virtualization platforms. The introduction of trusted computing technology to build a virtualized trusted platform has become one of the research hotspots in security of virtualization platform. Some research institutions have proposed implementation schemes of virtualized trusted platforms. Meanwhile, TCG also introduced an architecture specification for virtualized trusted platform. This following section will briefly introduce the virtualized trusted platform from the perspectives of specification, common architecture, technological realization and application.

5.5.1 Requirements and Specification

The implementation architecture of a platform that supports virtualization technology is different from that of a common computing platform. For example, a virtualized platform simultaneously executes multiple guest virtual machines, each of which requires providing the same security guarantees as the common computing platform. If we use the method of a common computing platform to build a trusted environment in the virtualized platform where multiple concurrent guest virtual machines directly access the single security chip, it will result in access conflicts of internal resources of the security chip (such as PCR operations and key operations) and a direct threat to security assurances provided by the platform based on security chip. Moreover, since the running status of guest virtual machines on the virtualized platform is uncertain (turn off and start up at any time), the direct use of the traditional chain of trust may lead to a loop of trust relationship. Therefore, when building a virtualized trusted platform, new standards and specifications support are needed.

In September 2011, TCG published the Virtualized Trusted Platform Architecture Specification for virtualized platforms [105]. It proposes the required functionalities of virtualized trusted platform such as trusted measurement, security migration and remote attestation by defining functions of various components of virtualized trusted platform and the interactive interfaces between these components. It proposes a generalized architecture of virtualized trusted platform and multiple optional deployment models and provides a general reference to design and develop a virtualized trusted platform. This specification does not focus on the specific implementation of each module in the virtualized trusted platform, but only gives the basic function definitions and an abstract architecture, which lays the foundation for a more detailed implementation specification of virtualized trusted platform in the future.

5.5.2 Generalized Architecture

The Virtualized Trusted Platform Architecture Specification takes into account many different ways that implement the virtualized trusted platforms in practice, so it only gives a conceptual abstract architecture to build trust in a virtual machine environment. It mainly defines what functional components should be included in a virtualized trusted platform and how to achieve the sharing of security chip by the interaction of these functional components. Taking into account the special nature of virtualized platform, the specification presents multilevel generalized architectures of virtualized trusted platform, including the architecture with privileged domain (i. e., a privileged virtual machine that is responsible for management functions) and the architecture without privileged domain. As an example, we briefly describe the functional hierarchy and key components of the three-layered virtualized trusted platform architecture with privileged domain (see Figure 5.6).

The virtualized trusted platform architecture in the figure includes three layers. The top layer provides execution environment to each virtual machine (VM). Each VM is isolated from the other VMs and operates independently, but all of them leverage the management services provided by the virtual machine monitor (VMM). In these VMs, there is a privileged VM as a management console that provides users with the management functions and interfaces of the whole virtualized platform. These management functions are achieved by executing VMM's privileged commands. The migration engine of virtualized platform is mainly used for migration of guest VMs,

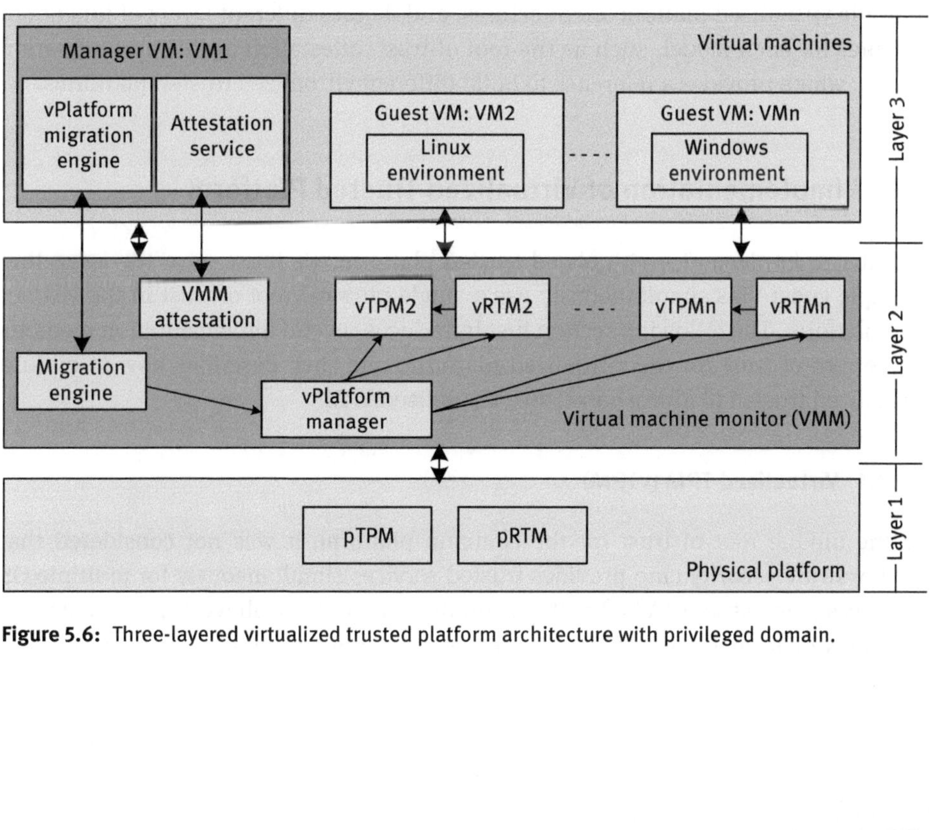

Figure 5.6: Three-layered virtualized trusted platform architecture with privileged domain.

while the component for attestation service provides proof of trust in a single guest VM or the whole virtualized platform by the interaction with the underlying VMM.

The second layer mainly includes the VMM. The VMM can provide the support of execution environment isolation for multiple VMs of upper layer. It is responsible to create, initialize, delete and manage the trust services related to each VM, such as creating a virtualized root of trust vTPM and a virtualized root of trust for measurement vRTM for a VM. Because of the complexity of this management service, this architecture uses a privileged VM (administrative domain) to implement the management and control of the requests from non-privileged VMs for a VMM.

The bottom layer is the physical hardware. This layer provides the physical roots of trust for the virtualized trusted platform (including a security chip and the root of trust for measurement). The physical roots of trust typically offer the basic trusted platform services for the upper-layer VMM, while the VMM constructs vTPM based on the physical root of trust and finally provides concurrent and collision-free trusted services to each VM.

The diversity of the virtualized platform architecture that makes the corresponding virtualized trusted platform can be implemented in different ways. These different platform architectures include the presence/absence of privileged administrative domain and the VM layer embedded in a new VM (i. e., virtualized platform architecture with nested *N* layer). In order to implement a virtualized trusted platform that is fit for the above architecture, TCG specially published the Virtualized Trusted Platform Architecture Specification. This specification gives corresponding abstract models for multiple virtualized platform architectures, and defines different layers of functional modules for each model, such as the root of trust, attestation agents and migration agents, which provides a reference to build different virtualized trusted platforms.

5.5.3 Implementation of Virtualized Trusted Platform

In order to implement a virtualized trusted platform, we must solve the issue that multiple guest VMs simultaneously use a single physical root of trust in the virtualized platform. The following section first introduces several implementation methods of the root of trust for the virtualized platform, and then describes how to build a virtualized trusted platform based on a virtualized TPM.

5.5.3.1 Virtualized TPM (vTPM)

As the unique root of trust for the common platform, it was not considered that the hardware security chip provides trusted services simultaneously for multiple OS instances (such as guest VMs) at the beginning. To meet the above requirements, obviously we can make use of the security features offered by a virtualized platform to provide trusted computing services for multiple VMs by virtualizing the hardware security chip.

There are two main approaches to virtualizing the security chip: software virtualization and hardware virtualization:

Software-based Virtualized Security Chip. The main purpose of software-based virtualized security chip is to provide an instance of the virtualized root of trust for each VM on VMM. In order to ensure that the virtualized root of trust has the same security features as the physical one, it requires that the design of virtualized root of trust should achieve the following security objectives:

(1) The virtualized root of trust should provide the same usage model and operation command set as the physical one.
(2) The virtualized root of trust should be correlated with VM's life cycle, for example, VM migration requires the entire migration of corresponding instance of virtualized root of trust and its status.
(3) It must maintain the strong correlation between virtualized root of trust and the TCB of virtualized platform.
(4) The security properties of virtualized root of trust and physical security chip are the same and indistinguishable.

The researchers at the University of Cambridge have implemented software vTPM for the TPM security chip based on the above-mentioned ideas. This solution is proposed based on separation device driver model provided by the XEN-based virtualized platform, whose core idea is to provide trusted computing services based on TPM emulator [123] and implement the management of multiple concurrent instances of vTPM in the administrative domain of virtualized platform. The basic architecture of vTPM is shown in Figure 5.7.

The architecture consists of two parts: vTPM manager and vTPM instances. There is only one vTPM manager, which is mainly used to manage vTPM instances of multiple guest VMs, including the creation, deletion and maintenance of these instances. There are multiple vTPM instances, each of which is corresponding to a guest VM. It requires that each user's vTPM instance runs independently. When implementing the architecture based on XEN virtualized platform, the vTPM can be seen as a special device of guest VM, whose functions are divided into two parts: one is located in privileged VM, namely, vTPM back-end drivers; the other one is located in guest VM, namely, vTPM front-end drivers. Using the communication mechanisms and isolation characteristics provided by XEN itself, a guest VM can use the corresponding vTPM instance to build its own trusted environment.

Hardware-based Virtualized TPM. The main purpose of the hardware-based virtualized security chip is to provide a vTPM instance for each VM inside the

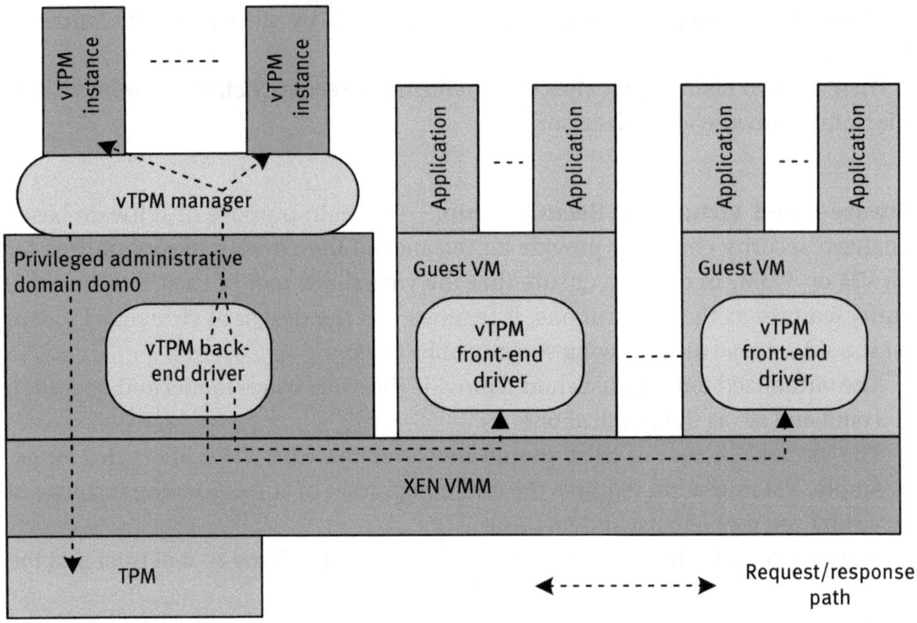

Figure 5.7: vTPM architecture.

hardware security chip, and then add a layer to provide interfaces of vTPM above the VMM for the upper guest VMs, which aim to coordinate the switching between multiple vTPMs inside the physical security chip.

The hardware virtualization needs to modify the existing structure of a security chip, thus it is necessary to update the existing trusted computing specifications and consult with the manufacturers, which makes it relatively difficult. This method has no substantive progress. IBM released the relevant extended draft specification for the TPM security chip in 2005. The specification defines the vTPM-related commands such as TPM_CreateInstance, which creates a vTPM instance inside the TPM and TPM_SetupInstance, which initializes a vTPM instance. Realizing that the TPM 1.2 specification does not provide enough support for virtualization platforms, TCG has presented enhancement and extension in the TPM 2.0 specification.

5.5.3.2 XEN-based Virtualized Trusted Platform

The typical virtualized trusted platforms are all designed based on the vTPM mentioned above and built on the XEN virtualized platform [18]. XEN is a VM monitor developed by the University of Cambridge. As an open-source para-virtualization scheme, it uses the four-ring privilege levels of X86 architecture to let VMM take complete control of other components. The privileged administrative domain dom0 interacts with VMM to achieve management function such as the creation, deletion and migration of the guest VMs. XEN offers a specific front-end and back-end driver model

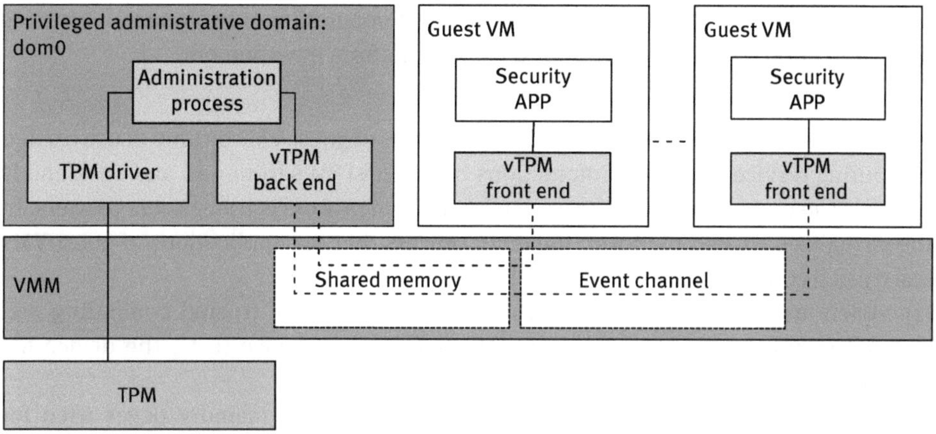

Figure 5.8: XEN-based virtualized trusted platform architecture.

to a device, which also provides sophisticated technical support for deployment of virtualized security chip.

Basic Architecture. The XEN-based virtualized trusted platform architecture is shown in Figure 5.8. It is similar to the generalized architecture mentioned in the Virtualized Trusted Platform Architecture Specification and mainly divided into three layers: hardware layer, VMM layer and VM layer.

In the above architecture, the hardware layer includes physical devices such as CPU, memory and the TPM chip. TPM is the hardware root of trust for building trusted environment of a virtualized platform and is the basis for building a virtualized trusted platform. VMM layer guarantees communication and isolation between the upper-layer guest VMs based on shared memory and event channel mechanism, including communication between vTPM front-end and back-end driver and monitoring and management of each guest VM's running. VM layer is divided into privileged administrative domain and guest VM. The administrative domain installs the driver of physical TPM chip, and creates corresponding vTPM back-end driver for each guest VM, which is managed and scheduled by the management process. The guest VM runs vTPM's front-end driver and uses the trusted computing functions by the communication between front-end and back-end drivers.

In the above XEN-based virtualized trusted platform, there are two phases to build trust. The first one is to construct a basic trusted operating environment based on the TPM chip, which includes a VMM, administrative domain kernel and key application tools (such as *xend*). The second one is the trusted execution environment of multiple guest VMs, that is, from the start-up process of guest VMs to the running of applications within them. The two phases of trust are based on hardware security chip TPM and virtualized root of trust vTPM, respectively. Cooperation of two phases of trust is needed to build a complete virtualized trusted platform environment.

vTPM Access Process. To make the applications of guest VMs be able to use trusted computing services, multiple interactions between vTPM's front-end and back-end is needed. The underlying communication interaction process is transparent to users. In the virtualized trusted platform, the main process that the applications of guest VMs use trusted computing services is illustrated as follows:

(1) Users use TSS to call the corresponding interfaces of trusted computing services and send a request using vTPM's front-end device (i. e., the device file */dev/tpm0*).
(2) The vTPM's front-end first applies for and initializes memory pages used for shared data between front-end and back-end. When trusted computing services request transferring data that will be copied to shared pages, they authorize the permission to access the shared pages for the back-end driver by sharing memory mechanism. Then they use event channel mechanism to notify vTPM's back-end driver to obtain the TPM request.
(3) Upon receiving the TPM request from the front-end driver, the back-end driver uses the function packet_read () to read it from the shared memory pages, copies it to a designated buffer and then delivers it to the vTPM management program. The vTPM management program distributes the request to the corresponding vTPM instance for processing according to the vTPM instance identifier.
(4) When the request has been processed, the back-end driver receives a response from the vTPM management program. It uses the function packet_write () to copy the response to shared pages, allows the front-end driver of guest VM to access the shared pages through authorization and uses the event channel to generate an interrupt to notify the front-end driver.
(5) Upon receiving the TPM response from the back-end driver, the vTPM front-end driver uses the function vtpm_recv () to read data from the shared memory, copies the data to the specified buffer and finally hands it to the application that initiates the TPM request.

5.5.3.3 Extended Virtualized Trusted Platform

With the increasing trusted computing functions, the daemon that handles the requests of trusted computing services becomes larger and larger in the amount of code. Such a growing process with large amount of code will lead to some problems such as reducing the running efficiency of the virtualized platform administrative domain and increasing the possibility of attacks. Research institutions improve and extend the above virtualized trusted platform architecture, whose main idea is to separate trusted computing functions from the administrative domain of virtualized platform.

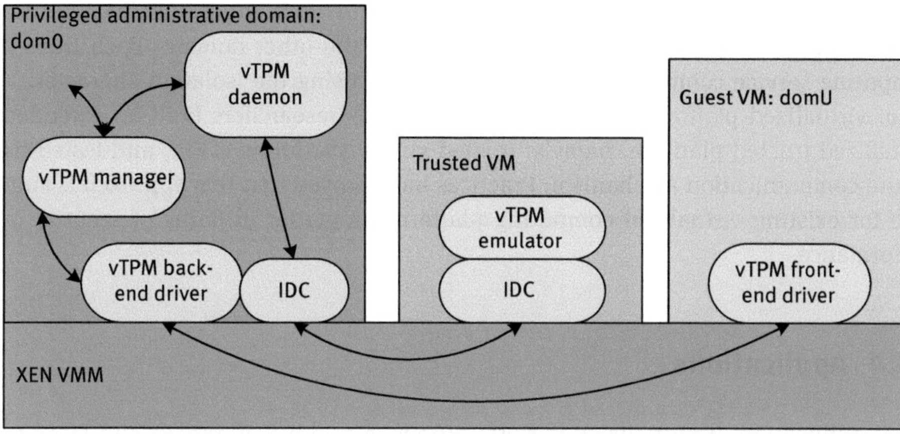

Figure 5.9: Architecture of extended virtualized trusted platform.

The trusted computing functions will serve as an independent functional domain that runs on the virtualized platform, so the functions are isolated from other management functions of administrative domain within the architecture of XEN-based virtualized trusted platform [124, 125]. The concept of driver domain presented in XEN-based virtualized platform provides technical support for the implementation of the above idea. Taking XEN-based virtualized platform as example, we briefly introduce the extended virtualized trusted platform architecture as follows, which is shown in Figure 5.9.

The above architecture adds a new trusted VM in addition to the original privileged administrative domain dom0 and the guest VM domU. The trusted VM is a virtualized domain with specific function, which mainly achieves the original trusted computing functions such as key generation and management. To ensure security, this domain is designed to be a lightweight and customizable function domain. In addition to the necessary libraries for trusted computing services and data communication, this domain does not run other application codes. Therefore, there still exists vTPM manager and vTPM daemon in the privileged administrative domain, which are used for coordination and management of user requests from guest VM.

When a user uses trusted computing functions in the extended virtualized trusted platform, the platform still uses the original vTPM's front end and back end to complete the user request, but the request is processed by the trusted service process within the trusted VM. It uses inter domain communication (IDC) mechanism between the trusted VM and the privileged administrative domain to complete data exchange. The administrative domain is more like a data-transfer agent in this process.

Based on the original vTPM's design, the architecture of extended virtualized trusted platform separates trusted computing function from the administrative domain. On the one hand, it reduces the amount of code of daemon within the administrative domain and reduces the possibility of attacks. On the other hand, it makes the running of trusted computing service independent of the other domain. Each trusted computing service component can be protected by using the isolation characteristics of virtualized platform. Based on this idea, HP's researchers built an extended virtualized trusted platform, namely, trusted virtual platforms (TVP), and tested its secure communication mechanism. Practices have proved that this approach is suitable for existing virtualized computing platform no matter in terms of security or performance.

5.5.4 Applications

Rapid application of virtualized platform attracts a number of attacks and leads to serious disasters that heavily threaten the security of critical services and application data. To enhance the security of virtualized platform, trusted computing technology is introduced. With the special requirement of building trust for the virtualized platform, there needs to be designed a virtualized root of trust that can support multiple guest VMs concurrently, so as to realize a virtualized trusted platform to meet the requirements.

The research and application of virtualized trusted platform has made great progress, and has been promoted and applied in many fields. In addition to above vTPM-based solutions of virtualized trusted platform, a solution proposed by Sirrix AG company in Germany provides strongly isolated execution and ensures trusted enforcement of security policy for virtualized platform (L4-Microkernel or XEN) by combining trusted computing technology with Turaya security kernel. It also provides trusted application services such as trusted virtualized desktop and trusted virtualized storage for virtualized platform users. IBM proposes a concept of Trusted Virtualized Domain (TVD) on the virtualized platform. It uses the centralized trusted service manager components to extend trust from a single virtualized platform to multiple virtualized platforms, so as to meet the requirement that multiple guest VMs in different virtualized platforms are located in the same logic trust domain. The solution has been promoted and applied in the large virtualized data centers.

A virtualized trusted platform is different from a common trusted computing platform. As a system architecture, it can be applied to different forms of computing platforms, such as the personal computing platform, the large server and even the mobile platform, all of which can use virtualized trusted platform to enhance their security. Virtualized trusted platform provides isolation protection for different guest VMs running concurrently on the one hand, and builds trust environment for the entire virtualized platform based on virtualized root of trust on the other hand. With the popularity of virtualization technology in large data centers, cloud computing environment and mobile computing environment, virtualized trusted platform will be further applied and promoted.

5.6 Applications of Trusted Computing Platform

Trusted computing platform takes a hardware security chip as the root of trust. It uses various trusted computing security mechanisms such as chains of trust, integrity measurement and remote attestation to establish a trusted execution environment for the local platform on the one hand, and to provide trust proof of its own environment to a remote platform on the other hand, which effectively enhances the platform security. With the rapid development of information technology, different forms of trusted computing platforms have appeared one after another, such as trusted personal computers, trusted servers, trusted mobile platforms and trusted embedded devices. Applications of trusted computing platform have gradually popularized into various industries and fields and provide security protection for state confidential information, corporate sensitive data and user privacy data. The following sections briefly describe the main applications of trusted computing platform in different fields.

5.6.1 Data Protection

Users need to protect sensitive data in the computing platforms. Trusted computing platform can be used to realize a data protection scheme more secure than traditional software-based encryption scheme. On the one hand, since data encryption keys are stored in a tamper-resistant security chip, attackers cannot crack encrypted file contents; on the other hand, it is assured that only a system passing the integrity check can decrypt the encrypted data by combining the integrity measurement mechanism during the operating system boot process.

Microsoft's Windows BitLocker is a full disk encryption scheme based on trusted computing platform, which can effectively prevent the data such as operating system data, user application data, and memory image data from being tampered with and stolen by attackers. It uses the key provided by TPM security chip to encrypt the entire disk, which can protect all of the data including operating system, Windows Registry and temporary files. Moreover, it compares the integrity of system start-up with the expected integrity in the release process of decryption key, and only a verified system can decrypt the data. This mechanism enhances the strength to protect operating system and user data. If the verification fails, then it refuses to release the secret key and terminates the system start-up. Since the required key to decrypt the disk data locates in the tamper-resistant TPM security chip, even if the user platform is stolen, the attacker cannot decrypt the data stored on the disk. In order to facilitate management of the platforms that use trusted computing services, Wave company has provided a management software named Wave for the BitLocker Management, which can provide centralized management for large enterprises' trusted computing platforms and remotely monitor users who use Windows BitLocker frequently.

The application of data protection scheme based on trusted computing platform is very popular. In China, Lenovo, Tongfang and other companies launched data protection applications and tools based on TCM. These applications include Wuyou U disk and secure cloud disk (data safe box). These applications mainly protect data such as user passwords and user sensitive files.

Compared with the pure software-based data encryption scheme, data protection implemented on a trusted computing platform has a higher security. Even if an attacker steals the trusted computing platform, he is unable to decrypt the encrypted data on the platform. Now, the data protection schemes based on trusted computing platform have been widely used in key fields such as health care, education, government and business, so as to provide protection for the sensitive data of these applications.

5.6.2 Security Authentication

Before using sensitive data or applications, there is a need to authenticate user or platform identities, especially when accessing critical sensitive application services, which requires two-factor authentication for user identities and platform identities. As traditional authentication schemes based on tokens or smart cards only provide user identity authentication, it cannot meet the high security authentication requirements. Authentication schemes based on trusted computing platform can simultaneously provide dual authentication of platform identity and user identity. By combining with fingerprint system, PIN code and the integrity measurement and verification mechanism, these schemes also can provide multifactor authentication (user, platform, environment, etc.) and implement platform authentications such as secure boot and network access.

Authentication schemes based on trusted computing platform have been promoted and applied. In China, Westone company implements the two-dimension (terminal and user) authentication system based on TCM security chip and USBKEY. This authentication system provides security control and protection for the use of terminals and removable storage devices and guarantees their resources to be used in a security and controlled environment, and prevents the lost token from being leaked and tampered. This system is the first security defending system that has been put into practice in China and is being used in many industries such as government, bank, taxation and aviation. Lenovo has launched a client security software CSS (Client Security Solution) based on trusted computing platform. The solution uses TPM security chip to provide password protection for users. The password inputted by the user is stored in the encrypted form on disk. The decryption key is always protected by hardware security chip to ensure the security of the password data. Moreover, combining with user fingerprint system, it can also provide single sign-on mechanism for multiple applications that require the user password. This allows the user to quickly access applications while ensuring the security of user password.

5.6.3 System Security Enhancement

User platforms are vulnerable to some attacks such as malicious codes and Trojan horses, resulting in a large number of sensitive data leaking and critical applications failing. In order to effectively solve these security problems, trusted computing mechanism based on hardware security chip is introduced to implement security enhancement for user platform. Starting from the operating system, the enhancement based on trusted computing platform mainly makes use of chain of trust and integrity measurement mechanism and combines some traditional security technologies such as authentication and access control to build a trusted execution environment for operating system and applications, which enhances the security of system services and data.

System security enhancement schemes based on trusted computing platform have been widely used. Platform vendors such as IBM and HP have launched a series of security enhancement products for terminal and server, such as HP ProLiant ML110 G6 and HP ProLiant ML150 G6. In China, typical applications are as follows:

(1) Tongfang company develops an EFI firmware supporting the full verification of chain of trust based on TCM. Under the premise of ensuring quick boot, this product provides integrity verification of the system's configuration. At the same time, they introduce security technology platform TST2.0, which provides system security enhancement based on TCM security chip. This platform stores the confidential information in a specific security area and enhances the usability for users by combining the user's fingerprint, such as binding the online banking payment and email login process with the user's fingerprint to complete sensitive operations.

(2) Lenovo also introduces a TCM-based security enhancement server (e. g., T168 G7 tower server). It can systematically solve key problems such as platform malicious code prevention, trusted identity identification and sensitive data protection and has been widely used in government, military and other classified industries.

5.6.4 Trusted Cloud Services

Cloud computing has become a hotspot in the current development of information technology. Many fields such as industry, academia and government pay close attention to its development, but its application has not been completely accepted. This is mainly because it cannot effectively solve the security problems when processing large-scale shared resource. Compared with traditional computing environment, cloud environment makes users lose control of data and applications. A privileged manager is free to read and disclose user data, which is a serious threat to the security of user privacy information and application data. For this reason, many cloud service providers (such as Amazon Elastic Compute Cloud EC2, IBM Blue Cloud, Google App Engine and Microsoft Azure), cloud computing organizations (such as Cloud Security Alliance CSA [126]) and research institutions (HP Research Institute) are looking forward to building a trusted cloud environment using the trusted computing technology to improve the security of cloud environments.

To build trusted cloud based on trusted computing technology, it mainly makes use of trusted computing mechanisms such as chain of trust establishment, integrity measurement, remote attestation and trusted network connection, so as to provide trusted execution environment for cloud servers (such as data storage server and business process server). Trusted cloud provides trust attestation of cloud environment for cloud service users on the one hand and verifies the trustworthiness of user platforms trying to use cloud services on the other hand. Many cloud service providers and research institutions have launched and popularized a number of trusted cloud schemes.

(1) In 2009, the University of Maryland proposed a solution to build trust environment for cloud infrastructure [127]. In this solution, before using cloud services, cloud users can take advantage of the Private Virtual Infrastructure (PVI) of cloud environment to measure and verify the integrity of cloud environment, so as to ensure the security of user applications and data in the cloud environment. Since cloud users are involved in the process of building trusted cloud environment, they build trust with cloud services.
(2) In 2010, Santos et al. proposed Trusted Computing Cloud Platform. This solution focuses on the issue that the privileged administrators of cloud services can maliciously tamper or steal the data of cloud users. They use the trusted computing services provided by TPM-embedded cloud service platform to implement the trusted registration and migration processes of VM instances in cloud service, and ensure the security of user data and applications in the cloud.
(3) The Cloud Security Alliance is a mainstream cloud security research organization, whose members include numerous security agencies and device manufacturers. The organization devotes to security enhancement of cloud computing environment, and puts forward a series of implementation schemes of secure cloud. The Trusted Cloud Initiative (TCI) program expects to use trusted computing technology based on hardware security chip to enhance authentication and access control of cloud devices and improve the security of cloud services.
(4) In China, DaoliNet Information Technology (Beijing) Co., Ltd. together with a number of scientific research institutions presented a relevant research project of trusted cloud. The project was expected to enable cloud users to verify the isolated execution and behavior security of cloud applications through a combination of trusted computing technology and hardware virtualization technology. Implementation of the project can strengthen the user data protection in the cloud storage services and enhance the trustworthiness and reliability of the execution of cloud environment.

Trusted clouds can establish basic trust environment for cloud services, enhance the security of cloud services and eliminate users' concern on the security of cloud applications. Therefore, no matter whether ordinary public clouds or private clouds used internally by some industries such as enterprises, government and health care, they make great efforts to promote research and application of trusted clouds. In 2010, TCG announced the establishment of a Trusted Multi-Tenant Infrastructure (TMI) working group. They want to solve the trust-establishment problem in the trusted cloud execution environment by integrating a variety of trusted computing mechanisms and provide a generalized reference model for building trusted cloud environment. With the rapid development and application of cloud computing, the trusted computing platforms meeting their security requirements will be further promoted.

5.6.5 Other Applications

With the increasing user demand for security, trusted computing platform is also used in mobile and embedded environments, such as mobile health, vehicle equipment and video processing. This improves the security of user sensitive data by providing a trusted execution environment for these applications.

5.6.5.1 Trusted Mobile Applications

Many business applications are integrated into mobile platforms, such as mobile bank, mobile health and mobile software downloading. In the process of using these applications on mobile platforms, users require protecting the security of their privacy data, and mobile application service providers also require preventing malicious users from breaking the application servers. For this reason, MTM-based trusted mobile platforms appear, which can satisfy above security requirements of mobile platform users and service providers. We can take mobile application downloading as example. On the one hand, the trusted mobile platform ensures the trustworthiness of its own execution environment by some mechanisms, such as secure boot and trusted measurement, and effectively prevents malicious software from damaging the client system. On the other hand, the trusted mobile platform proves to the application server that it satisfies some security properties based on the remote attestation mechanism and builds the trust from service providers to mobile user platforms.

5.6.5.2 Trusted Embedded Applications

Trusted computing platform can also be used to improve the security of embedded devices. Take as an example the embedded surveillance cameras used in transportation, automation control and so on. They are the target of many attackers who threaten the security of video data due to the sensitivity of video information. For this reason, trusted embedded video devices based on trusted computing technology have come up, which perform security monitoring on the running state of camera system and ensure the authenticity, confidentiality and integrity of video information to meet the security demands of embedded video devices.

With the rapid development of applications and increasing improvement of security requirements, application service providers together with many research institutions devote to the establishment, application and promotion of trusted computing platform.

(1) TCG together with platform vendors launched a series of trusted computing platform specifications and relevant products, and applied them in practice. Governments also supported major projects related to trusted computing platform to improve the security of information services. For example, the OpenTC project supported by European Commission [128] enhances the security of traditional computing platforms, mobile platforms and embedded systems via the introduction of trusted computing technology. Results of this project have been widely used in various fields such as servers, grid, mobile communication and industrial automation.
(2) In China, platform vendors such as Lenovo and Tongfang together with ISCAS (Institute of Software, Chinese Academy of Sciences) carried out research on trusted computing platform with independent intellectual properties and had made major breakthroughs in key technologies, standards, application and promotion. Trusted computing platform based on the independent security chip TCM has been applied in government, medical treatment, military and other industries.

With the rapid development of new computing models (such as cloud computing and Internet of Things) and applications (such as mobile and embedded devices), users have increasing requirements on information security. Trusted computing platform will be more widely applied in various fields of information technology because of its unique trust insurance mechanisms.

5.7 Summary

This chapter introduces the trusted computing platform. It first gives the basic concept and function architecture of trusted computing platform. According to different forms of trusted computing platforms, it elaborates related specifications, basic principles and applications of trusted mobile platforms such as trusted personal computer, trusted server, trusted mobile platform and virtualized trusted platform. It focuses on the key technologies of trusted computing platform in the mobile and virtualization scenarios. Finally, a brief description of prospects of the application and development of trusted computing platform is presented.

Trusted computing platform based on embedded security chip is a concrete representation of trusted computing technology. It can build a trusted execution environment for a user and an enterprise, and provide trust attestation to achieve security assurance for the execution of sensitive service. At present, a series of mature products of trusted computing platform have been launched and been widely used in many areas such as government, military and enterprise. However, it should be noted that there is still lack of trusted computing platform products that can be directly deployed in new application scenarios such as mobile and embedded devices. In addition, for the testing and evaluation of different trusted computing platforms, it also needs to develop appropriate verification criteria to provide security assessments support for manufacturers and users. Compared with the traditional system security technology, trusted computing platform can provide a trust-establishment mechanism based on a tamper-resistant security chip with a higher security level. With the increasing security requirements of various application fields, we believe that the trusted computing platform will be further promoted and applied.

6 Test and Evaluation of Trusted Computing

Trusted computing is irreplaceable in guaranteeing platform security and establishing chain of trust. For protecting personal, organizational and national interest, it is of great importance to ensure security and reliability of trusted computing technology through test and evaluation method. Test and evaluation is also useful for improving product's quality, enhancing interoperability and compatibility and even promoting development of trusted computing industry. Research achievement of test and evaluation could also provide scientific method and technical support for evaluating product quality and admitting market access.

Main research directions for test and evaluation of trusted computing technology include compliance test for TPM/TCM specification, analysis of trusted computing mechanisms and certification/evaluation of trusted computing products. Research trend for compliance test of TPM/TCM is promoting automation level, so as to achieve better performance and reduce influence of human factor on test result. Analysis of trusted computing mechanism mainly adopts formal methods such as theorem rover to verify all kinds of security properties of abstract protocols. Certification and evaluation of trusted computing products focus on carrying out security evaluation on overall quality of product with the idea of security assurance and process engineering.

6.1 Compliance Test for TPM/TCM Specifications

Compliance test for TPM/TCM specification is key part of test and evaluation research of trusted computing. First, specifications are relatively strict requirements on security and function correctness of product, thus compliance test is a primary method for testing these properties. Second, compliance test is helpful for vendors to find products' defects and improve products' quality and furthermore promotes development of trusted computing industry. Third, TPM products from different vendors or TPM and other software/hardware may interact with each other frequently, and compliance test is helpful to improve compatibility and interoperatibility and reduce cost of products' deploying and updating. Finally, research of compliance tests will provide not only scientific method for products certification and accreditation but also technical and instrumental support for test and evaluation institutions in China.

Currently, the main difficulty of compliance test research lies in automation of test method and quality analysis of test result. Existing researches, such as works on TPM compliance test given by Rulr University in German [46], perform completely in manual manner. This kind of test is usually time-consuming and expensive, and lacks acceptable analysis of test quality. For this problem, we have used extended finite state machine (EFSM) as theoretical basis and made breakthrough in several aspects of key technologies of trusted computing test and evaluation, including test model of trusted computing platform, test methods and quality analysis of test result [77].

DOI 10.1515/9783110477597-006

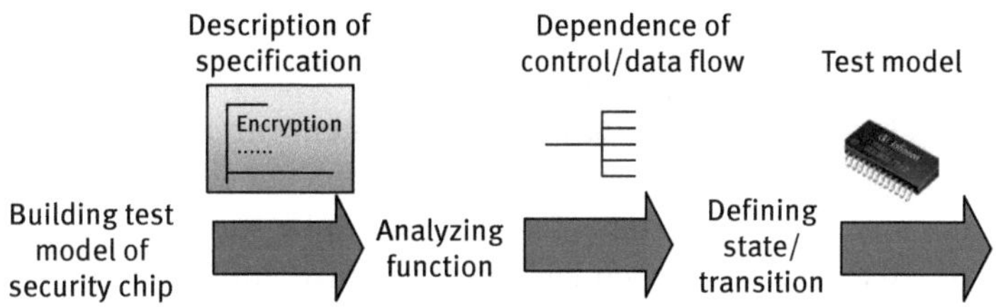

Figure 6.1: Compliance test steps for TPM/TCM.

6.1.1 Test Model

Formal test model could describe specification accurately and explicitly. It is fundamental to promote automation level and quality analysis of test. We build this model with the following steps, as is depicted in Figure 6.1.

(1) Describing specification: We adopt formal program-specifying language to describe trusted computing specifications. In this way, we divide TPM functions into related sets, and abstract concrete definitions into relatively simple descriptions. These descriptions avoid incompleteness and ambiguity of natural language description and eliminate interference of inessential content on the following test.

(2) Analyzing function of inner-module commands: Based on the description of specification, we analyze data flow and control flow dependencies between commands belonging to same function modules of TPM/TCM.

(3) Analyzing function of cross-module commands: Based on the description of specification, we analyze data flow and control flow dependencies between commands belonging to different function modules of TPM/TCM.

(4) Defining state and transition: According to the dependencies between internal commands of each function module, we define states and transitions of each TPM/TCM function module based on EFSM theory. We further combine states and transitions of different modules to construct an overall test model of TPM/TCM.

6.1.1.1 Describing Specification

The purpose of describing specification is abstracting and simplifying specification content and eliminating ambiguity or incompleteness of natural language. This work can be further divided into three steps: dividing functions, abstracting and simplifying functions and formally describing functions.

Dividing functions is the first step. The content of TPM/TCM-related specifications is divided into chapters, but granularities of different chapters are not balanced and dependent relationships between chapters are very complex. Based on specifications, we categorize specification contents into classes, which consist of high-cohesion and low-coupling functions. For example, we combine contents of key management and basic cryptographic service in protection of platform data into a cryptography subsystem, so as to depict TPM's basic cryptography functions.

Based on dividing function, function modules and subsystem can be abstracted and simplified. The purpose of this step is extracting core content and highlighting characteristic functions of each subsystem. Take cryptography subsystem as an example; although there are as many as seven key types, we take only three representative types into account: encryption, storage and signing keys. We ignore other types of keys as they are essentially similar to encryption, storage or signing keys. After simplifying key types, operations in cryptography subsystem can be divided into key management and key usage: The former includes creating, loading and evicting keys, and the latter includes encrypting, sealing and signing.

Finally, we precisely describe each subsystem by formal Z language. Z language is the most widely used program specification language. Its advantage for formal analysis has already been embodied and verified in several projects of large software engineering. In analysis work by Z language, analyzers usually first define data structures and variables and then give function operations. For cryptography subsystem, we introduce several abstract data types, including *KeyHandle*, *KeyType* (with three optional values) and global variable *maxcount* (for restricting maximum key count that a TPM/TCM can hold). These definitions are defined in Figure 6.2.

For key management operations, we define Z language functions *TPMCreateKey*, *TPMLoadKey* and *TPMEvictKey*, as illustrated in Figure 6.3. For key usage operations like *TPMEncrypt* and *TPMDecrypt*, we define input, output and critical internal processing steps, as is shown in Figure 6.4. Note that we must define the necessary system states and their initialization. For example, in Figure 6.5, key handles must be mapped onto different types by using *KeyHasType*, and SRK must exist when TPM initializes.

6.1.1.2 Analyzing Functions

Based on specification description, we can further analyze logic relationships between variables and operations within a function module. These logic relationships are embodied in both data flow and control flow aspects. The former indicates change of internal data and state of chip and its influence on other commands, and the latter indicates output parameters of a command and their influence on other commands.

Take cryptography subsystem as an example; *TPMLoadkey* needs the key blob outputted by *TPMCreatekey* as its input, but these two commands may be executed in different TPM life cycles (within one power-on life cycle, *TPMLoadKey* can be

```
[KeyHandle,KeyType]
maxcount: N;
   KeyType:=TCM_STORAGE\TCM_SIGN\TCM_BIND;
```

Figure 6.2: Data types and global variables.

TPMCreateKey

$\Xi TPMState$
$parentHandle? : KeyHandle$
$type? : KeyType$
$result! : \mathbb{N}$

$\exists h : KeyHandle \backslash h = parentHandle? \wedge$
$h \mapsto TPM\_STORAGE \in keyHasType$
$result! = 0$

TPMLoadKey

$\Delta TPMState$
$parentHandle? : KeyHandle$
$type? : KeyType$
$result! : \mathbb{N}$
$keyHandle! : KeyHandle$

$\exists h : KeyHandle \backslash h = parentHandle? \wedge$
$h \mapsto TPM\_STORAGE \in keyHasType$
$result! = 0$
$inKeyHandle! = \forall x : x \in KeyHandle \wedge x \notin keys$
$keys' = keys \cup \{inKeyHandle?\}$
$keyHasType' = keyHasType \oplus \{inKeyHandle? \mapsto\}\ type?\}$

TPMEvictKey

$\Delta TPMState$
$evictHandle? : KeyHandle$
$result! : \mathbb{N}$

$keys \neq \varnothing$
$evictHandle? \in keys$
$keys' = keys \,/\, \{evictHandle?\}$
$keyHasType' = \{evictHandle?\} \lhd keyHasType$

Figure 6.3: Key creating, loading and evicting.

TPMUnSeal

$\Xi TPMState$
$keyHandle? : KeyHandle$
$result! : \mathbb{N}$

$keyHandle? \in keys \wedge keyHasType(keyHandle?) = TPM\_STORAGE$
$keys' = keys$
$keyHasType' = keyHasType$

TPMSeal

$\Xi TPMState$
$keyHandle? : KeyHandle$
$result! : \mathbb{N}$

$keyHandle? \in keys \wedge keyHasType(keyHandle?) = TPM\_STORAGE$
$keys' = keys$
$keyHasType' = keyHasType$

Figure 6.4: Sealing and unsealing operations.

TPMState

$keys : \mathbb{P}\ KeyHandle$
$keyHasType : KeyHandle \mapsto KeyType$

$dom\ keyHasType : = keys$
$\#keys \leq maxcount$

Init

$keys = \{srkKeyHandle\}$
$keyHasType = \{srkKeyHandle \mapsto TPM\_STORAGE\}$

Figure 6.5: The definition of abstracted states of system and their initialization.

executed without previous execution of TPMCreatekey). Thus, there exists data flow relationship between these two commands but not control flow relationship. As a comparison, *TPMSeal*'s inputs include a key handle that is generated by *TPMLoadKey*, and any operation using a sealing key must be executed after a successful execution of *TPMLoadKey*. Thus, *TPMSeal* depends on *TPMLoadkey* in both aspects of data flow and control flow. Dependent relationships between key operations are illustrated in Figure 6.6.

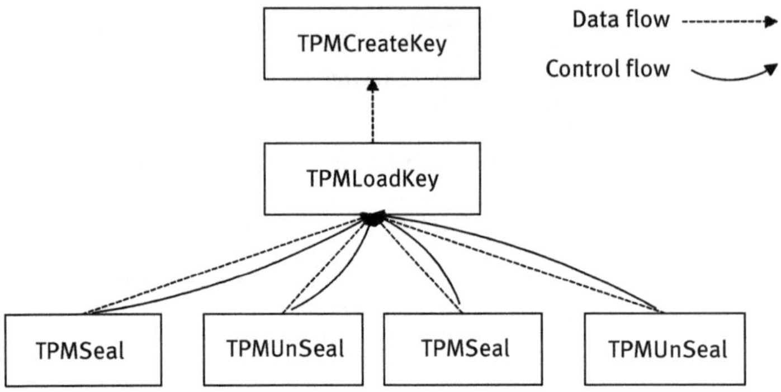

Figure 6.6: Dependent relationships between key operations.

6.1.1.3 Extracting State

Based on specification description and function analysis, we can construct an EFSM model of TPM. The key of this work is extracting states and transitions between them in the model. In the extracting state, we define system variables and initial state according to specification, and then divide initial state into several states according to the value of the variable.

Internal Variables and Initial State. The state of the TPM is decided by values of its internal variables, and these variables can be further classified into single-value variables and collective variables. Single-value variables are those variables that are assigned and changed in a single dimension. For example, the bool variables that indicate activation, enabling and ownership state of the TPM could only be assigned to TRUE or FALSE. Collective variables are those sets that range in multidimension and consist of several independent variables. As an example, the above-mentioned variable *keys*, which record information of loaded keys within the TPM, consist of key handle variables whose amount is at most *maxcount*.

Assume that the subsystem of TPM has state-related variables $x_1.x_i.x_n, A_1, \ldots, A_j, \ldots, A_l$. x_i represents some single-value variable, and its type ranges in $T_1, \ldots, T_n$. A_j represents some collective variable, and types of its internal elements are $TT_1, \ldots, TT_\ell$. Then, the initial state can be represented as (using Z language)

$$S_{Initial} = \{x_1, \ldots, x_n, A_1, \ldots., A_l | x_1 \in T_1, \ldots, x_n \in T_n, A_1 \in \mathbb{P}\, TT_1, \ldots, A_\ell \in \mathbb{P} TT_\ell\}$$

There are only one collective variable *key* in the Z language-based description of TPM cryptography subsystem and a constraint function *KeyHasType*. The initial state of the subsystem is

$$S_{Initial} = \{keys | \#keys \leq maxcount\}$$

Dividing State. Given the initial state, further division can be processed according to the values of state variables. For single-value variables, states can be divided according to a certain policy, such as the method of boundary value analysis and the method of category classification. A *Policy*-based division of state S according to the variable x_i is defined as follows:

$$Partition(S, x_i, policy) = \{AS_1, \ldots, AS_j, \ldots, AS_{m_i} | AS_j \triangleq (P_j(x_i) = true \wedge \\ \forall AS_{j1}, AS_{j2} : AS_{j1}(x_i) \cap AS_{j2}(x_i) = \emptyset \wedge \bigcup_{i=1}^{m_i} AS_i = T_i)\}$$

Here, AS_j represents substates of state S divided by variable x_i. P_j is the predicate to constraint x_i, such as x_i >=0; $AS_{j1}(x_i)$ represents value space for variable x_i in state AS_{j1}. For collective variables, usually a method based on set division is adopted to divide states space. We call a family of subsets π a partition of set A, if and only if π meets the following requirements: first, $\emptyset \notin \pi$; second, any two elements in π are nonintersect; third, union of all elements in π equals to A. If a function $f : T \rightarrow V$ reflects set T to type V, and V is a finite set that satisfies $ran(f) = \{v_1, v_2, \ldots, v_n\}$, then a division of function value of type T is as follows:

$$\pi = \{\{\forall t : T | f(t) = v_1\}, \{\forall t : T | f(t) = v_2\}, \ldots, \{\forall t : T | f(t) = v_n\}\}$$

Thus, state S can be divided by function f according to collective variable A_j, and the division result is

$$Partition(S, A_j, f) = \{BS_1, \ldots, BS_{k_j} | \\ \{\forall t : t \in BS_1(A_j) | f(BS_1(A_j)) = v_1\} \ldots \{\forall t : t \in BS_{k_j}(A_j) | f(BS_{k_j}(A_j)) = v_{k_j}\}\}$$

Here, $BS_1(A_j)$ represents a set of elements with type TT_j, which belong to collective variables A_j in state BS_1.

For cryptography subsystem, its states can be divided based on collective variables as follows:

$$Partition(S_{Initial}, keys, keyHasType) = \{S_{Sign}, S_{Storage}, S_{Bind}\}$$

Here, all elements in S_{Sign} are signing key handle, and $S_{Storage}$ and S_{Bind} are defined similarly. Up to now, combination number of states is $7(C_3^2 + C_3^1 + C_3^3 = 2^n - 1 = 7)$ and concrete states after dividing are $s_1 = \{S_{Sign}\}$, $s_2 = \{S_{Storage}\}$, $s_3 = \{S_{Bind}\}$, $s_4 = \{S_{Sign}, S_{Storage}\}$, $s_5 = \{S_{Storage}, S_{Bind}\}$, $s_6 = \{S_{Bind}, S_{Sign}\}$, and $s_7 = \{S_{Bind}, S_{Sign}, S_{Storage}\}$.

The final state space can be achieved by combining each state division. The count of state space after combination is $C_{k_j}^1 + C_{k_j}^2 + \cdots + C_{k_j}^{k_j} = 2^{k_j} - 1$. If variables within a state include both single-value ones $x_1, \ldots, x_n$ and collective ones $A_1, \ldots, A_l$, then the final state space is a complete combination of all variables. The count of final states is

$$\prod_{i=1,j=1}^{i=n,j=l} m_i \cdot (2^{k_j} - 1)$$

If there are too many state variables, then the final state space will expand dramatically. In this situation, there are two alternative choices. On one hand, state variables could be redivided into coarser granularity. On the other hand, some constraints can be imposed on final state space according to practical demands (such as test demands). For example, if we add constraint condition on the above result as follows, then the space will reduce to only four states (s_1, s_4, s_6, s_7):

$$P(S) = \{S | \forall key \in keys, keyHasType(key) = TPM\_SIGN\}$$

6.1.1.4 Extracting Transition

Extracting transition is the last step to construct an EFSM for TPM. Transition mainly consists of operation that causes states to transfer: For two TPM states s_i, s_j, if there is some operation OP that makes s_i transfer to s_j, then (s_i, s_j, OP) can be added to transition sets of model. Figure 6.7 depicts basic algorithms for extracting transition. In the figure, $def(s) = \{key | key \in s\}$, S is set of internal states and OP indicates set of TPM operations.

For cryptography subsystem, operations that cause transition include *TPMCreateKey*, *TPMLoadKey*, *TPMEvictKey*, *TPMSeal*, *TPMUnSeal*, *TPMSign*, *TPMVerify*, *TPMEncrypt* and *TPMDecrypt*. An EFSM model of cryptography subsystem achieved by applying the above method is illustrated in Figure 6.8, and concrete meaning about states and transitions is shown in Tables 6.1 and 6.2.

```
T = ∅        DrivingTransiton()
for all s_i ∈ S
        for all s_j ∈ S
          if exists op ∈ OP such that
                 ∃keys, keys' : ℙ KeyHandle
                 ∃keyHandle : KeyHandle
                 keys ∈ def(s_i) ∧ keys' ∈ def(s_j) ∧
                keys' = keys ∪ {keyHandle} ∧ # keys' ≤ maxcount
          add (s_i, s_j, op) to T
        else  break
```

Figure 6.7: Extraction algorithm of state transition.

Table 6.1: State description of EFSM.

State	Description	State	Description
s_0	Initial state: TPM is owned and enabled, and SRK is created	s_1	Only encryption keys exist in TPM
s_2	Only signing keys exist in TPM	s_3	Only storage keys exist in TPM
s_4	Both encryption and storage keys exist in TPM	s_5	Both signing and storage keys exist in TPM
s_6	Both encryption and signing keys exist in TPM	s_7	Encryption, signing and storage keys exist in TPM

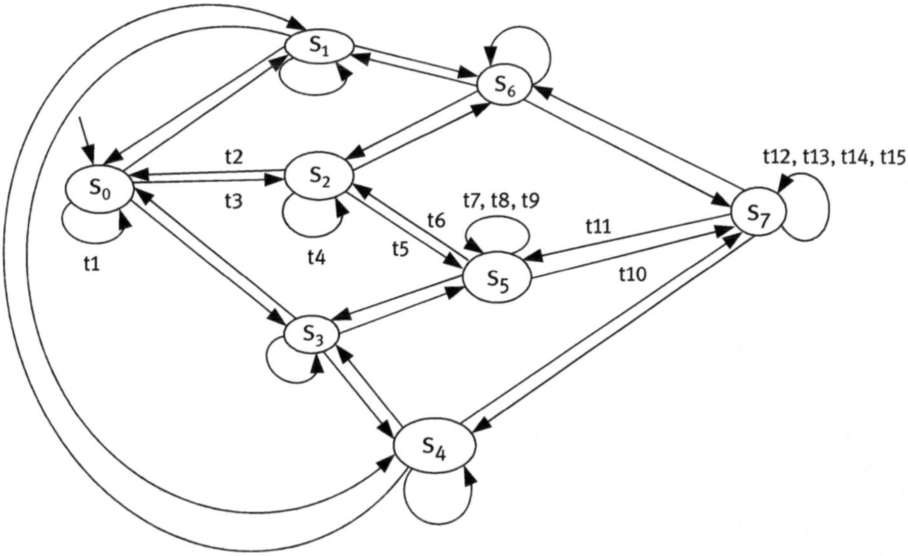

Figure 6.8: EFSM model of cryptography subsystem.

6.1.2 Test Method

6.1.2.1 Automatic Generation Method of Test Case

Automatic generation method of test cases is the key and most challenging part in compliance test for the TPM/TCM specification. To reduce the complexity of generation, abstract test case is generated automatically. Though not executable, this case identifies execution sequence of TPM/TCM commands and embodies data flow and control flow relationships between commands. In the second phase, the abstract cases are converted into practical ones. Through filling concrete parameters in test commands, internal function logic of each command is actually embodied, and the test cases are ready to be executed.

Table 6.2: State transition of EFSM.[1]

State transition	Description
t1	$\{s_0 - TPM\_CWK, P_{t3}/$ $< y_{retValue}(0), y_{ordinal}(TPM\_CWK), y_{tag}(RspTag), y_{keyType}(x_{keyType}) >, 0- > s_0\}$ Here $P_{t3} = (x_{tag}(auth1Tag), x_{keyHandle} \in keys)$
t2,t6,t11	$\{s_2(s_5, s_7) - TPM\_EK, P_{t2}/$ $< y_{retValue}(0), y_{ordinal}(TPM\_EK), y_{tag}(RSPTag) >, 0- > s_0(s_2, s_5)\}$ Here $P_{t2} =< x_{tag}(reqAuth), x_{keyHandle} \in keys >$
t3,t5,t10	$\{s_0(s_2, s_5) - TPM\_LK, P_{t3}/$ $< y_{retValue}(0), y_{ordinal}(TPM\_LK), y_{tag}(resAuth1) >, 0- > s_2(s_5, s_7)\}$ Here $P_{t3} = (x_{tag}(reqAuth1), x_{pkeyHandle} \in keys, x_{keyType}(SignKey))$
t4,t7,t12	$\{s_2(s_5, s_7) - TPM\_Sign, P_{t16}/$ $< y_{tag}(rspAuth2), y_{retValue}(0), y_{ordinal}(TPM\_Sign) >, 0- > s_2(s_5, s_7)\}$ Here $P_{t16} = (x_{tag}(reqAuth2))$
t8,t13	$\{s_5(s_7) - TPM\_Seal, P_{t10}/ < y_{tag}(rspAuth1), y_{retValue}(0) >, 0- > s_5(s_7)\}$ Here $P_{t10} = (x_{tag}(reqAuth1), x_{keyHandle} \in keys \wedge x_{keyType}(TPM\_STORAGE))$
t9,t14	$\{s_5(s_7) - TPM\_UnSeal, P_{t11}/$ $< y_{tag}(rspAuth2), y_{retValue}(0), y_{ordinal}(TPM\_UnSeal) >, 0- > s_5(s_7)\}$ Here $P_{t11} = (x_{tag}(reqAuth2))$
t15	$\{s_7 - TPM\_UB, P_{t9}/ < y_{tag}(repAuth1), y_{retValue}(0), y_{ordinal}(TPM\_UB) >, 0- > s_7\}$ Here $P_{t9} = (x_{tag}(reqAuth1), x_{KeyHandle} \in keys)$

[1]In identifier of transition **($s - x, P/op, y -> s'$)**, S represents source state of transition, s' represents destination state of transition, x represents input of transition, P represents condition of transition, op represents operations in transition and y represents output of transition. Input variables in this table include $x_{tag}, x_{ordinal}, x_{keyType}, x_{keyHandle}$. Output variables include $y_{tag}, y_{retValue}, y_{ordinal}, y_{keyHandle}, y_{keyType}$. Input commands include *TPM_CWK* (createkey), *TPM_EK, TPM_LK, TPM_UB, TPM_Seal, TPM_UnSeal, TPM_Sign*. The symbol y_{tag} (*value*) represents assign *value* to y_{tag}. Environment and global variable include *keys*(set of handles in TPM).

Basic steps of abstract generation are depicted in left part of Figure 6.9. For each command *A*, we first find its dependent relationship with other commands and then form a command sequence according to the dependent relationship. In this sequence, any command that *A* depends on should be located in a position before *A*, and any command that depends on *A* should be located after *A*. Then we adjust location of commands (except *A*) in the sequence and get an abstract test case of *A*. After repeating this process for all commands and merging some test cases when necessary, we can finally get abstract test cases of compound function, which consists of a series of commands.

Basic steps for practical test case are depicted in the right part of Figure 6.9. For any command *A*, we first find its data flow dependent relationship with other commands. Then, according to the associated parameters between commands embodied in the dependent relationship, we insert represent value of each equivalence class into

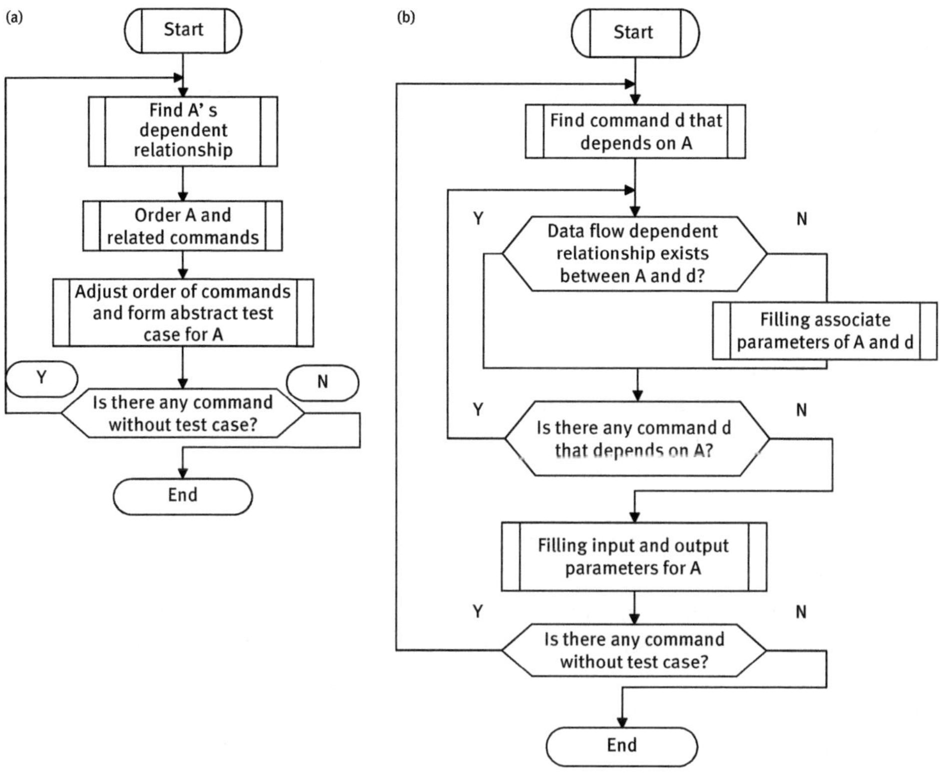

Figure 6.9: Basic steps for test case generation.

abstract test cases of A. Finally, according to input parameters of A and relationship of input/output parameters, we supplement necessary parameters and get the practical test case of A.

This method only needs small quantity of manual work in the initial phase of generation of test case. The relatively high degree of automation reduces the burden of testers and promotes work efficiency greatly. This method also supports accurate analysis of test quality, which builds trustworthiness of test result upon verifiable algorithm but not default trust on testers. This feature is helpful to exclude interference of artificial elements and enhance objectivity of test and clients' confidence in test result.

6.1.2.2 Analysis of Test Cases

Quality analysis of test cases is a critical method to quantify trustworthiness of test method. Given a relatively complete and universal test model, quality of test case actually depends on simplification of the model of test case generation and clipping of generated cases. In ideal situations, key index of quality like test coverage rate can be determined by analyzing principles of simplification and clipping. For example, if full-state coverage principle is adopted, then testers can guarantee that every optional value of every internal variable is covered by at least one test case. But in practice, it is often the case that full-state coverage is too expensive and coverage rate of state or transition beyond certain threshold is satisfactory for most cases. In other words, while generating test cases, coverage rate should be monitored. Generation process should immediately halt as long as this rate reaches some threshold value.

In completed test works, we typically set a threshold of test coverage rate as termination condition of test case generation. Thus, quality of test case can be measured by analysis tree of reachability. The so-called analysis tree of reachability is a tree structure graph describing FSM's behavior trace. Root of the tree (level-0 node) corresponds to the initial state of FSM, and nodes at Nth level indicate reachable states after N time transition from initial state. Some transitions may be blocked if the transition predicate of EFSM is judged to false under certain test inputs. Through depth-first or width-first traverse algorithm, the tree graph can be thoroughly traversed so as to analyze the test quality. Concrete algorithm to generate analysis tree of reachability is as follows:

(1) Set traverse depth l, do a depth-first traverse upon EFSM model of TPM/TCM starting from a designated initial node and get analysis tree of reachability.
(2) Put all reached nodes into a set $S_{traversal}$.
(3) Terminate the generation of analysis tree of reachability when traversal depth is greater than l.
(4) Every feasible path in the tree is correspondent to a test case. In order to get test coverage rate, the generated test cases should be reanalyzed according to the tree.

For the cryptography subsystem mentioned above, its test quality can be analyzed by an analysis tree of reachability. EFSM model of cryptography subsystem is illustrated in Figure 6.8. Exemplar paths in Figure 6.10 can be extracted from this model. In this figure, nodes represent model states (black node is the initial state) and paths represent transitions. The formula of coverage rate is $\#S_{traversal}/\#S_{total}$ where S_{total} is the total state/transition space. In order to make transition coverage rate of test cases of cryptography subsystem exceed 80%, we have actually generated over 70,000 test cases in the final.

6.1.3 Test Implementation

Based on the above-mentioned method, we have designed and implemented a comprehensive solution for compliance test for the TPM/TCM specification. Basic process of this solution is depicted in Figure 6.11. We first formally describe TPM/TCM

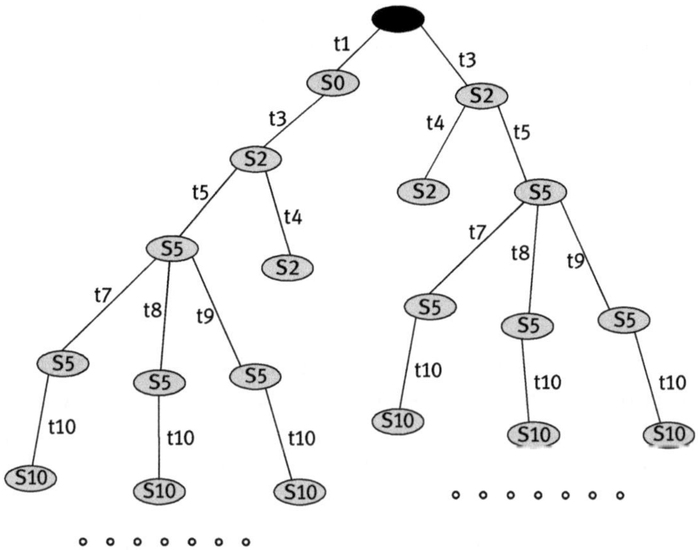

Figure 6.10: Analysis tree of reachability of cryptography subsystem.

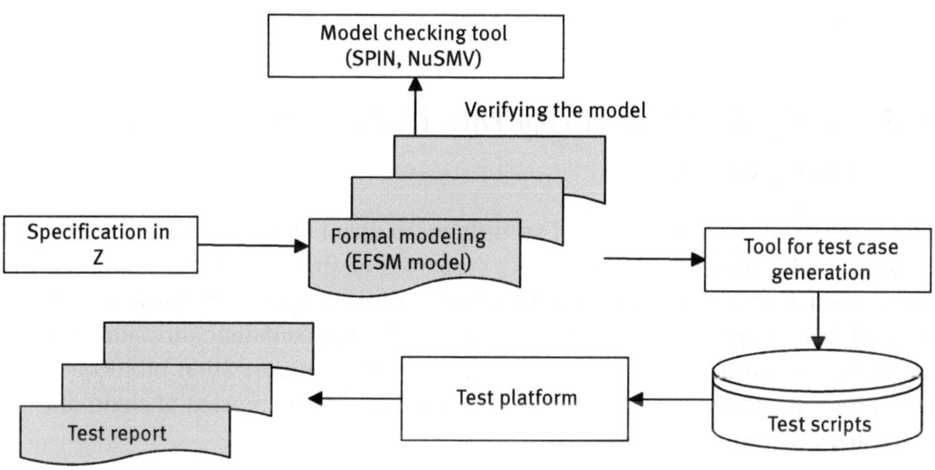

Figure 6.11: Basic steps for test implementing.

and establish the EFSM model. Then we automatically generate test cases and executable scripts by test case generation tool on EFSM, and finally get test report by inputting and executing the scripts on the test platform.

Currently, we have completed the compliance test on these TPM products, including Atmel AT97SC3203, NSC TPM 1.2 and Lenovo TPM 1.1b. It can be concluded that the actual situation of product quality is not optimistic, although compliance to TPMv1.2 specification is commonly claimed by TPM manufacturers. Parts of errors may cause attack and lead to serious loss. These errors are as follows:

- Error about resource handle: Resource handle should be generated randomly, but some products generate handles regularly. This leads to unfreshness of handles. If an attacker is able to release a handle in TPM/TCM, a man-in-the-middle attack may exist. For example, user loads a key *KEY2* into TPM and gets a handle 0×050000001, then attacker could release 0×050000001 and reload a new key *KEY1*. *KEY1* may be a corrupted key that shares the same usage authorization value with *KEY2*, and a TPM with this error may allocate 0×050000001 to *KEY1*. An insensitive user will not perceive these changes and continue to cite the key with handle 0×05000001 (now it is *KEY1*) to encrypt secret data, and ciphertext will finally be decrypted by attackers.
- Error about command ordinal: Ordinal is the parameter to identify a TPM command. We find that parts of ordinals in tested product are not compliant with specification. Although what kind of influence will be brought by this kind of error cannot be determined now, it will greatly influence interoperability and universality of the software that uses TPM.
- Error about return code: Parts of products sometimes return internal returning codes defined by vendors but not in specifications. This may give attackers chance that is useful for malicious purpose. Through analyzing these internal values, attacker may find vulnerabilities in TPM and even carrying out attacking.

6.2 Analysis of Security Mechanism of Trusted Computing

The research content of analysis of security mechanism of trusted computing is analysis and verification of various security properties of abstract protocols and running mechanism by theoretical and formal method. Typically, researchers use model checking and theorem proving methods to analyze and verify confidentiality, authenticity, anonymity and other security properties of TPM/TCM authorization protocols (AP), DAA protocols, PCR extending mechanism and establishing process of chain of trust in trusted computing platform.

6.2.1 Analysis Based on Model Checking

Model checking method depicts target system as an FSM system, describes properties that system supposed to have as logic formulas and uses automated means to verify whether each trace of (FSM of) target system satisfies the properties. The advantage of model checking is twofold. First, it is completely automatic. As long as the user gives logic description of target system and properties, model checking could complete all verification work automatically. Second, model checking could present vulnerabilities at the model layer in a relatively intuitive manner. If modeling method used in test work is relatively reasonable, the detected vulnerabilities are expected to be directly exploited in practical attacks. The disadvantage of model checking lies in that it can analyze only target with finite states. With expansion of target system, states of model (that need to be checked) will increase dramatically. Because potential behavior of verifying target like protocols is always infinite, model checking often suffers from state explosion problem and is doomed to be an imperfect method.

When using model checking method to analyze protocols, we must first give a clear description of protocol to avoid ambiguity in protocol description and prepare for modeling the protocol. Then we make assumptions about cryptography algorithms and attackers, and describe analysis target and properties by tool's modeling language. After all these preparation, we run tool to get and analyze the verification result. In the following sections, we give an example in which TCM authorization protocol is analyzed using SPIN [53], so as to illustrate concrete steps to analyze trusted computing protocols by model checking method.

6.2.1.1 Symbolic Definition of Protocol

TCM uses authorization protocol to protect its internal resources. A simple description of AP is illustrated in Figure 6.12.

For a formal definition of AP protocol, we introduce the following symbols and definitions:

- *AP*: ordinal of commands that establishes AP session
- *ET*: entity type that is protected by TCM
- *EV*: entity value that is protected by TCM
- *seq*: sequence number for preventing replay attack
- N_C: *CallerNonce*, nonce provided by caller
- N_t: *TCMNonce*, nonce generated and provided by TCM
- *CMD*: ordinal of commands that is to be executed (and access the resource)
- *D*1, *D*2: data needed in executing *CMD*

TCM_APCreate: commands for start establishing authorization session. Its internal operations are as follows:

1) If the entity type to access is TCM_none, then go to step 3, otherwise, verify the integrity of parameters and caller's preveledge to access the entity.
2) Based on shared authorization value *authData, callerNonce* (nonce given by caller) and *tcmNonce*(nonce generated by TCM), create shared secret data *shareSecret*=HMAC(*authData,callerNonce*//*TCMNonce*).
3) Create session and its handle.
4) Create replay initial sequence number for preventing replay attack.
5) Create HMAC for authorization data.

Figure 6.12: AP authorization protocol.

Phase of creating session
1. $User \rightarrow TCM : AP \parallel ET \parallel EV \parallel N_c \parallel HMAC(authData, ET \parallel N_c)$
2. $TCM \rightarrow User : R_S \parallel S \parallel N_t \parallel seq \parallel HMAC(shareSecret, N_t \parallel seq)$
Phase of running authorized command
3. $User \rightarrow TCM : CMD \parallel D_1 \parallel S \parallel HMAC(shareSecret, \mathrm{CMD} \parallel D_1 \parallel seq + 1)$
4. $TCM \rightarrow User : R_S \parallel D_2 \parallel HMAC(shareSecret, D_2 \parallel seq + 1)$

Figure 6.13: Execution flow of AP authorization session.

- S: identifier of authorization protocols
- R_S: return code representing successful execution

A concrete execution flow of AP is illustrated in Figure 6.13.

6.2.1.2 Modeling Target Protocols

The following assumptions should be made when analyzing AP protocol. First, cryptography algorithm used in protocol is secure. Second, honest users and malicious attackers coexist in running the protocol. Third, attacker cannot forge HMAC value, and HMAC computation is ignored in formal analysis. Fourth, attacker could intercept, tamper and forge any messages of user.

Under the above assumptions, we adopt PROMELA (PROcess MEta LAnguage) of SPIN to describe target protocol and expected properties. We set three roles in AP protocol: user *U* to start the protocol, attacker *A* and *TCM*. *A* acts between *U* and *TCM*, and is capable of tampering and intercepting all plaintext message. We introduce two half-duplex communication channels *User-to-A* and *A-to-TCM*. Assuming two concurrent AP sessions are supported by TCM, the following two global variables could be defined:
(1) *byte tcm_session[2]*, which indicates session between TCM and attackers.
(2) *byte user_session[2]*, which represents session between user and attackers.

For each session, there are two states *Success* and *Fail* to indicate successful and failure termination of session. Definition of message structure shared by all participants is as follows.

```
mtype={AP,ACK, CMD, ANSWER, FINISH}//message type
typedef padding{
   bit session; //session id
   short nc; //nonce provided by client
     shortnt; //nonce provided by TCM
   short seq; //sequence number
}
```

Message channel is defined as follows:

```
chan user_middle = [0]of{mtype, padding};
chan middle_tcm = [0]of{retype, padding}.
```

Finally, the behavior of user, attacker and TCM could be modeled. There are three processes modeled in SPIN, which represent user, TCM and attacker, respectively. The user process could initiate session, request to execute authorized commands and receive result. The TCM process could actually open session, execute commands and send result. Attacker is active and his behavior is not restricted by any specification. He can do any operation such as message interception, tampering and forgery. For example, an attacker could request to open a session by impersonating a user, send valid message to TCM or user, store all intermediate message, replay previous message and terminate sessions.

Depicting Target Property. Description of target property by natural language is as follows: Let S be a session set, T_S represent the state of session between TCM and attacker and U_S represent the state of session between user and attacker. Then it is expected that for any $s \in S$, states of T_S and U_S should be consistent with each other.

The target property described by PROMELA is as follows:

#definesessionProperty(tcm_session[0]==user_session[0])&&rtcm_session[1] ==user_session[1]).

Analyzing Result. Based on the above model checking method, we have found a kind of replay attack against AP authorization protocol, as is depicted in Figure 6.14. This attack consists of three phases. The first phase is attack phase. User creates an AP session according to the specification of AP protocol, and then attacker intercepts and saves the concrete information of command and forces to terminate the session. The second phase is user's normal execution phase. User is completely unaware of any abnormity and opens another authorization session. In this way, the session that is actually not closed in the previous phase is maintained. The last phase is replay attack phase. The attacker leverages information saved in the first phase to re-execute the TCM command that user wants to execute previously, so as to change the TCM's internal state of resources that will not be perceived by the user.

6.2.2 Analysis Based on Theorem Proving

Besides model checking, research institutions have also carried out works on analysis of security mechanism of trusted computing, such as authorization protocol, chain of trust and DAA protocol, by belief logic, logic of secure system and applied pi calculus. The methods like belief logic typically take all behaviors of target into

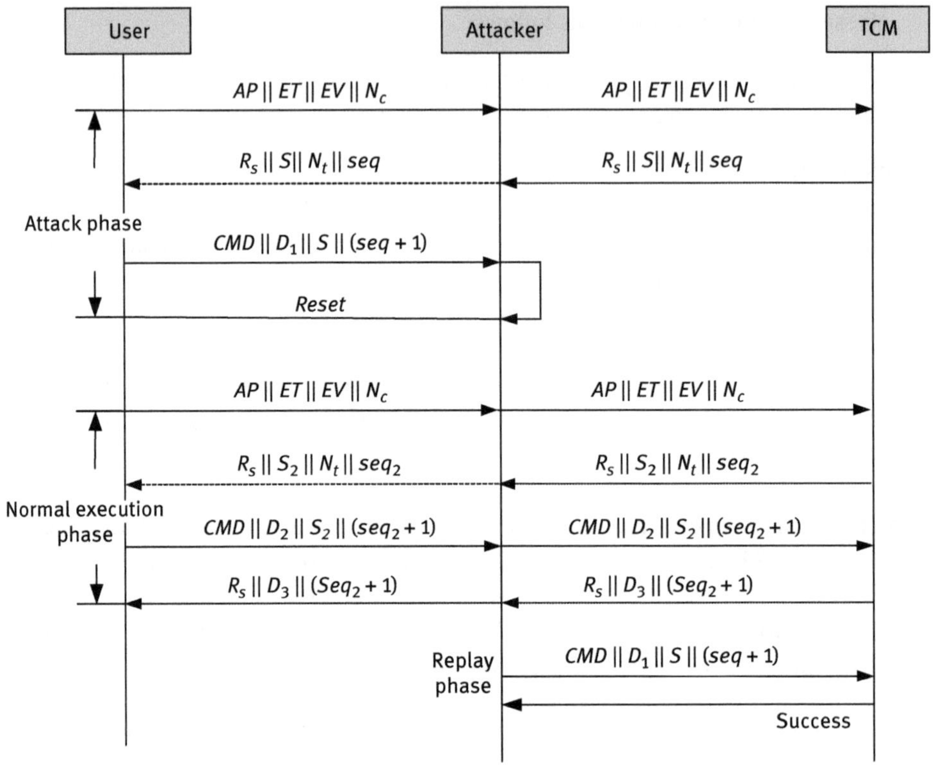

Figure 6.14: Sequence of commands in replay attack of AP.

account and dedicate to proving properties that their behaviors satisfy; thus, we classify the analysis works into theorem proving category. Theorem proving methods are based on strict method of logical analysis, so their advantage lies in soundness of analysis. Namely, once a security property is proved, it is determinately correct (in the model set by theorem proving system). Generally speaking, theorem proving method dedicates to proving security properties of protocols but not finding their defects, and it is inferior to model checking in the aspect of automation degree. But as the development of secure logic theory and technology, these disadvantages have been gradually remedied.

Currently, security mechanism analysis of trusted computing based on theorem proving is still in its infancy. First, construction methods of trusted execution environment and related security technologies are constantly emerging, so analysis works are unable to keep up with the pace of technology development. Second, against concrete problems in practical applications of trusted computing, such as combination scheme of remote attestation, TNC and secure channel, there has not been any compellent result yet. Last but not least, for complex analysis target like DAA and trusted virtualization platform, existing formal description methods and definition of security properties are not mature enough. Thus, it still needs to be thoroughly discussed how to use all kinds of analysis methods especially theorem proving in trusted computing area. In the following sections, we briefly introduce several existing works of analyzing security mechanism of trusted computing using theorem proving.

6.2.2.1 Analysis of Trusted Computing Protocols

Researchers from Saar University in Germany have successfully described zero-knowledge proof (ZKP) and ZKP-based DAA protocol using equivalence theory of applied pi calculus [51]. Based on extended applied pi calculus, the researchers leverage ProVerif tool to propose the first mechanical (i. e., not using theory of provable security based on computation) verification result of DAA and successfully detect a security defect: authenticity in the process of issuing credential cannot be ensured. In other words, the attacker may make DAA credential issuer fail to figure out which platforms actually hold DAA credentials.

Researchers from HP company in UK find that authorization data of TPM key are likely to be shared in practical application. In this situation, the malicious user could impersonate TPM to communicate with other users. If the malicious user (like administrator) knows authorization data of SRK, he can forge the whole storage hierarchy [129]. Though transportation protection can be used to partially avoid this situation, authorization protocol is still vulnerable to offline-dictionary attack. To handle these problems, the author proposes a new authorization protocol and proves its security against the above two attacks by ProVerif.

Chinese researchers successfully find a session substitution attack in implementation of OSAP [130] using SVO logic (which is a kind of belief logic). In detail, if implementation of OSAP does not bind session handle and its corresponding entity, a malicious user may use an OSAP session created by himself to access unauthorized internal resource in TPM.

6.2.2.2 Analysis of Critical Mechanisms of Trusted Computing

From the view of protocol composition, researchers from Carnegie Mellon University in USA have proposed Logic of Secure System (LS^2) for system analysis. By introducing predicates and deriving formula for describing security function and properties of system into existing protocol composition analysis logic, LS^2 gets strong description ability while inheriting local reasoning property (attacker behavior could be excluded in reasoning) and is regarded to be a powerful tool for system security analysis. Based on LS^2, researchers find a defect of dynamic root of trust-based integrity collection and reporting. That is, a program may actually not run even if it is measured and extended into PCR [52].

Researchers from CNRIA of France have analyzed state-related security mechanism [131, 132], such as PCR extending. Researchers find that analysis process in ProVerif tool may not terminate when analyzing state-related security mechanism.

The tool may also present false attacks. Against this problem, researchers have carried out specialized theoretical analysis on PCR extending mechanism and confirmed that minimum complete set of PCR extending mechanism is finite. This conclusion makes it possible for the analysis tool to verify global security of the system quickly by actually verifying finite system variation. To solve the false attack problem, researchers have extended the ProVerif tool eliminating the false attack and proved its correctness theoretically.

6.3 Evaluation and Certification of Trusted Computing

Compared with test and formal analysis, security evaluation is more comprehensive and expensive. Besides security of specification and products, security evaluation also pays close attention to production process. Up to now, TCG have already proposed directive documents for guiding evaluation organization to carry out security evaluation of trusted computing. TCG have also carried out certification projects on TPM and TNC. These projects verify correctness and rationality of security evaluation, and conclude an authoritative and overall judgment on the trusted computing products. This judgment is a valuable guidance for product selection, and a positive evaluation is of great importance for enhancing users' confidence.

6.3.1 Common Criteria

The primary basis for product evaluation given by TCG is common criteria (CC). The core purpose of CC is to introduce principle of security engineering into evaluation. Namely, the whole process of evaluation target, including designing, developing and application, will be enforced under principle of security engineering to ensure the product security.

The common criteria consists of two relative independent parts – demands on security assurance and demands on security function – and seven evaluation assurance levels (EAL) are set according to security assurance demands. Besides demands on security assurance and security function, CC further requires authority to formulate security demands for specific types of products, which is called as "Protection Profile (PP)." PP should fulfill requirements of certain users, be with certain level of abstraction and be independent of specific product. Given one or more PPs, manufacturers can form concrete security demands about its products, and these demands are called "Security Target" (ST). Evaluation organizations can evaluate PP and ST, and complete evaluation of target product. In overview of specification architecture, TCG has explicitly specified purpose, implementation environment, implementation processed security evaluation and relationship between evaluation and certification. As the most influential industry alliance of trusted computing, TCG has already drawn up PP for TPM in PC.

6.3.2 TPM and TNC Certification

Based on security evaluation and with reference to compliance test result, TCG carries out TPM and TNC certification and accreditation projects.

- Compliance test. TCG develops its own software for compliance test for TPM specification, and accepts self-test results carried out by vendors themselves.
- Security evaluation. TCG develops its own PP for TPM in PC, admits CC evaluation results carried out by vendors and requires that the level of the results is no more than EAL4.

Currently, SLB9635TT1.2 from Infineon Technologies in Germany is the first TPM product certified by TCG, which is claimed to be compliant to TPMv1.2 revision 103.

TNC certification is based on the following two aspects of evidences:

- Compliance test. TCG develops its own software for compliance test for TNC specification, and accepts results of self-test carried out by vendors themselves.
- Interoperability test. TNC compliance workgroup of TCG performs interoperability test work one or two times a year. Vendors are forced to participate in and complete this test.

Currently, IC4500 access control suites, EX4200 switches and StrongSwan etc. TNC-related produces from Juniper Technologies in USA and Hochschule Hannover in Germany have been certified by TCG. These products implement various interfaces in TNC specification, and are typically tested as a component of TNC architecture. For example, EX4200 switch implements IF-PEP-REDIUS1.0 interface, and is certified as policy enforcement point (PEP) of TNC.

6.4 Comprehensive Test and Analysis System of Trusted Computing Platform

Currently, for representative trusted computing products such as security chip and trusted software, industrial administration urgently needs effective comprehensive and effective methods to test and analyze compliance of product and security of cryptography algorithm, so as to meet practical requirements on quality inspection, market admittance and government procurement. Trusted computing vendors also need help from professional test and evaluation organizations, in order to improve product quality, enhance product compliance and get professional reference for product updating and revising.

For the above-mentioned practical requirements, we design and implement a comprehensive test and analysis system for trusted computing platform. Our system is based upon methods of compliance test for TPM specification presented in Section 6.2

and research achievements of analysis of trusted computing protocols mentioned in 6.3.1. It also references mature specifications and methods of test and analysis given by researchers all over the world. The system mainly targets on trusted computing-related products like Chinese domestic security chips and trusted computers, and implements multiple functions including compliance test for TPM specification, test for cryptography algorithm correctness and performance, test for randomness and protocol emulation.

The system is now put into practice by Chinese domestic test and evaluation organizations of information security. In works of testing multiple Chinese products, the system shows its great test scalability and good test ability. The system also gets good praise from all application organizations. The following section first introduces the architecture and functions of system and then explains in detail each function, including compliance test of security chip, test of cryptography algorithm, randomness test and protocol emulation. Finally, practical application of the system is also briefly mentioned.

6.4.1 Architecture and Functions of System

The system adopts client/server architecture. It consists of test controller, test agent and supporting database, as shown in Figure 6.15. Test agent is the agent software that is embedded into the target platform to be tested. For example, when performing compliance test for security chip specification, test agent runs as a daemon in target platform where security chip is located and waits for test instructions from the test controller. Test controller is the center of the whole system, which supports control

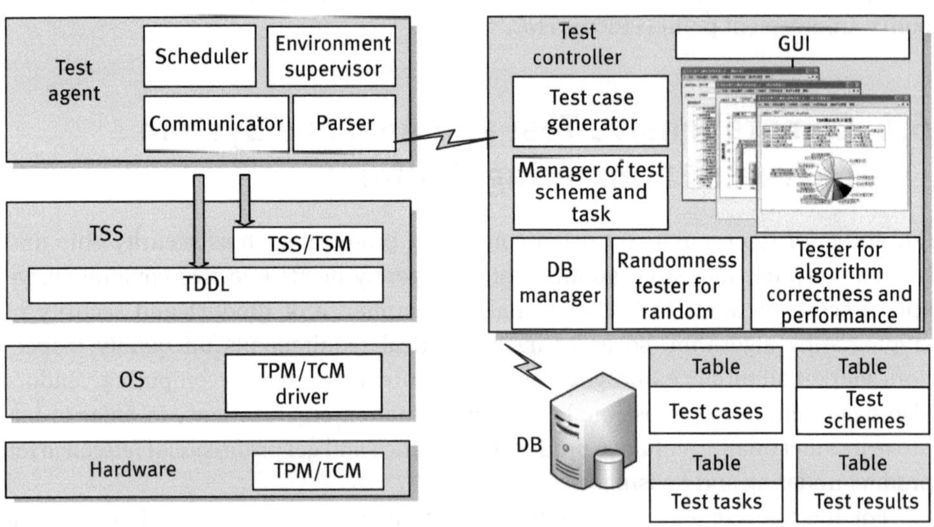

Figure 6.15: Architecture and interfaces of system.

and administration interfaces to test engineers. Supporting database independently stores test cases and test results needed in test work. The design of system aims at supporting simultaneously concurrent tests on several trusted computing products. It also significantly enhances the flexibility and elasticity of device deployment. All these features facilitate test work as much as possible.

- Test controller. Test controller is the center of the system. It is a cross-platform control tool that provides administration and control GUI to test engineers. On test controller, test engineers could carry out works like test case generation, test scheme and task management, test result analysis and test report generation. While test engineers assign any of these works, test controller conducts a concrete test activity by interacting with the test agent, that is, sending instructions to test agent, receiving and analyzing test results and generating test report. Test controller is also responsible for database management, namely, storing and retrieving test schemes, tasks, results and reports.
- Test agent. Test agent is the module to execute concrete test instructions. It is deployed on the platform to be tested, which supports TPM/TCM security function. On receiving test controller's test instructions, test agent invokes TSS or TDDL interfaces, completes actual tests and data collection of security chip and returns test results or collected data to test controller.
- Supporting database. Database is deployed on a dedicated database server, and is responsible for storing test cases, schemes, tasks and results.

Our system is implemented according to the above-mentioned architecture. It supports flexible and comprehensive test and evaluation upon TPM/TCM and trusted computers. Its functions include the following:

- Comprehensive compliance test for TPM/TCM and TSS/TSM specification. The system could conduct compliance test for specification upon all kinds of functions of TPM/TCM and TSS/TSM according to trusted computing specification. Composition of test cases can be flexibly adjusted according to test demands and desired reliability.
- Correctness and performance test of cryptography algorithm. By executing test cases that contain series of pre-defined test vectors for commands, the system could perform correctness and performance test upon various encryption and signing algorithms of security chips or algorithm libraries such as RSA, SM2 and SM4.
- Randomness test of randoms. The system could conduct tests on SHA1 and SM3 hash algorithms implemented by products. These tests are compliant to FIPS-140-2 specification, including frequency test, frequency in block test, runs test, poker test, matrix rank test, linear complexity test and approximate entropy test.
- Emulation of security chip and protocol. Through emulation of functions of security chip and environment of trusted computing protocols, the system provides effective and convenient emulation experiment environment for designers of

security chip and trusted computing protocols, which can be used to verify feasibility, security and performance of new functions, new protocols and new interfaces.

- Comprehensive analysis of test results. For results of any test task, the system not only provides original test logs but also various advanced statistics information of test. Users could select demonstration styles within multiple contents and layers and export reports in different formats.

6.4.2 Compliance Test for TPM/TCM Specification

Compliance test for TPM/TCM specification is one of the main functions of this system. This kind of test mainly relies on TPM-related specifications and Chinese domestic specification – Functionality and Interface Specification of Cryptographic Support Platform for Trusted Computing. The system is capable of doing compliance test upon logic relationship of inputs and outputs of most trusted computing commands. It can also conduct test upon data flow and control flow relationships of multiple commands. The test cases can either be generated manually by test engineers or be generated randomly by test system according to index of test quality designated by test engineers. This kind of test is a black box-type test, which is executed through invoking TSS/TSM software interfaces or TDDL interfaces.

Concrete execution of test task relies on the test agent that is deployed on the platform to be tested. Completely according to controller's instructions, the test agent is mainly responsible for initializing security chip (activating and enabling security chip and taking ownership), parsing instructions, carrying out concrete tests and returning results. Besides, because some test cases may influence each other and some even corrupt TPM (for example, after test command *TPM_SetStatus*, TPM may enter an idle state and not respond to any request), the test agent must monitor the state of test environment at real time, eliminate undesired influences between test cases and recover corrupted test environment. If some test cases cannot be executed due to the interference from external factors, the test agent must notify controller in time to get manual intervention.

Test control and administration relies on test controller, which is deployed upon control terminal. Test controller can generate and manage test cases, schemes and tasks, and is also responsible for demonstrating and exporting test results. The test cases can be divided into command-level class and function-level class. The former focuses on noncompliance of output parameters under correct and error input parameters of one command, and the latter concentrates on compliance of compound functions of multiple commands. A test scheme consists of several test cases, and typically represents a concrete test target in technical aspect. A test task is composed of a test scheme and concrete information of test object, test engineer and test conditions, and depicts all aspects of information about an independent test work. While starting a test work, test engineer can directly retrieve pre-stored test scheme from database, attach additional information and execute the test work using test task as a unit. The test results will be demonstrated as the test engineer has configured. Test engineer could query original test logs, such as input or output parameters of arbitrary commands in arbitrary test case, or directly lookup statistics of test result in figure or table mode, or export test result as a standard test report.

6.4.3 Tests of Cryptography Algorithms and Randoms

Cryptography algorithms test is a function specially developed for verifying security foundation of trusted platform. According to specifications about trusted computing and cryptography algorithms, the system could execute correctness and performance tests upon encryption and signing algorithms used by security chip and trusted software stack. The test is mainly composed of pre-defined test cases and executed in black box form. For SM2 and SM4 algorithms in TCM/TSM, the test cases are defined according to the following specifications: "Public Key Cryptographic Algorithm SM2 based on Elliptic Curves" and "SM4 Block cipher Algorithm" published by OSCCA. The system executes tests by invoking interfaces to do encryption, signing and hash computation on random messages and verifying correctness of the results. For RSA algorithms in TPM/TSS, including RSA-OAEP encryption and signing algorithm with standards of PKCS#11 v1.5 or PSS (Probabilistic Signature Scheme) padding, the test cases are generated according to corresponding specifications like RSA PKCS#1 and test vectors recommended by PKCS-related specifications. The test cases are executed in the same way as testing TCM/TSM.

In the aspect of randomness test of random, the system mainly tests SHA1 and SM3 hash algorithms implemented in products according to Chinese or international specifications. After retrieving 1,000 random files with length of 128 KB by invoking interfaces of product, test agents could execute more than ten kinds of tests on these files as follows:

- Frequency Test. This test judges whether probability distribution of random is uniform. Namely, the test collects statistics of bit0 and 1, and ideally the probability distribution of bit0 and 1 are identical.
- Frequency Test in Block. This test is similar to frequency test, but the concrete test target is a subset in random string with designated length but not the whole random string.
- Runs Test. This test examines runs of 0 and 1 in a target string. A run of 0 or 1 consists of several continuous 0 or 1 bits, and a run with length k includes k same bits.
- Longest Runs Test in Block. This test examines the longest run in a certain M-bits length block. Purpose of this test is to judge whether longest run in target bit string conforms to the situation of the whole random string.

- Poker Test. This test divides target strings into binary substrings with length m (m is arbitrary and there are 2^m kinds of possible substrings), and examines whether counts of these substrings are largely the same.
- Matrix Rank Test. This test examines rank of non-intersect submatrixes in target string, so as to check the linear correlation of fixed length substrings.
- Discrete Fourier Test. This test checks features of fast discrete Fourier transform. In detail, the test checks periodical feature of random string, and this kind of feature embodies the difference between ideal random and target string.
- General Statistical Test. This test examines the number of bits between different matching patterns, so as to check whether the target string can be significantly compressed without loss of any information. If so, the randomness of target string is poor.
- Linear Complexity Test. This test examines length of feedback register, so as to judge whether target string is complex enough to be considered as random. A feature of random string is that it has relatively long feedback register. On the contrary, a relatively short feedback register indicates relatively poor randomness.
- Approximate Entropy Test. This test examines overlapped m-bits patterns, so as to compare appearing frequency of overlapped blocks in two strings with adjacent length (e. g., two strings with length m and $m + 1$).
- Accumulation Sum Test. This test examines offset of accumulation relative to 0, so as to check whether accumulation sum of substring of target string is too large or too small compared to that of a random string.

6.4.4 Simulation of Security Chip and Protocol

Research of trusted computing technology is constantly emerging, and a mount of new protocols and mechanisms are published. These new research achievements often add new functions to current security chip or change internal function logic of current security chip. In this situation, we integrate simulation function of security chips and protocols into our system, so as to verify correctness and feasibility of these new achievements in software simulation and test their performance in different environments and parameters. These test results can provide valuable reference for further research.

In the aspect of security chip simulation, the system implements a simulation and management tool of security chip. This tool aims at providing a scalable customization function of TPM/TCM to researchers. In order to test trustworthiness and performance of new functions, researchers could get a new simulator with new functions by implementing new interfaces and corresponding functions and integrating them into emulator through appropriate configuration of management tool of security chip. In this way, researchers could add new functions to security chip without changing or recompiling original code. Hence, researchers could focus on their innovations on new protocols and functions, and efficiency of development and research will be significantly promoted.

In the aspect of protocol simulation, the system implements tests of security chip interfaces involved in protocols and analysis of protocol performance.

The first is test and evaluation on security chip interfaces in trusted computing protocols. Parts of interfaces of security chip are used in trusted computing protocols, which embody function of security chip in computation and communication of protocols. Security chip often plays important role in protocols, but its resource and computation capability is rather limited. Hence, the design of interfaces directly affects security and performance of protocols. Currently, we have implemented various new protocol schemes of DAA, PBA, trusted channel and trusted data distribution that have been proposed by academic fields in recent years. Based on the implementation, we have also verified implementation feasibility of interfaces in protocols, and evaluated influence of these interfaces on other functions of security chip.

The second is performance analysis of trusted computing protocols. As a relatively theoretical work, performance analysis of trusted computing protocols only considers quantity of pure algebraic computations. This work cannot embody complex factors that influence protocol's performance in practical environments. To solve this problem, our system integrates all kinds of parameters that will influence implementation of trusted computing protocols, including security level, algebraic structure (such as elliptic curve on which algebraic computation of protocol runs), basic cryptography algorithm (such as algorithms of encryption, signing and bilinear mappings) and running environment (such as the number of processing cores). Researchers could select appropriate parameters and test and simulate protocol performance conveniently and effectively. The test results will provide scientific basis and guidance to design and implementation of practical protocols.

6.4.5 Promotion and Application

The system has been promoted and applied in Chinese domestic governmental departments and vendors of trusted computing products. After several improvements and update, the system was formally accepted by Chinese supervision departments of cryptography-related products and vendors of trusted computing products in 2009. As far as we know, the system is the only practically applied test system for trusted computing platform and cryptography algorithms in China.

Up to now, the system has worked well on testing TCM products from major chip vendors and security computers from mainstream vendors in China. In these works, series of problems have been detected by our system, such as poor compliance and interoperability. Through feedback and communication with vendors, most of problems have been fixed in time. This process is of great importance for improving products' quality and avoiding negative influence of defects on products' availability

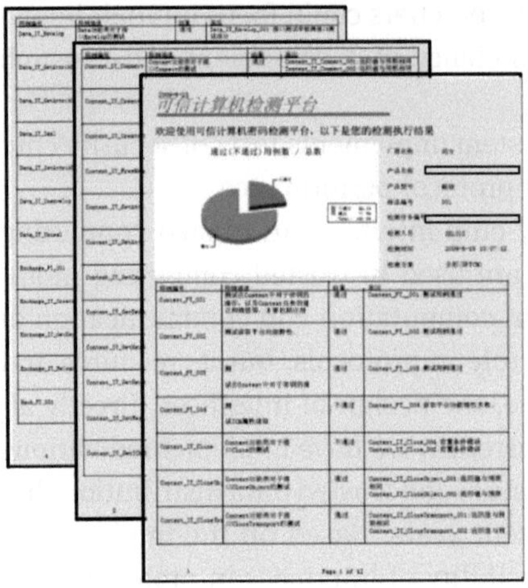

Mods	Cases	Err	Pass%
TCM	13	1	97
Cert	2	1	50
Key Mig	3	0	100
Enc	14	2	86
Sig	10	3	70
Hash	12	4	63
Other	24	4	83

Figure 6.16: Test results of some type of Chinese domestic TCM product.

and security. Problems of Chinese domestic trusted computing specifications have also been found in test. For example, parts of descriptions and regulations about key management, key certification, command audit, counter and locality are found to be incomplete and implicit. These findings provide concrete basis for improving and updating of specifications.

Figure 6.16 presents test results of some type of Chinese domestic TCM product and its corresponding TSM. The left graphs are test reports exported by system in default format. These reports record all original information about test tasks and execution results of each test case. From the reports, errors can be concluded as shown in the right graph. The detected errors cover nearly all function modules of the TCM and TSM, and most of the errors are led by implementation with poor compliance (logic of functions are not compliant to specifications) and incompleteness (part of functions defined in specifications are not implemented). The main errors are as follows:

- Incomplete support for command parameters. For example, all the TCM products in earliest work do not support all parameters of *Tspi_TCM_GetCapability()* in specification. Similar to this, some vendors restrict format or length of part of input parameters, which makes valid inputs to be rejected by TCM.
- Deviation in comprehending specification. For example, due to deviation in comprehending specification, some vendors confuse the usage of „*rgbExternalData*" and „*rgbValdationData*" domains in „*pValidataionData*" parameter of *Tspi_TCM_Quote()*, and swap their functions in design and implementation.
- Poor robustness of functions. This kind of error influences reliability of trusted computing application. For example, specification specifies that a „NULL" value of parameter „*rgbMemory*" of *Tspi_Context_FreeMemory()* indicates that memory

space bound to context has been released. But in some TSM products, TSM process cannot handle this case and even falls into memory error and immediate crash.

Implicit descriptions and definitions of Chinese domestic trusted computing specifications, have also been found in test. Some of these problems are listed below.

- In the aspect of key management, the specification specifies that in some situation TSM key object could be used without any authorization data. This facilitates TSM users, but brings potential security vulnerabilities. We have found that some vendors in our test work do not obey this rule in implementation for better security.
- In the aspect of locality, the specification has not defined format of parameter „*localityValue*" of *Tspi_PcrComposite_SetPcrLocality()*, and different vendors adopt different formats.
- In the aspect of command audit, the specification specifies that *Tspi_TCM_GetAuditDigest()* should return "number of commands to be audited." This implicit description leads to different explanations. Some products generate only one audit record when same command executes several times, but others generate multiple audit records for multiple executions of the same command.

6.5 Summary

Research of test and evaluation of trusted computing mainly focuses on compliance test for TPM/TCM specification, analysis of trusted protocols and mechanisms and certification and evaluation of products. In the aspect of compliance test for TPM/TCM specification, current works typically model security chip based on FSM theory, automatically generate test cases based on the model and perform test work. In the aspects of analysis of protocols and mechanisms, current works often adopt formal methods, such as model checking, programming logic, belief logic and logic of secure system, to verify various security properties of DAA, authorization protocols and process of establishing chain of trust. In the aspect of product evaluation and certification, TCG has issued projects to evaluate TPM and TNC products according to common criteria and achieved comprehensive conclusion about product security. To meet requirements of test and evaluation on trusted computing products, we have implemented a comprehensive test and analysis system for trusted computing platform. This system integrates functions like compliance test for TPM/TCM specification, correctness and performance test on cryptography algorithms, randomness test of random and analysis and simulation of trusted computing protocols. Currently, the system has already been put into practice and is widely accepted.

Test and evaluation of trusted computing are of great importance for improvement of product quality, advance of related technology, healthy development of industry and enhancement of Chinese information security. But as mentioned in Chapter 1, current research works on test and evaluation of trusted computing is relatively scarce, and they are required to be improved in both aspects of coverage and deepness. First, test and evaluation of trusted computing lags behind trusted computing technology. There are few effective methods to examine security and reliability properties of latest trusted computing technology, such as dynamic root of trust and ARM TrustZone. Second, existing methods focus on relatively simple products and mechanisms, which are components but not the whole computing platform. In other words, research on overall security of complex target, such as trusted computing platform or trusted execution environment, is the blank condition. Third, products or mechanisms like chain of trust lack corresponding specifications, thus they can hardly been tested or analyzed.

7 Remote Attestation

Remote attestation is one of the most important functionalities of the trusted computing. The Trusted Platform Module (TPM)/Trusted Cryptography Module (TCM) user can complete the attestation of the trusted computing platform identity and the platform configuration integrity by using security chip. From a certain point of view, even the TPM/TCM can be regarded as a dedicated security chip to do remote attestation. Remote attestation can attest the hardware, firmware and software of the trusted computing platform. It can attest all the softwares running on every layer of the software stack, and even the running states of the virtual machine on the platform in communication with the remote verifier. Remote attestation can attest both the identity of the security chip and the platform states at the same time, which greatly improves the security of the network communication terminals.

Remote attestation is the extension of the trust of the trusted computing platform from the terminal to the network. In practice, it can satisfy the security requirements of the users in many aspects: (1) It can help determine whether or not the computing platform in communication is trusted, namely whether or not it can support the trusted computing capabilities. (2) It can help detect the integrity of the input and output of the softwares running in the platform as well as the platform configuration. (3) It can help verify whether or not the current platform configuration satisfies the verifier security policy. Remote attestation can be widely used in PC, network servers, embedded devices, mobile Internet, cloud computing and other different environments. It is one of the most important applications of the trusted computing.

In a narrow sense, the remote attestation refers to the attestation of the platform integrity of the current platform configuration and the running state by the TPM/TCM security chip, but in practice, the trusted computing platform will inevitably attest the platform identity in the attestation of the platform configuration. Therefore, the platform identity based on TPM/TCM can also be included in the category of the remote attestation. Remote attestation can be divided into two categories according to the different attested objectives, namely the Attestation of Platform Integrity and the Attestation of Identity. There is also a more generalized interpretation of the remote attestation. It includes the attestation of all the entities in the trusted computing platform. In addition to the identity and integrity, the attestations of the key and data in the trusted computing platform are also regarded as the remote attestation. For example, the key certification is to attest that the key is generated by the TPM chip and it is bound with the TPM. The Subject Key Attestation Evidence (SKAE) is the mechanism to attest the key source (can be seen as the key identity), and to support the subject key certificate extension. The certification of data unsealing requires the configuration state for unsealing the data is the same to that for sealing data. It essentially attests that the current configuration state is exactly the same to that for the unsealing and can be regarded as the attestation of the use of data. These are both the extension of the remote attestation semantics and belong to the category of the

DOI 10.1515/9783110477597-007

generalized attestation of the trusted computing platform. However, in this chapter we use the common classification of the remote attestations and divide them into the attestations of platform integrity and identity to discuss.

7.1 Remote Attestation Principle

Remote attestation is an advanced security service provided by the TPM/TCM security chip. It needs the auxiliary supports of other basic functions such as key management and integrity measurement. In general, the remote attestation principle is to outline the procedure of attestation from the macroscopic view, but in this section, we will give a comprehensive introduction of the detailed remote attestation principle from the view of the foundation, the protocol, the interfaces and other aspects.

7.1.1 Technology Foundation

Remote attestation involves what the content in the platform is to be attested and how to attest by the TPM/TCM. These are the technology foundations for the remote attestation (or the necessary conditions). TPM/TCM security chip must provide these basic functions to support attestation. Integrity measurement and quoting of the identity key are the two most critical basic security functions. Integrity measurement and reporting are to solve the problem of what to be attested. The TPM/TCM identity keys and quoting are to solve the problem of how to attest.

7.1.1.1 Integrity Measurement

Integrity measurement is the process for the TPM/TCM security chip to acquire the platform software and hardware characteristic values of trust degree. Usually, these values are extended into the Platform Configuration Registers (PCRs) in the form of digests. The starting point of the integrity measurement is called the Root of Trust for Measurement (RTM), which is located within the TPM/TCM security chip, and is trust by default. When the computer starts, the trusted computing platform begins to execute the integrity measurement process. From BIOS, bootloader, OS to the applications, each entity will be measured by the TPM/TCM. For every measurement, the security chip will create a measurement event, which contains the measured values (characteristic value of the executed program code or the data) and the measurement digest (the hash value of the characteristic value), which is extended into the PCRs. The measurement event$e$, which is caused by any changes in the integrity at any system layer, will inevitably make the system transit from one trusted state to another trusted state. For example, $S_i \rightarrow^{e_{i+1}} S_{i+1} \cdots \rightarrow^{e_{i+j}} S_{i+j}$ represents the sequence of events $e_{i+1}, e_{i+2}, \ldots, e_{i+j}$, which lead to the transitions of the state sequence $S_{i+1}, S_{i+2}, \ldots, S_{i+j}$. If S_i and each measurement event e is known to be trusted, the state sequence is transited from S_i to S_j, the final state S_j is trusted.

By using the integrity measurement, the trusted computing platform can record the integrity states of the executions of all modules (hardware and software) in the platform to build the chain of trust of the trusted computing platform. If there is any module that has been maliciously infected, its digest value must be changed so that we can know which module in the system has problems. The integrity measurement values need to be stored following a specific format, which forms the storage measurement list (SML). The list might be very large and need to be stored outside the security chip. It records all the integrity measurement events during the system startup and running. Based on SML, the TPM/TCM chip can attest the integrity configurations and running states of the trusted computing platform identified by SML.

7.1.1.2 Platform Identity Key Quote

TPM/TCM security chip supports multiple key types. TPM defines seven key types including the signing key, the storage key, the identity key, the endorsement key (EK), the binding key, the migratable key and the certified key. Although the TCM adopts different cryptographic algorithms, it also defines the similar key types. Among these key types, only the platform identity key (PIK) can be used for remote attestation. The PIK in the TPM specification is called the attestation identity key (AIK), and is called the PIK) in the TCM specification. AIK is an RSA key and PIK is an elliptic curve cryptology (ECC) key. Except for these key types, they are the same for the other aspects.

The PIK can only be created and used by the trusted computing platform owner. Common users can neither use the PIK nor do the remote attestation. The TPM owner can use the command *TPM_MakeIdentity* to create the AIK with the type of identity key. This key can be used to do remote attestation by signing the TPM internal PCRs. In addition, when used in the remote attestation, the AIK should be used with the AIK certificate. Thus the TPM specification specifies that the trusted third-party Privacy CA can issue the AIK certificate. The certificate can be imported into the platform for use through the TPM command *TPM_ActivateIdentity*. In the remote attestation, the remote verifier usually determines the TPM identity by checking the validity of the AIK certificate. Then it can verify the signature in the TPM remote attestation by using the public key of the AIK, and finally complete the integrity verification.

The signing process of TPM remote attestation is also called PIK quote. TPM uses the command *TPM_Quote* to sign the integrity measurement value stored in the internal PCR. Before the remote attestation, the TPM owner first loads the PIK AIK. When the verifier starts the remote attestation challenge, the TPM owner chooses the PCR to be attested which represents the platform integrity. Then the owner inputs the challenge nonce and the selected PCR to invoke the TPM command *TPM_Quote*. The TPM outputs the signature of the corresponding remote attestation. The detailed process will be given in the following interface implementation (Section 7.1.3) of the remote attestation.

7.1.2 Protocol Model

Remote attestation is achieved by the attestation protocol based on the TPM/TCM cryptographic functions. Although there are a variety of different specific protocols, they all have a unified protocol model. In this section, we will take as an example the most basic remote attestation based on AIK to discuss the remote attestation protocol model. In the remote attestation model, the main participants include the trusted computing platform, the remote verifier and the trusted third party. It is presented in Figure 7.1.

- The trusted computing platform includes the TPM/TCM security chip and the host, which together complete the attestation of the platform integrity. The host is mainly to measure and report the platform integrity, and the TPM/TCM security chip is mainly to generate signature in the remote attestation.
- The remote verifier is the challenger of the remote attestation. It requests the trusted computing platform to attest the integrity states of the current system, and according to the corresponding verification policy it verifies the trusted computing platform integrity log and the signature from the security chip. Before the remote attestation, it must obtain the public key of the AIK and the trusted third party, in order to ensure the trusted relationship between the participants of remote attestation and to prevent that the attacker forges the identity to deceive other participants.
- The trusted third party in the basic remote attestation protocol is the Privacy CA. It issues the certificate for the identity key of trusted computing platform and provides checking of the validation of the certificates. When the trusted third party issues the AIK certificate for the trusted computing platform, it must verify the EK of the TPM/TCM chip so as to ensure the authenticity of the TPM/TCM identity.

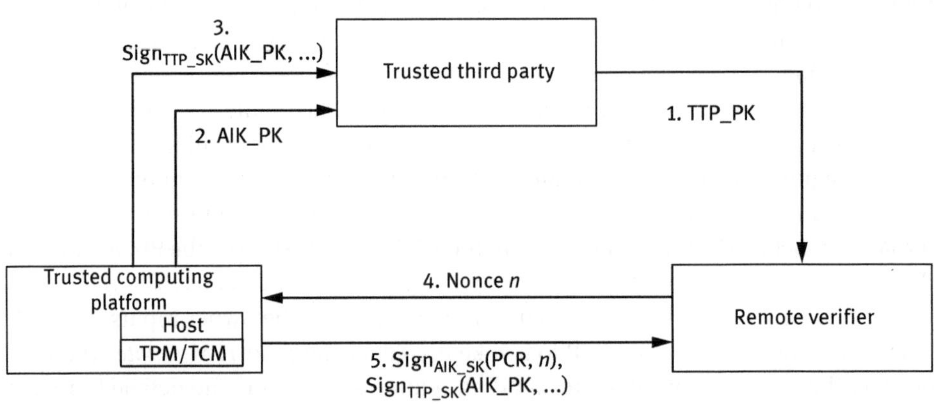

Figure 7.1: Remote attestation model.

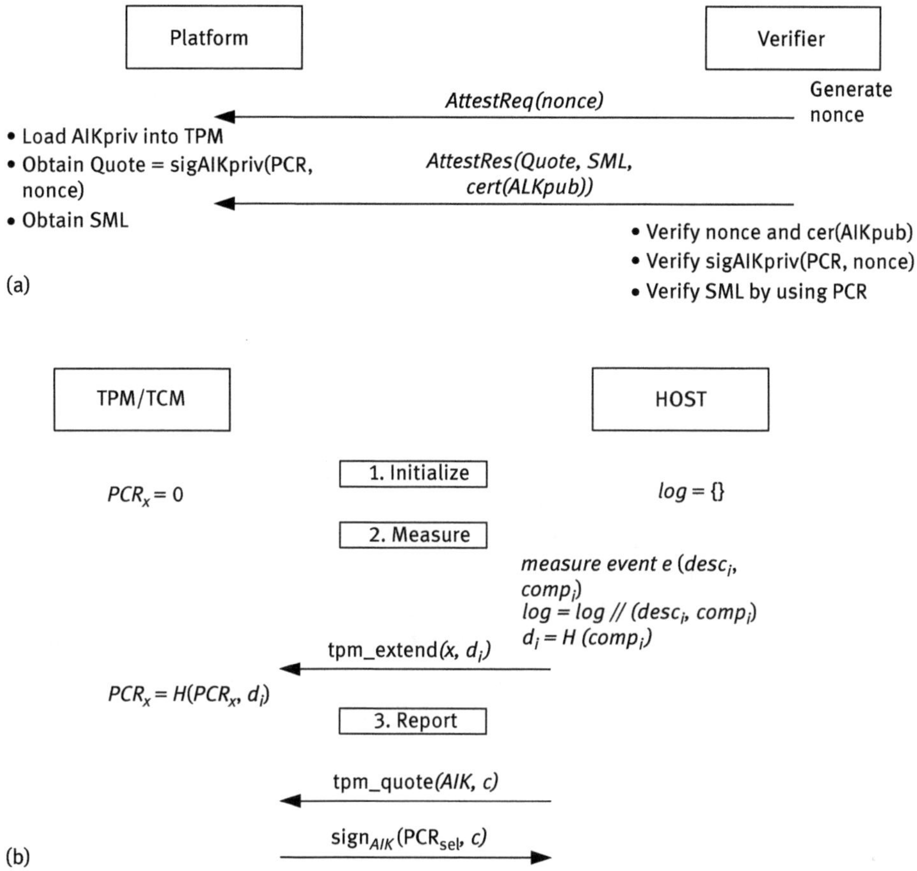

Figure 7.2: Remote attestation process: (a) protocol process between trusted computing platform and verifier and (b) protocol process in trusted computing platform.

The core step of the remote attestation occurs between the trusted computing platform and the remote verifier. It is a typical two-party protocol that is composed of the remote challenge request *AttestReq (nonce)* and the response *AttestRes (quote, SML, cert (AIKpub))*. The detailed process is shown in Figure 7.2: Figure 7.2(a) describes the main steps of the trusted computing platform and the verifier; Figure 7.2(b) describes the process of the attestation in the trusted computing platform between the host and the TPM/TCM, where log is the SML, x denotes the index of the extended PCR and *comp* denotes the measured components.

7.1.3 Interface Implementation

Remote attestation is achieved by using the TPM/TCM security chip to sign the platform integrity value (represented by PCR). The security chip interface to complete the remote attestation is *TPM_Quote*. The TPM security chip provides a variety of different layers of operation interfaces, mainly including the TPM kernel driver interface, TDDL interface, Trusted Core Service (TCS) service layer interface and TSPI application layer interface. The interfaces for each layer can realize the function of quote. TPM_Quote is the command interface that can be directly identified and executed by the TPM security chip. The other interfaces, such as TDDL, TCS and TSPI, only provide the package of this command function. For example, *Tspi_TPM_Quote* is the packaging application interface of *TPM_Quote* by the TSPI layer. Except the differences in the uses and the interface names, the principles of the interface Quote are exactly the same. The interface of the upper layer is easy to use and that of the lower layer requires complex settings.

TPM_Quote is essentially the process of signing TPM internal PCR by using the identity key AIK and then outputting the signature of quote. The outputting signature contains two parts: the original message *QuoteInfo* and the signature *SignatureOnQuoteInfo*. The command TPM_Quote can be described as *SignedInfo* = *QuoteInfo* || *SignatureOnQuoteInfo* = *TPM_Quote(selectedPCR, serverNonce)*. Its interface diagram (Figure 7.3) is described as follows.

The first part of the TPM_Quote signed message *QuoteInfo* is a 48-byte data object which has the data structure *TPM_QUOTE_INFO*. The second part *SignatureOnQuoteInfo* is a 256-byte digital signature on *QutoeInfo* which follows the format RSASSA-PKCS1-v1.5, namely the signature result of the selected PCR by using the private key of AIK.

```
Type defstructtdTPM_QUOTE_INFO{
TPM_STRUCT_VER version;
BYTE fixed[4];
TPM_COMPOSITE_HASH digestValue;
TPM_NONCE externalData;
} TPM_QUOTE_INFO;
```

The specific meaning of each item in the data structure *TPM_QUOTE_INFO* of *QuoteInfo* is as follows:

Figure 7.3: TPM_Quote interface.

- The item *version* denotes the version number of the TCG (Trusted Computing Group) specification. If it follows the TPM specification v1.1, the two bytes of version are defined as 0×01 and 0×01. For the TPM specification v1.2, they are 0×01 and 0×02.
- The item *fixed* is a default value, filled as the ASCII strings of "QUOT."
- The item *digestValue* contains the SHA1 digest values of all the selected PCR values with the data structure *TPM_PCR_COMPOSITE*.
- The item *externalData* denotes the challenge nonce sent by the verifier, which is a 160-bit nonce (in the form of the output strings of the SHA1 algorithm).

When the remote verifier receives the attestation message *SignedInfo* = *QuoteInfo* || *SignatureOnQuoteInfo*, it first divides *SignedInfo* into two parts and does the verification as follows:

(1) It verifies whether *QuoteInfo* is the valid data structure of TPM_QUOTE_INFO. It needs to check whether the item *version* meets the requirement of the TCG and the item *fixed* is a default ASCII string of "QUOT."
(2) It verifies whether the item *externalData*in*QuoteInfo* is the same with the nonce used as the challenge nonce by the verifier.
(3) It uses the public key certificate of AIK to verify whether *SignatureOnQuoteInfo* is a signature of *QuoteInfo*.

For the command *TPM_Quote*, we have implemented the corresponding interface in remote attestation system prototype. The followings are the codes of the *TPM_Quote* interface by using the Java. It performs the following *TPM_Quote* interface to output the TPM remote attestation signature.

```
import iscas.tcwg.attestation.tpm.TPMConst;
importiscas.tcwg.attestation.tpm.struct.*;
importiscas.tcwg.attestation.util.*;

// TPMOSAPSession is associated
public class TPM_Quote extends TPMCommandAuth1
{
private intkeyHandle;
private TPM_NonceexternalData = null;
private TPM_PCR_SelectionpcrSel = null;

// sel = 0x0000ff select pcr0-pcr7
public TPM_Quote(TPMOSAPSession session, intkeyHandle,
   intsel,
```

```
 TPM_NoncesNonce) {
      super(session, TPMConst.TPM_TAG_RQU_AUTH1_COMMAND,
           TPMConst.TPM_ORD_Quote);
this.keyHandle = keyHandle;
this.externalData = new TPM_Nonce(sNonce);
this.pcrSel = new TPM_PCR_Selection(sel);
this.auth1 = computeAuth1();
      intlen = TPMConst.TPM_COMMAND_HEADER_SIZE +
               computeBodyLength(this.keyHandle,
               this.externalData, this.pcrSel,
               this.authHandle, this.nonceOdd,
               this.continueAuthSession, this.auth1);
setParamSize(len);
}
// Override TPMCommand interface
public byte[] toBytes() {
      Debug.println("keyHandle = " +
                 EncodeUtil.to32HexString(this.keyHandle));
      Debug.println("Server Nonce = " +
                 EncodeUtil.toHexString(this.externalData.
                 toBytes ()));
      Debug.println("TPM_PCR_SELECTION : " +
                 EncodeUtil.toHexString(this.pcrSel.
                 toBytes()));
      Debug.println("authHandle = " +
                 EncodeUtil.to32HexString(this.authHandle));
 return CreateCommandBlob(this.keyHandle, this.externalData,
this.pcrSel,
  this.authHandle, this.nonceOdd, this.continueAuthSession,
 this.auth1);
 }

 public void fromBytes(byte[] source, int offset) {
  super.fromBytes(source, offset); // parse the Header
    and Auth1
Block
 // other body field
```

```
int off = offset + TPMConst.TPM_COMMAND_HEADER_SIZE;
this.keyHandle = ByteArrayUtil.ReadUInt32LE(source, off);
off += 4;
      byte[] nonce = ByteArrayUtil.ReadBytes(source, off,
 TPM_Digest.TPM_DIGEST_SIZE);
 off += TPM_Digest.TPM_DIGEST_SIZE;
 if(this.externalData == null) {
  externalData = new TPM_Nonce(nonce);
 }
 else {
  externalData.fromBytes(nonce, 0);
 }
      byte[] bytePCRSel = ByteArrayUtil.ReadBytes(source,
        off, TPM_Digest. TPM_DIGEST_SIZE);
 if(this.pcrSel == null) {
  pcrSel = new TPM_PCR_Selection(bytePCRSel);
 }
 else {
  pcrSel.fromBytes(bytePCRSel, 0);
  }
 }
 private byte[] computeParamDigest() {
  byte[] ord = ByteArrayUtil.toBytesUInt32BE(this.
    getOrdinal());
  byte[] nonce = this.externalData.toBytes();
  byte[] pcrSelBytes = this.pcrSel.toBytes();
  byte[] paramAuth = null;
  paramAuth = CryptoUtil.computeSHA1Hash(ord, nonce,
    pcrSelBytes);
  return paramAuth;
 }
 private byte[] concatAuthSetupParam() {
  byte[] even = this.authSession1.getNonceEven().toBytes();
  byte[] odd = this.nonceOdd.toBytes();
  byte[] c =
    ByteArrayUtil.toBytesBoolean(this.continueAuthSession);
```

```
  return CryptoUtil.byteArrayConcat(even, odd, c);
 }

 // implement TPMCommandAuth1
 public TPM_AuthData computeAuth1() {
  TPM_Secretss = ((TPMOSAPSession) authSession1)
    .getSharedSecret();
  byte[] p1 = computeParamDigest();
  byte[] p2 = concatAuthSetupParam();
  byte[] auth = CryptoUtil.computeTpmHmac(ss, p1, p2);
  return new TPM_AuthData(auth);
 }

 public boolean verifyAuth1(TPM_AuthDataauth) {
  TPM_AuthDatacurAuth = computeAuth1();
  if (curAuth.toBytes().equals(auth.toBytes())) {
   return true;
 } else {
  return false;
 }
 }
}
```

7.2 Comparison of Remote Attestation Researches

Based on the TPM/TCM security chip, the remote attestation mechanism achieves the attestation of the platform identity and integrity state. It is an important technological method to assure the trust of the platform computing environment and to enhance the security of network communications. The security problems in the remote attestation that need to be solved are in many aspects. Its main security goals are to ensure the unforgeability (authenticity) of attestation of the platform identity and integrity, and to assure that the platform identity and the platform integrity configuration cannot be leaked (anonymity/privacy). Moreover, it needs to prevent TOCTOU (time of check/time of use) attacks, replay attacks, man-in-the-middle attacks, etc. To solve these problems, many researchers in different institutions have conducted in-depth researches, put forward some innovations to solve the security issues and achieved a lot of research results.

7.2.1 Attestation of Platform Identity

The main method to attest platform identity is to certify that the trusted computing platform is a communication entity whose identity can be trusted by remote verifier through a series of platform-related certificates. The identity of the trusted computing platform is identified by the TPM EK credential. The role of the credential is to provide the evidence that a legitimate TPM has been embedded into the trusted computing platform, and to show the binding relationship between the security chip and the platform. The direct use of EK credential for remote attestation can obviously disclose the platform identity. Thus in the TCG specification, it uses the method based on the trusted third-party Privacy CA to help TPM complete the attestation of platform identity and avoid the platform identity leakage. The attestation method based on Privacy CA is to identify the identity by issuing the AIK certificate for the TPM identity key. In the attestation, the verifier needs to confirm the correctness of the AIK identity with Privacy CA. This method requires an online CA. Compared with the commonly used offline CA, it needs a high level of trust assurance and requires a higher security level of CA.

In 2004, Brickell et al. proposed the TPM-based Direct Anonymous Attestation (DAA) scheme [21]. It adopts the zero-knowledge proof, group signature and other cryptographic techniques to anonymously attest platform identity. Through the DAA signature, the remote verifier can confirm that the party in communication is a genuine trusted computing platform embedded with a legitimate TPM. It can also avoid the disclosure of the platform authentic identity. DAA currently has been accepted as part of the TCG TPM v1.2 specification, and the TPM chips have supported the DAA protocol. However, since the original DAA scheme uses too many zero-knowledge proofs, it has high complexity in the implementation and its practical applications are infeasible. Therefore, many researchers have put forward the continuous improvement and innovation of the DAA scheme and proposed many improved schemes [22, 24, 26, 29, 133, 134].

He et al. proposed an improved DAA scheme [22] for embedded devices. Since the DAA scheme based on the RSA cryptosystem has the disadvantages that the signature length is long and the efficiency is low, Brickel et al. proposed the first DAA scheme [24] based on ECC and bilinear map. It adopts the LRSW assumptions and the CL-LRSW signature. Both its computation efficiency and communication performance have been greatly improved. Subsequently, Feng et al. also proposed an improved DAA scheme [26] based on the q-SDH assumption and the BBS+ signature, which further improves the computation and communication efficiency. In recent years, Chen et al. have performed an in-depth research on DAA. By using new cryptographic assumptions and the optimization method, they fully studied the possibility of protocol improvement and promoted the protocol computational optimization to a higher level [29, 134].

Table 7.1 lists the comparison of several representative schemes. The latest DAA schemes have experienced a very large increase in the computational efficiency. In the

Table 7.1: Comparison of direct anonymous attestation schemes.

Scheme	Subprotocol	Computation cost		Signature length	Security assumption
		TPM	Host		
BCC04	Join	$3G_p+2G_N$^3	$1G_p+1G_N$^2+P_v	20555 bits	Strong RSA, DDH
	Sign/Ver	$3G_p+1G_N$^3	1 $G_p+1G_N+1G_N$^2+2 G_N^3+ $1G_N$^4		
BCL08	Join	$3G_1$	6P	7584 bits	LRSW, DBDH
	Sign/Ver	$3G_T$	$3G_1+1G_T+3P$		
CF08	Join	$3G_1$^2+$1G_2$+2P	2P	8352 bits	q-SDH, DDH
	Sign/Ver	$2G_1+1G_T$^2	$1G_1+2G_1$^2+$1G_1$ ^3+$1G_T$^3		
Ch09	Join	$2G_1$	$1G_1$+2P	1952 bits	q-SDH, DDH
	Sign/Ver	$2G_1+1G_T$	$1G_1+1G_T$^3		
CPS10	Join	$3G_1$	1P^4	1952 bits	LRSW, DDH
	Sign/Ver	$3G_1$	$4G_1$		
BL10	Join	$2G_1$	$1G_2$+2P	1952 bits	q-SDH, DDH
	Sign/Ver	$3G_1$	$1G_1+1G_T$^3		

development of DAA researches, the main idea of the improvements is to use the latest elliptic curve cryptosystem to improve the DAA signing efficiency based on bilinear map. It reduces the computation cost of DAA Join and Sign, especially the cost of the TPM chip. At the same time, it reduces the DAA signature length so as to adapt to the bandwidth of the mobile and wireless network environments.

7.2.2 Attestation of Platform Integrity

Based on the security chip TPM/TCM, the basic way to attest the platform integrity is the TCG binary remote attestation. In it, the TPM uses the AIK to sign the PCR values which represents the platform integrity, and then sends to the remote verifier the TPM signature and the integrity measurement log in order to attest the current running state of the platform. IBM Integrity Measurement Architecture (IMA) and tcglinux system [135] are based on this idea to implement the binary remote attestation system. The binary attestation mechanism has many disadvantages. On the one hand, it discloses the local software and hardware configuration information of the trusted computing platform, which somewhat makes the platform more vulnerable to various attacks. On the other hand, the problem is the diversity of the platform state information. Considering that the types and versions of the system softwares and hardwares are varied, and the system needs to be updated, it is very difficult to check the validity of the system integrity configuration in practice.

In order to overcome the shortcomings of the binary remote attestation mechanism, in 2004, Sadeghi and Stüble of Ruhr University Bochum in Germany adopt the idea of integrity and property mappings to propose the property-based attestation (PBA) [32]. Then IBM proposed the implementation of PBA [31]. In 2006, Chen et al. proposed the first PBA protocol [33]. It gave out the theoretical method to achieve the concrete PBA protocol, and thus began a more in-depth study on PBA. Through the definition of the trusted computing platform security properties, PBA can give out the mappings between the platform configurations and properties. In the remote attestation, it directly attests the properties and their mappings so as to avoid the disclosure of the specific platform configurations. Among the remote attestation methods, PBA overcomes several faults of the original remote attestation, such as high complexity, leakage of privacy and abuse of the attestation results. It is the most promising and practical method to do the remote attestation.

Researchers have focused on the extension of the PBA protocols and proposed the PBA without the trusted third-party issued property certificates (referred to as PBA-RS protocol [34]). It uses the ring signature to attest that the target platform configurations and states meet the verifier's requirements. It does not need the support of the trusted third party and protects the privacy of platform. The general way of PBA is to attest the commitments on platform configuration based on the property certificates by using the zero-knowledge proof method. However, they are all based on an offline trusted third party. The verification of the property revocation is complex and the attestation efficiency is not high enough. Chinese researchers have carried out in-depth study [67, 69]. By fining the granularity, they proposed the component property-based remote attestation [69]. This method is adapted to the small-scale computing environment. It is easy to issue, verify and revoke the property certificates. According to the features of the TCM security chip, the property-based remote attestation protocol based on bilinear mapping [67] was proposed to further reduce the computation cost of the PBA protocol and the signature length of the property attestation.

In the implementation of PBA, researchers in Ruhr University Bochum use the property certificate issued by the online trusted third party to convert the binary measurement value in boot to properties [35], and achieve the system attestation and scaling based on the properties. The study is based on the online trusted third party, which is convenient for the integrity management and security property management. It uses the Certificate Revocation List (CRL) to validate the revocation of the properties. However, it lacks the practical protocol to protect the privacy of the platform configurations.

In addition to the researches on binary attestation and property-based attestation, there are some other works on the semantics and the specific application scenarios of the remote attestation. In the extension study of remote attestation semantics, Haldar et al. proposed the semantic remote attestation [36]. Its basic idea is to use a language-based trusted virtual machine and achieve the attestation by checking the security policy of the running code in the virtual machine. However, the trusted virtual machine still needs the support of binary attestation. Researchers in Carnegie Mellon University proposed a fine-grained attestation [12] which can dynamically attest the program code semantics by using the secure kernel provided by the CPU. This method has the obvious advantage for the attestation of the sensitive kernel. Moreover, it solves the problem of TOCTOU. Zhang et al. proposed the behavioral attestation [136], which is based on the access control policy and system semantics of usage control (UCON) policy. It is suitable to the checking and verification of the subject behaviors in the policy model. In specific application scenarios of the remote attestation, the works are quite rich. We do not list them here. The representative works include the software-based attestation for embedded devices [37], attestation for Web Service [137], etc.

7.3 Attestation of Platform Identity

7.3.1 Attestation of Platform Identity Based on Privacy CA

Attestation of platform identity is to attest the authentic identity of trusted computing platform by using the identity credential. In general, the identity of trusted computing platform is identified by the security chip, namely the attestation of platform identity is essentially the authentication of the identity of the TPM/TCM security chip. Among the many attestation methods of platform identity, the widely accepted and the most practical method is the attestation based on Privacy CA. Since it is compatible with the existing PKI authentication architecture and has advantages of convenient deployment and simple operation, many solutions based on security chips utilize this method to attest platform identity.

In TCG Privacy CA-based attestation architecture, the platform is identified by the TPM EK. Once this key is disclosed, the platform identity will be completely exposed. Thus TCG does not adopt the attestation based on EK. Instead, it uses the identity key AIK as the alias of EK to authenticate the identity. Even in this way, Privacy CA-based attestation method with the assistance of the trusted third party just reduces the risk of leaking the privacy of platform identity. However, this method does not guarantee the privacy of the platform identity. Attestation of platform identity based on Privacy CA can be divided into two main processes: issuing the platform identity certificate and attestation of the platform identity.

7.3.1.1 Issuing Platform Identity Certificate

When the TPM owner purchases a trusted computing platform, the TPM does not have an identity. The TPM owner must apply for the platform identity from a trusted third-party Privacy CA to obtain the platform identity certificate. Its main steps are as follows (Figure 7.4):

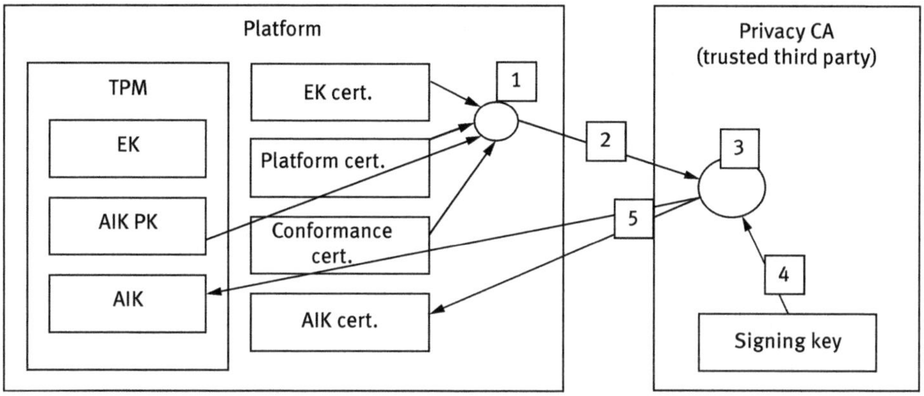

Figure 7.4: Issuing process of platform identity certificate.

(1) The TPM owner uses the TPM security chip to create an RSA key with the key type of identity key (i. e. AIK). Then he executes the command *TPM_MakeIdentity* to wrap the public key of AIK, the EK certificate, the platform certificate and the conformance certificate.
(2) The trusted computing platform sends these wrapped data to the Privacy CA as an application for the AIK certificate.
(3) Privacy CA verifies the application for AIK certificate by authenticating the certificates such as the EK certificate and the platform certificate.
(4) Privacy CA uses its own signing key to sign the AIK certificate and uses the public key of EK to encrypt the AIK certificate.
(5) Privacy CA sends to the TPM the response of the AIK certificate. The TPM owner executes the command *TPM_ActivateIdentity* to decrypt and obtain the AIK certificate.

After the trusted computing platform obtains the AIK certificate, the TPM can use the AIK and the AIK certificate to attest the platform identity. Then it has the capability to attest the platform integrity, namely the capability to do remote attestation.

7.3.1.2 Attestation of Platform Identity

The main steps for the attestation of the platform identity are as follows (Figure 7.5):
(1) The owner of platform A sends a request of attestation to the platform B.
(2) The platform B sends to the platform A the challenge nonce and specifies the selected PCR to be attested.
(3) The owner of platform A loads the AIK and then uses the private key of AIK to sign the selected PCR value.
(4) Platform A sends to the verifier of platform B the remote attestation signature and the integrity log.

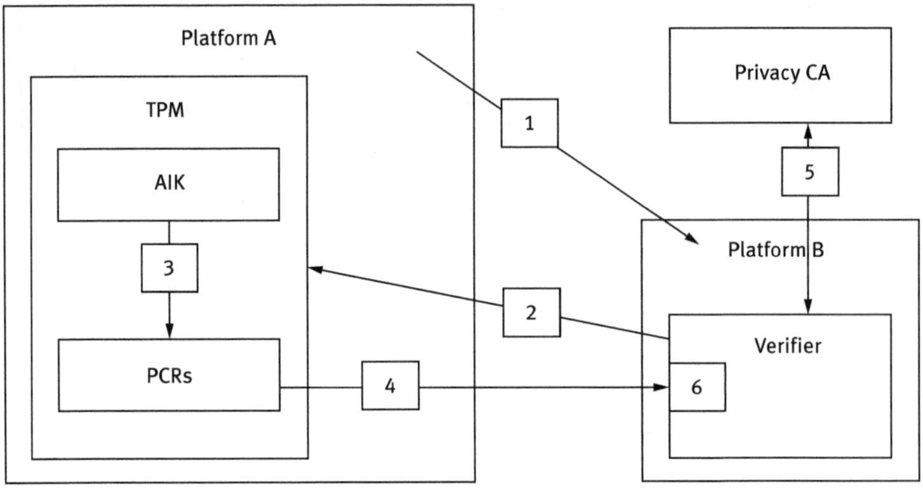

Figure 7.5: Attestation of platform identity.

(5) Platform B sends a request to Privacy CA to query whether or not the identity of the TPM in platform A is trusted.
(6) Platform B verifies the remote attestation signature of platform A, as well as the platform configuration integrity log.

The last two steps of the platform identity attestation achieve both the authentication of the platform identity and the evaluation of the trustworthiness of the platform environment configurations. This ensures the trustworthiness of the platform identity and the platform states for both sides, and helps to enhance the ability to resist a variety of malicious software. Since a trusted computing platform can theoretically generate an infinite number of AIKs and certificates, when the trusted computing platform is in communication, only the trusted third-party Privacy CA knows the authentic identity of the user. The verifier does not know it. Thus, to some extent, it reduces the exposure of the privacy of platform identity. However, it does not achieve completely anonymity.

7.3.2 Direct Anonymous Attestation

Although attestation based on the Privacy CA provides a certain degree of the privacy protection of platform identity, the privacy CA knows the TPM's authentic identity. So if the verifier and the privacy CA collude, the privacy of the TPM identity has no guarantee. In addition, since the verifier needs to query the Privacy CA every time in the verification of the platform identity, the performance of Privacy CA will become a major bottleneck in the attestation of platform identity.

To compensate the defects in the attestation based on the Privacy CA, TCG proposed the DAA for authenticating identity of TPM, and supports DAA in the TPM specification v1.2. DAA uses the cryptographic technologies such as group signature and zero-knowledge proof to attest the identity anonymously so as to ensure that the remote attestation is indeed from an authentic TPM, but the remote verifier does not know which one of TPMs. DAA scheme originates from the study of anonymous credential systems. The issuer in DAA does not provide any identification. Instead, it issues the anonymous credential. The TPM can use the zero-knowledge proof method to prove its identity to the remote verifier by using the pseudonym.

7.3.2.1 DAA Model

DAA mainly includes three participants: issuer, prover and verifier. The prover can be divided into host and TPM/TCM security chip according to the different computing entities in the DAA protocol. They both collaborate to complete the process of the TPM/TCM anonymous credential application and the anonymous attestation.

- Issuer: It is responsible to set up the DAA system parameters, issue the DAA credential for the TPM/TCM security chips and verify whether the identity of the TPM/TCM security chip has already been revoked. In general, the TPM/TCM manufacturers can be regarded as the issuer. Different security chip manufacturers can choose different DAA parameters. Or an independent authority can act as the DAA issuer. The management of all the TPM/TCM anonymous credentials is centralized.
- Prover: It is the platform embedded with the TPM/TCM security chip, such as security PC, laptop and other trusted computing platforms that support the DAA specification. The main functionality of the prover is the application of DAA anonymous credentials and the attestation of the anonymous identity.
- Verifier: It mainly verifies the DAA signature to authenticate the TPM/TCM anonymous identity so as to make sure that the DAA signature is indeed from an authentic TPM/TCM. During the verification of the anonymous identity, the verifier also needs to query the issuer that whether the TPM/TCM identity has been revoked.

In a DAA scheme, the anonymous identity key and its credential can be created for many times, but one remote attestation can only use one anonymous identity. The private key f of anonymous identity identifies the TPM/TCM anonymous identity. It can only be stored in TPM/TCM internal memory and cannot be exported. The DAA anonymous credential can be stored in the host platform outside the chip, or in other storage devices. The TPM/TCM anonymous attestation commands (including *DAA_Join* and *DAA_Sign*) can only be invoked by the TPM/TCM owner, and only the TPM/TCM owner can clear the existing insecure private key of anonymous identity.

The main procedures in the DAA protocol include four sub-protocols: Setup, Join, Sign and Verify. Among them, the most important sub-protocols are DAA Join and DAA Sign.

(1) Setup: Set up the public parameters of the DAA system and generate the key pair (sk_I, pk_I) for the issuer to sign the anonymous credentials, where sk_I is the issuer's private key and pk_I is the issuer's public key.
(2) DAA Join: The TPM/TCM sends to the issuer the application and then obtains the anonymous credential.
(3) DAA Sign: With the anonymous private key f and its anonymous credential, the TPM/TCM uses the zero-knowledge proof method to generate the DAA signature.
(4) Verify: The verifier verifies whether the DAA signature is valid, and further checks whether the TPM/TCM identity is revoked.

The DAA protocol is mainly to solve the problem of how to anonymously attest the TPM/TCM identity to the remote verifier, namely to ensure the privacy of TPM/TCM identity. It requests that the remote verifier cannot know the specific identity of the TPM/TCM security chip and cannot link multiple DAA sessions to distinguish whether or not they are from the same TPM/TCM identity. Thus the DAA protocol must satisfy the following security properties:

(1) Unforgeability: Only the TPM/TCM that has applied for the anonymous credentials can do the anonymous attestation. Any other attacker without the knowledge of the anonymous identity cannot forge the DAA signatures.
(2) Anonymity: In the case that the TPM/TCM cryptographic algorithms are not compromised, the attacker cannot obtain the authentic identity of the TPM/TCM through the protocol data.
(3) Unlinkability: The verifier cannot distinguish the correlation between two DAA sessions. That is to say, for two different DAA sessions, the verifier cannot determine whether or not they are from the same TPM/TCM.
(4) Rogue TPM Detection: When the corresponding private key of the anonymous credential of the TPM/TCM is disclosed, the verifier and the issuer can detect the disclosure in the running process of the protocol in time.

Although there are various DAA protocols, all of them follow the above basic DAA model. The difference is mainly due to the different group signature schemes and the different zero-knowledge proof methods used in the DAA protocol design. Figure 7.6 shows the main process of the original DAA protocol, which is based on the CL signature [20] and DDH assumptions to ensure its security. The subsequent DAA protocol researches are all based on its design.

7.3.2.2 Researches on DAA

In recent years, many works have been done on the DAA protocol from the original RSA-DAA scheme in 2004 to the following ECC-DAA scheme based on the elliptic

Platform (Host/TPM)		Issuer (I)
1. Create Join request $U := R_0^{f_0} R_1^{f_1} S^{v'} \bmod n$ $N_I := \zeta_I^{f_0+(f_1)2'f} \bmod \Gamma$	$\xrightarrow{N_I,\, U}$	
		2. Check for rogue TPM $N_I \overset{?}{\not\equiv} \zeta_I^{f_0'+(f_1')2'f} \bmod \Gamma$
3. Zero-knowledge proof f $SPK\{(f_0, f_1, \upsilon') \mid U = R_0^{f_0} R_1^{f_1} S^{v'} (\bmod n) \wedge$ $N_I = \zeta_I^{f_0+(f_1)2'f} (\bmod \Gamma)\}(n_t, n_i)$	$\xrightarrow{c,\, n_t,\, Sf_0,\, Sf_1,\, S_{\upsilon}'}$	
	$\xleftarrow{c',\, S_e,\, (A,\, e,\, \upsilon'')}$	4. Check and generate DAA credential $A := (\frac{Z}{US^{\upsilon''}})^{1/e} \bmod n$ $SPK\{(d) \mid A = (\frac{Z}{US^{\upsilon''}})^{d} (\bmod n)\}(n_h)$
5. Save DAA credential Save $(A, e, \upsilon' + \upsilon'')$		

Platform (Host/TPM)		Verifier (V)
	$\xleftarrow{n_{\upsilon},\, bsn_V}$	1. Challenge n_{υ}, bsn_V
2. Anonymously attest TPM identity $\zeta \in_R \langle \Upsilon \rangle$ or $\zeta := (H_{\Gamma}(1 \parallel bsn_V))^{(\Gamma-1)/\rho \bmod \Gamma}$ $N_V := \zeta_I^{f_0+(f_1)2'f}$ $T_2 := g^{\omega} h^{e} (g')^{r}$ $T_1 := A h^{\omega} \bmod n$ $SPK\{(f_0, f_1, \upsilon, e, \omega, r, ew, ee, er) \mid N_V = \zeta^{f_0+(f_1)2^l f} \wedge$ $Z = T_1^{e} R_0^{f_0} R_1^{f_1} S^{\upsilon} h^{-ew} \wedge T_2 = g^{\omega} h^{e} g'^{r} \wedge$ $1 = T_2^{e} g^{e\omega} h^{ee} g'^{er})\}(n_t, n_v, b, m)$ $\delta := (\zeta, (T_1, T_2), N_V, c, n_t, s_v, s_{f0}, s_{f1}, s_e,$ $s_e e, s_w, s_e w, s_r, s_e r)$	$\xrightarrow{\delta}$	
		3. Verify DAA attestation Verify the signature δ $N_V \overset{?}{\not\equiv} \zeta_I^{f_0'+(f_1')2'f} \bmod \Gamma$

Figure 7.6: The DAA Join phase (above) and DAA Sign phase (below) of BCC04 scheme.

curve and bilinear map. Its proof is simplified, and its computation cost and the signature length are reduced. DAA research has experienced a great breakthrough. In this section, we take our schemes as examples to discuss the related issues of the DAA research.

Design of DAA Protocol Based on Pairing. Since the BCC04 scheme based on RSA was proposed in 2004, many researchers have improved the DAA protocols. Under the same security level, elliptic curve cryptosystem is more efficient than the RSA cryptosystem, and it has the shorter private key and signature length. Thus the elliptic curve and pairing are more suitable for the design of the next-generation trusted computing DAA protocols. In 2008, we improved the DAA protocol by using ECC and put forward the next-generation trusted computing DAA protocol [26, 64]. It greatly improves the efficiency of the DAA protocol and promotes the improvement of the DAA protocol. The protocol skeleton of the scheme is as follows:

- DAA Join
  (1) TPM/TCM chooses the private key $f \in_R \mathbb{Z}/p\mathbb{Z}$ and the nonce $t' \in_R \mathbb{Z}/p\mathbb{Z}$, computes the Pedersen commitment $C = g^f h^{t'}$ and sends it to the issuer. Then the TPM/TCM proves it has the private dataf, t'.
    (a) Randomly chooses $r_f, r_t' \in_R (\mathbb{Z}/p\mathbb{Z})^2$, computes $C' = g^{r_f} h^{r_t'}$ and sends to the issuer.
    (b) Issuer randomly chooses $c \in_R \mathbb{Z}/p\mathbb{Z}$ and sends it to the TPM/TCM.
    (c) TPM/TCM computes $s_f = r_f + cf, s_t' = r_t' + ct'$ and sends s_f, s_t' to the issuer.
    (d) Issuer checks $C' \stackrel{?}{=} C^{-c} g^{s_f} h^{s_t'}$.
  (2) Issuer chooses $x \in_R \mathbb{Z}/p\mathbb{Z}, t'' \in_R \mathbb{Z}/p\mathbb{Z}$, computes$A = \left(g_1 C h^{t''}\right)^{1/(y+x)}$ and sends A, x, t'' to the host.
  (3) Host storesA, x and sends t'' to the TPM/TCM.
  (4) TPM/TCM computes $t = t' + t''$, stores f, t and checks the following equation:

$$e(A, Yg_2^x) = e(g_1, g_2) \cdot e\left(g^f, g_2\right) \cdot e\left(h^t, g_2\right).$$

- DAA-Sign
  (1) Host randomly chooses $w \in_R \mathbb{Z}/p\mathbb{Z}$, computes $T_1 = (Ah^w)$, $T_2 = g^w h^{-x}$, where T_1, T_2 are the commitments onA, x, and then proves the following two equations:

$$e(T_1, Y)/e(g_1, g_2) = e(h, Y)^w e(h, g_2)^{wx+t} e(g, g_2)^f / e(T_1, g_2)^x,$$
$$T_2 = g^w h^{-x} T_2^{-x} g^{wx} h^{-xx} = 1.$$

(2) Host (including TPM/TCM) proves it has the witnesses f, x, w, t which satisfy the above equations, and computes the auxiliary values$\delta_1 = wx$, $\delta_2 = -xx$.
   (a) TPM/TCM randomly chooses $r_f \in \mathbb{Z}/p\mathbb{Z}$, $r_t \in \mathbb{Z}/p\mathbb{Z}$, computes $\tilde{R}_1$ and sends $\tilde{R}_1$ to the host:

$$\tilde{R}_1 = e(g, g_2)^{r_f} e(h, g_2)^{r_t}.$$

   (b) Host chooses $r_x, r_w, r_{\delta_1}, r_{\delta_2} \in \mathbb{Z}/p\mathbb{Z}$ and computes

$$R_1 = \tilde{R}_1 e(h, Y)^{r_w} e(T_1, g_2)^{r_x} e(h, g_2)^{r_{\delta_1}},$$
$$R_2 = g^{r_w} h^{r_x},$$
$$R_3 = T_2^{r_x} g^{r_{\delta_1}} h^{r_{\delta_2}}.$$

   (c) Host computes $c_h = H(g\|h\|g_1\|g_2\|g_T\|Y\|T_1\|T_2\|R_1\|R_2\|R_3)$ and sends $c_h$to the TPM/TCM.
   (d) TPM/TCM chooses $n_t \in_R \mathbb{Z}/p\mathbb{Z}$ and computes $c = H(H(c_h\|n_t)\|m)$.
   (e) Host computes $s_x = r_x + c(-x)$, $s_{\delta_1} = r_{\delta_1} + c\delta_1$, $s_w = r_w + cw$, $s_{\delta_2} = r_{\delta_2} + c\delta_2$. TPM/TCM computes $s_f = r_f + cf$, $s_t = r_t + c(-t)$.

(3) Host outputs the signature $\sigma = (T_1, T_2, c, n_t, s_f, s_x, s_t, s_w, s_{\delta_1}, s_{\delta_2})$.

– DAA-Verify
(1) Given the signature $\sigma = (T_1, T_2, c, n_t, s_f, s_x, s_t, s_w, s_{\delta_1}, s_{\delta_2})$of the message $m$and the public key$(p, g_1, g_2, g_T, Y, g, h)$, the verifier computes

$$R_1' = e(g, g_2)^{s_f} e(h, Y)^{s_w} e(h, g_2)^{s_{\delta_1}+s_t} e(T_1, g_2)^{s_x} (e(T_1, Y)/e(g_1, g_2))^{-c},$$
$$R_2' = T_2^{-c} g^{s_w} h^{s_x},$$
$$R_3' = T_2^{s_x} g^{s_{\delta_1}} h^{s_{\delta_2}}.$$

(2) Verifier checks the following equation:

$$c \stackrel{?}{=} H(H(H(g\|h\|g_1\|g_2\|g_T\|Y\|T_1\|T_2\|R_1'\|R_2'\|R_3')\|n_t)\|m).$$

The above scheme is based on the q-SDH assumption and DDH assumption. It is the first DAA scheme based on bilinear mapping and q-SDH assumption. Reference [26] uses the ideal/real system model to prove the security of the protocol. The method mainly simulates the protocol running by designing the simulator S of the ideal system, which makes the environment to not distinguish between the ideal and real systems, thus proving the protocol is secure under the DDH assumption and q-SDH assumption. This scheme essentially uses the BBS+ signature to issue the anonymous credential (A, x, t) for the TPM/TCM and uses the characteristics of the pairing and the zero-knowledge signature to anonymously prove the platform identity and its credential. Since it uses the ECC and pairing, the signature length is shortened by 90 % compared with the original DAA scheme, and the computation cost is reduced significantly, which greatly improves the efficiency of the DAA protocol. In order to further reduce the computation cost of DAA Join, we propose a new DAA protocol [64] based on the improved BB signature by using the similar design method. The computational efficiency of the Join process is nearly doubled.

Although the above scheme is not perfect, the efficiency of its knowledge signature is not high. However, it highlights the way to design DAA protocols based on the q-SDH assumption. A lot of following researches are based on this scheme and constantly improve the BBS+ signature. The current research in this field has gradually become mature.

Forward-Secure DAA Protocol. The basic security properties of the DAA protocol are the user-controlled anonymity and user-controlled traceability. It considers less about the leakage of the TPM internal secret f. Once f leaks, it not only breaks the security of the DAA scheme but also affects the security of the DAA signatures signed before the leakage. To solve this problem, reference [65] puts forward a new protocol to support forward-secure DAA signature, and researched the extension of security of DAA scheme.

The forward-secure DAA scheme extends the original model with the key f updating algorithm. It periodically updates f to ensure that even if the current f leaks, the attacker cannot break the anonymity and unlinkability of the DAA signature signed before. The protocol is based on the strong RSA assumption and DDH assumption. The issuer uses a way that is similar to the CL signature to issue the anonymous credential (A, e, t) for the initial cycle f_0. The TPM DAA private key is updated by using one-way function on each cycle. The key f_i updated after the first i cycle follows the verification equation of anonymous credential:

$$A^e = a^{f_i^{s^{T-i}}} b^t \bmod n.$$

The DAA signing and verification are similar to those of the original DAA scheme. The difference is that in DAA Sign, it needs to use the root discrete logarithm signature of knowledge method to compute the signature of knowledge by using the private key f_i of the latest cycle. Under the strong RSA assumption, the proposed scheme can be proved to be secure. The protocol not only satisfies the basic security properties of the DAA model but also provides the forward security for DAA scheme and enhances security when the DAA private key is disclosed. At present, the research on the extension and enhancement of the DAA security is still preliminary. There are many problems to be solved.

Application of DAA Protocol. Although the TPM/TCM provides the support for DAA protocol, its direct applications in the real network system still confront many security issues, such as the DAA cross-domain problem, DAA network connection and so on.

DAA scheme is mainly designed for the small-scale network environment where the boundary is determined. In general, it is a single network domain. For the multi-domain application scenarios, in addition to the problem that they cannot be mutually authenticated, it also faces man-in-the-middle attack in the cross-domain. Reference [66] proposed a cross-domain DAA scheme to solve the TPM anonymous authentication problem in trusted multi-domain. The basic idea in cross-domain DAA is as follows. A trusted computing platform A (host/TPM A) in domain A needs to attest its identity to the verifier B in domain B. First of all, platform A needs to apply for a passport certificate from the local passport issuer, which certifies the identity of the trusted platform A in the trust domain A. Then the trusted computing platform A uses the passport certificate to apply for the visa certificate from the visa issuer in domain B. Finally, the trusted computing platform A uses the passport certificate and the visa certificate to anonymously attest its identity to the verifier B in trust domain B. The system architecture is shown in Figure 7.7. The major improvement of the cross-domain DAA protocol is to extend the original DAA protocol with two sub-protocols IDAA-IssuePassport and IDAA-IssueVisa for obtaining the passport certificate and the visa certificate, respectively. It achieves the anonymous attestation in multi-domain environments.

Following the protocol, we implement the prototype system of the cross-domain DAA and conduct the experiment to test and analyze the cross-domain DAA scheme. Compared with the original DAA scheme, its computational overhead increases a little, but the computational overhead of the TPM almost has no increase. The increased computation is mainly done by the host. The test results (as in Table 7.2) show that the performance of the cross-domain DAA scheme meets the requirements of the practical application even extended with the cross-domain anonymous attestation.

In addition to the application in security PC, DAA protocols can also be widely applied in wireless terminals, mobile phones and other embedded devices. The DAA protocol needs to be improved to adapt to these applications. The existing DAA design has become gradually mature, but there are still many technical problems to be solved for the practical application of the DAA protocol. Thus the implementation and security analysis of the DAA schemes is an important research direction in DAA's development.

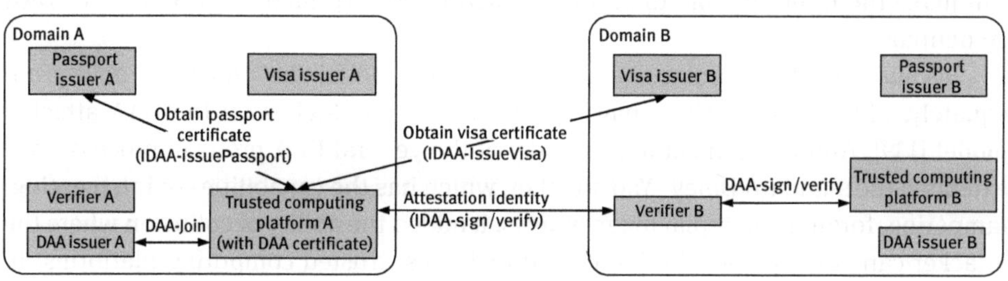

Figure 7.7: Crossdomain DAA system architecture.

Table 7.2: Evaluation results of the crossdomain DAA system.

Sub-protocol	Scheme	Time for host	Time for TPM
Join	Cross-domain DAA-IssuePassport	1,053	928
	Cross-domain DAA-IssueVisa	1,147	946
	Original DAA	718	910
Sign	Cross-domain DAA	1,921	875
	Original DAA	937	826
Verify	Cross-domain DAA	2,547	0
	Original DAA	1,523	0

7.3.2.3 Security Analysis and Test of DAA Protocols

Security Analysis of DAA Protocols. In the design of the DAA protocols, it is proved that the TPM/TCM DAA scheme is secure. It is not feasible to computationally break the DAA in the case that the cryptographic building block used in the scheme is secure. DAA protocol is not adequate to only ensure the security in cryptography. It also needs to conduct the security analysis from multiple aspects such as the logic analysis of protocol process, the attacker model checking and the API analysis, and in this way to ensure the security of the implementation of DAA protocol.

Security analysis achievements of the simple protocols in trusted computing (such as the authorization protocols [AP]) are very rich. The researchers in the University of Milan used the tool SPIN to detect the TPM OIAP and found the replay attacks [49]. The researchers in the University of Birmingham analyzed the TPM AP and found the off-line dictionary attack [138]. The researchers in HP laboratories used the protocol analysis tool ProVerif to detect that there exists the impersonation attack in the case of shared secret information [50]. Chinese researchers have analyzed the TCM AP and found the security deficiencies of replay attack and the off-line dictionary attacks [53]. However, there are few works for the security analysis of complex protocols (such as DAA protocol) in trusted computing. The researchers in Saarland University adopted π calculus to model the DAA protocol [51] and used the tool ProVerif to give the DAA mechanized verification results. They found a tiny security flaw: in the process of issuing, the authentication of the security chip cannot be guaranteed. The adversary can make the issuer unable to accurately figure out how many platforms have DAA credentials.

Because the DAA protocol analysis does not model the attackers' ability adequately, Chinese researchers have conducted the researches on the DAA attacker model [139]. Aiming at the attacker model of the general DAA protocol process, they extended the standard Dolev–Yao attacker, which has the capabilities of intercepting, tampering, forging and replaying messages. It added the ability of collusion where the attacker can collude with the issuer and dishonest trusted computing platforms. In order to simplify the analysis process, it does not distinguish the TPM and the host

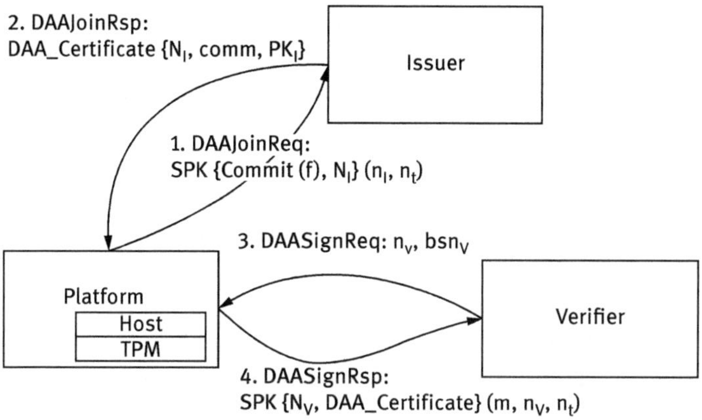

Figure 7.8: DAA communication process.

and ignores the communications between them. The simplified DAA protocol process is shown in Figure 7.8.

According to the above simplified message flows, we can respectively establish the states of finite state machines for the DAA protocol participants: issuer, platform, verifier. Then according to the attacker model, we can determine the attacking rules, and such that the DAA protocol analysis model can be established. We use the model checking tool Murphi to check the above DAA analysis model (the checking results are in Table 7.3). We find the link attack by using issuer base name, Rudolph attack and the masquerading attack by replaying DAA requests. These attacks are relatively simple but not easy to be found, especially when an attacker colludes with a participant. Due to the extension of the attacker's ability, it makes the security analysis of DAA protocol more in depth. It is of great significance for the improvement of the DAA protocol design and system implementation.

Simulation Test of DAA Protocols and Result Analysis. The theoretical research of DAA protocol has experienced a breakthrough, but for these schemes, there is a certain distance away from the practice application, especially for the schemes based on ECC and bilinear mapping (the so-called ECC-DAA). There are many problems to be

Table 7.3: The verification result using Murphi tool.

	Issuer number	Platform number	Verifier number	Size of network	States	Time (s)
Link attack	1	2	2	1	114	0.11
Rudolph attack	2	2	2	1	19,881	0.85
Masquerading attack	1	2	2	1	404	0.10
Fix above all	1	2	2	1	2,91,850	9.14

solved in the specific parameters, interfaces and implementation ways. To solve these problems, we have carried on the tests of ECC-DAA schemes [140] and attempted to give good suggestions for the tests and implementation of the DAA system.

We adopt the TPM simulation method to analyze and evaluate several critical factors that can affect security and efficiency of the DAA protocol, including the elliptic curve selection, parameter selection, preprocessing, optimization of point multiplication and pairing, signature length and so on. Through the simulation test of the DAA protocol, we find that the most influential factors are the elliptic curve and the parameter selection. We take as an example the analysis of the supersingular curves and the MNT curves. We choose the supersingular curve parameters such that it is with the length $|q| = 512$ of the finite field F_q, the cyclic groups G_1, G_2 order $|r| = 160$, embedding degree k =2, symmetric pairing and MNT curve parameters such that $|q| = |r| = 159$ (denoted by MNT159), embedding degree $k = 6$, asymmetric pairing. The algorithm strength with the above two curves selection is approximately equal to 80 bits security level. In addition, we have chosen the curves MNT201 and MNT224 with a higher security strength. The experiment results are depicted in Figure 7.9:

For the curve selection, supersingular curve is the most efficient curve, which is at least 3 times faster or more than MNT curve in every stage of DAA sub-protocol. However, the security strength of the supersingular curve only has 80 bits, which cannot satisfy the higher application requirement. The DAA signature length is 6,386 bits if supersingular curve is chosen, which is almost 0.5 times longer than that of the MNT159 curve of 4,216 bits. Thus for the application with a low security strength requirement, DAA with supersingular curve is certainly the best selection. For the applications with a high-level security, MNT curves support multiple security strength and are more flexible. Preprocessing can significantly decrease the running time for DAA scheme. In the stage of DAA sign, for supersingular curves and MNT curves, the computation cost can be, respectively, reduced by 36.85 % and 37.6 % with preprocessing. In the stage of DAA verify, it is reduced by 57.78 % and 65.96 %. Thus preprocessing is an important way to reduce the computation cost of the DAA protocol.

The above research gives out some preliminary test results of DAA schemes. In the future, we will make a more in-depth test, give out more efficient DAA optimization methods and define secure API for ECC-DAA schemes so as to provide a more scientific guideline for design and implementation of ECC-DAA systems.

7.3.3 Research Prospects

In this section, we discuss the attestation of platform identity based on TPM/TCM. We introduce the principle and method of the attestation based on Privacy CA and focus on the model of DAA and some related research results. In the field of engineering,

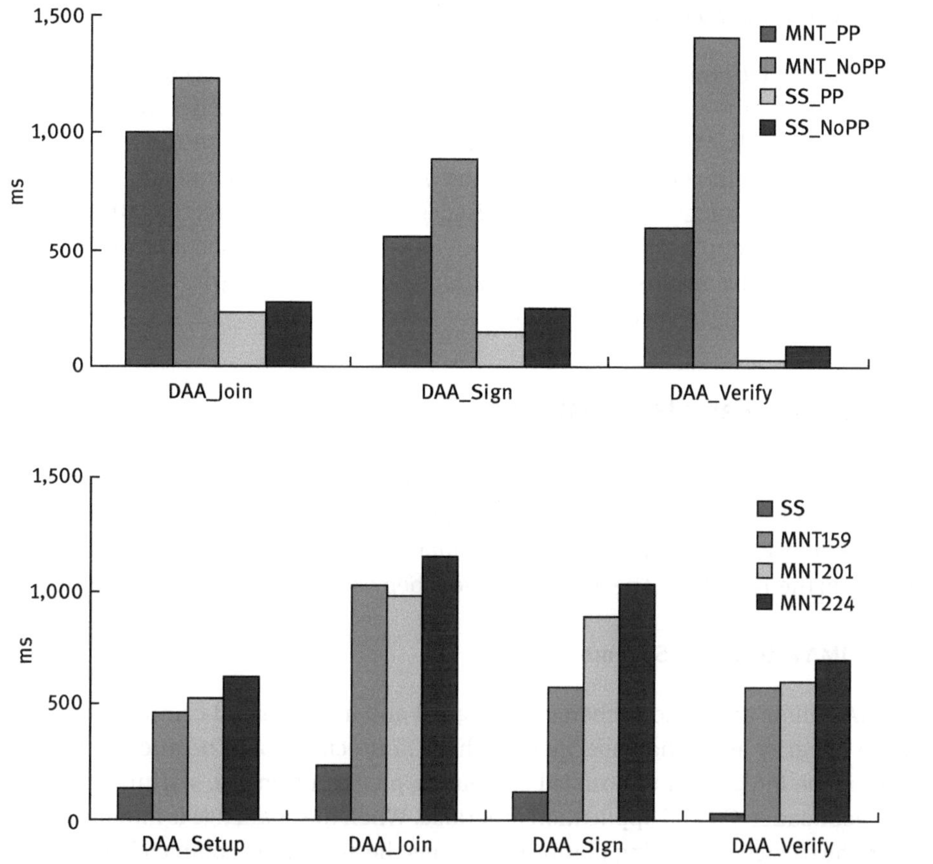

Figure 7.9: Simulation test results of ECC-DAA.

the currently most practical way to attest platform identity is based on the Privacy CA, which is built on the mature PKI certificate architecture. This method is easy to be implemented and deployed. In the academic field, researches focus on ECC-DAA. Many researchers in this field have continued to improve and develop it.

In the future, the research on the attestation of identity based on TPM/TCM must be more practical and secure. Since the research on DAA protocol has already solved the main problem of the TPM/TCM anonymous attestation on PC and other common platforms, the improvement space of the protocol is limited. However, the existing ECC-DAA schemes have a certain distance away from the practice application. The DAA research on standardization and DAA system will become the focus. DAA protocols in some specific application platforms (such as mobile phones and embedded devices) are required to be further studied. It needs to build different DAA models according to the specific application requirements for the platforms other than the PC platforms, which is also the future direction for DAA research.

7.4 Attestation of Platform Integrity

Attestation of platform integrity based on TPM/TCM is one of the most important research issues in the trusted computing. It is concerned by both the industrial and the academic fields. Many solutions have been proposed (such as the binary integrity attestation, semantic remote attestation, software attestation for embedded environments, etc.), which focus on the critical issues on the platform remote attestations, especially on the applications of the remote attestation. In this section, we focus on some representative results on the attestations of platform integrity to discuss from the perspective of the research method.

7.4.1 Binary Remote Attestation

The binary remote attestation is the most basic attestation method of the platform integrity. The other attestation methods are derived from it. Just as its name implies, the binary remote attestation directly uses the binary hash value to represent the platform integrity in the TPM/TCM. The representative schemes include IMA and PRIMA [10, 11].

7.4.1.1 IMA Attestation Scheme

The IMA remote attestation scheme is designed and implemented completely following the integrity attestation specified by the TCG specification. The attested content in IMA is the integrity of the trusted computing platform from the startup, including BIOS, bootloader, OS and application programs. When the challenge is initialized by a server, the trusted computing platform performs the attestation completely in accordance with the remote attestation presented in Section 7.1. It uses the AIK to compute the remote attestation signature of the platform integrity. Based on IMA, IBM implemented the prototype of the mutual attestation system based on TPM, which can check the running state of the system by remote attestation and can find the tampering of the system integrity, as depicted in Figure 7.10. TCG integrity measurement and attestation only establish the trust of the system booting process, but the IMA attestation scheme extends the TCG static booting sequence and implements the integrity attestation of the operating system dynamic running. Although the IMA attestation exposes all the system's integrity configuration to the verifier, which leads to a risk of disclosure of configuration privacy, it is still the most practical remote attestation scheme. The IMA measurement module has been integrated into the Linux kernel codes as part of the Linux security mechanisms, which can be widely applied to all kinds of security applications.

7.4.1.2 Policy-Reduced Integrity Measurement Architecture Attestation Scheme

The IMA scheme achieves the basic goal of TCG remote attestation, but it also has some deficiencies. For example, it cannot reflect the dynamic behaviors of the system

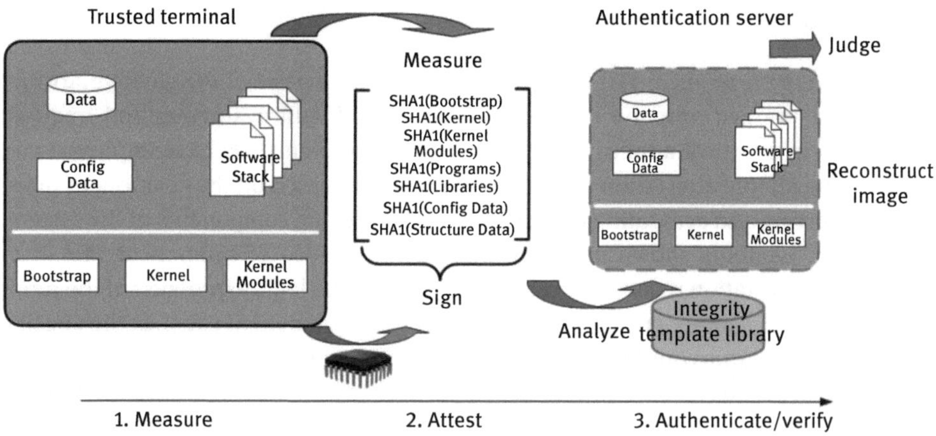

Figure 7.10: TPM-based integrity measurement and attestation architecture.

and requires the integrity attestation of the whole system. To solve these problems, the IBM Research Center extended the IMA scheme with the integrity measurement of the system information flow and proposed the PRIMA (Policy-Reduced Integrity Measurement Architecture) scheme. PRIMA scheme extends the IMA scheme such that the remote verifier can check the integrity of the information flow on trusted computing platform. It supports the Biba and Clark–Wilson model of information flow integrity. The PRIMA prototype system implemented by IBM Research Center adopts the more practical CW-Lite model. It provides the verification of information flow integrity in the common Linux system by using SELinux policy. The PRIMA attestation scheme is also the binary-based remote attestation. It extends the IMA scheme with restriction of information flow integrity, simplifies the attestation scope of system integrity and improves the efficiency of remote attestation. However, it essentially is still the binary-based remote attestation such that the privacy issue of the platform integrity still remains.

7.4.2 Property-Based Remote Attestation

The property-based attestation overcomes the problems of the binary remote attestation, such as the low efficiency and the leakage of the privacy of configuration. It is the most popular research direction in the field of integrity attestation. The research on attestation of platform integrity is developed in a more and more practical and extendable way. As the most practical and efficient attestation method, the property-based attestation has been rapidly developed. At present, the property-based attestation has already experienced the breakthrough in the system model, architecture design and concrete protocol design. In the following, we will introduce some research results [67–69] of the PBA from the granularity and efficiency of attestation, and combination with DAA.

7.4.2.1 Fine-Grained Component PBA Scheme

The original PBA protocol [33] is used to attest the properties of the whole platform. This coarse-grained property has the problems of difficult evaluation and frequent revocation in practical application. To solve these problems, we have improved and realized the remote attestation protocol and its system based on the component properties by testing and evaluating the software and hardware components of the system. The system model is shown in Figure 7.11. The basic idea of component PBA is to convert the attestation request of system properties to the logic expression of the properties of several components, and to attest that each component satisfies the specific component properties one by one. The component PBA uses the zero-knowledge proof method to prove that the commitments on platform component measurement satisfy the requirement of the component property certificate. The whole scheme is proved to be secure in the RO model. In the component PBA system, the TPM first commits and signs on the component measurement. Then the host randomizes the CL component properties certificate and proves to the verifier that the TPM committed component integrity configurations satisfy the requirements of the component properties in the attestation. Finally under the assistance of the property authority, the verifier checks whether the properties are revoked, or the signatures of commitments are all valid.

The component PBA scheme consists of four main algorithms: *Setup*, *Attest*, *Verify* and *Check*. *Setup* algorithm is used to establish the public parameters of the system and to issue the component property certificates. *Attest* algorithm is used by the TPM and the host to attest the security properties of the platform. *Verify* algorithm is used for the verification of the component property attestation. *Check* algorithm is used to check whether the security properties have been revoked.

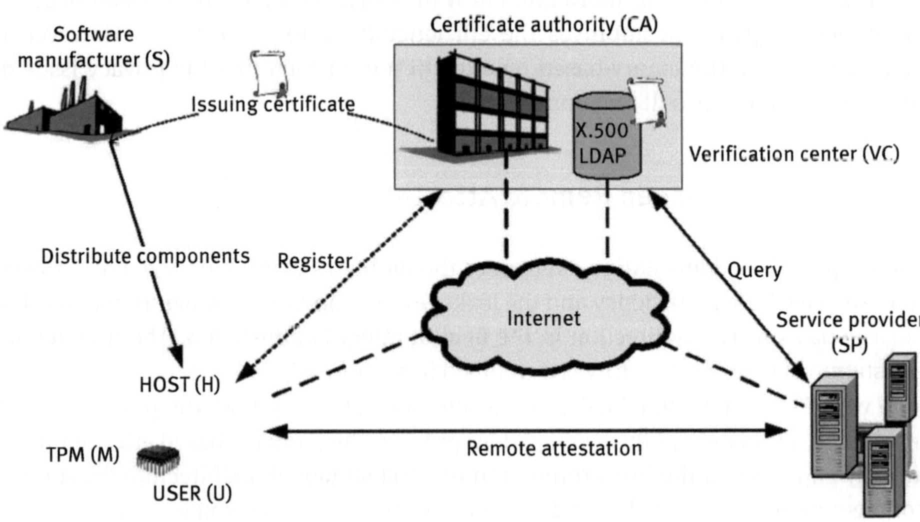

Figure 7.11: Component PBA model.

– Setup

The Certificate Authority $\mathscr{CA}$ generates the public parameters of the RSA algorithm $n = pq, p = 2p' + 1, q = 2q' + 1$, where p, q, p, q' are all primes, and the length of n is l_n.

Let g_0 be the generator of the group of quadratic residues QR_n, randomly choose $x_0, x_1, x_2, x_g, x_h, x_s, x_z \in [1, p'q']$ and compute:

$$\begin{aligned} g &= g_0^{x_g} \bmod {}_n, \\ h &= g_0^{x_h} \bmod n, \\ S &= h^{x_s} \bmod n, \\ Z &= h^{x_z} \bmod {}_n, \\ R_0 &= S^{x_0} \bmod {}_n, \\ R_1 &= S^{x_1} \bmod {}_n, \\ R_2 &= S^{x_2} \bmod n. \end{aligned}$$

Thus we have $g, h, S, Z, R_0, R_1, R_2 \in \langle g_0 \rangle$, and the public parameters of $\mathscr{CA}$ are $parm_{\mathscr{CA}} = (n, g_0, h, S, Z, R_0, R_1, R_2)$. Let $parm_{\mathscr{VC}} = (g_0, g, h, n, y)$ be the parameters of the Verification Authority $\mathscr{VC}$, where $y = g^x \bmod n$ is its public key and x is its private key. Suppose the configuration of the component $\hat{c}_i$ is $(id_i, \chi, \hat{p}_i)$, where id_i is the identity ID of the component $\hat{c}_i$ ID, χ_i is the measurement of the component $\hat{c}_i$ and $\hat{p}_i$ is the security property that should be satisfied by the component. $\mathscr{CA}$ issues the CL signature of the property certificate $(id_i, \chi_i, \hat{p}_i)$, (A_i, e_i, v_i) for the component $\hat{c}_i$, which satisfies the following equation:

$$Z \equiv A_i^{e_i} R_0^{id_i} R_1^{\chi_i} R_2^{\hat{p}_i} S^{v_i} \bmod n$$

$\mathscr{CA}$ assigns $(sk_{\mathscr{U}}, vk_{\mathscr{U}})$ to the user $\mathscr{U}$ in the cyclic group $G = \langle g \rangle$, where $vk_{\mathscr{U}} = g^{sk_{\mathscr{U}}} \bmod n$. Similarly, it assigns the public key and private key pairs $(sk_{\mathscr{SP}}, vk_{\mathscr{SP}})$ and $(sk_{\mathscr{VC}}, vk_{\mathscr{VC}})$, respectively, for $\mathscr{SP}$ and $\mathscr{VC}$, where $sc_{\mathscr{VC}} = x$, $vk_{\mathscr{VC}} = y = g^x \bmod {}_n$. The private keys are stored secretly and the public keys are published.

– Attest

Component PBA Protocol.

(1) The user ($\mathscr{U}$) requires the service provider ($\mathscr{SP}$) to provide the service and sends the TPM AIK certificate to $\mathscr{SP}$, which includes the public key $vk_{\mathscr{M}}$ of the TPM AIK.

(2) $\mathscr{SP}$ sends the requests $PAR\left\{\bigwedge_{i=1}^{\bar{n}} \hat{p}_i \Rightarrow \hat{p}\right\}$ and the challenge nonce N_v to $\mathscr{U}$, and requires the attestation that the computing platform of $\mathscr{U}$ satisfies the security property $\hat{p}$.

(3) $\mathscr{U}$ does the component PBA $CAP\left\{\bigwedge_{i=1}^{\bar{n}} \hat{c}_i \Rightarrow \hat{p}\right\} = CPA\left\{\left(\bigwedge_{i=1}^{k} \hat{c}_i\right) \wedge \left(\bigwedge_{i=k+1}^{\bar{n}} (\bigvee_{j \in \mathscr{I}_i} \hat{c}_{i,j})\right) \Rightarrow \hat{p}\right\}$.

TPM Measuring and Signing.

(1) TPM measures the system components and executes the system component measurement algorithm. The measurement of the component $\hat{c}_i(i = 1, \ldots, k)$ is χ_i. For the component $\hat{c}_i(i = k + 1, \ldots, n)$, the optional component for user $\mathscr{U}$ is $\hat{c}_{i,i^*}$. The measurement of $\hat{c}_{i,i^*}$ is χ_i. Since the platform is not configured or does not run the optional component $\hat{c}_i$ other than $\hat{c}_{i,i^*}$, then the TPM does not measure the optional components $\hat{c}_{i,j}, j \in \mathscr{J}_i, j \neq i^*$ of $\hat{c}_i$.

(2) TPM chooses the nonce $N_t \in_R \{0, 1\}^{l_\emptyset}$ and the nonce $w_i \in \{0, 1\}^{l_n + l_\emptyset}$, and computes the commitments of the attested components $C_i = g_0^{id_i} g^{\chi_i} h^{w_i} \bmod n$ $(i = 1, \ldots, n)$, and $K = DH(vk_{\mathscr{S}\mathscr{P}}, sk_{\mathscr{U}})$, $h_i = h^{w_i}$, $g_i = g^{w_i}$. Then, the TPM uses sk_{TPM} to sign the commitments of the components $\sigma = Sign_{sk_{TPM}}(parm_C \| C_1 \| \ldots \| C_n \| K \| N_v \| N_t)$.

(3) TPM returns the computation results C_i, h_i, g_i, K, σ to the host.

Host Computes the Component Property-Based Signature.

(1) It chooses the nonce $u_i \in_R \{0, 1\}^{l_n + l_\emptyset}$ and computes $a_i = g^{u_i} \bmod n$, $b_i = id_i \cdot y^{u_i} \bmod n (i = 1, \ldots, \bar{n})$.

(2) $\mathscr{U}$ runs the signature of knowledge protocol:

$$SKP\left\{ \begin{array}{l} (id_i, \chi_i, v_i, e_i, w_i, r_i, e_i w_i, e_i e_i, e_i r_i)_{i=1,\ldots,n} | \bigwedge_{i=1}^{\bar{n}} (Z/R_2^{\hat{p}_i} \equiv T_{i,1}^{e_i} R_0^{id_i} R_1^{\chi_i} S^{v_i} h^{-e_i w_i} \bmod n \wedge \\ T_{i,2} = g^{w_i} h^{e_i} g_0^{r_i} \bmod n \wedge 1 = T_{i,2}^{-e_i} g^{e_i w_i} h^{e_i e_i} g_0^{e_i r_i} \bmod n \wedge C_i = g_0^{id_i} g^{\chi_i} h^{w_i} \bmod n \wedge \\ \chi_i \in \{0, 1\}^{l_\chi + l_\emptyset + l_{\mathscr{H}} + 2} \wedge (e_i - 2^{l_e}) \in \{0, 1\}^{l'_e + l_\emptyset + l_{\mathscr{H}} + 1}) \} (N_v, N_t) \end{array} \right\}.$$

(a) The configuration of the component $\hat{c}_i$ is $(id_i, \chi_i, \hat{p}_i)$. The property certificate is (A_i, e_i, v_i). Host $\mathscr{H}$ randomly chooses $r_i \in \{0, 1\}^{l_n + l_\emptyset}$ and computes $Z'_i = Z/R_2^{\hat{p}_i} \bmod n$, $T_{i,1} = A_i h_i \bmod n$, $T_{i,2} = g_i h^{e_i} g_0^{r_i} \bmod n$

(b) TPM chooses the nonces $r_{id_i} \in_R \{0, 1\}^{l_{id} + l_\emptyset + l_H}$, $r_{\chi_i} \in_R \{0, 1\}^{l_\chi + l_\emptyset + l_H}$, $r_{w_i} \in_R \{0, 1\}^{l_n + 2l_\emptyset + l_H}$, and then computes $\tilde{C}_i = g_0^{r_{id_i}} g^{r_{\chi_i}} h^{r_{w_i}} \bmod n$. TPM sends $\tilde{C}_i$ to the host.

(c) $\mathscr{H}$ chooses the nonces:

$$r_{v_i} \in_R \{0, 1\}^{l_v + l_\emptyset + l_H},$$

$$r_{e_i} \in_R \{0, 1\}^{l'_e + l_\emptyset + l_H},$$

$$r_{r_i} \in_R \{0, 1\}^{l_n + 2l_\emptyset + l_H},$$

$$r_{e_i e_i} \in_R \{0, 1\}^{2l_e + l_\emptyset + l_H + 1},$$

$$r_{e_i w_i}, r_{e_i r_i} \in_R \{0, 1\}^{l_e + l_n + 2l_\emptyset + l_H + 1}.$$

$\mathscr{H}$ computes:

$$\tilde{Z}_i' = T_{i,2}^{-r_{e_i}} g^{r_{e_i w_i}} h^{r_{e_i e_i}} g_0^{r_{e_i r_i}} \bmod n,$$

$$\tilde{T}_{i,2} = g^{r_{w_i}} h^{r_{e_i}} g_0^{r_{e_i r_i}} \bmod n,$$

$$\tilde{T}_{i,2}' = T_{i,2}^{-r_{e_i}} g^{r_{e_i w_i}} h^{r_{e_i e_i}} g_0^{r_{e_i r_i}} \bmod n. c_{\mathscr{H}}$$

$$= H(parm_C || C_i || Z_i' || T_{i,1} || T_{i,2})_{i=1,\dots,\bar{n}} || (\tilde{C}_i || \tilde{Z}_i' || \tilde{T}_{i,2} || \tilde{T}_{i,2}')_{i=1,\dots,\bar{n}} || N_v)$$

Host sends $c_{\mathscr{H}}$ to the TPM.

(d) TPM computes $c = H(c_h || N_t) \in [0, 2^{l_H - 1}]$, and then it computes:

$$s_{id_i} = r_{id_i} + c \cdot id_i,$$

$$s_{\chi_i} = r_{\chi_i} + c \cdot \chi_i,$$

$$s_{w_i} = r_{w_i} + c \cdot w_i.$$

It sends $c, N_t, s_{id_i}, s_{\chi_i}, s_{w_i}$ to the host

$\mathscr{H}$ computes the signature of knowledge:

$$s_{v_i} = r_{v_i} + c \cdot v_i,$$

$$s_{e_i} = r_{e_i} + c \cdot (e_i - 2^{l_e - 1}),$$

$$s_{r_i} = r_{r_i} + c \cdot r_i,$$

$$s_{e_i w_i} = r_{e_i w_i} + c \cdot e_i \cdot w_i,$$

$$s_{e_i e_i} = r_{e_i e_i} + c \cdot e_i^2,$$

$$s_{e_i r_i} = r_{e_i r_i} + c \cdot e_i \cdot r_i.$$

(3) $\mathscr{H}$ computes the signature of the component properties:

$$\sigma_{CPBA} = (\sigma, N_t, K, c, (C_i, T_{i,1}, T_{i,2}, s_{id_l}, s_{\chi i}, s_{v_i}, s_{e_i}, s_{w_i}, s_{r_i}, s_{e_i w_i}, s_{e_i e_i}, s_{e_i r_i})_{i=1,\dots,\bar{n}})$$

User platform $\mathscr{U}$ sends the signature of the component properties σ_{CPBA} to $\mathscr{SP}$.

– Verify

$\mathscr{SP}$ verifies the TPM signature and the signature of knowledge, and then sends $(C_i, \ T_{i,1}, a_i, b_i, \hat{p}_i)_{i=1,\dots,n}$ to the $\mathscr{VC}$ to check whether the component property certificates are revoked. If the component property certificates have not been revoked, it finally verifies the agreement key K.

Verify the TPM Signature. It checks the validity of the AIK certificate and the fresh nonce N_v, and then it verifies $Verify_{vkTPM}(parm_C || C_1 || \dots || C_n || K || N_v || N_t, \sigma)$.

Verify the Component Property Certificate. $\mathcal{SP}$ uses the public key $parm_C = (n, g_0, g, h, S, Z, R_0, R_1, R_2)$ to verify the component property signature σ_{CPBA} of the messages N_v, N_t.

(1) $\mathcal{SP}$ sends $(C_i, T_{i,1}, a_i, b_i, \hat{p}_i)_{i=1,\dots,n}$ to $\mathcal{VC}$ to check whether or not the component property certificates are revoked. $\mathcal{VC}$ executes the check algorithm.

(2) $\mathcal{SP}$ computes $Z_i' = Z/R_2^{\hat{p}_i} \bmod n$, and then computes:

$$\hat{C}_i = C_i^{-c} g_0^{s_{id_i}} g^{s_{\chi_i}} h^{s_{w_i}} \bmod n,$$

$$\hat{Z}_i' = Z_i'^{-c} T_{i,1}^{s_{e_i}+c\cdot 2^{l_e-1}} R_0^{s_{id_i}} R_1^{s_{\chi_i}} S^{s_{v_i}} h^{-s_{e_iw_i}} \bmod n,$$

$$\hat{T}_{i,2} = T_{i,2}^{-c} g^{s_{w_i}} h^{s_{e_i}+c\cdot 2^{l_e-1}} g_0^{s_{r_i}} \bmod n,$$

$$\hat{T}_{i,2}' = T_{i,2}^{-(s_{e_i}+c.2^{l_e-1})} g^{s_{e_iw_i}} h^{s_{e_ie_i}} g_0^{s_{e_ir_i}} \bmod n.$$

(3) Verify the following relations:

$$c \stackrel{?}{=} \mathcal{H}(parm_C||(C_i||Z_i'||\ T_{i,1}||T_{i,2})_{i=1,\dots,\tilde{n}}||(\hat{C}_i||\hat{Z}'_i||\ \hat{T}_{i,2}||\hat{T}_{i,2}')_{i=1,\dots,\tilde{n}}||N_v||N_t),$$

$$C_i \stackrel{?}{\in} \langle g_0 \rangle,$$

$$s_{\chi_i} \stackrel{?}{\in} \{0,1\}^{l_\chi+l_\emptyset+l_H+1},$$

$$s_{e_i} \in \{0,1\}^{l_e'+l_\emptyset+l_H+1}.$$

It verifies the agreement key K for $K \stackrel{?}{=} DH(vk_{\mathcal{U}}, sk_{\mathcal{SP}})$. If the agreement key is equal, then there the impersonation attack of $\mathcal{U}$ does not exist.

– Check

(1) $\mathcal{VC}$ computes the component ID, $id_i = b_i/a_i^x \bmod n$. Then it uses $(id_i, \hat{p}_i)$ as the index to query the property certificate library and get the configuration and certificate of the component $\hat{c}_i$:$(id_i, \chi_i, \hat{p}_i)$,$(A_i, e_i, v_i)$.

(2) It checks whether or not the component property and configuration have been revoked. If not, it checks the commitment must match with the component. $\mathcal{VC}$ verifies the following equation:

$$Z * [C_i/(g_0^{id_i} g^{\chi_i})]^{e_i} \stackrel{?}{=} T_{i,1}^{e_i} R_0^{id_i} R_1^{\chi_i} R_2^{\hat{p}_i} S^{v_i}.$$

If it is valid, the component property attested by $\mathcal{U}$ has not been revoked, and the committed message is real.

(3) $\mathcal{VC}$ sends the verification results of the property certificates to $\mathcal{SP}$.

The advantages of the remote attestation scheme based on component property are as follows: (1) It has the semantic and property expression ability. Its properties are fine-grained, convenient to be verified and scalable. (2) It does not need the temporary property certificate. The revocation and verification of the property are simple and efficient. (3) It can protect the privacy of the platform components. (4) It can prevent the impersonation attack on TPM remote attestation. The component PBA scheme can deepen the research of property-based remote attestation from the aspect of attestation granularity. It solves the basic problem of the application of property-based remote attestation from the aspects of the protocol design and the system implementation. However, since it adopts the RSA cryptosystem, the efficiency of zero-knowledge proof is low. It leaves improvement space for the efficiency of PBA by adopting pairing in future research.

7.4.2.2 Efficient PBA Based on Pairing

For the traditional PBA based on the RSA cryptosystem, it has the problems of large amount of zero-knowledge proof computation and low efficiency. Reference [67] proposed an efficient PBA based on pairing with the support of TCM. The security model of PBA based on pairing is the same to that of the traditional RSA PBA. It requires the security properties of unforgeability of attestation and the configuration privacy. The protocol identifies the platform properties by issuing the property certificate $\sigma = (a, A, b, B, c)$ of CL-LRSW pairings for the platform configuration property pairs (cs, ps). The platform uses the signature proof of knowledge to prove the binding relationship among the commitments of the platform configurations, the randomized property certificates and the TPM attestation, namely the following equation:

$$SPK\{(cs, r_0, r, t_1, t_2) | v_x v_{xy}^{cs} v_{xyz}^{ps} = v_s^r \wedge C = g_T^{cs} h_T^{r_0} \wedge d_1 = X^{t_1} \wedge d_2 = Y^{t_2}\}(N_v, N_t).$$

The procedure of PBA protocol based on pairing is similar to that of the component PBA. It just adopts the pairing to simplify the attestation and improve the efficiency. The main algorithms of PBA protocol based on pairing is as follows:

Setup. Set the security parameters in the attestation system: l_q, l_H, l_φ, where l_q is the order length of the prime q order group (e. g., if q is of 256 bits, its length l_q is 256); l_H is output length of hash function for Fiat–Shamir heuristic; l_φ is the length of security parameter used to control zero-knowledge proof. Let H be a strong collision-resistant hash function, $H : \{0,1\}^* \to \{0,1\}^{l_H}$. $\mathcal{T}$ chooses two groups $G = \langle g \rangle$, $G_T = \langle g_T \rangle$ of prime order q and a bilinear map $e : G \times G \to G_T$, and then set private key $sk = (x, y, z)$ and public key $pk = (q, G, G_T, g, g_T, e, X, Y, Z)$ according to the CL-LRSW signature scheme.

Issue. $\mathcal{P}$ carries out the integrity collection for the platform configuration and then requests the property certificate from $\mathcal{T}$ with the current platform configuration cs. $\mathcal{T}$ evaluates the configuration information for the security property. Suppose the evaluated property is ps. $\mathcal{T}$ issues the configuration property certificate $\mathfrak{cre}$ for $(cs,$

ps), which is CL-LRSW signature using the issuer's private key, and the signature is (a, A, b, B, c), where $a \in_R Ga \in_R G$, $A \leftarrow a^z$, $b \leftarrow a^y$, $B \leftarrow A^y$, $c \leftarrow a^{x+x\cdot y\cdot cs} A^{x\cdot y\cdot ps}$. Let $\sigma = (a, A, b, B, c)$, then the configuration property certificate is $\mathfrak{cre} = ((cs, ps), \sigma)$. $\mathcal{T}$ sends the property certificate to $\mathcal{P}$; $\mathcal{P}$ checks the validation of certificate by the following equations and saves the certificate for the further attestation:

$$e(a, Z) \stackrel{?}{=} e(g, A), \quad e(a, Y) \stackrel{?}{=} e(g, b), \quad e(A, Y) \stackrel{?}{=} e(g, B),$$
$$e(X, a) \bullet e(X, b)^{cs} \bullet e(X, B)^{ps} \stackrel{?}{=} e(g, c).$$

The CL-LRSW signature issued by $\mathcal{T}$ has the randomization property. Choose $r' \in Z_q^*$ at random and compute $a' = a^{r'}$, $b' = b^{r'}$, $A' = A^{r'}$, $B' = B^{r'}$, $c' = c^{r'}$. Then randomized $\sigma' = (a', A', b', B', c')$ is also the CL-LRSW signature for (cs, ps).

Attest. $\mathcal{V}$ challenges $\mathcal{P}$ with a random number $N_v \in_R \{0, 1\}^{l_H}$ for the property attestation. The host $\mathcal{H}$ invokes TCM chip ($\mathcal{M}$) to attest the platform configuration after $\mathcal{P}$ receives the request. $\mathcal{M}$ generates random number $r_h, r_0 \in_R Z_q^*$,, $N_t \in_R \{0, 1\}^{l_\varphi}$ with random number generator inside the security chip, computes $h_T = g_T^{r_h} \in G_T$, generates commitment $C = g_T^{cs} h_T^{r_0}$ on $c\ s$ following Pederson commitment scheme and signs the commitment with PIK in TCM chip. The final signature is defined as $\delta = Sig_{\mathcal{M}}(C, N_v || N_t)$.

$\mathcal{M}$ sends $g_T, h_T, C, r_0, \delta, N_t$ to host $\mathcal{H}$ for the property attestation signature.

$\mathcal{H}$ randomizes the signature σ on the property certificate and gets $a' = a^{r'}$, $b' = b^{r'}$, $A' = A^{r'}$, $B' = B^{r'}$, $c' = c^{r'r^{-1}}$, where $r', r \in_R Z_q^*$. $\mathcal{H}$ chooses random number $t_1, t_2 \in_R Z_q^*$, and computes $\sigma_o = \sigma \bullet g^{t_1+t_2}$ and the following parameters:

$$v_x = e(X, a') v_{xy} = e(X, b') \quad v_s = e(g, c') \quad v_{xyz} = e(X, B').$$

We can optimize the protocol computation at this step. Host $\mathcal{H}$ can precompute the pairing according to property certificate, $\bar{v}_x = e(X, a)$, $\bar{v}_{xy} = e(X, b)$, $\bar{v}_s = e(g, c)$,$\bar{v}_{xyz} = e(X, B)$. When $\mathcal{H}$ receives the attestation challenge, $\mathcal{H}$ can easily compute $v_x = (\bar{v}_x)^{r'}$, $v_{xy} = (\bar{v}_{xy})^{r'}$, $v_s = (\bar{v}_s)^{r'}$, $v_{xyz} = (\bar{v}_{xyz})^{r'}$ based on the precomputing result.

Next $\mathcal{H}$ executes the signature proof of knowledge on (N_v, N_t) according to the following steps:

$$SPK\{(cs, r_0, r, t_1, t_2) | v_x v_{xy}^{cs} v_{xyz}^{ps} = v_s^r \wedge C = g_T^{cs} h_T^{r_0} \wedge d_1 = X^{t_1} \wedge d_2 = Y^{t_2}\}(N_v, N_t).$$

(1) $\mathcal{H}$ chooses the random number $R_1, R_2, R_3, R_4, R_5 \in_R Z_q^*$ and computes $\tilde{T}_1 = v_s^{R_3}(v_x v_{xy}^{R_1} v_{xyz}^{ps})^{-1}$, $\tilde{T}_2 = g_T^{R_1} h_T^{R_2}$, $\tilde{d}_1 = X^{R_4}$, $\tilde{d}_2 = Y^{R_5}$.

(2) $\mathcal{H}$ computes $\begin{aligned} c_H = H(&q||g||X||Y||a'||b'||c'||A'||B'||g_T||h_T||C||\sigma_0 \\ &||d_1||d_2||v_x||v_{xy}||v_{xyz}||v_s||\tilde{d}_1||\tilde{d}_2||\tilde{T}_1||\tilde{T}_2||N_v||N_t) \end{aligned}$.

(3) $\mathcal{H}$ computes $s_1 = R_1 - c_H \cdot cs \bmod q$, $s_2 = R_2 - c_H \cdot r_0 \bmod q$, $s_3 = R_3 - c_H \cdot r \bmod q$, $s_4 = R_4 - c_H \cdot r_1 \bmod q$, $s_5 = R_5 - c_H \cdot r_2 \bmod q$.

At last $\mathcal{H}$ outputs the property attestation signature $\sigma_{PBA} = (\delta, C, a', b', c', A', B', c_H, s_1, s_2, s_3, s_4, s_5)$ and sends the attestation result to $\mathcal{V}$.

Verify. The verifier $\mathcal{V}$ knows the public key $pk = (q, G, g, G_T, e, X, Y, Z)$ that is used by $\mathcal{T}$ to verify the property certificate and the security property ps that needs to be verified is pre-negotiated by the participants $\mathcal{P}$ and $\mathcal{V}$ during the communication. When $\mathcal{V}$ receives the property attestation signature σ_{PBA} on (N_v, N_t), $\mathcal{V}$ verifies the result in the following steps:

(1) $\mathcal{V}$ verifies $h_T \overset{?}{\in} G_T$, and then uses TCM public key to verify the signature on commitment: $Verf_{\mathcal{M}}(\delta, C, N_v, ||N_t) \overset{?}{=} true$.

(2) $\mathcal{V}$ verifies $e(a', Z) \overset{?}{=} e(g, A')$, $e(a', Y) \overset{?}{=} e(g, b')$, $e(A', Y) \overset{?}{=} e(g, B')$.

(3) $\mathcal{V}$ computes

$$\hat{v}_x = e(X, a'), \quad \hat{v}_{xy} = e(X, b'), \quad \hat{v}_s = e(g, c'), \quad \hat{v}_{xyz} = e(X, B')$$
$$\widehat{T}_1 = v_s^{s_3} v_{xy}^{-s_1} (v_x v_{xyz}^{ps})^{c_H - 1}, \quad \widehat{T}_2 = g_T^{s_1} h_T^{s_2} C^{c_H}, \quad \widehat{d}_1 = X^{s_4} d_1^{c_H}, \quad \widehat{d}_2 = Y^{s_5} d_2^{c_H}.$$

(4) Next, $\mathcal{V}$ verifies

$$c_H \overset{?}{=} H(q||g||Y||a'||b'||c'||A'||B'||g_T||h_T||C||\sigma_o)$$
$$||d_1||d_2||v_x||v_{xy}||v_{xyz}||v_s||\widehat{d}_1||\widehat{T}_1||\widehat{T}_2||N_v||N_t).$$

(5) $\mathcal{V}$ sends (σ_o, d_1, d_2, ps) to $\mathcal{T}$, and requests $\mathcal{T}$ to check whether the pair (cs, ps) on the configuration and property is revoked.

(6) If all of above verifications are passed, $\mathcal{V}$ outputs **ACCEPT**, otherwise outputs **REJECT**.

Check. $\mathcal{V}$ requests $\mathcal{T}$ to check whether the property on cs is revoked with (σ_o, d_1, d_2, ps). $\mathcal{T}$ computes $\sigma = \sigma_0 / \left(d_1^{1/x} d_2^{1/y}\right)$, and queries the property pair in certificate database by ps and σ. If $\mathcal{T}$ gets the relevant certificate, it indicates that the property on cs is still valid. Otherwise $\mathcal{T}$ notifies $\mathcal{V}$ to reject the attestation when (cs, ps) has been revoked. T can improve the efficiency of revocation verification when precomputing $1/x$ and $1/y$.

The PBA scheme based on pairing simplifies the property-based remote attestation. It uses the cryptographic method to prove the security of the protocol from the two aspects of unforgeability of remote attestation and the protection of configuration privacy. Under the assumptions of LRSW and DDH, there is no forgery on remote attestation or no identification on specific platform configuration by security property in the protocol. Compared with the original scheme of PBA protocol, the computation cost is reduced by about 32 %, the signature length is reduced by about 63 %. It can be seen that the PBA scheme based on pairing has a significant improvement in the performance.

7.4.2.3 Anonymous Property Attestation Combining PBA and DAA

DAA and PBA are two different application categories of the remote attestation. PBA just attests that the platform integrity configuration satisfies the specific security property. It can use either the TPM AIK or the anonymous identity to attest. The former method is very simple. However, if the practical trusted computing applications have a high security requirement, where it requires the property attestation and anonymous attestation, it needs the hybrid of DAA and PBA (it is the so-called Anonymous Property-Based Attestation, APA). DAA and PBA themselves are very complex. If the attestation is divided into two stages to attest sequently, this method will greatly affect the efficiency of remote attestation. Therefore, APA in trusted computing application is required to attest the anonymous identity and the platform properties simultaneously in one attestation procedure.

Reference [68] proposed an efficient APA scheme which is a hybrid of PBA and DAA. The basic idea of the scheme is to embed the authentication of DAA anonymous identity into the property-based remote attestation. The trusted third party first verifies the DAA anonymous identity and then issues the property certificate on the anonymous identity and the platform configuration property pair (f, cs, ps). Its advantage is that running PBA protocol once is able to complete the remote attestation. It greatly improves the efficiency of remote attestation. The anonymous credential issued by the trusted third party is $cre = ((N_I, cs, ps), \sigma)$, where $\sigma = (a, A_1, B_1, b, B_1, B_2, c)$ is a CL signature on (N_I, cs, ps), N_I is the pseudonym of the DAA private key f based on the issuer base name. This is to prevent the leakage of the DAA secret f. Since the trusted third party issues a temporary APA credential, the anonymous property attestation uses the following equation of zero-knowledge proof to attest both the anonymous identity and the platform properties:

$$SPK\{(cs, r_0, r, t_1, t_2) | v_x v_{xy}^{f} v_{xyz_1}^{cs} v_{xyz_2}^{ps} = v_s^{r} \wedge C = g_T^{cs} h_T^{r_0} \wedge d_1 = X^{t_1} \wedge d_2 = Y^{t_2}\}(N_v, N_t).$$

The APA attestation just uses the temporary credential to do the attestation. The trusted computing platform could use the original DAA credential to attest the anonymous identity. It can also use the security property certificate for the PBA. The APA scheme provides good application flexibility and is fully compatible with the existing remote attestation framework. The APA scheme does not lower the security of the original remote attestation. The protocol also satisfies the security properties such as unforgeability, anonymity, configuration privacy and so on. Reference [68] conducts the proof using sequence of games. It has proved the security of the protocol. Under the same security strength, the APA scheme can significantly improve the efficiency

Table 7.4: Performance and signature length comparison of APA.

	DAA + PBA scheme	Our APA scheme
Attest phase	30673 **S** + 16351 **M**	3390 **S**+1699 **M**
Verify phase	23651 **S** + 11844 **M**	2480 **S**+1247 **M**+15 **P**
Signature length	2972 bytes	894 Bytes

of the attestation in the protocol. The computation cost for attestations is reduced by about 89 %. The signature length is reduced by about 72 %. The comparison results are shown in Table 7.4.

7.4.3 Research Prospects

In this section, we discuss integrity attestation of trusted computing platform. We introduce a number of representative platform integrity attestation schemes and focus on the research of property-based remote attestation. Binary-based remote attestation is the most basic method. It is designed and implemented following the TPM specification completely. It is currently the only remote attestation method that has been applied to the practical Linux system. However, there are still many security deficiencies in the binary-based remote attestation. Thus researchers focus on the study of property-based remote attestation method and are devoted to proposing more secure and practical method of platform integrity remote attestation.

There are still many security problems in the platform integrity attestations. The perfect remote attestation scheme must be able to resist various forms of attackers, such as the local attackers, the network attackers and the malicious verifiers. The local attacker is able to tamper the integrity measurement value to carry out fraudulent attacks and to implement TOCTOU attack. The network attacker is able to replay the signature of remote attestation and to impersonate an honesty platform to spoof the remote verifier. The malicious verifier is able to analyze the attestation data to break the privacy of platform integrity or to break the anonymity by linking the remote attestation sessions. In summary, the remote attestation system still faces many security threats, and there are still no perfect solutions. It requires an in-depth research. Only if these problems are solved can the platform integrity remote attestation be applied in practice.

7.5 Remote Attestation System and Application

As one of the most important functions of trusted computing, the remote attestation has experienced not only the important breakthrough in theoretical research but also many research achievements in its applications and the development of remote attestation systems. The research scale on remote attestation systems and applications is very wide, such as security PC, mobile phone platforms, trusted channel establishment, trusted network connection, cloud computing node authentication and so on. The researches on remote attestation systems and applications mainly introduce remote attestation security mechanisms on the basis of the original systems so as to enhance the application security. It requires that the remote attestation scheme combined with the original system should have good compatibility, fine scalability and high efficiency. In this section, we will describe three representative works, which are the remote attestation system in security PC, integrity verification application on mobile platform and remote attestation integrated with the TLS protocol.

7.5.1 Remote Attestation System in Security PC

According to the trusted computing remote attestation principle, we implement the attestation system on PC platforms. In aspect of hardware, it supports the TPM and TCM security chip. In aspect of operation system, it supports the Linux and Windows operating systems. Part of the system has been used in the practical application. Remote attestation system insecurity PC implements the security functions such as the establishment of the whole chain of trust from the PC booting to the application running, the platform binary integrity attestation and the component integrity attestation, and the management and verification of integrity of the trusted PC terminal platforms. It is one of the most representative achievements in trusted computing in China.

Platform integrity measurement and collection are the basis of the remote attestation. The remote attestation system supports three ways of integrity measurement: the loading-time measurement, the runtime measurement and the component measurement. The loading-time measurement is to measure the integrity of the system program when it is loaded into the memory. The most typical system is IBM IMA architecture. The runtime measurement (or called dynamic measurement) is to measure the characteristics of the system program runtime state when it is running. It can reduce time interval between the time of measurement and the time of attestation, which can mitigate the TOCTOU problem. The component measurement is to measure the executable code of the system program and its direct dependent code, namely to measure the context associated with the measured program. To determine whether a component is trusted, it can measure the executable image loaded into the memory, or the text section of the component, or the kernel module called by the component, or the system dynamic link library loaded into the memory during the running and so on. These features, which can describe the component trustworthiness from the various aspects, are defined as the measurement categories. The specific measured terms, which can describe the component runtime states, are defined as the component measurement variables. Currently the measurement categories implemented in the security PC remote attestation system include the following:

(1) Executable image: When the program runs, it measures the executable image loaded into the process space.

(2) Component dynamic link library: the dynamic link library is released with the component. It is measured when the component program dynamically loads it. When the component is running, not all of its dynamic link libraries need to be measured. Only when the executable program calls the dynamic link library, it is loaded into the memory and measured.
(3) System dynamic link library: it measures the system dynamic link library required by the components running. The measurement category acts as the system dependence for the runtime component. Since each system configuration of hardware and software varies greatly, the system dynamic link libraries for the same component in different systems might be completely different.
(4) System kernel module: the kernel module which is the dependence of the component also needs to be measured. Its measurement is completed by the trusted operating system.

In addition to these measurement categories, the trusted runtime states of the components can also be described by the measurement categories such as the component configurations, component text section and the runtime critical data structure of the components. The following figures show the remote attestation system architecture for the Linux system based on the component measurement as well as the component measurement and the attestation results[1] of the browser Firefox.

Figure 7.12 shows the remote attestation system architecture of security PC in Linux. The attestation service is responsible for the management of the component PBA data. It drives the component measurement agents to classify and measure the system components, and then the TPM signs the measurement values. In addition to the component integrity measurement and attestation, the system also includes a dynamic measurement agent, which can dynamically measure the programs running in the system. It improves the real-time performance of the remote attestation. Firefox component attestation includes the Firefox browser executable file *firefox-bin*, Firefox component dynamic link libraries */usr/lib/firefox-1.5.0.1/components/libmork.so*, */usr/lib/firefox-1.5.0.1/components/libeditor.so* and so on; the system dynamic link libraries */usr/lib/libssl3.so*, */lib/libpthread-2.4.so*, */lib/libdl-2.4.so* and so on; and other dynamic link libraries, such as GTK, GNOME and so on. The integrity of these measurement variables assures the security of the browser Firefox components. The template instance of the Firefox attestation data is shown in Figure 7.13. When remote attestation challenge is sent out by the verifier service, the system attestation service creates the attestation data according to the measurement log, requests the TPM to

1 The running environment of the test results: National Semiconductor TPM security chip in compliance with the TPM 1.2 specification, Federa Core 5 Linux OS, DDR2 1GB memory, Intel Pentium4 3 GHz CPU.

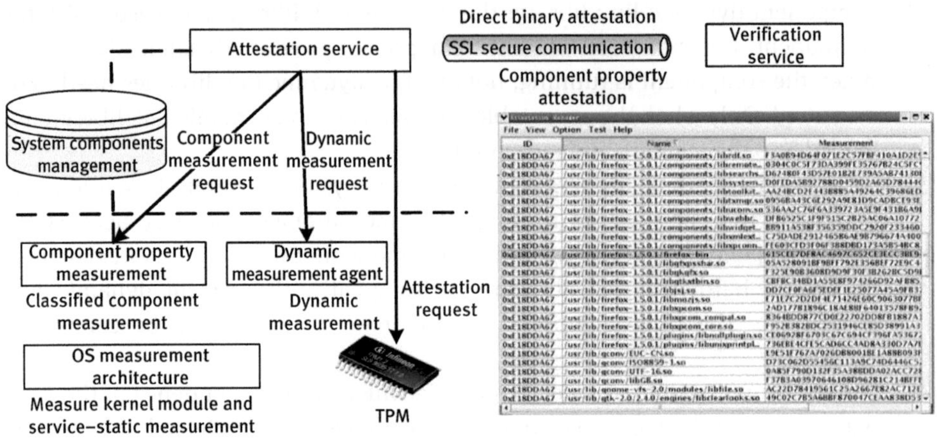

Figure 7.12: Remote attestation system architecture and interface in security PC.


```xml
<?xml version="1.0" encoding="UTF-8" ?>
- <ComponentAttest>
- <Component ID="0xE18DDA67">
- <ComponentItem>
  <ID>0xE18DDA67</ID>
  <Name>/usr/lib/firefox-1.5.0.1/firefox-bin</Name>
  <Hash>615CEE7DF8AC4697C652CE3ECC3BE94B50F3B125</Hash>
  <Timestamp>2007-11-9 14:16:14</Timestamp>
</ComponentItem>
..........
..........
- <ComponentItem>
  <ID>0xE18DDA67</ID>
  <Name>/usr/lib/gtk-2.0/2.4.0/loaders/libpixbufloader-png.so</Name>
  <Hash>CB7825FEDE533059CB511A65BEA16D814BFA9E7F</Hash>
  <Timestamp>2007-11-9 14:16:14</Timestamp>
</ComponentItem>
</Component>
- <TPMQuote>
  <QuoteInfo>0101000051554F546B00BD8547414A76755CBB9A6616A9BBAA9A5E440ABF3CE5AE5E536
1E3F6AD2C1499C3B898927C62</QuoteInfo>
  <Signature>1AB60D42AF81C55BD85B66DE51DDDD12FBF6AA6886C7C40F34B17391750D0C99D0DECB
286622BBED4D9665EC67FD003BB9D77371C4A52E9D1F6AF2A11FC0F6BEBB53A42BEA1B2E3FB1EF
8519E4D6F6019D94894D5A6DB9FBB55823810D9B8B8755F89ECE19620046C1414FA6EB791507AE7FA
5599B1BFDC03EFBF23F234A6D805A00EBEDF46F8FF2AD73CFE99F5D6904EA8623089B793710AEA94
E975DDBF1D50DC796A098A29CA957ACE7A54A1222968EF31E258CCFA9B651B27D87D902D7EF09634
853563E77FCE5ED01675A2065986C433E659E5ECD76251E3264EAC7A16E7AF1B09E5E8CDB83A43EE6
049BC489523D2969CA64EBAD9DEC37CEA9772E3A4F</Signature>
  </TPMQuote>
  </ComponentAttest>
```


Figure 7.13: Attestation data instance of browser Firefox.

sign the integrity measurement values and then through the SSL channel attests to the verifier that the platform runtime components satisfy the specific security properties.

Based on the same principle, we also implement the remote attestation system of security PC in the Windows platform based on the TCM security chip. In

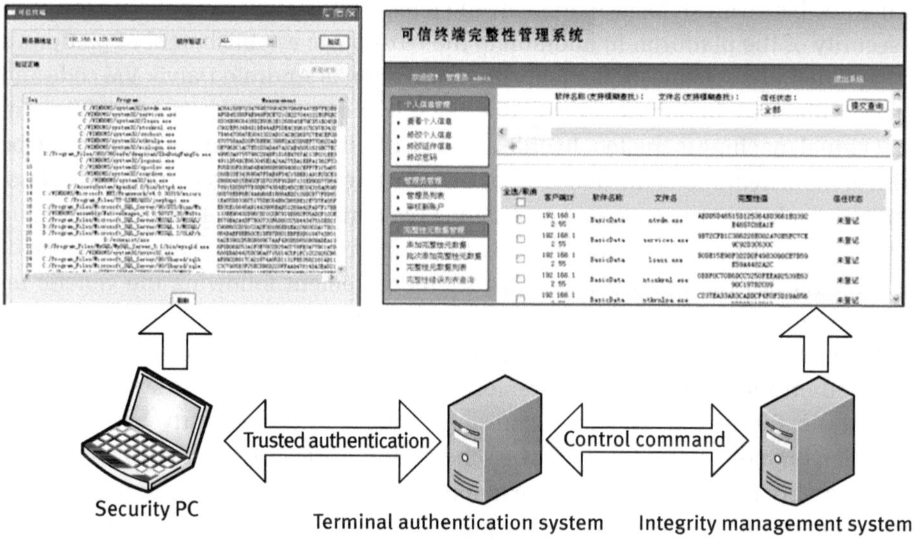

Figure 7.14: Graphical user interface of remote attestation in windows platform.

addition to the different implementation method of the Windows measurement technology, it enhances the TCM platform identification and authentication, and integrity management and verification of the trusted computing platform. Figure 7.14 shows the architecture and graphical user interface of the system[2].

7.5.2 Integrity Verification Application on Mobile Platform

Early research on mobile platform mainly includes the trusted computing architecture, Mobile Trusted Module (MTM). The researchers in Nokia Research Center did a lot of work. Through the extension of the mobile platform SoC architecture with trusted computing, Nokia designed and implemented the MTM, which includes the minimum code and data, to provide security services to mobile platform users, manufacturers, and mobile operators.

With the rapid development of mobile Internet, the integrity attestation and verification of application-oriented mobile phone has attracted a lot of attentions. In the smart phone Android platforms, some research institutions proposed the integrity attestation and verification schemes at Android kernel level [141]. Android is unable to determine whether the running application is trusted. The traditional method based on verification of application signatures cannot solve the problem. The introduction of

2 The running environment of the test results: Nationz Technologies TCM security chip in compliance with the China's trusted computing specification, Microsoft Windows XP SP3 OS, DDR2 3.25 GB memory, Intel Core2 Duo 2.80 GHz CPU.

the method based on MTM measurement and remote attestation can enhance the overall security of the platform. In addition to the most basic establishment of platform's chain of trust, the scheme implements the verification of Android Dalvik VM code and Java core libraries, in order to ensure that the initial running environment of the Android virtual machine is trusted. In order to ensure that each loaded application can be verified, the scheme adds the hooks at the entry where the Android kernel loads Class, measures each application code and extends the corresponding measurement value to the MTM. If it needs to verify whether the current running application is trusted, the MTM verifies the signature on integrity measurement following the generic remote attestation method. The scheme is suitable for the Android smart phone platform because of its ease of use, small amount of computation and power consumption.

Based on the application requirements of the vehicle electronic system, the researchers in the Nokia Research Center also proposed the property based remote attestation on mobile devices [142]. The scheme adopts the application ID and the security property mapping method. The mapping relation is stored in smart phones as application certificates. Then it uses the property based remote attestation to convince the users that the current running applications can use the vehicle electronic devices in a trusted way. In the smart phone, it uses TrustZone to build an isolated TrEE (trusted execution environments). The keys and confidential data used in PBA based on the MTM are protected by TrEE. The application has an urgent practical need. It uses the remote attestation method to establish the trust among users, smart phones and electronic devices, which allows the users to easily use the mobile Internet applications. The smart phones act as controllers, which can conveniently communicate with the external mobile devices. The users can verify that this application threatens neither the smart phone nor the mobile electronic devices.

7.5.3 Remote Attestation Integrated with the TLS Protocol

The researchers in Ruhr University Bochum have done a lot of research on the hybrid of the remote attestation protocol and the TLS/SSL protocol [44, 45]. They tried to establish the network communication protocol that can be fully compatible with the TLS/SSL protocol and has a higher efficiency. The initial idea is to extend the SKAE within the TLS X.509 V3 certificate to attest the platform identity. Then it starts the new configuration exchange stage in the TLS handshake protocol to attest the platform integrity. Since this is the first combination of TLS and the remote attestation, it has the problems that it is not compatible with the TLS protocol and uses the public key to encrypt and transfer the platform integrity data inefficiently. Then a more thorough improvement is made on the trusted channels based on OpenSSL. It uses the extended message *SupplementalData* of the TLS handshake protocol to transfer the platform integrity information and the remote attestation signature information. The scheme is fully compatible with the TLS/SSL protocol. Through the application tests of the scheme implemented by OpenSSL, both the security and the communication efficiency could meet the practical application requirements.

The DAA protocol can be integrated to the TLS protocol, just like the remote attestation based on the platform integrity. The researchers in the University of Turin in Italy propose a practical anonymous authentication method [143], which combines the DAA protocol and the TLS protocol. The scheme uses the approach that is similar to the one used by the researchers in Ruhr University of Bochum. It uses the *SupplementalData* to transfer the DAA attestation message. The DAA Sign subprotocol is integrated with the TLS handshake protocol. The scheme studies in detail the feasibility of the combination of the two protocols, defines the format and interface of each extended message and extends the OpenSSL library to implement the system which combines the DAA and the TLS. The compatibility and feasibility are considered in the scheme design. The scheme is a good way to implement the DAA system.

In summary, in trusted computing applications, integration of the remote attestation protocol with the applications of the network communication protocols (TLS protocol, IPSec protocol) is a very good idea, which not only is compatible with the existing protocols, applications and systems but also improves the security of network communication. Moreover, it is convenient for large-scale application of trusted computing.

7.6 Summary

Remote attestation is able to determine the trust level of the platform integrity at the remote verifier. It is an important technology to establish the trust between the platforms and the trust in the network space. Research on the remote attestation involves a wide range of contents, which mainly includes the TPM security chip, the integrity measurement architecture and the remote attestation protocol. The remote attestation mechanism is supported by the security chip functions and interfaces, such as TPM quote, AIK, PCR, and DAA. The integrity measurement architecture is to measure the integrity of platform hardware and software through the measurement agent and to obtain the platform configurations, which can provide trusted data for the remote attestation. The most typical scheme is the IBM IMA architecture. The remote attestation protocol is to use the specific cryptographic protocol to attest the platform identity and integrity. It focuses on the security properties such as the unforgeability, anonymity, privacy and so on.

If only the theoretical methods are concerned, the remote attestation methods are varied and developed rapidly. The research results in related fields are abundant. However, the application of remote attestation is very limited because of the complexity and diversity of the platform configuration integrity. It also faces many technical problems that hinder its applications, such as platform integrity verification, platform integrity updating and so on. Although the property-based remote attestation overcomes some disadvantages of the traditional binary attestation, it still has some problems in the property definition, property revocation and property management of the trusted third party. Recently, it is only limited to some simple applications. In the future, the remote attestation schemes will be developed toward a more practical and more efficient direction. It is a good idea to integrate the remote attestation scheme within the traditional network communication protocol, which is convenient for the upgrade of the system and the extension of the application. It is also an important development trend to establish the isolated execution environment based on dynamic root of trust for measurement, which can greatly reduce the scope and the size of the TCB to be attested.

8 Trust Network Connection

Trusted network connection (TNC) is an application of trusted computing technology in network access control (NAC) framework, and it is an open NAC solution that can strengthen the trustworthiness of network environment. TNC is designed by Trusted Computing Group (TCG) to be compatible with other network access control solutions. TCG proposes a complete series of standards and specifications, including architecture, component interfaces and supporting technology. Since the proposal of TNC architecture, a variety of TNC prototypes are implemented based on all kinds of network access technologies. In order to accelerate the commercialization of TNC, some TCG members have designed products in compliance with TNC specifications, and have applied these products in various industrial fields. In the aspect of standards, TCG is working hard to evolve TNC specifications to more popular international standards, and has made some achievements. In China, many manufacturers have proposed their network security solutions based on TNC.

In this chapter, we first introduce the background of TNC, including NAC framework and existing commercial solutions and their defects. Then we take an overview of TCG's work on TNC, including TNC architecture, working principle, advantages and current problems of TNC in the aspect of NAC. We also review some research work in TNC, including our ISCAS TNC system. Finally, we introduce the development of TNC in industrial fields and development trends of TNC in the future.

8.1 Background of TNC

The network access control framework, launched by CISCO and other network manufacturers, aims to protect the network security, especially the security of enterprise network. NAC framework requires verifying the terminal's identity and security status before it accesses network, and guarantees that only legitimate and trusted terminals can access network. Because of the inherent advantages in protection of platform identity and trustworthiness, trusted computing technology is very suitable for NAC framework. In this background, the TNC architecture is proposed, which is the application of trusted computing technology to NAC framework. This section mainly introduces the TNC's background, that is, the NAC framework, overviews popular commercial NAC solutions and summarizes the defects of the existing NAC solutions and TNC's advantages in the aspect of NAC.

8.1.1 Introduction to NAC

8.1.1.1 Requirements of NAC Framework

With the development of network, more and more network attacks appear and the emergence of viruses, worms and Trojans threatens network users and enterprises.

DOI 10.1515/9783110477597-008

First, malicious attackers can illegally get resources or do some damage after they access the network without permission. Second, even a legitimate user might be infected accidentally in the external network and bring the malicious code into the internal network, which will infect the network.

Although traditional security solutions, such as firewalls and antivirus software, have been developing for years, they cannot control the spread of malicious codes in the network. This situation makes malicious codes (such as viruses, worms and Trojans) cause great losses every year and even lots of enterprise security accidents, which have great impact on economy. Therefore, the traditional security solutions alone cannot solve security problems caused by malicious codes. CISCO is the first enterprise that proposes the NAC framework, which combines terminals' security status check and network control technology to ensure that all devices in the network meet security requirements.

The NAC framework improves the security of network by bringing in user's identity authentication and status authentication mechanisms. First, it requires that users must provide their identity information when accessing network, and only allows legitimate users accessing the network. This identity authentication can effectively block unauthorized users. Second, it requires to authenticate the terminal's security status, and the terminal should report its security status (e.g., whether the OS is updated, and whether antivirus and firewall start) to the network access server, and terminals are allowed to access the network only if they meet server's security policy. The NAC framework can prevent illegal users and insecure terminals (such as terminals affected by malicious codes) by authenticating terminals' identities and security status. In this way, the NAC guarantees the security of network environment.

8.1.1.2 NAC Framework

The NAC framework is composed of four parts: NAC client agency, NAC policy enforcement point, NAC server and NAC policy server. The details of NAC framework are depicted in Figure 8.1. For the convenience of users, NAC provides an isolated domain that is used to repair terminals that fail to access the network. In the following, we will explain components in the NAC architecture.

(1) NAC client agency: It starts access request and collects security information of clients.
(2) NAC policy server: Network administrator gives security policies in this server, and this server performs user identity authentication and security status authentication.
(3) NAC server: It gives access decisions by authentication results of NAC policy server.
(4) NAC policy enforcement point: Usually it is a network access device, which enforces access policies given by the NAC server.
(5) Isolated domain: An isolated network domain, in which terminals that fail to access the network can remedy their system components that do not meet the security requirements.

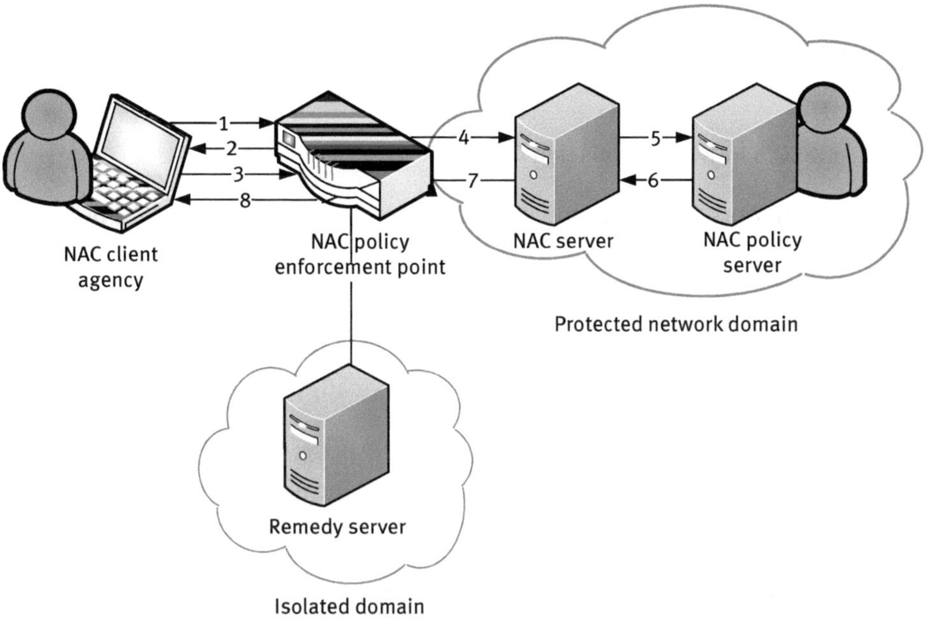

Figure 8.1: NAC architecture.

Figure 8.1 depicts the processes that a terminal accesses the network:

(1) NAC client agency starts the access request.

(2) NAC policy enforcement point requires the terminal to send user identity and security status information of the terminal.

(3) NAC client agency collects terminal's security status and identity information, and sends them to NAC policy enforcement point.

(4) NAC policy enforcement point transfers received information to the NAC server.

(5) NAC server transfers received information to the NAC policy server for authentication.

(6) NAC policy server gives authentication results based on user identity information and platform security information.

(7) NAC server gives access decisions based on authentication results: access allowed or access isolated.

(8) NAC policy enforcement point enforces access decisions and notifies the terminal.

8.1.2 Commercial NAC Solutions

As the NAC framework can effectively improve the security of the network environment, many NAC products under various network access control frameworks have been put on the market. The most typical solutions are CISCO's Network Admission Control (NAC) solution and Microsoft's Network Access Protection (NAP) solution.

8.1.2.1 CISCO's Network Admission Control

The NAC framework is first proposed by CISCO, which launched the NAC project in 2003. After the project, CISCO finally proposed the NAC solution. This solution combines traditional security solutions such as antivirus, security enhancement with network access technology to ensure that all the terminals in the network meet the requirements of administrator's security policies (such as the requirement of running latest version antivirus and firewall), and thus can greatly reduce security risks caused by malicious codes.

The CISCO's NAC architecture is compatible with NAC framework, and its processes are as follows: When a terminal tries to access the network, the network access devices (such as switches, wireless access points or VPNs) demand the terminal to submit its security status information collected by the client agency. After the terminal submits its status information, the NAC server will compare the status information according to security policies, and gives access decision by the comparison results. The terminals meeting the security requirements are allowed to access the network directly. The terminals that do not meet the security requirements are usually isolated to some LAN or redirected to some LAN to restrict their network access. In addition, the isolated terminals can repair their components using the remedy server to meet security policies. After the terminals remedy their components, they are allowed to access the network if they meet the security policies.

The security policy of CISCO's NAC solution includes the following aspects:

(1) Check whether the terminal runs OS with legitimate version.
(2) Check whether the OS installs the patches, and whether they are updated in time.
(3) Check whether the terminal is deployed with antivirus software.
(4) Ensure that the antivirus software is running.
(5) Check whether the terminal installs network security software such as firewall; check whether they are configured correctly.
(6) Check whether the images of the OS and firmware are tampered.

CISCO proposes the CISCO Clean Access series products based on the aforementioned NAC solution. The Clean Access products can be integrated with many antivirus and security management software and provide a powerful capability of network access control. Their advantages are as follows:

(1) Scalability: Clean Access can be directly deployed in the network access environment, and their components can be integrated into other CISCO's network access control products.

(2) Rapid deployment: Provide a set of solutions that can be deployed rapidly and conveniently.
(3) Flexibility: A variety of operating systems in the network are supported.

8.1.2.2 Microsoft's Network Access Protection

Following CISCO, Microsoft proposed the NAP solution that is similar to the CISCO's NAC solution. The NAP architecture is composed of system components added to Windows (Windows Server series, Windows Vista, Windows XP etc.), and provides security status authentication when terminal is trying to access the network. The NAP architecture ensures the security of clients in the network, and the clients not meeting the security requirement will be isolated to a network domain with constraint access privilege and cannot access the network until their running status meet the security requirements.

The NAP solution adds some components to Windows, including NAP client, policy enforcement point and policy decision point, and defines the interfaces that these components should provide. Users and enterprises can leverage the interfaces to implement products that are compatible with NAP. NAP does not specify network devices, and needs the support of physical network devices in the bottom layer. With the support of network infrastructure, Microsoft's NAP solution provides the following functions:
(1) Security status verification: Check whether access terminals satisfy the security policy.
(2) Network access isolation: Isolate the terminals that do not satisfy the security policy.
(3) Auto remedy: Remedy the terminals that do not satisfy the security policy without participant of users.
(4) Auto update: Update terminals on time to satisfy the security policy that is updated continuously.

Currently, NAP solution can implement control for a variety of network access technologies:
(1) IPsec: Implement the control of security communication at network layer by managing IPsec certificates.
(2) 802.1X: Provide access control based on port at the data link layer by leveraging 802.1X framework.
(3) VPN: Control remote VPN connection.
(4) DHCP: Implement the DHCP control by providing IP from a pool with limited permission for clients whose security status does not satisfy security requirements.

8.1.3 Defects of Current Solutions and TNC Motivation

8.1.3.1 Defects of Current Solutions

With the application of network access control products, defects of current products (such as CISCO's NAC and Microsoft's NAP) appear because of patents and technologies used by these products:

(1) Bad interoperability and scalability: Most manufacturers' solutions are not compatible and do not support multiplatform. Due to the protection acts on intellectual property, critical source code and key interactive interfaces, mainstream products between different manufacturers are hard to interoperate, and the support for noncommercial operating system platform is extremely limited. For example, CISCO's NAC architecture contains some special technology protected by patents, so the implementation of NAC architecture must rely on CISCO's own network equipment; Microsoft's NAP architecture leverages some non-public source codes and system calls, which do not support non-Windows platforms such as Linux.

(2) Status forgery: Due to lack of strong terminal status authentication mechanism, current schemes cannot prevent forgery behaviors. By ways such as forging system state, a client can meet the requirements of access control and then access the controlled network freely. In Black hat 2007, hackers gave an example of such attacks. Although such attacks require a certain level of technology and attack costs, the benefits of these attacks may be very high.

(3) Lacking control after access in network: Obtaining illegal benefits by changing configuration after access of the network is a much more practical way of attacking compared to the aforementioned forging attack, but current architectures lack control after clients are connected, so there exist security risks.

8.1.3.2 Motivation of TNC

To solve the aforementioned security problems, TCG proposes an open network access control solution: Trusted Network Connection, and launches a series of standards. TNC highlights openness of the architecture, and does not limit the implementation technologies so as to support all kinds of popular computation platforms, network devices and OS. Another feature of TNC is that it combines with trusted computing technology.

In the aspect of openness, the interoperability of TNC products is obviously ensured by the nature of TCG as an industry alliance. Now, some TCG members have proposed products compliant with TNC specifications, especially Microsoft's latest NAP version, which is also compatible with TNC.

In the aspect of combination with trusted computing technology, TNC uses security chips embedded on the platforms to implement identity authentication and integrity status verification, and solves the problems of terminal status authentication and network control after access:

(1) Platform identity authentication: By the non-migratable identity keys AIK (attestation identity key) provided by TPM, the TNC is capable of authenticating clients' identities when they are trying to access the network.
(2) Platform integrity attestation: TPM measures key components of the platform when it powers on and stores the measurement results in the TPM. These integrity information can be used to verify the integrity status of the access terminal.

8.2 Architecture and Principles of TNC

8.2.1 Standard Architecture

The TCG's TNC workgroup designs an open network access control framework according to the existing requirements of network access applications, and develops a series of TNC specifications. TNC specifications consist of architecture, component and supporting technology specifications:
(1) Architecture specification [90]: This specification defines the overall architecture of TNC and basic communication process, analyzes the compatibility with other network access control systems and illustrates principles that how trusted computing technology can enhance the security of network access control.
(2) Component interoperability interface specifications [144–146]: These specifications define internal basic functions and interfaces of components in the TNC architecture.
(3) Supporting technology specifications [147, 148]: These specifications define special functions and components implemented by trusted computing technology. Although these specifications are not mandatory, they provide mature references and technical ideas for developers to implement trusted network access system.

The TNC specifications are developing continuously. TNC workgroup updates TNC specifications by improving and revising current specifications. TCG actively participates in the development of IETF standard, aiming to upgrade TNC specifications to international standards. TNC workgroup has made some achievements in this aspect: The TNC IF-TNCCS2.0 and IF-M specifications have been upgraded to RFC 5793 and RFC 5792, respectively. With the development of TNC technology, we believe that TNC specification family will attract more and more focus and support and be upgraded to international standards accepted by industrial fields.

8.2.2 Overall Architecture

The architecture of TNC, as is shown in Figure 8.2, consists of three participants and three logic layers. The three participants are Access Requester (AR), Policy Enforcement Point (PEP) and Policy Decision Point (PDP). The AR is the terminal requesting

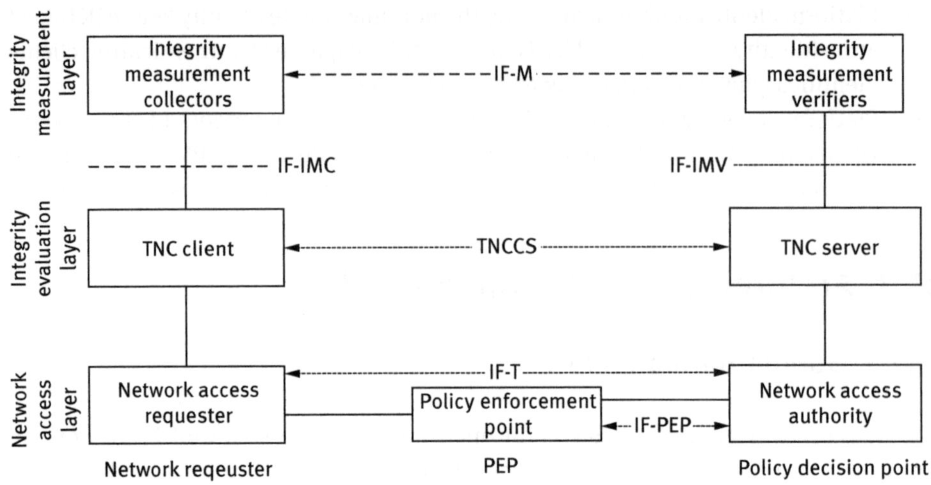

Figure 8.2: TNC architecture.

access to the network, the PEP enforces network access and the PDP authenticates clients and gives access policy. TNC can be divided into three logic layers according to the roles in the network access: integrity measurement layer, integrity evaluation layer and network access layer. As there exists interoperability between participating entities and logic layers, TNC defines interface specifications between components at the same layer (such as the integrity measurement collector (IMC) and integrity measurement verifier (IMV) and the interface relationship between components in the same participant (such as the IMC and TNC clients).

8.2.2.1 Main Participants

TNC has three participants: AR, PEP and PDP. AR is the client trying to access the network, which collects platform's integrity information and actively transfers access request to PDP. PDP's role is to check the security status of AR and determine AR's access request according to security policy. PEP enforces the access decision given by the PDP. TNC splits the decision of access policy and access enforcement, which increases its elasticity and flexibility.

AR includes network access requester (NAR), TNC client (TNCC) and IMC. NAR issues the access request to apply for access to the network. TNCC calls IMC to collect the platform's integrity measurement information and measures and reports IMC own integrity information. IMC measures each component's integrity information in AR, and each AR can deploy multiple IMCs to collect integrity information of different components.

PDP includes three components: network access authority (NAA), trusted network connection server (TNCS) and integrity measurement verifier. NAA decides whether an AR should be granted access according to TNCS's verification result. TNCS verifies whether AR's integrity information satisfies PDP's security policy, and returns the verification result to PDP. Besides, TNCS collects verification results from all of IMVs and then forms a global network access decision. IMV verifies integrity measurement information of AR's components.

PEP controls network access. In particular, PEP performs some operation (*allow*, *deny* or *isolation*) according to the decision of PDP. For example, in 802.1X framework, PEP takes the role of authenticator, that is, switch or wireless AP.

8.2.2.2 Logic Layer

TNC architecture consists of three layers: the integrity measurement layer, the integrity evaluation layer and the network access layer. The integrity measurement layer deals with original integrity measurement data, which has no relationship with specific access policy. In this layer, AR needs to collect platform integrity data, and the corresponding PDP needs to verify the correctness of the integrity data. The integrity evaluation layer deals with the network access policy and assessment of the integrity verification results. In this layer, AR finishes collection of integrity data by resolving the network access policy, and PDP gives access decision according to the access policy. The network access layer deals with the underlying network communication data. In this layer, AR and PDP establish a reliable communication channel, and PEP allows, denies or isolates AR's network access according to PDP's decision.

8.2.2.3 Interoperate Interface

TNC architecture needs to define standard interoperate interface between components in the architecture, which can cooperate TNC's overall function. On the one hand, functions for different layers in one participant are divided into different components, which enhances the elasticity and flexibility of architecture. These components require proper interoperate interface, such as IF-IMC and IF-IMV interface specifications defined by TNC. On the other hand, different participants in the same layer require indirect logic communication, which also require proper interoperate interface, such as IF-M, IF-TNCCS and IF-T interface specifications defined by TNC.

8.2.2.4 Architecture with PTS Extension

TNC architecture is a general network access control framework, and the implementation of corresponding components does not always adopt trusted computing technology. However, the chain of trust and remote attestation mechanism based on security chips can effectively improve the integrity attestation and identity authentication for access terminals; so TCG has developed the platform trust service (PTS) specification [14] for TNC, which illustrates the combination of TNC and TPM's integrity measurement and attestation. This specification provides technical guidance for implementation of TNC based on TPM.

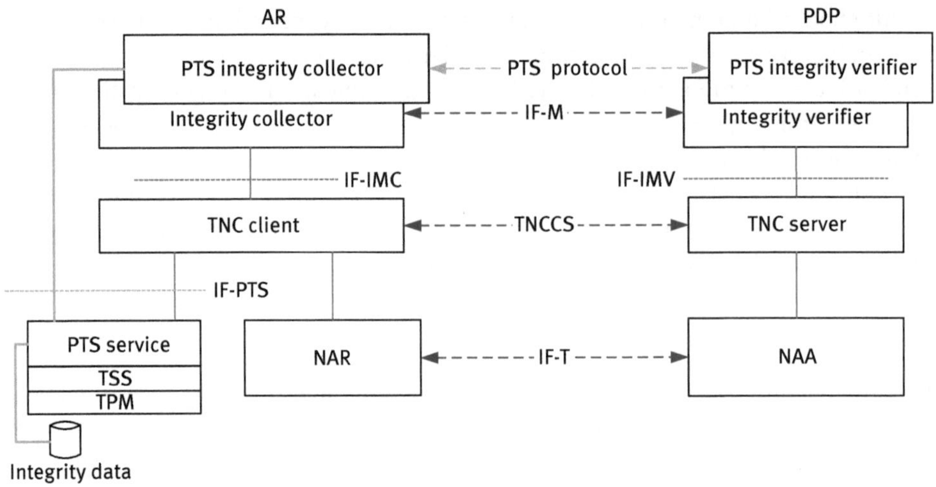

Figure 8.3: TNC architecture with PTS extension.

The TNC architecture with PTS extension is shown in Figure 8.3. There are two changes in the extended architecture: (1) AR is equipped with TPM security chip and trusted software stack (TSS), and other components of AR can invoke PTS; (2) in the original integrity measurement layer, TNC defines PTS protocol used by PTS to collect and verify integrity information above the IF-M interface, and the PTS protocol standardizes the PTS's interoperate way in integrity collection and verification.

8.2.2.5 Network Supporting Technology

As an open general specifications on trusted network access, TNC only specifies the overall architecture, component function, each layer's interface and basic workflow. It does not make any mandatory requirement on the implementation technology. In fact, TNC architecture can smoothly integrate all kinds of network access technology. We can also implement network control compliant with TNC specification based on current network access technology.

From the TNC architecture, we can see that its underlying network access layer leverages existing network access control technology, which makes it convenient for TNC to be compatible with existing network access control system. In order to be compatible with other network technology, TCG proposes a series of TNC specifications on network protocol compatibility. For example, in order to be compatible with 802.1X framework and VPN, TCG defines a protocol standard used to exchange TNC data at IF-T layer, a protocol bound with EAP method [149] and a protocol bound with TLS under 802.1X framework. These specifications compatible with current network technologies greatly promote the development and application of TNC standards and technology. Currently, many open-source projects and network products on the market have begun to support TNC specifications such as IF-T protocol.

8.2.3 Workflow

TNC framework ensures the terminals to access the network securely by a number of steps. Figure 8.4 describes the TNC access procedure, and the details are as follows:

(1) Before all terminals access the network, the TNCC must find and load each relevant IMC in the platform. Then TNCC initializes the IMC. Similar to TNCC, the TNCS must load and initialize each relevant IMV.

(2) When the user requires to access the network, the NAR sends an access request to PEP.

(3) Upon receiving a network access request from the NAR, the PEP sends a network access decision request to NAA.

(4) Usually the NAA is 3A authentication server, such as RADIUS and Diameter. The NAA authenticates the user, and then informs the TNCS that a new access request needs to be dealt with.

(5) The TNCS performs platform identity authentication with TNCC.

(6) After the successful completion of platform identity authentication, the TNCS notifies the IMV that a new access request has arrived. Similarly, the TNCC notifies IMCs that a new access request has arrived. IMCs respond to TNCC with some platform integrity information.

(7) This step is used by PDP to perform integrity authentication of AR, and is divided into three substeps:

   (a) The TNCS and TNCC begin the exchange of messages related to the integrity check. These messages will be transferred through the NAR, PEP and NAA, and will continue until the TNCS collects enough integrity information sent by TNCC for integrity check.

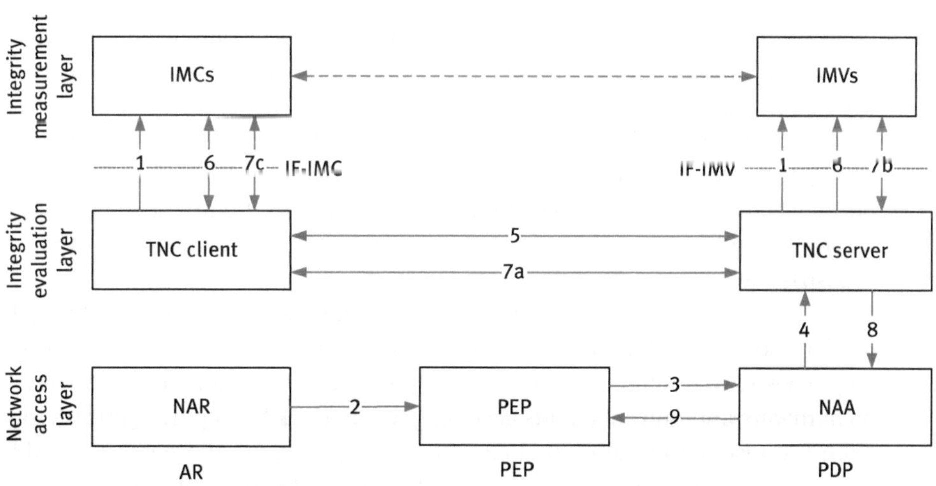

Figure 8.4: TNC workflow.

(b) The TNCS passes each integrity information collected by IMC to the corresponding IMV for integrity check. Each IMV analyzes the IMC message. If an IMV needs TNCC to provide more messages, it sends integrity request message to the TNCS through the IF-IMV interface. If an IMV gives a check result, it gives it to the TNCS through the IF-IMV interface.

(c) The TNCC will forward integrity request from the TNCS to the corresponding IMC, and send integrity information returned from the IMC to the TNCS.

(8) When the TNCS has completed integrity check with TNCC, it sends network access decision to the NAA.

(9) The NAA then sends the network access decision to the PEP, which enforces network access control according to the access policy. The NAA also returns the access decision to the AR.

If the AR does not pass the integrity check, the TNCS will isolate the AR to the remedy network, and AR can rerequest to access the network after it remedies its integrity.

8.2.4 The Advantages and Disadvantages of TNC

8.2.4.1 The Advantages of TNC

(1) Openness: The TNC architecture, proposed by TCG, is an open general network access framework supporting heterogeneous network environment, and now has been supported by a series of complete technology specifications. The openness of TNC makes each manufacturer design and develop products compatible with TNC standard. TCG also launched the TNC product certification plan, so that manufacturers can perform the test on TNC specification compatibility for their products. At present, more and more manufacturers have announced support for TNC specifications in their products, and more and more products have passed the TNC certification [150].

(2) Standard completeness: TNC workgroup developed a complete set of standards and specifications, including the architecture, component interfaces and supporting technology. The completeness of the standard facilitates the TNC solution to be adopted by manufacturers, and promotes the development of TNC in industrial fields.

(3) Security chip support: Besides the traditional network access control, TNC adds platform identity authentication and integrity verification based on the security chip. These two functions not only provide platform status authentication based on hardware and prevent clients accessing the network by forging status information but also apply the trusted computing technology to the network. In this way, it extends the trustworthiness of client to the network environment.

(4) Technical compatibility: TNC architecture does not specify its network technology, which enables it to be implemented on current network technologies (such

as 802.1X, IPsec, TLS). Compared with other network access control, TNC greatly reduces the development difficulties and also the user's economic burden of updating user's network devices.

8.2.4.2 Problems of TNC

Currently, TNC lacks theoretical security proof. The technology of TNC proceeds ahead of its theory, and currently theoretical security model and proof method for TNC have not been built. How to extend the trust from terminals to network and construct a trustworthy network environment are problems that TNC need to solve urgently.

Privacy leakage problem caused by binary attestation: The TNC architecture, which is based on security chips such as TPM or TCM, adopts the binary attestation scheme [10] recommended by TCG specifications, which has some disadvantages: First, the integrity management of terminal platform is complex, which requires the network access server must manage all platforms' integrity configuration status, and these integrity information must cover various software and different versions of the same software, which brings great management burden to the network access server; second, this scheme leaks the terminal's integrity configuration information, leading that all platforms' configuration information is completely exposed in the network, which can be used by malicious attackers to attack terminals by exploiting vulnerabilities of terminals' configuration.

Lack of security protection after network access: TNC only provides identity and integrity authentication when clients connect the network, and provides no security protection after clients access the network. This protection mechanism only guarantees the security at the moment of network access, and cannot guarantee the security of network after terminals' access.

8.3 Research on Extension of TNC

8.3.1 Overview of the TNC Research

Since TCG releases the open TNC architecture and TNC specifications, a large number of open-source projects have begun to support TNC. A number of research institutions have started the research work on TNC. In the following, we will introduce some open-source projects related to TNC and TNC-based systems developed by research institutions.

With the wide application of TNC, a large number of open-source projects implement functions of TNC. In the following, we will introduce these projects:

(1) libTNC [151]: This project aims to build an OS-independent open-source TNC system, and now has supported Windows, some UNIX-like OS and Mac OS. libTNC has implemented interfaces of the integrity evaluation layer and the integrity

measurement layer, and an integrity measurement component that assesses OS by setting security policies.

(2) Open1X [152]: This project is sponsored by the OpenSEA alliance [153], which aims to develop an open-source 802.1X supplicant supporting cross-platform. Open1X implements 802.1X framework and security standard of wireless LAN 802.11i. The product Xsupplicant in Open1X project now supports EAP-TNC method.

(3) strongSwan [154]: This project is an implementation of IPsec for Linux, and now has implemented the integrity evaluation layer of TNC and provides interfaces of integrity evaluation layer and integrity measurement layer. strongSwan has obtained TCG's TNC certification.

The Trust@FHH [155] research group of Hochschule Hannover University of applied sciences and arts is a member of TNC workgroup, and implements the TNC@FHH and tNAC systems based on TNC, which are relatively comprehensive TNC solutions in open-source projects. Based on the TNC architecture, the Institute of Software, Chinese Academy of Sciences (ISCAS) proposes the ISCAS TNC system, which are based on user identity, platform identity and platform integrity authentication. This section focuses on tNAC and TNC@FHH systems implemented by TNC@FHH group, and the ISCAS TNC system implemented by ISCAS.

8.3.2 Trust@FHH

8.3.2.1 TNC@FHH

In order to test TNC's functions, operability and usability, the Trust@FHH research team develops the open-source system TNC@FHH, which implements all core components and interfaces of the TNC architecture, and has passed TCG's TNC certification tests.

The architecture of TNC@FHH is shown in Figure 8.5. TNC@FHH implements TNCS, some IMCs, some IMVs and EAP-TNC method, and also implements interfaces of IF-TNCCS, IF-M, IF-IMC and IF-IMV. The network access requester can adopt the open-source projects Xsupplicant or wpa_supplicant, and the network access authority adopts FreeRadius. which are widely deployed and has implemented EAP-TNC method in it.

TNC@FHH implements the whole TNC architecture based on open-source products Xsupplicant, wpa_supplicant and FreeRadius, and has the following features:

(1) The TNC server can run as an extension of FreeRadius.

(2) The system implements some IMCs and IMVs, and simple terminal integrity attestation can be performed.

(3) The system implements basic policy management.

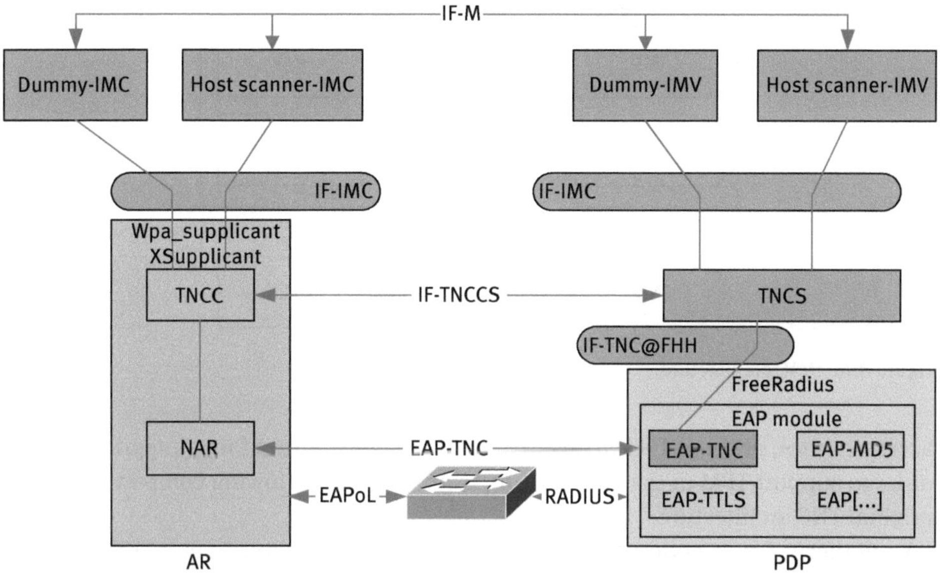

Figure 8.5: The architecture of TNC@FHH.

(4) The system is compatible with other TNC products, such as Xsupplicant, wpa_supplicant and libtnc.
(5) The system is implemented by C++ language.

Since the TNC architecture requires the security policy maker to determine which part of the client's integrity information is checked, PDP is able to examine all the configuration information of the platform, which leads to the privacy leakage issue of clients. To solve this issue, TNC@FHH proposes a privacy protection mechanism by extending a policy manager (PM) (and its communication interface IF-PM between TNCC and PM), which can communicate with TNCC on TNC architecture. Every time the TNCC sends a message to the TNCS, it first queries the PM using IF-PM interface. PM determines whether the message is allowed to be sent according to user's policy and returns the decision result to TNCC. TNCC will decide whether the decision result can be sent. Users can use policy to guarantee that the TNCC can only send the integrity information of some components, and cannot send the integrity information of some other components. In this way, TNC@FHH achieves the goal of clients' privacy protection.

8.3.2.2 tNAC

The TNC@FHH project does not combine the TNC architecture with TPM. In 2008, the Trust@FHH workgroup proposes trusted network access control (tNAC) project, as is shown in Figure 8.6 which implements trusted network access control based on TNC@FHH and trusted platform Turaya. The TNC@FHH is responsible for network

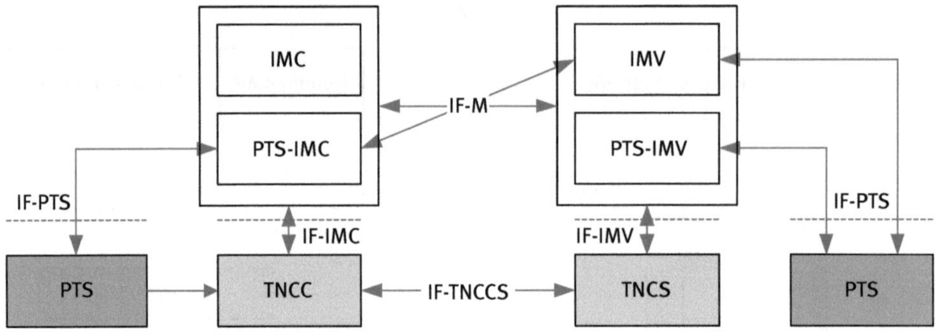

Figure 8.6: tNAC architecture.

access control, and the Turaya ensures that the client cannot forge integrity data. In order to support TPM in the architecture, tNAC adds the following components to the original TNC architecture:

(1) Platform Trust Services (PTS): Both the client and the server require PTS support. At the client side, PTS obtains the client's integrity report by querying the TPM. At the server side, PTS checks the integrity report sent by the client.

(2) PTS-IMC: This IMC informs the PTS to measure corresponding components and collect integrity report, and finally sends the integrity report to the IMV of server side.

(3) PTS-IMV: This IMV sends to the client a request of integrity measurement values of chain of trust and other components. When receiving the measurement values, it invokes PTS to perform integrity verification.

(4) Other IMVs: These IMVs can obtain measurement results of any file in the client by requesting PTS-IMC. When PTS-IMC receives the request, it notifies the PTS to perform measurement and then report the integrity report to the IMV. After the IMV receives the integrity report, it can invoke PTS to perform integrity verification.

8.3.3 ISCAS Trusted Network Connection System

For the requirements of network access and network management of terminal platforms, we develop a trusted network connection system (ISCAS TNC) supporting TNC specifications, which is based on the ISCAS chain of trust system. This TNC system uses trust established by chain of trust of the platform to perform platform identity authentication and integrity attestation, and builds a trusted network computing environment. Taking the application requirement of Chinese TCM chip into account, the TNC system adds support for TCM, and it achieves the integrity attestation of terminal platforms and the trusted network connection based on two kinds of security chips: TPM and TCM. To deal with the privacy leakage of platform configuration during the binary integrity attestation of traditional trusted network connection system, we propose a method named property-based TNC that adds terminal configuration privacy protection to the general trusted network connection schemes.

8.3.3.1 Architecture and Functions of ISCAS TNC System

ISCAS TNC system is a trusted network connection system, which follows TCG standards. When the terminal accesses the network, the system checks the security status of terminals based on TPM chips to achieve the end-to-end security, which ensures the security of terminals accessing the network. Figure 8.7 and Figure 8.8 show the architecture and user interface of ISCAS TNC system respectively.

ISCAS TNC system consists of three entities: network access terminal, network access device (PEP) and AAA server (PDP), and they correspond to access requester, policy enforcement point and policy decision point of TNC architecture, respectively. The internal design architecture and the communication logic of the three entities also follow TNC specifications. In the aspect of functions, ISCAS TNC system implements platform identity registration, trusted network connection and integrity component management functions based on trusted computing technology.

(1) Platform identity registration: A terminal needs to apply for a legitimate platform identity for the first network connection. It sends a platform identity request based on TPM/TCM identity to the TNC server, and the server will issue a TPM/TCM identity credential to a legitimate terminal.

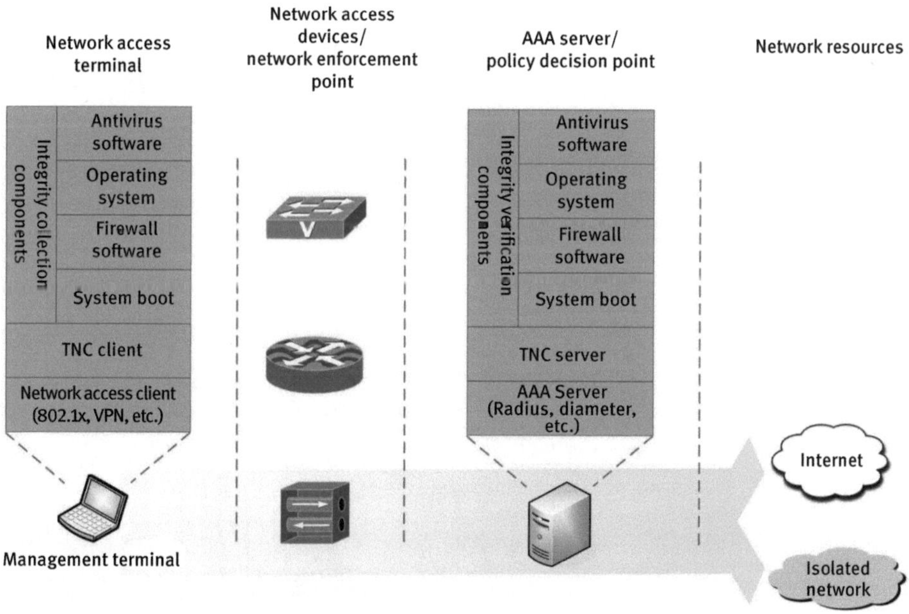

Figure 8.7: Architecture of ISCAS TNC system.

(2) Trusted network connection: The TNC server first authenticates the user identity, the platform identity and the integrity state of the terminal, and then enforces the network access control of the terminal according to the authentication result.
(3) Integrity component management: This function is used to add, update and delete an integrity collector or an integrity verifier, and to query and manage the integrity of application components of a terminal.

ISCAS TNC system strengthens the terminal authentication function of traditional trusted network connection systems. In the aspect of identity authentication, ISCAS TNC implements a two-factor identity authentication method based on user identity and platform identity, and supports both TPM and TCM security chips. In the aspect of platform attestation, (1) the system verifies platform integrity collected during start-up process of the terminal based on its chain of trust; (2) the system leverages the dynamic measurement method to verify the running antivirus software and firewall in real time; (3) the system measures and verifies important system patches of Windows system.

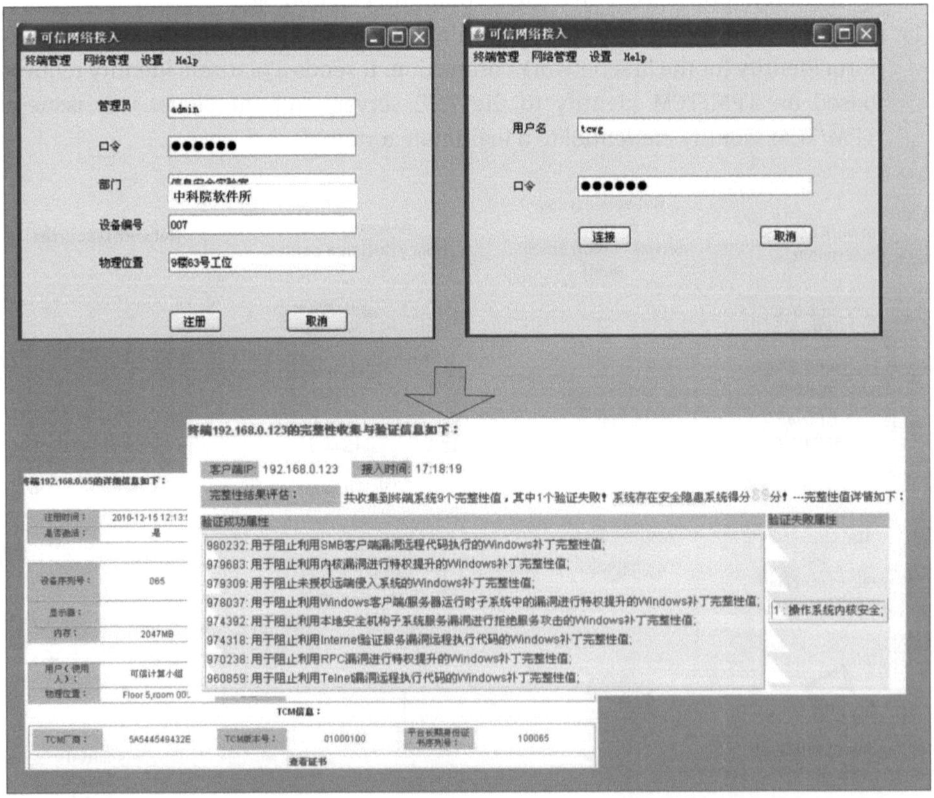

Figure 8.8: The graphic user interface of ISCAS TNC system.

8.3.3.2 Technical Implementation and Characteristics of ISCAS TNC System

In order to meet different requirements of network connection control, the ISCAS TNC system implements two network connection schemes (the deployment of the network connection system is shown in Figure 8.9) in the network access layer based on the third layer of the network (i. e., the network layer) and the second layer of the network (i. e., the data link layer), respectively. The first scheme enforces the network access control at the network layer, and communication messages of system components are all forwarded at this layer. TNCS server provides iptables connection policy after authenticating a terminal, and then the policy enforcement point leverages the iptables policy to implement terminal control based on IP. The network connection control at data link layer follows the 802.1X framework. TNC server gives the final connection control policy based on VLAN, which is deployed on the ports of switch/router. In this way, the ISCAS TNC achieves isolation of terminals based on ports or VLAN.

The control granularity and the application scope of the connection control schemes at the network layer and the data link layer are different. The connection control scheme at network layer controls IP address, and it has low deployment costs, which is suitable for small-scale network connection. The connection control scheme at data link layer controls switch/router ports or VLAN, and it needs support of a certain type of switch/router, which is suitable for large-scale network connection. Figure 8.10 shows the trusted network access time and the authentication time of the two schemes. It can be seen from the figure that the data link layer scheme costs significantly less access time than the network layer scheme and enjoys better performance under the support of network devices such as switch/router.

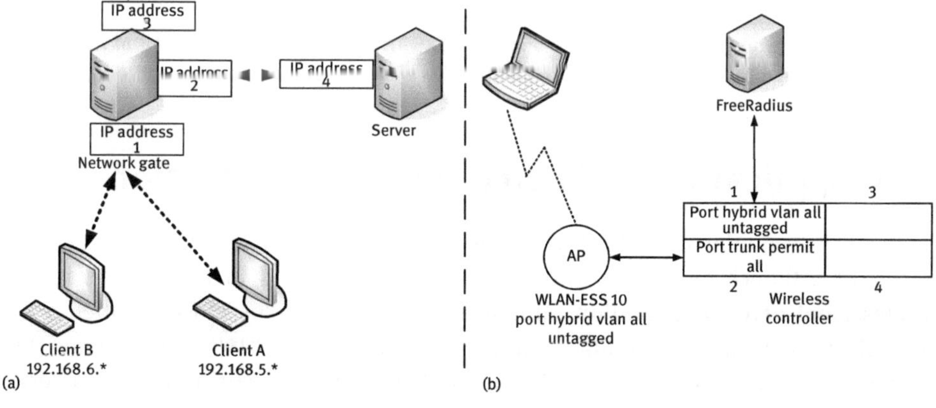

Figure 8.9: The deployment of network connection control. (a) At the third layer, (b) At the second layer.

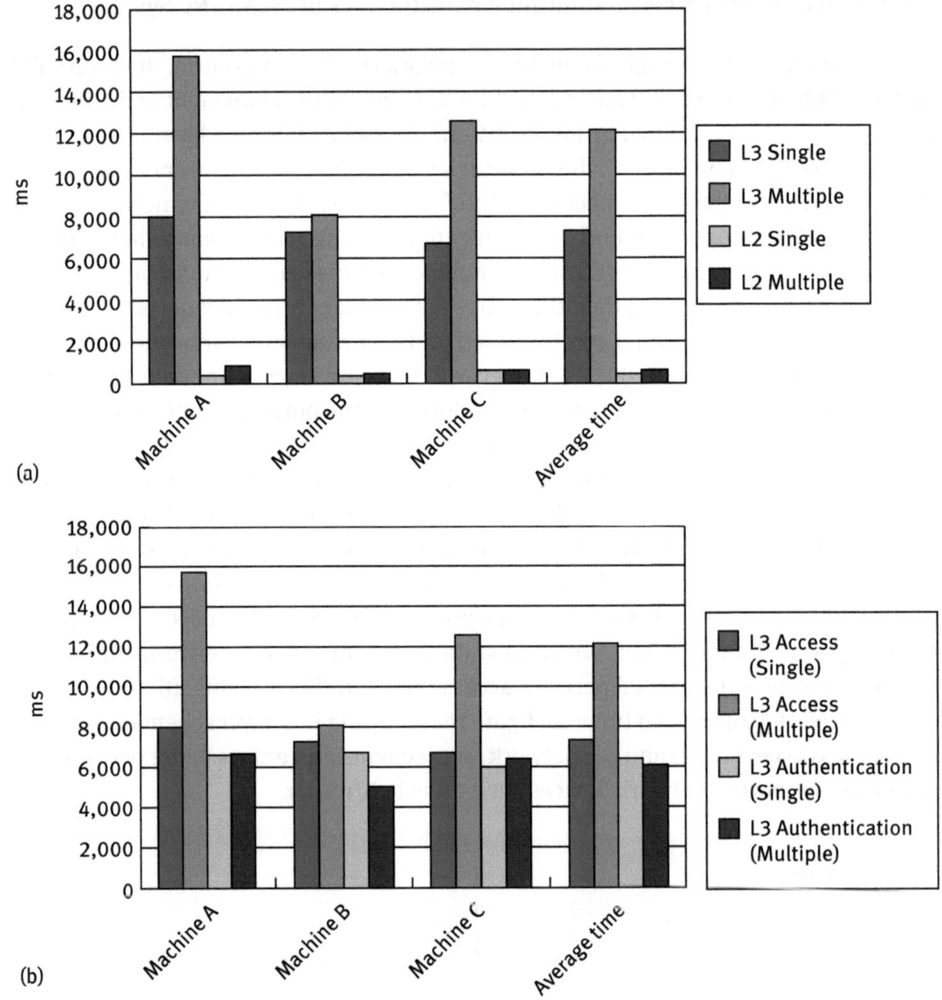

Figure 8.10: Network connection performance of ISCAS TNC system. (a) Comparison of Access Performance between Layer 3 and Layer 2, (b) Comparison of Access and Authentication Performance of L3 TNC.

8.4 Application of Trusted Network Connection

In order to popularize TNC, TCG members Infoblox, Juniper Networks, Lumeta, OpenSEA Alliance and HP Networking jointly participated in the world's largest professional network exhibition: American Information Industry Expo (Interop Las Vegas) in 2010. In the exhibition, they proposed a slogan "TNC Everywhere: Unified Security," and showed how TNC guarantees network security through a series of demonstration. Since then, numerous TNC-supporting network equipment and network access authentication servers have been promoted and placed on the market.

TCG announced the TNC certification program the same year. The main content of the program is compliance test and interoperability test for products to be verified. Products must first pass an automated compliance test suite to ensure that they implement the TNC specifications correctly, and then they must pass interoperability test with other certified products for compatibility. This program aims to ensure for the user that the certified products implement the TNC specifications correctly. Many products of Juniper Networks Company have been certified. Readers can view the list of certified products in Ref. [150].

In China, Huawei, Topsec, AnchTech and other companies have launched their own network connection control solutions based on TNC. Huawei launched the EAD terminal connection control solution [156], which aims to create a trusted computing network environment. Topsec Company launched a trusted network framework TNA [157], which is now upgraded to version 2.0. TNA comprehensively improves the overall protection capability of a network by combining the trusted network connection control mechanism. AnchTech developed a Trusted Network Connection system based on the Chinese security chip TCM [158]. The system uses TCM chip to authenticate terminal users, and provide users with more secure access authentication method. It also uses TCM chips as platform identities to implement device authentication of terminals.

8.5 Summary

This chapter first describes the network access control framework, and then focuses on the open network access control solution TNC proposed by TCG, and TNC's open architecture and standards. TNC verifies the platform identity and integrity of access terminals to ensure the validity of their identities and the security of the terminals. Compared with other commercial network access control solutions, TNC has advantages of openness, standard completeness, security chip support and technology compatibility. But TNC is not perfect in theoretical security proof, integrity attestation and protection after connecting, and it still needs further research.

Currently, TNC is relatively mature, and research institutions have launched their own prototype systems. There are a variety of TNC-based network access control products designed by a number of manufacturers in industrial fields. To promote TNC continually, the TNC workgroup designs an architecture that combines PTS with TNC to facilitate the integrity management. To ensure compatibility of TNC products, the TNC workgroup launches the TNC certification program, which performs compliance test on TNC products and ensures the interoperability of TNC products on the market.

Appendix A: Foundations of Cryptography

Cryptography can effectively ensure the confidentiality, integrity, authenticity and nonrepudiation of information, which is the core foundation of information security. The focus of the appendix is to introduce some common cryptographic algorithms and basic knowledge in trusted computing research, including block ciphers algorithm, public-key cryptography algorithm, digital signature algorithm, hash function and key exchange protocol.

A.1 Block Cipher Algorithm

The main goal of the cryptographic algorithm is to provide data confidentiality. A cryptographic algorithm is defined as a pair of data transformation. One of the transformation is applied to the original data, known as plaintext, and the corresponding transformation result is called ciphertext, while the other transformation is applied to the ciphertext to recover the plaintext. These two transformations are called encryption transformation and decryption transformation. We call them encryption and decryption usually. Encryption and decryption operations are usually performed under the control of a set of keys, called encryption key and decryption key, respectively. There are two general types of key-based algorithms: symmetric algorithms and public-key algorithms. The characteristic of symmetric algorithms is that the encryption key and decryption key are the same or they can be deduced from each other easily. The characteristic of public-key algorithms is that the encryption key is different from the decryption key and any of them cannot be deduced by the other one.

Symmetric algorithms can be divided into two categories. One is the encryption operations on the plaintext bit by bit, which is called stream cipher. The other is the encryption operation on the plaintext block by block (each block contains multiple bits), which is called block cipher. Block cipher is an important research direction of modern cryptography, with advantages of high speed, easy standardization and convenient implementation in software and hardware.

Here, we introduce two block cipher algorithms: AES and SMS4.

A.1.1 AES

On 15 April 1997, the United States National Institute of Standards and Technology (NIST) set up a working group and launched Advanced Encryption Standard (AES: Advanced Encryption Standard) collecting activities to make a nonclassified data encryption standard that is free worldwide. On 12 September 1997, the Federal Register (FR) announced a notice for AES candidate algorithms. On 20 August 1998, NIST convened the first meeting of AES candidates, announcing 15-candidate algorithms.

DOI 10.1515/9783110477597-009

Held on 22 March 1999, the second meeting of AES candidates announced the results of the discussion of the 15-candidate algorithms, from which they chose five candidates. On 25 April 2000, NIST held the AES Candidate Conference for the third time and discussed the five-candidate algorithms again. On 2 October 2000, NIST announced the final result of the candidate, and the Rijndael algorithm was selected as the candidate algorithm. On 26 November 2001, NIST published the Rijndael algorithm as the Federal Information Processing Standard FIPSPUB197 [159].

The block length of AES is 128 bit, and the key length may be 128, 192 or 256 bits. The key length is expressed by 4 bytes word as unit, and is denoted by N_k, with $N_k = 4$, 6 or 8. The block length is denoted by $N_b(= 4)$.The number of AES iteration round is denoted byN_r. As shown in Table A.1, N_r and N_k have the following relationship:

A.1.1.1 The Mathematical Basis of AES

Some operations of the AES are defined by byte, and a byte can be seen as an element of a finite field GF(2^8). Some other AES operations are defined by 4 bytes and a 4-byte word can be seen as a polynomial with the coefficient on GF(2^8) and the degree less than 4.

1) Finite Fields GF(2^8). AES chooses the polynomial to denote the elements of the finite fields GF(2^8). All the elements of GF(2^8) are the polynomial with all the coefficients on GF(2) and the degree less than 8. A polynomial can be seen as a byte made up of $b_7b_6b_5b_4b_3b_2b_1b_0$.

$$b_7x^7 + b_6x^6 + b_5x^5 + b_4x^4 + b_3x^3 + b_2x^2 + b_1x + b_0.$$

Here, $b_i \in \mathrm{GF}(2)$, $0 \le i \le 7$. Thus, an element of GF(2^8) can be considered as a byte. For example, the polynomial corresponding to a byte with a value equal to 57 (01010111 expressed in binary) in hexadecimal representation is

$$x^6 + x^4 + x^2 + x + 1.$$

The sum of two elements in the finite field GF(2^8) is a polynomial, the coefficient of which is addition of corresponding coefficients of the two elements modulo 2. The

Table A.1: The relationship between the number of rounds and the key lengths

	Key length (N_k)/word	Block length (N_b)/word	The number of rounds (N_r)
AES-128	4	4	10
AES-192	6	4	12
AES-256	8	4	14

multiplication of two elements in the finite domain GF(2^8) is polynomial multiplication under 8-degree irreducible polynomials in GF(2) and the multiplication is denoted by •. The irreducible polynomial selected by AES is as follows:

$$m(x) = x^8 + x^4 + x^3 + x + 1.$$

$M(x)$ is 0000000100011011 by binary representation (2 bytes), and is 011b by hex.

Multiplication • meets the associative law and 0x01 is the identity of multiplication. For any polynomial $b(x)$ coefficient in binary field GF(2) with degree less than 8, $a(x)$ and $c(x)$ can be calculated by using the Euclidean algorithm, making

$$a(x)b(x) + c(x)m(x) = 1$$

Therefore, $a(x)b(x) \bmod m(x) = 1$ means that the inverse element of $b(x)$ is $b^{-1}(x) = a(x) \bmod m(x)$.

2) Polynomial with Coefficients on GF(2^8). Coefficients of the polynomial can be defined as the element in GF(2^8). Through this approach, a 4-byte word corresponds to a polynomial with degree less than 4. The polynomial addition is simply the sum of the corresponding coefficient. Multiplication is complicated. We assume that two polynomials on GF(2^8) are as follows:

$$a(x) = a_3x^3 + a_2x^2 + a_1x + a_0,$$
$$b(x) = b_3x^3 + b_2x^2 + b_1x + b_0.$$

Their product is

$$c(x) = c_6x^6 + c_5x^5 + c_4x^4 + c_3x^3 + c_2x^2 + c_1x + c_0.$$

Here,

$$\begin{aligned}
c_0 &= a_0 \bullet b_0,\\
c_1 &= a_1 \bullet b_0 \oplus a_0 \bullet b_1,\\
c_2 &= a_2 \bullet b_0 \oplus a_1 \bullet b_1 \oplus a_0 \bullet b_2,\\
c_3 &= a_3 \bullet b_0 \oplus a_2 \bullet b_1 \oplus a_1 \bullet b_2 \oplus a_0 \bullet b_3,\\
c_4 &= a_3 \bullet b_1 \oplus a_2 \bullet b_2 \oplus a_1 \bullet b_3,\\
c_5 &= a_3 \bullet b_2 \oplus a_2 \bullet b_3,\\
c_6 &= a_3 \bullet b_3.
\end{aligned}$$

Obviously, $c(x)$ can no longer be represented as a 4-byte word. We can get a polynomial with degree less than 4 by computing the remainder of $c(x)$ modulo a 4-degree polynomial. The modulo polynomial selected by AES is $M(x) = x^4 + 1$. Two polynomial multiplication on GF(2^8) in AES is defined as multiplication modulo $M(x)$, donated by $\otimes$.

Assuming that $d(x) = a(x) \otimes b(x) = d_3x^3 + d_2x^2 + d_1x + d_0$, by above discussion, we can know that

$$\begin{aligned} d_0 &= a_0 \bullet b_0 \oplus a_3 \bullet b_1 \oplus a_2 \bullet b_2 \oplus a_1 \bullet b_3, \\ d_1 &= a_1 \bullet b_0 \oplus a_0 \bullet b_1 \oplus a_3 \bullet b_2 \oplus a_2 \bullet b_3, \\ d_2 &= a_2 \bullet b_0 \oplus a_1 \bullet b_1 \oplus a_0 \bullet b_2 \oplus a_3 \bullet b_3, \\ d_3 &= a_3 \bullet b_0 \oplus a_2 \bullet b_1 \oplus a_1 \bullet b_2 \oplus a_0 \bullet b_3. \end{aligned}$$

Easy to see, operation $\otimes$ on fixed polynomial $a(x)$ and polynomial $b(x)$ can be written as a matrix multiplication, which is as follows:

$$\begin{bmatrix} d_0 \\ d_1 \\ d_2 \\ d_3 \end{bmatrix} = \begin{bmatrix} a_0 & a_3 & a_2 & a_1 \\ a_1 & a_0 & a_3 & a_2 \\ a_2 & a_1 & a_0 & a_3 \\ a_3 & a_2 & a_1 & a_0 \end{bmatrix} \begin{bmatrix} b_0 \\ b_1 \\ b_2 \\ b_3 \end{bmatrix}.$$

Here, the matrix is a cyclic matrix. Due to that x^4+1 is not an irreducible polynomial on GF(2^8), it is not always invertible when multiplied by a fixed polynomial. AES chooses a fixed polynomial with inverse element as follows:

$$\begin{aligned} a(x) &= \{03\}\,x^3 + \{01\}\,x^2 + \{01\}\,x + \{02\}\,, \\ a^{-1}(x) &= \{0b\}\,x^3 + \{0d\}\,x^2 + \{09\}\,x + \{0e\}\,. \end{aligned}$$

A.1.1.2 AES Algorithm Description

1) AES Encryption Algorithm. Figure A.1(a) is the diagram of AES encryption algorithm. Each iteration round of AES is made up of four phases, as shown in Figure A.1(b).

The description of round transformation of AES encryption algorithm using pseudo code is as follows:

```
Round(byte state[4,Nb],word w[Nb*(Nr+1)])
Begin
SubBytes(state)
ShiftRows(state)
MixColumns(state)
AddRoundKey(state,w[r*Nb,(r+1)*Nb-1])
end
```

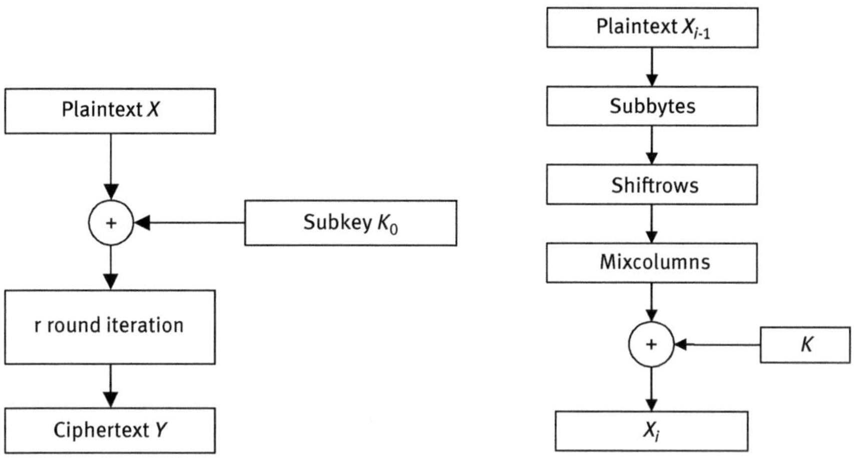

Figure A.1: AES encryption algorithm. (a) AES encryption algorithm diagram, (b) Each iteration round of AES.

The final round transformation is slightly different, defined as follows:

```
FinalRound(byte state[4,Nb],word w[Nb*(Nr+1)])
Begin
SubBytes(state)
ShiftRows(state)
AddRoundKey(state,w[r*Nb,(r+1)*Nb-1])
end
```

(1) Byte Substitution Transformation SubBytes ()

Byte substitution transformation SubBytes () is a nonlinear transformation of the byte, which transforms each byte of the state into another byte. Each byte does the following two steps: First, a byte is transformed into its multiplicative inverse element of a finite field GF(2^8). Specify 00 to 00 (that's itself). Then, an affine transformation is done for the above results.

$$\begin{bmatrix} b'_0 \\ b'_1 \\ b'_2 \\ b'_3 \\ b'_4 \\ b'_5 \\ b'_6 \\ b'_7 \end{bmatrix} = \begin{bmatrix} 1&0&0&0&1&1&1&1 \\ 1&1&0&0&0&1&1&1 \\ 1&1&1&0&0&0&1&1 \\ 1&1&1&1&0&0&0&1 \\ 1&1&1&1&1&0&0&0 \\ 0&1&1&1&1&1&0&0 \\ 0&0&1&1&1&1&1&0 \\ 0&0&0&1&1&1&1&1 \end{bmatrix} \begin{bmatrix} b_0 \\ b_1 \\ b_2 \\ b_3 \\ b_4 \\ b_5 \\ b_6 \\ b_7 \end{bmatrix} + \begin{bmatrix} 1 \\ 1 \\ 0 \\ 0 \\ 0 \\ 1 \\ 1 \\ 0 \end{bmatrix}.$$

You can also lookup the table to transform (in form of Hex):

63	7c	77	7b	f2	6b	6f	c5	30	01	67	2b	fe	d7	ab	76
ca	82	c9	7d	fa	59	47	f0	ad	d4	a2	af	9c	a4	72	c0
b7	fd	93	26	36	3f	f7	cc	34	a5	e5	f1	71	d8	31	15
04	c7	23	c3	18	96	05	9a	07	12	80	e2	eb	27	b2	75
09	83	2c	1a	1b	6e	5a	a0	52	3b	d6	b3	29	e3	2f	84
53	d1	00	ed	20	fc	b1	5b	6a	cb	be	39	4a	4c	58	cf
d0	ef	aa	fb	43	4d	33	85	45	f9	02	7f	50	3c	9f	a8
51	a3	40	8f	92	9d	38	f5	bc	b6	da	21	10	ff	f3	d2
cd	oc	13	ec	5f	97	44	17	c4	a7	7e	3d	64	5d	19	73
60	81	4f	dc	22	2a	90	88	46	ee	b8	14	de	5e	0b	db
e0	32	3a	0a	49	06	24	5c	c2	d3	ac	62	91	95	e4	79
e7	c8	37	6d	8d	d5	4e	a9	6c	56	f4	ea	65	7a	ae	08
ba	78	25	2e	1c	a6	b4	c6	e8	dd	74	1f	4b	bd	8b	8a
70	3e	b5	66	48	03	f6	0e	61	35	57	b9	86	c1	1d	9e
e1	f8	98	11	69	d9	8e	94	9b	1e	87	e9	ce	55	28	df
8c	a1	89	0d	bf	e6	42	68	41	99	2d	0f	b0	54	bb	16

(2) Row Shift Transformation ShiftRows ()

Row shift transformation ShiftRows () rotate each row of a state to the left with different displacement. Zeroth row is not shifted and keeps the same, while the first row is rotated one byte to the left, the second row is rotated two bytes to the left and the third row is rotated three bytes to the left.

$$\begin{bmatrix} s_{00} & s_{01} & s_{02} & s_{03} \\ s_{10} & s_{11} & s_{12} & s_{13} \\ s_{20} & s_{21} & s_{22} & s_{23} \\ s_{30} & s_{31} & s_{32} & s_{33} \end{bmatrix} \xrightarrow{ShiftRows()} \begin{bmatrix} s_{00} & s_{01} & s_{02} & s_{03} \\ s_{11} & s_{12} & s_{13} & s_{10} \\ s_{22} & s_{23} & s_{20} & s_{21} \\ s_{33} & s_{30} & s_{31} & s_{32} \end{bmatrix}.$$

(3) Column Mixing Transformation MixColumns()

MixColumns () transforms a state column by column, and it treats each column of a state as a polynomial on finite field GF(2^8).

$$\begin{bmatrix} s_{00} & s_{01} & s_{02} & s_{03} \\ s_{10} & s_{11} & s_{12} & s_{13} \\ s_{20} & s_{21} & s_{22} & s_{23} \\ s_{30} & s_{31} & s_{32} & s_{33} \end{bmatrix} \xrightarrow{MixColumns()} \begin{bmatrix} s'_{00} & s'_{01} & s'_{02} & s'_{03} \\ s'_{10} & s'_{11} & s'_{12} & s'_{13} \\ s'_{20} & s'_{21} & s'_{22} & s'_{23} \\ s'_{30} & s'_{31} & s'_{31} & s'_{33} \end{bmatrix}.$$

Let

$$s_j(x) = s_{3j}x^3 + s_{2j}x^2 + s_{1j}x + s_{0j},\ 0 \le j \le 3,$$
$$s_j^{/}(x) = s_{3j}^{/}x^3 + s_{2j}^{/}x^2 + s_{1j}^{/}x + s_{0j}^{/},\ 0 \le j \le 3.$$

We have $s_j^{/}(x) = a(x) \otimes s_j(x),\ 0 \le j \le 3$, among them $a(x) = \{03\}\, x^3 + \{01\}\, x^2 + \{01\}\, x + \{02\}$, $\otimes$ represents multiplication modulo $x^4 + 1$. $s_j^{/}(x) = a(x) \otimes s_j(x)$ could be expressed as a matrix multiplication as follows:

$$\begin{bmatrix} s_{0j}^{/} \\ s_{1j}^{/} \\ s_{2j}^{/} \\ s_{3j}^{/} \end{bmatrix} = \begin{bmatrix} 02\ 03\ 01\ 01 \\ 01\ 02\ 03\ 01 \\ 01\ 01\ 02\ 03 \\ 03\ 01\ 01\ 02 \end{bmatrix} \begin{bmatrix} s_{0j} \\ s_{1j} \\ s_{2j} \\ s_{3j} \end{bmatrix}, 0 \le j \le j3.$$

That is,

$$s_{0j}^{/} = \{02\} \bullet s_{0j} \oplus \{03\} \bullet s_{1j} \oplus s_{2j} \oplus s_{3j},$$
$$s_{1j}^{/} = s_{0j} \oplus \{02\} \bullet s_{1j} \oplus \{03\} \bullet s_{2j} \oplus s_{3j},$$
$$s_{2j}^{/} = s_{0j} \oplus s_{1j} \oplus \{02\} \bullet s_{2j} \oplus \{03\} \bullet s_{3j},$$
$$s_{3j}^{/} = \{03\} \bullet s_{0j} \oplus s_{1j} \oplus s_{2j} \oplus \{02\} \bullet s_{3j}.$$

(4) Subkey Addition Transformation AddRoundKey ()

Subkey addition transformation AddRoundKey() simply XOR a state with a round subkey bitwise. The length of the round subkey is four words (128 bits), and a word is 4 bytes (32 bits). The round subkeys are taken from the expanded key in order. The expanded key is obtained by expanding the original key. The length of the expanded key is $N_b(N_r + 1)$ words.

$$\begin{bmatrix} s_{00}\ s_{01}\ s_{02}\ s_{03} \\ s_{10}\ s_{11}\ s_{12}\ s_{13} \\ s_{20}\ s_{21}\ s_{22}\ s_{23} \\ s_{30}\ s_{31}\ s_{32}\ s_{33} \end{bmatrix} \xrightarrow{\text{AddRoundKey()}} \begin{bmatrix} s_{00}^{/}\ s_{01}^{/}\ s_{02}^{/}\ s_{03}^{/} \\ s_{10}^{/}\ s_{11}^{/}\ s_{12}^{/}\ s_{13}^{/} \\ s_{20}^{/}\ s_{21}^{/}\ s_{22}^{/}\ s_{23}^{/} \\ s_{30}^{/}\ s_{31}^{/}\ s_{32}^{/}\ s_{33}^{/} \end{bmatrix}$$

$$(s_{0j}^{/}, s_{1j}^{/}, s_{2j}^{/}, s_{3j}^{/}) = (s_{0j}, s_{1j}, s_{2j}, s_{3j}) \oplus (k_{0j}, k_{1j}, k_{2j}, k_{3j}) \quad 0 \le j \le 3.$$

Here, $(k_{0j}, k_{1j}, k_{2j}, k_{3j})$ represents the $(r * N_b + j)$th word in the expanded key, $0 \le j \le N_r$.

2) AES Decryption Algorithm. The structure of AES decryption algorithm is the same as that of the encryption algorithm and the transformation is the inverse transformation of the encryption algorithm. Here we do not depict it in detail.

3) AES Key Expansion Algorithm. In the process of encryption, we need $r + 1$ sub-keys and establish 4 $(r + 1)$ 32-bit words. When the seed key is 128 and 192 bits, the programs are the same for establishing $4(r + 1)$ 32-bit word. While the seed key is 256 bits, a different program is used to establish $4(r + 1)$ 32-bit word. The key scheme consists of two parts: the key expansion and the round key selection.

(1) Key Expansion Process

The expanded key is an array of 32-bit words, and is denoted as $W[4(r + 1)]$. The key is contained in the first N_k32-bit words, and the other words are obtained by previous processed words.

When $N_k = 4$, $r = 10$ or $N_k = 6$, $r = 12$, the key expansion process is as follows:

```
KeyExpansion(CipherKey,W)
 {
  For (i=0;i<N_k;i++)        W[i]=CipherKey[i];
 For (j=N_k;j<N_k(r+1);j+=N_k)
   {
    W[j]=W[j-N_k] ^S(Rotl(W[j-1])) ^RC[j/N_k];
    For(i=1;i<N_k && i+j<4(r+1);i++)
          W[i+j]=W[i+j-N_k] ^W[i+j-1];
   }
 }
```

When $N_k = 8$, $r = 14$, the key expansion process is as follows:

```
KeyExpansion(CipherKey,W)
 {
  For (i=0;i<N_k;i++)  W[i]=CipherKey[i];
 For(j=N_k;j<N_k(r+1);j+=N_k)
 {
 W[j]=W[j-N_k] ^S(Rotl(W[j-1])) ^RC[j/N_k];
   For(i=1;i<4;i++)
 W[i+j]=W[i+j-N_k]   ^W[i+j-1];
     W[j+4]=W[j+4-N_k] ^S(Rotl(W[j+3]));
 For(i=1;i<N_k && i+j<4(r+1);i++)
        W[i+j]=W[i+j-N_k] ^W[i+j-1];
 }
}
```

Among them, Rot1 (W) represents cyclic rotation operation on the byte of the word W. For example, if inputting byte of a word is (a, b, c, d), the output is (b, c, d, a). RC[] is a sequence of 8-bit round constant whose cycle is 8. And it is expressed in hexadecimal as RC[1] = 01, RC[2] = 02, RC[3] = 04, RC[4] = 08, RC[5] = 10, RC[6] = 20, RC[7] = 40, RC[8] = 80. Its recursive relation formula is $\mathrm{RC}[i+1] = \mathrm{RC}[i] \ll 1$, $\mathrm{RC}[i] \ll 1$, indicating that the $\mathrm{RC}[i]$ is rotated one bit to the left.

(2) Round Key Selection

The round key K_i is composed of words in the key buffer from $W[4i]$ to $W[4(i+1)]$.

A.1.2 SMS4

In January 2006, the Office of State Commercial Cryptography Administration (OSCCA) announced the recommendation cryptography algorithm applied in wireless LAN products, including the SMS4 block cipher algorithm [160]. SMS4 is an iterative block cipher algorithm and the lengths of both the block and the key are 128 bits. The encryption algorithm and key expansion algorithm adopt 32-round nonlinear iterative structure. The decryption and encryption algorithms have the same architecture. However, they have the reverse order on the usage of round key. Decryption round keys are the reverse order of encryption round keys.

A.1.2.1 SMS4 Encryption Algorithm

The SMS4 encryption process is shown in Figure A.2. The input of plaintext is $(X_0, X_1, X_2, X_3) \in (F_2^{32})^4$. The output of ciphertext is $(Y_0, Y_1, Y_2, Y_3) \in (F_2^{32})^4$. The round key is $\mathrm{rk}_i \in F_2^{32}$ $(i = 0, 1, \ldots, 31)$. Encryption transformation is

$$\begin{aligned} X_{i+4} &= F(X_i, X_{i+1}, X_{i+2}, X_{i+3}, rk_i) \\ &= X_i \oplus T(X_{i+1} \oplus X_{i+2} \oplus X_{i+3} \oplus rk_i)\ (i = 0, 1, \cdots, 31) \end{aligned}$$

$$(Y_0, Y_1, Y_2, Y_3) = R(X_{32}, X_{33}, X_{34}, X_{35}) = (X_{35}, X_{34}, X_{33}, X_{32}).$$

Round function: SMS4's round function F is defined as follows:

$$F(X_i, X_{i+1}, X_{i+2}, X_{i+3}, rk_i) = X_i \oplus T(X_{i+1} \oplus X_{i+2} \oplus X_{i+3} \oplus rk_i).$$

Synthetic permutation T: $F_2^{32} \to F_2^{32}$ is an invertible transformation, compounded by nonlinear transformation τ and linear transformation L, that is, $T(\bullet) = L(\tau(\bullet))$.
Nonlinear transformation: τ is composed of four parallel S-boxes. Set the input to $A = (a_0, a_1, a_2, a_3) \in (F_2^{32})^4$, the output to $B = (b_0, b_1, b_2, b_3) \in (F_2^{32})^4$, then

$$(b_0, b_1, b_2, b_3) = \tau(A) = (S(a_0), S(a_1), S(a_2), S(a_3)).$$

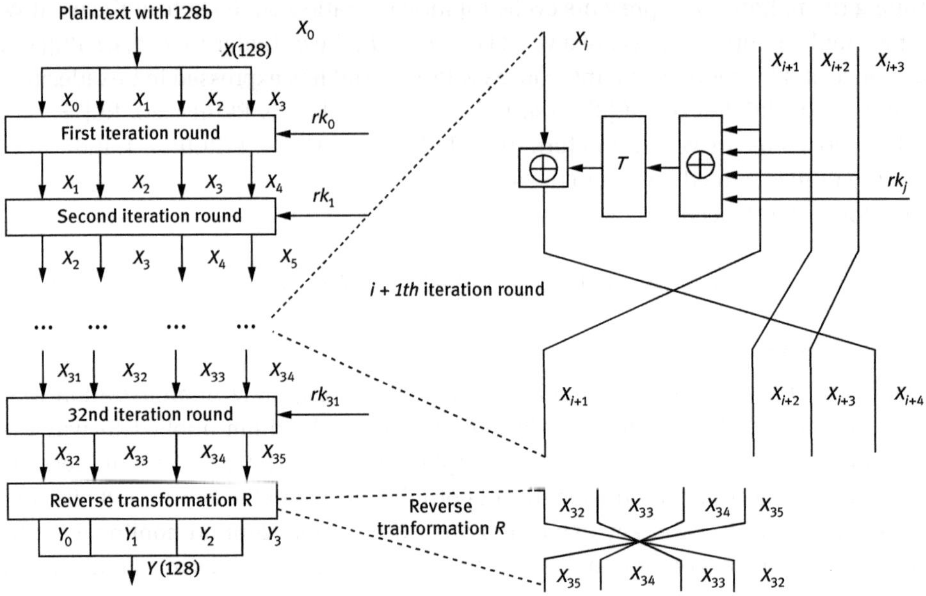

Figure A.2: SMS4 encryption algorithm.

S-boxes are as follows:

	0	1	2	3	4	5	6	7	8	9	a	b	c	d	e	f
0	d6	90	e9	fe	cc	e1	3d	b7	16	b6	14	c2	28	fb	2c	05
1	2b	67	9a	76	2a	be	04	c3	aa	44	13	26	49	86	06	99
2	9c	42	50	f4	91	ef	98	7a	33	54	0b	43	ed	cf	ac	62
3	e4	b3	1c	a9	c9	08	e8	95	80	df	94	fa	75	8f	3f	a6
4	47	07	a7	fc	f3	73	17	ba	83	59	3c	19	e6	85	4f	a8
5	68	6b	81	b2	71	64	da	8b	f8	eb	0f	4b	70	56	9d	35
6	1e	24	0e	5e	63	58	d1	a2	25	22	7c	3b	01	21	78	87
7	d4	00	46	57	9f	d3	27	52	4c	36	02	e7	a0	c4	c8	9e
8	ea	bf	8a	d2	40	c7	38	b5	a3	f7	f2	ce	f9	61	15	a1
9	e0	ae	5d	a4	9b	34	1a	55	ad	93	32	30	f5	8c	b1	e3
a	1d	f6	e2	2e	82	66	ca	60	c0	29	23	ab	0d	53	4e	6f
b	d5	db	37	45	de	fd	8e	2f	03	ff	6a	72	6d	6c	5b	51
c	8d	1b	af	92	bb	dd	bc	7f	11	d9	5c	41	1f	10	5a	d8
d	0a	c1	31	88	a5	cd	7b	bd	2d	74	d0	12	b8	e5	b4	b0
e	89	69	97	4a	0c	96	77	7e	65	b9	f1	09	c5	6e	c6	84
f	18	f0	7d	ec	3a	dc	4d	20	79	ee	5f	3e	d7	cb	39	48

Linear transformation *L*: Take the output of the nonlinear transformation τ as the input, assuming that the input is $B \in (F_2^{32})^4$ and the output is $C \in (F_2^{32})^4$, then

$$C = L(B) = B \oplus (B <<< 2) \oplus (B <<< 10) \oplus (B <<< 18) \oplus (B <<< 24).$$

Reverse order transformation R:

$$R(A_0, A_1, A_2, A_3) = (A_3, A_2, A_1, A_0), A_i \in F_2^{32}, i = 0, 1, 2, 3.$$

A.1.2.2 SMS4 Key Expansion Algorithm

The round key of SMS4 encryption algorithm is generated by the encryption key using the key expansion algorithm. The encryption key is denoted by MK = (MK_0, MK_1, MK_2, MK_3), $MK_i \in F_2^{32}(i = 0, 1, 2, 3)$; Let $K_i \in F_2^{32}(i = 0, 1, \ldots, 35)$ and round keys $rk_i \in F_2^{32}(i = 0, 1, \ldots, 31)$ The round key generation method is as follows:

First, the initial transformation is carried out.

$$(K_0, K_1, K_2, K_3) = (MK_0 \oplus FK_0, MK_1 \oplus FK_1, MK_2 \oplus FK_2, MK_3 \oplus FK_3).$$

Then, perform the following operations on $i = 0, 1, \ldots, 31$:

$$rk_i = K_{i+4} = K_i \oplus T'(K_{i+1} \oplus K_{i+2} \oplus K_{i+3} \oplus CK_i).$$

The transformationT' is basically the same with T in round function encryption, only modifying the linear transformation L to L':

$$L'(B) = B \oplus (B <<< 13) \oplus (B <<< 23).$$

The system parameter value FK= (FK_0, FK_1, FK_2, FK_3), represented by hex, is as follows:

$$\mathrm{FK}_0 = (\mathrm{A3B1BAC6}),\ \mathrm{FK}_1 = (\mathrm{56AA3350}), \mathrm{FK}_2 = (\mathrm{677D9197}),$$
$$\mathrm{FK}_3 = (\mathrm{B27022DC}).$$

The method for determining the value of 32 fixed parameters is: assuming that the jth byte of CK_i $(i = 0, 1, \ldots, 31; j = 0, 1, 2, 3)$, that is, $CK_i = (ck_{i,0}, ck_{i,1}, ck_{i,2}, ck_{i,3})$, we have $ck_{i,j} = (4i + j) \times 7 \bmod 256$.

A.2 Public-Key Cryptography Algorithm

Public-key cryptography algorithm was first proposed by Diffie and Hellman in 1976. Different from the symmetric cryptography algorithm, public-key cryptography algorithm separates encryption function from decryption function by two different keys.

One key is called the private key, which is kept secret as in a symmetric cryptography algorithm. The other key is called the public key, which does not need to be kept secret. The public-key cryptography algorithm must have the following important property: Given the public key, it is not feasible to determine the private key.

For algorithm designers, the design of the public-key cryptography algorithm is more challenging than that of symmetric cryptography algorithm, because the public key provides some information for the attack algorithm. The security foundation of public-key cryptography algorithm lies on the hard problems in mathematics. There are two most popular problems: one is based on the large integer factorization problem, such as RSA public-key encryption algorithm; the other is based on discrete logarithm problem, such as elliptic curve encryption algorithm, and SM2 publickey encryption algorithm. This section focuses on several commonly public-key encryption algorithms.

A.2.1 RSA

In 1977Rivest, Shamir and Adleman proposed the first relatively mature public-key cryptography algorithm, namely, the well-known RSA algorithm [161]. RSA is the most widely used public-key cryptography algorithm by far. Its security is based on large integer factorization problem: Given the large integer N, it is difficult to calculate prime factors p and q ($N = pq$). The detailed description of RSA algorithm is as follows:

(1) Key Pair Generation. Randomly generate two large odd primes p and q, calculate $n = p\,q$, make n public and keep p, q as secret. e, a randomly selected integer, is less than $\varphi(n) = (p-1)\,(q-1)$ and it is an inter-prime positive integer. d was calculated with extended Euclid algorithm, s.t. $ed \equiv 1 \bmod \varphi(n)$. The public key of algorithm is $\{e, n\}$, and the private key is $\{d, p, q\}$.

(2) Encryption. First of all, we group the plaintext bit string into blocks, ensuring that the corresponding decimal number of each block is less than n. That is to say, the length of each block is less than $\log_2(n)$. Then, for each plaintext block m, do encryption computation: $c = m^e(mod\, n)$.

(3) Decryption. Do the decryption computation: $m = c^d(mod\ n)$ to the ciphertext block c.

A direct method for breaking the RSA algorithm is to use some existing decomposition method to decompose modulus n. If modulus n of RSA is successfully decomposed into $p \times q$, we get $\varphi(n) = (p-1)\,(q-1)$ immediately. Depending on $\varphi(n)$, we can determine the multiplicative inverse element d of e modulo $\varphi(n)$, namely $ed \equiv 1 \bmod \varphi(n)$.This means we launch a successful attack. Therefore, the strength of RSA depends on the equipment cost and time consumption for large prime decomposition With the lower prices of equipment and the improvement of computing capability, modulus n of RSA algorithm must increase. Now it is able to decompose 155-bit decimal integers. Usually, we recommend using the modulus whose length is more than 1024 bits.

Compared with the symmetric cryptography algorithm, the shortcoming of RSA algorithm is that encryption and decryption speeds are too low. However, RSA public-key cryptography algorithm is applied widely, such as in digital signature, key management and authentication.

A.2.2 Elliptic Curve Public-Key Encryption Algorithm

In 1985, Koblitz and Miller independently proposed elliptic curve cryptography (ECC) [162, 163]. The security of ECC is based on discrete logarithm problem of elliptic curve group. ECC algorithm can use a shorter key to get a higher-level security, and the encryption speed is faster than RSA. Therefore, ECC has been widely applied in many resource-constrained environments. Standardization organizations such as ISO and IEEE have formulated a draft standard of ECC.

The elliptic curve over a finite field is widely used in cryptography. One of the most commonly used is the elliptic curve E over finite field F_p. Assuming that p is a prime greater than 3, elliptic curve E over a finite field F_p is defined as a point set. It is composed of all solutions of cubic equation in the affine plane: $y^2 = x^3 + ax + b(mod\, p)$ and infinite point O, denoted by $E(F_p) = \{(x, y)|y^2 = x^3 + ax + b, (x, y) \in F_P * F_P\} \cup \{O\}$. Among them, $a, b \in F_p$, and this equation satisfies $4a^3 + 27b^2(mod\, p) \neq 0$. By defining the addition operation rules on $E(F_p)$, we make them form a commutative group.

The hard problem of computing discrete logarithm on the elliptic curve group is: given $Q = k\,P$, and $Q, P \in E(F_p)$, the calculation is difficult to get k by Q, P. Elliptic curve public-key encryption algorithm is designed based on this hard problem. The concrete description of the algorithm is as follows:

Assuming that the elliptic curves over finite fields is $E(F_p)$, we select the base point G of $E(F_p)$ on condition that the order of G is a big prime number n.

(1) Key Generation. Randomly select the integer $d \in [1, n-1]$ and calculate $Q = dG$. The public key of algorithm is $\{G, Q\}$, and the private key is $\{d\}$.
(2) Encryption. Transform the plaintext message m to be encrypted into a point P_m in $E(F_p)$. Then, randomly select $k \in [1, n-1]$ and compute ciphertext $C_m = \{kG, P_m + kQ\}$.
(3) Decryption. Do the decryption operation on the ciphertext C_m: $P_m = (P_m + kQ) - d(kG)$.

A.2.3 SM2 Public-Key Encryption Algorithm

In December 2010, OSCCA announced the SM2 elliptic curve public-key cryptography algorithm [164], including public-key encryption algorithm, digital signature algorithm and key exchange protocol. The specific description of the SM2 public-key encryption algorithm is as follows:

Supposing elliptic curve $E(F_p)$ over finite field, select the base point G in $E(F_p)$ on the condition that the order of G is a big prime n.

(1) Key Generation. Randomly select integer $d \in [1, n-1]$ and calculate $Q = dG$. The public-key algorithm is $\{G, Q\}$, and the private key is $\{d\}$.
(2) Encryption. Let the plaintext message to be encrypted be the bit string M and $klen$ be the bit length of M.
 (a) Randomly select k $\in [1, n-1]$ to compute the ciphertext: $C_1 = kG = (x_1, y_1)$, $kP = (x_2, y_2)$.
 (b) Calculate $t = KDF(x_2||y_2, klen)$, where KDF is the key derivation function with output length equal to $klen$.
 (c) Calculate $C_2 = M \oplus t$, $C_3 = \text{Hash}(x_2||M||y_2)$. Here, Hash is the hash function. The final ciphertext is : $C = C_1||C_2||C_3$.
(3) Decryption. In order to decrypt the ciphertext $C = C_1||C_2||C_3$, the following steps should be implemented:
 (a) Take out the bit string C_1 from the C, convert the data type of C_1 to the point on the elliptic curve and verify whether it satisfies the elliptic curve equation. If not, report errors and exit.
 (b) Calculate $dC_1 = (x_2, y_2)$, and convert the data type of x_2 and y_2 to bit string.
 (c) Calculate $t = KDF(x_2||y_2, klen)$. If t is the bit string t with all zeros, report errors and exit.
 (d) Take out the bit string C_2 from the C and calculate $M = C_2 \oplus t$. Then calculate $u = Hash(x_2||M||y_2)$ and take out the bit string C_3 from the C. If $u = C_3$, M is the plaintext by decryption.

A.3 Digital Signature Algorithm

Digital signature is a method of signing the message in electronic form. The digital signature algorithm is that a signer generates the digital signature for data, and a verifier verifies the validity of signature. Every signer has a public key and a private key. The private key is used to generate the digital signature and the verifier takes signer's public key to verify the signature. A digital signature scheme should have the following basic characteristics:
(1) Unforgeability: Without knowing the signer's private key, no other person can forge the signature.
(2) Non-repudiation: The signer cannot deny his signature on the message.
(3) Ensurance of the Message's Integrity: Any change to the message will lead to failure of the signature verification. The characteristic of the digital signature plays an important role in electronic commerce and electronic government system, which makes the digital signature widely popular in application protocols such as electronic payment, bidding, auction, lottery tickets and voting.

Public-key cryptography algorithm can provide a powerful digital signature scheme, without the need for the receiver keeping the verification key in secret. Currently,

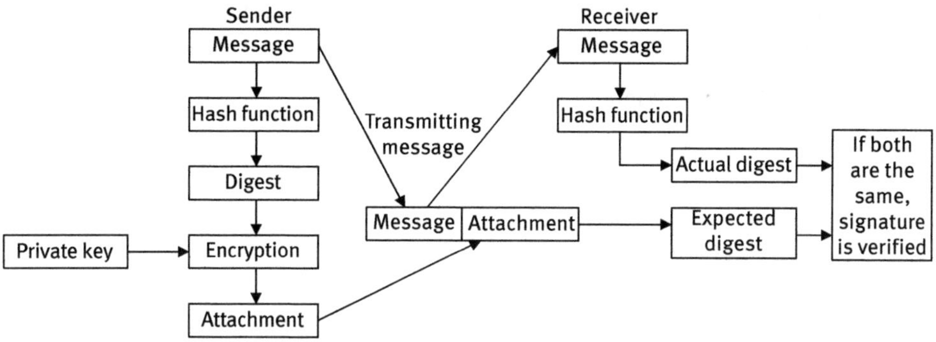

Figure A.3: Digital signature based on public-key encryption algorithm.

many digital signature schemes are based on public-key cryptography algorithms. Figure A.3 describes the digital signature scheme using public-key encryption algorithm like RSA.

In addition to the RSA digital signature scheme, there are several other digital signature schemes with different functions and types. Here, we introduce two important digital signature schemes: the ISO digital signature standard ECDSA, and the SM2 elliptic curve digital signature of Chinese commercial cryptography algorithm.

A.3.1 ECDSA Digital Signature Algorithm

ECDSA digital signature algorithm [165] uses an elliptic curve to simulate digital signature algorithm DSA. ECDSA became ISO standards in 1998, the ANSI standard in 1999, the standard of IEEE and FIPS in 2000.

ECDSA is a variant of ElGamal public-key cryptography algorithm, whose security depends on the discrete logarithm hard problem on elliptic curve. The concrete description of the ECDSA digital signature algorithm is as follows:

Supposing the elliptic curve $E(F_p)$ in finite field, select the basis point G in the $E(F_p)$ with the order of G being a big prime n.

(1) Key Generation. Randomly select the integer $d \in [1, n-1]$, calculate $Q = dG$. The public key of the algorithm is $\{G, Q\}$ and the private key is $\{d\}$.
(2) Signature. Assuming that the message to be signed is m, execute the following operations:
   (a) Randomly select $k \in [1, n-1]$ to calculate $kG = (x_1, y_1)$.
   (b) Calculate $r = x_1 \bmod n$. If $r = 0$, return to (a).
   (c) Calculate $s = k^{-1}\ (hash(m)+dr)\ mod\ n$. If $s = 0$, return to (a). Here, *hash* is hash function.

   In the end, the signature of the message m is (r, s).
(3) Signature Verification. In order to verify the received message m and its digital signature (r', s'), the verifier should perform the following calculations:

(a) Check whether $r' \in [1, n-1]$ and $s' \in [1, n-1]$. If not, the signature is invalid.
(b) Calculate $e = hash\left(m'\right)$; $w = s'^{-1} \bmod n$.
(c) Calculate $u_1 = ew \bmod n$, $u_2 = r'w \bmod n$.
(d) Calculate $X = u_1G + u_2Q$. If $X = O$, the signature is invalid. Otherwise, $X = \left(x_1', y_1'\right)$ and calculate$v = x_1' \bmod n$.

If $v = r' \bmod n$, signature is valid.

A.3.2 SM2 Digital Signature

In December 2010, OSCCA announced the recommended SM2 elliptic curve public-key cryptography algorithms [164], including public-key encryption algorithm, digital signature algorithm and key exchange protocol. Similar to the ECDSA digital signature algorithm, security of SM2 digital signature algorithm also depends on the discrete logarithm hard problem on elliptic curve group. The detailed description of the SM2 digital signature algorithm is as follows:

Supposing the elliptic curve in finite field is denoted by $E(F_p)$, select the basic point G in the $E(F_p)$ with the order of G being a big prime n.

(1) Key Generation. Randomly select the integer $d \in [1, n-1]$ and calculate $Q = dG$. The public key of the algorithm is $\{G, Q\}$ and the private key is $\{d\}$.
(2) Signature. Assuming that the message to be signed is m, perform operations as follows:
   (a) Set $\overline{m} = Z||m$, where Z is the signer's identity, a part of system parameters and hash value of signer's public key.
   (b) Calculate $e = hash(\overline{m})$. Here, *hash* is the hash function.
   (c) Randomly select $k \in [1, n-1]$ and calculate $kG = (x_1, y_1)$.
   (d) Calculate $r = (e + x_1) \bmod n$. If $r = 0$ or $r + k = n$, return to (c).
   (e) Calculate $s = ((1 + d) - 1(k - rd)) \bmod n$. If $s = 0$, return to (c).
   In the end, the signature of the message m is (r, s).
(3) Signature Verification. In order to verify the received message m' and its digital signature $\left(r', s'\right)$, the verifier should achieve the following steps:
   (a) Check whether $r' \in [1, n-1]$ and $s' \in [1, n-1]$. If not, the signature is invalid.
   (b) Set $\bar{m}' = Z \parallel m'$.
   (c) Calculate $e' = hash\left(\overline{m}'\right)$.
   (d) Calculate $t = \left(r' + s'\right) \bmod n$. If $t = 0$, the signature is invalid.
   (e) Calculates $\left(x_1', y_1'\right) = s'G + tQ$ and $v = \left(e' + x_1'\right) \bmod n$.

If $v = r' \bmod n$, signature is valid.

A.4 Hash Function

The hash function can compress message with arbitrary length to a hash value with fixed length. Hash functions must have the following properties:

(1) One-way. For a given hash value, it is not feasible in calculation to construct an input message to map it to the value.

(2) Collision Resistance. It is not feasible in calculation to construct two different messages and map them to the same hash value.

Hash function can be used to construct block ciphers, stream cipher and message authentication code. It is also an important component of the digital signature. It may break the algebraic structure of input, and do the message source authentication. Besides, it is also used to construct pseudorandom number generator, do the key derivation and so on. It is a formidable task to design a safe and efficient hash function. Many different hash functions have been proposed, but most of them have been confirmed with some vulnerabilities. Common hash functions are: hash functions based on block ciphers algorithm; MD series hash functions, such as MD2, MD4 and MD5, all with a 128-bit output; SHA series hash functions, including SHA1, SHA-224, SHA-256, SHA-384 and SHA-512, designed by the National Security Agency (NSA), which are the US standards. SHA1 is widely used in many security protocols, including SSL, PGP, SSH, S/MIME and IPsec. But the security of SHA1 is now seriously challenged by the cryptographers. The last four algorithms are sometimes referred to as SHA-2. The effective attack has not yet appeared on the SHA-2. The National Institute of Standards and Technology (NIST) has formulated new hash function standard algorithm (SHA-3) in the form of public solicitation. This section details the two important hash functions: SHA-256 algorithm [166], and Chinese commercial cipher algorithm SM3 [167].

We will use the following notations:

mod: modular arithmetic

$\wedge$: 32 bits *and* operations

$\vee$: 32 bits *or* operation

$\oplus$: 32 bits *XOR* operation

$\neg$: 32 bits *not* operation

+: $\bmod 2^{32}$ arithmetic addition operation

$\leftarrow$: Left to assignment operator

$S^n(X)$: X rotate n bits to right

$L^n(X)$: X rotate n bits to left

$R^n(X)$: X shift n bits to right.

A.4.1 SHA-256 Hash Algorithm

For the message m whose length is l ($l < 2^{64}$), the output length is 256 bits, that is, eight words after padded and iteratively compressed by SHA-256 hash algorithm.

A.4.1.1 Message Padding

Assume that length of message m is l bits. First, add bit "1" to the end of the message m, and then add k bits "0" again, where k is the minimum nonnegative integer meeting $l + 1 + k \equiv 448 \ mod \ 512$. Next add a 64-bit string, which is the binary representation of length l. The bit length of the padded message is in multiples of 512, that is, $m' = m||1||0^k||f$. Here f is the binary representation of the length l.

A.4.1.2 Message Extension

There are n 512-bit message blocks after the message is padded: $m' = B^{(0)}B^{(1)}\ldots B^{(n-1)}$. Each message block is divided into 16 words with lengths of 32 bits, for example, $B^{(i)} = W_0W_1\ldots W_{15}$. These 16 message blocks are extended to 64 message blocks $W_0W_1\ldots W_{63}$ by the message extension algorithm in the following way:

FOR j = 16 to 63

$$W_j = \sigma_1\left(W_{j-2}\right) + W_{j-7} + \sigma_0\left(W_{j-15}\right) + W_{j-16}$$

ENDFOR

Among them, $\sigma_0(X) = S^7(X) \oplus S^{18}(X) \oplus R^3(X)$, $\sigma_1(X) = S^{17}(X) \oplus S^{19}(X) \oplus R^{10}(X)$.

A.4.1.3 Iterative Compression

For the message $m' = B^{(0)}B^{(1)}\ldots B^{(n-1)}$, SHA-256 hash algorithm is constructed as follows:

FOR i = 0 to n - 1

$$V^{(i+1)} = CF\left(V^{(i)}, B^{(i)}\right)$$

ENDFOR

Among them, CF is the compression function, $V^{(0)}$ is a 256-bit initial value. $V_1^{(0)}$ = 6a09e667, $V_2^{(0)}$ = bb67ae85, $V_3^{(0)}$ = 3c6ef372, $V_4^{(0)}$ = a54ff53a, $V_5^{(0)}$ = 510e527f, $V_6^{(0)}$ = 9b05688c, $V_7^{(0)}$ = 1f83d9ab, $V_8^{(0)}$ = 5be0cd19 and the output of SHA-256 hash algorithm is $V^{(n)}$.

Setting A, B, C, D, E, F, G, H as shift registers, the specific calculation process of compression function $Vi(i+1i) = CF(V^{(i)}, B^{(i)})(0 \leq i \leq n-1)$ is described as follows:

(1) First of all, using $V^{(i)}$ give the initial value to the shift registers A, B, C, D, E, F, G, H, that is, $A \leftarrow V_1^{(i)}, B \leftarrow V_2^{(i)} \dots, H \leftarrow V_8^{(i)}$.

(2) Perform computations as follows:

$FOR\ j = 0\ to\ 63$

$T_1 \leftarrow H + \sum_1 (E) + Ch(E, F, G) + K_j + W_j$

$T_2 \leftarrow \sum_0 (A) + Maj(A, B, C)$

$H \leftarrow G$

$G \leftarrow F$

$F \leftarrow E$

$E \leftarrow D + T_1$

$D \leftarrow C$

$C \leftarrow B$

$B \leftarrow A$

$A \leftarrow T_1 + T_2$

$ENDFOR$

(3) Calculate $V^{(i+1)}$: $V_1^{(i+1)} \leftarrow A + V_1^{(i)}, V_2^{(i+1)} \leftarrow B + V_2^{(i)}, \dots, V_8^{(i+1)} \leftarrow H + V_8^{(i)}$. Here $K_0, \cdots, K_{63}$ are taken from the first 32 bits of fractional part of the first 64 prime cube roots. The corresponding logic functions are as follows:

$$Ch(X, Y, Z) = (X \wedge Y) \oplus (\neg X \wedge Z);$$

$$Maj(X, Y, Z) = (X \wedge Y) \oplus (X \wedge Z) \oplus (Y \wedge Z);$$

$$\sum_0 (X) = S^2(X) \oplus S^{13}(X) \oplus S^{22}(X);$$

$$\sum_1 (X) = S^6(X) \oplus S^{11}(X) \oplus S^{25}(X)$$

A.4.2 SM3 Hash Algorithm

In order to meet the application requirements like electronic authentication service system, OSCCA released the SM3 hash algorithm in December 2010, which is used in digital signature and verification, message authentication code generation and verification and random number generation of commercial cryptographic applications. The parameter designs of SM3 and SHA-256 are similar.

For the message m whose length is $l(l < 2^{64})$, after padded and iteratively compressed by SM3 hash algorithm, the output length of m is 256 bits in length, which is eight words.

A.4.2.1 Constants and Functions

Initial vectors are as follows:

IV_1 = 7380166f IV_2 = 4914b2b9 IV_3 = 172442d7 IV_4 = da8a0600
IV_5 = a96f30bc IV_6 = 163138aa IV_7 = e38dee4d IV_8 = b0fb0e4e
SM3 algorithm uses the following constants:

$$T_j = \begin{cases} \text{79cc4519} & 0 \le j \le 15 \\ \text{7a879d8a} & 16 \le j \le 63 \end{cases}.$$

The SM3 algorithm uses the following Boolean functions:

$$FF_j(X, Y, Z) = \begin{cases} X \oplus Y \oplus Z & 0 \le j \le 15 \\ (X \wedge Y) \vee (X \wedge Z) \vee (Y \wedge Z) & 16 \le j \le 63 \end{cases},$$

$$GG_j(X, Y, Z) = \begin{cases} X \oplus Y \oplus Z & 0 \le j \le 15 \\ (X \wedge Y) \vee (\neg X \wedge Z) & 16 \le j \le 63 \end{cases}$$

SM3 algorithm uses the following permutation functions:

$$P_0(X) = X \oplus L^9(X) \oplus L^{17}(X),$$
$$P_1(X) = X \oplus L^{15}(X) \oplus L^{23}(X).$$

A.4.2.2 Message Padding and Message Extension

Message padding algorithm is the same as SHA-256. The length of padded message m' is a multiple of 512 bits.

The padded message has n 512-bit message blocks: $m' = B^{(0)}B^{(1)}\ldots B^{(n-1)}$. Every message block $B^{(i)} = W_0W_1\ldots W_{15}$ is extended from 16 words to 132 words $W_0, W_1, \ldots, W_{67}, W'_0, W'_1, \ldots, W'_{63}$ by the message extension algorithm as follows:

```
FOR j = 16 to 67
```

$$W_j \leftarrow P_1(W_{j-16} \oplus W_{j-9} \oplus L^{15}(W_{j-3})) \oplus L^7(W_{j-13}) \oplus W_{j-6}$$

```
ENDFOR

FOR j = 0 to 63
```

$$W'_j = W_j \oplus W_{j+4}$$

```
ENDFOR
```

A.4.2.3 Iterative Compression

For the message $m' = B^{(0)}B^{(1)}\ldots B^{(n-1)}$, the iterative compression process of SM3 algorithm is as follows:

FOR $i = 0$ to $n - 1$

$$V^{(i+1)} = CF\left(V^{(i)}, B^{(i)}\right)$$

ENDFOR

Among them, CF is the compression function, $V^{(0)}$ is the 256-bit initial value IV and $V^{(n)}$ is the output result of SM3 hash algorithm.

Let A, B, C, D, E, F, G, H be word registers, SS1, SS2, TT1, TT2 be intermediate variables, then the specific calculation process of compression function $V^{(i+1)} = CF(V^{(i)}, B^{(i)})(0 \le i \le n-1)$ is described as follows:

(1) $ABCDEFGH \leftarrow V^{(i)}$

(2) FOR $j = 0$ to 63

$SS1 \leftarrow L^7(L^{12}(A) + E + Lj(T_j))$

$SS2 \leftarrow SS1 \oplus L^{12}(A)$

$TT1 \leftarrow FF_j(A, B, C) + D + SS2 + W'_j$

$TT2 \leftarrow GG_j(E, F, G) + H + SS1 + W_j$

$D \leftarrow C$

$C \leftarrow L^9(B)$

$B \leftarrow A$

$A \leftarrow TT1$

$H \leftarrow G$

$G \leftarrow L^{19}(F)$

$F \leftarrow E$

$E \leftarrow P_0(TT2)$

ENDFOR

(3) $V^{(i+1)} \leftarrow ABCDEFGH \oplus V^{(i)}$

A.5 Key Exchange Protocols

In general, the communication participants need to assure confidentiality and authentication of data as transmitting data in the open network environment. To achieve this goal, data must be encrypted and authenticated, which requires using the session key. The key exchange protocol is a process in which two or more parties establish the secret session key in the open network environment. The session key is a parameter of input function generated by the protocol participants.

Usually, key exchange protocol needs to meet the following security properties:

(1) Implicit Key Authentication: The protocol participants can be convinced that no one can get the secret session key except the designated entity.
(2) Key Confirmation: The participants of protocol can determine that the other party has got a specific session key.
(3) Explicit Key Authentication: If the implicit key authentication and key confirmation properties are satisfied simultaneously.
(4) Known Key Security (KKS): The leakage of a session key does not affect the security of the other session keys.
(5) Forward Security (FS): The leakage of the participant's long-term key does not affect the security of the session key established earlier.
(6) Key Compromise Impersonation Resilience (KCIR): When one side's long-term private key is compromised, for example, Alice's, the adversary can explicitly impersonate Alice to communicate with any other side, Bob. However, we would like to guarantee that the adversary cannot impersonate the other side, Bob, to communicate with Alice and so establishes the same session key successfully even in above case.
(7) Unknown Key-Share Resilience (UKSR): Assume adversary Malice makes Alice consider herself to have established a session key K with Bob and Bob establishes the same session key K with Malice. These two sessions should be independent in essence. However, their keys are the same. So, adversary Malice can get K from Bob to break Alice's session. The protocol that can resist this kind of attack is called UKSR.

In the following section, we introduce two important two-side key exchange protocols: MQV key exchange protocol, and SM2 key exchange protocol.

A.5.1 MQV Key Exchange Protocol

MQV protocol was first proposed by Menezes et.al. in 1995 [168]. This protocol is adopted as cryptography standard by many authoritative standard organizations in the world, such as ANSI, IEEE and NIST. MQV is also incorporated into "next-generation cryptography" standard system by NSA for protecting the important and sensitive data whose level is up to national secrets. The concrete description of MQV key exchange protocol is as follows.

A.5.1.1 System Settings

Users A and B want to negotiate shared session key K. Let G be a cyclic group whose prime order is q and generator is g. User A randomly selects $d_A \in [1, q-1]$ as the private key, and calculates $P_A = g^{d_A}$ as A's public key. Similarly, user B randomly selects $d_B \in [1, q-1]$ as his private key and calculates $P_B = g^{d_B}$ as the public key.

A.5.1.2 Key Exchange

User A randomly selects $x \in [1, q-1]$, then calculates $X = g^x$ as his own ephemeral public-key value. User B randomly selects $y \in [1, q-1]$, then calculates $y \in [1, q-1]$ as his own ephemeral public-key value. Both the users exchange their identity and ephemeral public-key values, that is, user A sends message (A, B, X) to user B and user B sends message (B, A, Y) to user A.

After receiving the message, A verifies whether Y $\neq$ 0. If yes, A computes session key K $= \mathrm{H}\left(\left(YP_B^{\bar{Y}}\right)^{x+\bar{X}d_A}\right)$. Similarly, B verifies whether $X \neq 0$. If yes, B computes session key K $= \mathrm{H}\left(\left(XP_A^{\bar{X}}\right)^{y+\bar{Y}d_B}\right)$. Here, $\bar{X} = 2^l + \left(X mod 2^l\right)$, $\bar{Y} = 2^l + \left(Y mod 2^l\right)$ and $l = |q|/2$.

A.5.2 SM2 Key Exchange Protocol

In December 2010, OSCCA announced the SM2 elliptic curve public-key cryptography recommended algorithms [164], including public-key encryption algorithm, digital signature algorithm and key exchange protocol. SM2 key exchange protocol is suitable for the key exchange in commercial cryptographic application. This protocol allows both sides in communication to compute and obtain a shared session key jointly through two-time or optional three-time information transfer process.

The system settings for the SM2 key exchange protocol are as follows: Users A and B want to negotiate shared session key K with *klen*-bit length. Based on the elliptic curve $E(F_p)$ in finite field, select the basic point G with order being a big prime n. User A randomly selects $d_A \in [1, n-1]$ as his private key, and calculates $P_A = d_A G$ as his public key. Similarly, user B randomly selects $d_B \in [1, n-1]$ as his private key, and calculates $P_B = d_B G$ as his public key. In the protocol, Z_A and Z_B are hash values of user A and user B identities, respectively, and h is the cofactor, $h = \#E(F_q)/n$. Here, $\#E(F_q)$ is the order of elliptic curve $E(F_q)$; w $= \lceil(\lceil \log_2 n \rceil/2)\rceil - 1$, among them, $\lceil x \rceil$ is the smallest integer that is greater than or equal to x.

In order to obtain the same session key, both users should achieve the following operations:

(1) User A performs the following operations:
   (a) Generate random number $r_A \in [1, n-1]$, compute $R_A = r_A G = (x_1, y_1)$ and send R_A to user B.
   (b) Compute $t_A = (d_A + \bar{x}_1 r_A) mod n$, here, $\bar{x}_1 = 2^w + (x_1 \& (2^w - 1))$.

(2) User B performs the following operations:
   (a) Generate random number $r_B \in [1, n-1]$, compute $R_B = r_B G = (x_2, y_2)$ and send R_B to user A.
   (b) Compute $t_B = (d_B + \bar{x}_2 r_B) mod n$, here, $\bar{x}_2 = 2^w + (x_2 \& (2^w - 1))$.

(c) Verify whether R_A satisfies elliptic curve equation. If not, the key negotiation fails; otherwise, compute

$$V = (h \cdot t_B)(P_A + \bar{x}_1 R_A) = (x_V, y_V).$$

If V is the infinite point, the negotiation fails, otherwise, compute

$$K_B = KDF(x_V \parallel y_V \parallel Z_A \parallel Z_B, klen).$$

Here, *KDF(·, klen)* is the key derivation function whose output length is *klen*.

(d) Calculate $S_B = Hash\,(0x02||y_v||Hash(x_v||Z_A||Z_B||x_1||y_1||x_2||y_2))$; here, *Hash*(·) is the hash function.

(e) Send R_B (or S_B) to user A.

(3) User A performs the following operations:

(a) Verify whether R_B satisfies elliptic curve equation. If not, the key negotiation fails; otherwise, calculate

$$U = (h \cdot t_A)(P_B + \bar{x}_2 R_B) = (x_U, y_U).$$

If U is infinite point, the key negotiation fails; otherwise calculate

$$K_A = KDF(x_U \parallel y_U \parallel Z_A \parallel Z_B, klen).$$

(b) Calculate S_1 =Hash $(0x02||y_u||Hash\,(x_u||Z_A||Z_B||x_1||y_1||x_2||y_2))$ and check whether $S_1 = S_B$. If not, the key confirmation from B to A fails.

(c) Calculate S_A =Hash $(0x03||y_u||Hash\,(x_u||Z_A||Z_B||x_1||y_1||x_2||y_2))$ and send S_A to user B.

(4) User A performs the following operations:

Calculate S_2 = Hash $(0x03||y_v||Hash\,(x_v||Z_A||Z_B||x_1||y_1||x_2||y_2))$ and verify whether $S_2 = S_A$. If not, the key confirmation from A to B fails.

References

[1] Common Criteria Project Sponsoring Organisation. Common Criteria for Information Technology Security Evaluation. ISO/IEC International Standard 15408, Version 2.1. Genevese: Common Criteria Project Sponsoring Organisation, 1999.

[2] Avizienis A, Laprie JC, Randell B, et al. Basic Concepts of Dependable and Secure Computing. IEEE Transactions on Dependable and Secure Computing, New York: IEEE Press, 2004, 1(1): 11–33.

[3] Trusted Computing Group. TCG Specification Architecture Overview, Version 1.2. 2003 [25 January 2011]. https://www.trustedcomputinggroup.org

[4] Office of Security Commercial Code Administration. Technical Specification of Cryptographic Support Platform for Trusted Computing. 2007 [25 January 2011]. http://www.oscca.gov.cn

[5] Trusted Computing Group. TPM Main Specification, Version 1.2. 2003 [25 January 2011]. https://www.trustedcomputinggroup.org

[6] Microsoft. Security Model for the Next-Generation Secure Computing Base. 2002 [25 January 2011]. http://www.microsoft.com/resources/ngscb/documents/ngscb_security_model.doc

[7] Intel. Trusted Execution Technology Architecture Overview. 2003 [25 January 2011]. http://www.intel.com/technology/security/arch-overview.pdf

[8] Petroni N Jr, Fraser T, et al. Copilot – A Coprocessor-based Kernel Runtime Integrity Monitor. Proc of the 13th Conference on USENIX Security Symposium. San Diego: USENIX Association, 2004: 13.

[9] Seshadri A, Luk M, Shi E, et al. Pioneer: Verifying Code Integrity and Enforcing Untampered Code Execution on Legacy Systems. Proc of the 12th ACM Symposium on Operating Systems Principles. New York: ACM Press, 2005: 1–16.

[10] Sailer R, Zhang XL, Jaeger T, et al. Design and Implementation of a TCG-based Integrity Measurement Architecture. Proc of the USENIX Security '04. Berkeley: USENIX Association, 2004: 223–238.

[11] Jaeger T, Sailer R, Shankar U. PRIMA: Policy-reduced Integrity Measurement Architecture. Proc of the 11th ACM Symposium on Access Control Models and Technologies. New York: ACM Press, 2006: 19–28.

[12] Shi E, Perrig A, Doorn LV. BIND: A Fine-Grained Attestation Service for Secure Distributed Systems. Proc of the 2005 IEEE Symposium on Security and Privacy. Washington, DC: IEEE Computer Society, 2005: 154–168.

[13] Peng GJ, Pan XC, Zhang HG, et al. Dynamic Trustiness Authentication Framework Based on Software's Behavior Integrity. Proc of the 9th International Conference for Young Computer Scientists (ICYCS 2008). Hunan: IEEE Press, 2008: 2283–2288.

[14] Xu ZY, He YP, Deng LL. An Integrity Assurance Mechanism for Run-time Programs. Proc of the Information Security and Cryptology. Berlin: Springer-Verlag, 2009: 389–405.

[15] Loscocco PA, Wilson PW, Pendergrass JA, et al. Linux Kernel Integrity Measurement Using Contextual Inspection. Proc of the 2nd ACM Workshop on Scalable Trusted Computing. New York: ACM Press, 2007: 21–29.

[16] Azab AM, Ning P, Sezer EC, Zhang X. HIMA: A Hypervisor-based Integrity Measurement Agent. Proc of the 2009 Annual Computer Security Applications Conference. Washington: IEEE Press, 2009: 461–470.

[17] Azab AM, Peng N, Wang Z, et al. HyperSentry: Enabling Stealthy In-context Measurement of Hypervisor Integrity. Proc of the 17th ACM Conference on Computer and Communications Security. New York: ACM, 2010: 38–49.

[18] Berger S, Cáceres R, Goldman KA, et al. vTPM: Virtualizing the Trusted Platform Module. Proc of the 15th USENIX Security Symposium. Berkeley: USENIX Association, 2006: 305–320.

DOI 10.1515/9783110477597-010

[19] Sadeghi AR, Stüble C, Winandy M. Property-based TPM Virtualization. Proc of the 11th International Conference on Information Security. Berlin: Springer-Verlag, 2008: 1–16.

[20] Camenisch J, Lysyanskaya A. A Signature Scheme with Efficient Protocols. 3rd International Conference on Security in Communication Networks. Heidelberg: Springer-Verlag, 2003: 268–289.

[21] Brickel E, Camenisch J, Chen L. Direct Anonymous Attestation. Proc of the ACM Conference on Computer and Communications Security. New York: ACM, 2004: 132–145.

[22] Ge H, Tate SR. A Direct Anonymous Attestation Scheme for Embedded Devices. Proc of the Public Key Cryptography. Heidelberg: Springer-Verlag, 2007: 16–30.

[23] Camenisch J, Lysyanskaya A. Signature Schemes and Anonymous Credentials from Bilinear Maps. CRYPTO 2004. Heidelberg: Springer-Verlag, 2004: 56–72.

[24] Brickel E, Chen LQ, Li JT. A New Direct Anonymous Attestation Scheme from Bilinear Maps. Proc of the Trusted Computing – Challenges and Applications. Heidelberg: Springer-Verlag, 2008: 166–178.

[25] Boneh D, Boyen X. Short Signatures without Random Oracles. EUROCRYPT 2004. Heidelberg: Springer-Verlag, 2004: 56–73.

[26] Chen XF, Feng DG. Direct Anonymous Attestation for Next-Generation TPM. Journal of Computers, 2008, 43(50): 43–50, 10.4304/jcp.3.12.43-50

[27] Chen LQ, Morrissey P, Smart NP. DAA: Fixing the Pairing-based Protocols. Cryptology ePrint Archive. 2009 [25 January 2011]. http://eprint.iacr.org/2009/198

[28] Chen LQ. A DAA Scheme Using Batch Proof and Verification. International Conference of on Trust and Trustworthy Computing. Heidelberg: Springer-Verlag, 2010: 166–180.

[29] Chen LQ, Page D, Smart NP. On the Design and Implementation of an Efficient DAA Scheme. IFIP Conf of 9th Smart Card Research and Advanced Application. Heidelberg: Springer-Verlag, 2010: 223–238, 10.1007/978-3-642-12510-2_16

[30] Sailer R, Doorn VL, Ward JP. The Role of TPM in Enterprise Security. New York: IBM Research, 2004.

[31] Poritz J, Schunter M, Herreweghen EV, et al. Property Attestation Scalable and Privacy Friendly Security Assessment of Peer Computer. Zurich: IBM Research, 2004.

[32] Sadeghi AR, Stüble C. Property-based Attestation for Computing Platforms: Caring about Properties, Not Mechanisms. Proc of the 2004 Workshop on New Security Paradigms. Nova Scotia: ACM Press, 2004: 67–77.

[33] Chen LQ, Landfermann R, Löhr H, et al. A Protocol for Property-based Attestation. Proc of the 2006 ACM Workshop on Scalable Trusted Computing. Alexandria: ACM, 2006: 7–16.

[34] Chen LQ, Lohr H, Manulis M, et al. Property-based Attestation without a Trusted Third Party. Proc of the 11th International Conference on Information Security. Heidelberg: Springer-Verlag, 2008: 31–46.

[35] Kühn U, Selhorst M, Stüble C. Realizing Property-based Attestation and Sealing with Commonly Available Hard- and Software. Proc of the 2007 ACM Workshop on Scalable Trusted Computing. New York: ACM Press, 2007: 50–57.

[36] Haldar V, Chandra D, Franz M. Semantic Remote Attestation: A Virtual Machine Directed Approach to Trusted Computing. Proc of the USENIX Virtual Machine Research and Technology Symposium. Berkeley: USENIX Association, 2004: 3.

[37] Seshadri A, Perrig A, Doorn LV, et al. SWATT: Software-based Attestation for Embedded Devices. Proc of the IEEE Security & Privacy Conference. Washington: IEEE Press: 2004: 272–282.

[38] Li XY, Zuo XD, Shen CX. System Behavior-based Trustworthiness Attestation for Computing Platform. Chinese Journal of Electronics, 2007, 35(7): 1234–1239.

[39] Cisco System. Network Admission Control (NAC) Executive Overview. 2009 [25 January 2011]. http://www.cisco.com/en/US/solutions/collateral/ns340/ns394/ns171/ns466/ns617/net_implementation_white_paper0900aecd8051fc24.pdf

[40] Microsoft Corporation. Network Access Protection Platform Architecture. 2008 [25 January 2011]. http://download.microsoft.com/download/3/9/f/39ff0ca3-56d1-4d93-af46-98f92134d040/NAPArch.doc
[41] Trusted Computing Group. TNC Architecture for Interoperability. [25 January 2011]. http://www.trustedcomputinggroup.org/resources/tnc_architecture_for_interoperability_specification
[42] Zhang HG, Chen L, Zhang LQ. Research on Trusted Network Connection. Chinese Journal of Electronics, 2010, 33(4): 706–717.
[43] Goldman K, Perez R, Sailer R. Linking Remote Attestation to Secure Tunnel Endpoints. Proc of the 2006 ACM Workshop on Scalable Trusted Computing. New York: ACM Press, 2006: 21–24.
[44] Gasmi Y, Sadeghi AR, Stewin P, et al. Beyond Secure Channels. Proc of the 2007 ACM Workshop on Scalable Trusted Computing. Alexandria: ACM Press, 2007: 30–40.
[45] Armknecht F, Gasmi Y, Sadeghi AR, et al. An Efficient Implementation of Trusted Channels Based on OpenSSL. Proc of the 2008 ACM Workshop on Scalable Trusted Computing. New York: ACM Press, 2008: 41–50.
[46] Sadeghi AR, Selhorst C. Stüble C, et al. TCG Inside? – A Note on TPM Specification Compliance. Proc of the 2006 ACM Workshop on Scalable Trusted Computing. New York: ACM Press, 2006: 47–56.
[47] Cui Q, Shi WX. An Approach for Compliance Validation of TPM Through Applications. Graduate School of Chinese Academy of Science. 2008, 25(5): 649–656.
[48] Zhang HG, Yan F, Fu JM, et al. Research on Theory and Key Technology of Trusted Computing Platform Security Testing and Evaluation. Science China, 2010, 53(3): 434–453, 10.1007/s11432-010-0062-4.
[49] Bruschi D, Cavallaro L, Lanzi A, et al. Replay Attack in TCG Specification and Solution. Proc of the 21st Annual Computer Security Applications Conference. Washington: IEEE Press, 2005.
[50] Chen LQ, Ryan M. Attack, Solution and Verification for Shared Authorisation Data in TCG TPM. 6th International Workshop on Formal Aspects in Security and Trust. Berkeley: USENIX Association, 2009: 201–216
[51] Backes M, Maffei M, Unruh D. Zero-Knowledge in the Applied Pi-calculus and Automated Verification of the Direct Anonymous Attestation Protocol. Proc of the 2008 IEEE Symposium on Security and Privacy. Washington: IEEE Press, 2008: 202–215.
[52] Datta A, Franklin J, Garg D, et al. A Logic of Secure Systems and Its Application to Trusted Computing. Proc of the 2009 IEEE Symposium on Security and Privacy. Washington: IEEE Press, 2009: 221–236.
[53] Chen XF, Feng DG. Model Checking of Trusted Cryptographic Module. Journal on Communications, 2010, 31(1): 59–65, 10.3969/j.issn.1000-436X.2010.01.009
[54] Chen J. Security Analysis and Application of Trusted Platform Module. Beijing: Institute of Computation Technology Chinese Academy of Science, 2006.
[55] Trusted Computing Group. TCG Certification Program Announcement. [25 January 2011]. http://www.infineon.com/cms/en/corporate/press/news/releases/2009/INFCCS200912-015.html;
http://www.trustedcomputinggroup.org/certification
[56] Trusted Computing Group. Protection Profile of PC Client Specific Trusted Platform Module TPM Family 1.2. [25 January 2011]
http://www.trustedcomputinggroup.org/resources/tpm_12_protection_profile/
[57] Trusted Computing Group. Security Conformance Evaluation of the Infineon TPM Confirmed by Common Criteria Certificate. [25 January 2011].
http://www.infineon.com/cms/en/corporate/press/news/releases/2009/INFCCS200912-015.html

[58] Wang D, Feng DG. Trust Degree-based Model of Chain of Trust. 7th Chinese Conference of Information and Communication Security. New Jersey: Science Press, 2010: 1–5.
[59] Nie XW, Feng DG. Modified Security Model Based on Dynamic Trusted Degree. Journal on Communications, 2008, 29(10): 37–44.
[60] Liu ZW, Feng DG. TPM-based Dynamic Integrity Measurement Architecture. Journal of Electronics & Information Technology, 10.3724/SP.J.1146.2009.00408, 2010, 32(4): 875–879.
[61] Hu H, Feng DG. BIFI: Architectural Support for Information Flow Integrity Measurement. Proc of the 2008 International Conference on Computer Science and Software Engineering. Washington: IEEE Computer Society, 2008: 605–609.
[62] Qin Y, Feng DG, Liu CY. TPM Context Manager and Dynamic Configuration Management for Trusted Virtualization Platform. Wuhan University Journal of Natural Sciences, 2008, 13(5): 1–8.
[63] Chen XF, Feng DG. Direct Anonymous Attestation Based on Bilinear Maps. Journal of Software, 10.3724/SP.J.1001.2010.03579, 2010, 21(8): 2070–2078.
[64] Chen XF, Feng DG. A New Direct Anonymous Attestation from Bilinear Maps. Proc of the 2008 International Symposium on Trusted Computing. Washington: IEEE Computer Society, 2008: 2308–2313.
[65] Feng DG, Xu J, Chen XF. An Efficient Direct Anonymous Attestation Scheme with Forward Security. WSEAS Transactions on Communications, 2009, 10(8): 1076–1085.
[66] Chen XF, Feng DG. A Direct Anonymous Attestation Scheme in Multi-Domain Environment. Chinese Journal of Computers, 2008, 31(7): 1122–1130, 10.3321/j.issn:0254-4164.2008.07.007
[67] Feng DG, Qin Yu. A Property-based Attestation Protocol for TCM. Science China, 2010, 53(3): 454–464, 10.1007/s11432-010-0057-1
[68] Qin Y, Feng DG. Component Property-based Remote Attestation. Journal of Software, 2009, 20(6): 1625–1641, 10.3724/SP.J.1001.2009.03343
[69] Qin Y, Feng DG, Xu Z. An Anonymous Property-based Attestation Protocol from Bilinear Maps. Proc of the International Conference on Computational Science and Engineering. Washington: IEEE Computer Society, 2009: 732–738.
[70] Yu AM, Chu XB, Feng DG. Research of Platform Anonymous Identity Management Based on Trusted Chip. Chinese Journal of Computers, 2010, 33(9): 1–10, 10.3724/SP.J.1016.2010.01703
[71] Wang D, Feng DG, Xu Z. An Approach to Data Sealing Based on Trusted Virtualization Platform. Journal of Computer Research and Development, 2009, 46(8): 1325–1333.
[72] Li H, Qin Y, Feng DG. Virtual Monotonic Counters Using Trusted Platform Module. Journal of Computer Research and Development, 2011, 48(3): 415–422.
[73] Chu XB, Qin Y. A Distributed Usage Control System Based on Trusted Computing. Chinese Journal of Computers, 2010, 33(1): 93–102, 10.3724/SP.J.1016.2010.00093.
[74] Li H, Hu H. UCFS: Building a Usage-controlled File System with a Trusted Platform Module. Proc of the 1st Chinese Conference on Trust Computing Theory and Practice. Beijing: Tsinghua University Press, 2009: 10–23.
[75] Yu AM, Feng DG, Liu R. TBDRM: A TPM-based Secure DRM Architecture. Proc of the International Conference on Computational Science and Engineering. Washington: IEEE Computer Society, 2009: 671–677.
[76] Hu H, Li H, Feng DG. L-UCON: Towards layered Access Control with UCON. Proc of the International Conference on Computational Science and Engineering. Washington: IEEE Computer Society, 2009: 823–829.
[77] Chen XF. The Formal Analysis and Testing of Trusted Platform Module. Chinese Journal of Computers, 2009, 32(4): 27–34, 10.3724/SP.J.1016.2009.00646.
[78] Li H, Hu H, Chen XF. Research on Compliant Testing Method of Trusted Cryptography Module. Chinese Journal of Computers, 2009, 32(4): 1–10, 10.3724/SP.J.1016.2009.00654.

[79] Feng DG. Research Progress of Trusted Computing, Development Report of Chinese Cryptography 2008. Beijing: Publishing House of Electronics Industry, 2009: 343–360.
[80] Shen CX, Zhang HG, Feng DG, et al. Survey of Information Security. Science in China (Series E), 2007, 37(2), 10.3321/j.issn:1006-9275.2007.02.001.
[81] Feng DG. Theory and Practice of Security Protocol. Beijing: Tsinghua University Press, 2011.
[82] Feng DG, Qin Y, Wang D, Chu XB. Research on Trusted Computing Technology. Journal of Computer Research and Development, 2011, 48(8): 1332–1349.
[83] Lampson B, Abadi M, Burrows M, Wobber E. Authentication in Distributed Systems: Theory and Practice. ACM Transactions on Computer Systems (TOCS). New York: ACM Press, 1992, 10(4): 265–310. DOI:10.1145/121132.121160
[84] Trusted Computing Group. Mobile Trusted Module Specification, Reversion 1. [25 January 2011]. https://www.trustedcomputinggroup.org/specs/mobilephone
[85] China TCM Union. [25 January 2011]. http://www.tcmu.org.cn
[86] Office of Security Commercial Code Administration. Functionality and Interface Specification of Cryptographic Support Platform for Trusted Computing. [25 January 2011]. http://www.oscca.gov.cn/UpFile/File64.PDF
[87] Trusted Computing Group. TCG PC Client-specific TPM Interface Specification (TIS), Version 1.21 Revision 1.00. [25 January 2011]. http://www.trustedcomputinggroup.org/developers/pc_client
[88] Trusted Computing Group. TCG Generic Server Specification, Version 1.0 Revision 0.8. [25 January 2011]. https://www.trustedcomputinggroup.org
[89] Trusted Computing Group. TCG Software Stack (TSS) Specification, Version 1.10. [25 January 2011]. http://www.trustedcomputinggroup.org/developers/software_stack
[90] Trusted Computing Group. TCG Specification Trusted Network Connect – TNC Architecture for Interoperability Revision 1.1. [25 January 2011]. http://www.trustedcomputinggroup.org
[91] ISO/IEC 11889-1. Information Technology – Trusted Platform Module, 2009.
[92] ISO/IEC 11889-1:2015. Information Technology – TPM Library, 2015.
[93] Intel Corporation. Hardware-based Technology for Enhancing Server Platform Security. [25 January 2011]. http://www.intel.com/technology/security/downloads/arch-overview.pdf
[94] Intel Corporation. Intel Virtualization Technology: Hardware Support for Efficient Processor Virtualization. [25 January 2011]. http://en.wikipedia.org/wiki/AMD-V#AMD_virtualization_.28AMD-V.29
[95] ISO/IEC International Standard 15408: Common Criteria for Information Technology Security Evaluation, 1999.
[96] Avizienis A, Laprie J, Randell B, et al. Basic Concepts and Taxonomy of Dependable and Secure Computing. IEEE Transactions on Dependable and Secure Computing, 2004, 1(1):11–33.10.1109/TDSC.2004.2
[97] Intel Corporation. LaGrande Technology Preliminary Architecture Specification. Intel Publication no. D52212, May 2006.
[98] Kauer, B. OSLO: Improving the Security of Trusted Computing. SS'07: Proc of the 16th USENIX Security Symposium on USENIX Security Symposium. Berkeley, CA: USENIX Association, 2007: 1–9.
[99] Trusted GRUB Web site. [25 January 2011]. http://projects.sirrix.com/trac/trustedgrub
[100] Maruyama H, Seliger F, Nagaratnam N, et al. Trusted Platform on Demand (TPod). [25 January 2011]. http://citeseerx.ist.psu.edu/viewdoc/summary?doi=10.1.1.207.5700
[101] England P, Lampson B, Manferdelli J, et al. A Trusted Open Platform. IEEE Computer, 2003, 36(7): 55–62.

[102] Sailer R, Jaeger T, Zhang X, et al. Attestation-based Policy Enforcement for Remote Access. Proc of the 11th ACM conference on Computer and Communications Security. New York: ACM Press, 2004: 308–317.

[103] McCune JM, Parno BJ, Perrig A, et al. Flicker: An Execution Infrastructure for TCB Minimization. ACM SIGOPS Operating Systems Review. New York: ACM Press, 2008, 42(4): 315–328.

[104] McCune JM, Li Y, Qu N, et al. TrustVisor: Efficient TCB Reduction and Attestation. 2010 IEEE Symposium on Security and Privacy. IEEE, 2010: 143–158.

[105] Trusted Computing Group. TCG Virtualized Trusted Platform Architecture Specification, Version 1.0. [8 August 2017]. https://www.trustedcomputinggroup.org/wp-content/uploads/TCG_VPWG_Architecture_V1-0_R0-26_FINAL.pdf

[106] Challener D, Yoder K, Catherman R, Safford D, et al. A Practical Guide to Trusted Computing. Indianapolis: IBM Press, 2008: 77–102.

[107] Stüble C, Zaerin A. µTSS – A Simplified Trusted Software Stack. Lecture Notes in Computer Science. Berlin: Springer Verlag, 2010: 124–140.

[108] Pearson S. Trusted Computing Platforms, the Next Security Solution. HP Laboratories Bristol: Trusted E-Services Laboratory, 2002.

[109] Trusted Computing Group. TCG PC Client specific Implementation Specification for Conventional BIOS, Version 1.20 FINAL Revision 1.00. 2005. [25 January 2011]. http://www.trustedcomputinggroup.org/developers/pc_client

[110] Trusted Computing Group. TCG Platform Reset Attack Mitigation Specification, Version 1.00 Revision 1.00. 2008 [25 November 2011]. https://www.trustedcomputinggroup.org/developers/pc_client

[111] Trusted Computing Group. TCG EFI Platform Specification, Version 1.20 Final Revision 1.0. 2006. [25 January 2011]. https://www.trustedcomputinggroup.org/developers/pc_client

[112] Trusted Computing Group. TCG EFI Protocol, Version 1.20 Final Revision 1.00. 2006. [25 January 2011]. https://www.trustedcomputinggroup.org/developers/pc_client

[113] Trusted Computing Group. Mandatory and Optional TPM Commands for Servers, Version 1.0 Revision 1.1. 2007. [25 January 2011]. https://www.trustedcomputinggroup.org/developers/server

[114] Trusted Computing Group. TCG ACPI Specification, Version 1.00 – FINAL Revision 1.00. 2005. [25 January 2011]. https://www.trustedcomputinggroup.org/developers/server

[115] Trusted Computing Group. TCG Itanium Architecture-based Server Specification, Version 1.0. 2006. [25 January 2011]. https://www.trustedcomputinggroup.org/developers/server

[116] Trusted Computing Group. TCG Mobile Reference Architecture Specification, Version 1.0 Revision 1. [25 January 2011]. https://www.trustedcomputinggroup.org/developers/mobile

[117] Trusted Computing Group. TCG Mobile Abstraction Layer Specification, Version 1.0 Revision 2.03. [25 January 2011]. http://www.trustedcomputinggroup.org/developers/mobile

[118] Trusted Computing Group. Mobile Trusted Module 2.0 Use Cases Specification, Version 1.0. [25 January 2011]. https://www.trustedcomputinggroup.org/developers/mobile

[119] Dietrich K. An Integrated Architecture for Trusted Computing for Java-enabled Embedded Devices. Proc of the 2007 ACM Workshop on Scalable Trusted Computing. New York: ACM Press, 2007: 2–6.

[120] Dietrich K, Winter J. Implementation Aspects of Mobile and Embedded Trusted Computing. Proc of the 2nd International Conference on Trust and Trustworthy Computing. Heidelberg: Springer Verlag, 2009: 29–44.

[121] Dietrich K, Winte J. Towards Customizable, Application-specific Mobile Trusted Modules. Proc of the 5th ACM Workshop on Scalable Trusted Computing. New York: ACM Press, 2010: 31–40.

[122] Ekberg JE, Kylänpää M. Mobile Trusted Module (MTM) – An Introduction. Helsinki, Finland: Nokia Research Center, 2007.

[123] Strasser M. Department of Computer Science Swiss Federal Institute of Technology Zurich. A Software-based TPM Emulator for Linux. [25 January 2011]. http://tpm-emulator.berlios.de/
[124] Murray D G, Milos G, Hand S. Improving Xen Security Through Disaggregation. Proc of the 4th ACM SIGPLAN/SIGOPS International Conference on Virtual Execution Environments. New York: ACM Press, 2008: 151–160.
[125] Anderson M J, Moffie M, Dalton C I. Towards Trustworthy Virtualization Environments: Xen Library OS Security Service Infrastructure. HP Laboratories Bristol: Trusted Systems Laboratory, 2007.
[126] Cloud Security Alliance. [25 January 2011]. https://cloudsecurityalliance.org/
[127] Krautheim F J, Phatak D S, Sherman A T. Introducing the Trusted Virtual Environment Module: A New Mechanism for Rooting Trust in Cloud Computing. Proc of the 3rd International Conference on Trust and Trustworthy Computing. Berlin: Springer Verlag, 2010: 211–227.
[128] Official website of OpenTC. [25 January 2011]. http//www.opentc.net
[129] Chen LQ, Ryan M. Attack, Solution and Verification for Shared Authorization Data in TCG TPM. FAST'09 Proc of the 6th International Conference on Formal Aspects in Security and Trust. Berlin, Heidelberg: Springer-Verlag, 2010: 201–216.
[130] Chen J. Security Analysis and Application of Trusted Platform Module. Beijing: Institute of Computation Technology Chinese Academy of Science, 2006.
[131] Arapinis M, Ritter E, Ryan M. StatVerif: Verification of Stateful Processes. Proc of the 24th IEEE Computer Security Foundations Symposium (CSF 2011).Washington, DC: IEEE Computer Society, 2011: 33–47.
[132] Delaune S, Kremer S, Ryan M, Steel G. Formal Analysis of Protocols Based on TPM State Registers. Proc of the 24th IEEE Computer Security Foundations Symposium (CSF 2011).Washington, DC: IEEE Computer Society, 2011: 66–82.
[133] Chen LQ. A DAA Scheme Requiring Less TPM Resources. Lecture Notes in Computer Science. Berlin: Springer Verlag, 2011: 350–365. DOI: 10.1007/978-3-642-16342-5_26
[134] Brickell E, Li J. A Pairing-based DAA Scheme Further Reducing TPM Resources. Lecture Notes in Computer Science. Berlin, Heidelberg: Springer, 2010: 181–195. DOI: 10.1007/978-3-642-13869-0_12
[135] Safford D, Zohar M. A Trusted Linux Client (TLC). [25 January 2011]. http://www.research.ibm.com/gsal/tcpa/tlc.pdf
[136] Alam M, Zhang XW, Nauman M, Ali T, Seifert JP. Model-based Behavioral Attestation. Proc of the 13th ACM Symposium on Access Control Models and Technologies (SACMAT'08). New York: ACM Press, 2008: 175–184. DOI:10.1145/1377836.1377864
[137] Yoshihama S, Ebringer T, Nakamura M, Munetoh S, Maruyama H. WS-Attestation: Efficient and Fine-grained Remote Attestation on Web Services. ICWS'05 Proc of the IEEE International Conference on Web Services. Washington, DC: IEEE Computer Society, 2005: 743–750. DOI: 10.1109/ICWS.2005.136
[138] Chen LQ, Ryan M. Offline Dictionary Attack on TCG TPM Weak Authorisation Data, and Solution. Proc of Future of Trust in Computing, Vieweg&Teubner, 2008. DOI: 10.1007/978-3-8348-9324-6_20
[139] Qin Y, Chu XB, Feng DG, Feng W. DAA Protocol Analysis and Verification. Proc of the 3rd International Conference on Trusted Systems (INTRUST 2011). Berlin, Heidelber: Springer-Verlag, 2011: 338–350. DOI:10.1007/978-3-642-32298-3_21
[140] Qin Y, Wu QX, Chu XB. Design and Analysis on Direct Anonymous Attestation for Security Chip. Intelligence Information Processing and Trusted Computing (IPTC). Washington, DC: IEEE Computer Society, 2011: 13–18. DOI: 10.1109/IPTC.2011.11
[141] Nauman M, Khan S, Zhang XW, Seifert JP. Beyond Kernel-level Integrity Measurement: Enabling Remote Attestation for the Android Platform. Proc of the 3rd International Conference

on Trust and Trustworthy Computing (TRUST'10). Berlin, Heidelberg: Springer-Verlag, 2010: 1–15. DOI: 10.1007/978-3-642-13869-0_1

[142] Kostiainen K, Asokan N, Ekberg JE. Practical Property-based Attestation on Mobile Devices. Lecture Notes in Computer Science. Berlin, Heidelberg: Springer-Verlag, 2011: 78–92. DOI: 10.1007/978-3-642-21599-5_6

[143] Cesena E, Lohr H, Ramunno G, Sadeghi AR, Vernizzi D. Anonymous Authentication with TLS and DAA. Proc of the 3rd International Conference on Trust and Trustworthy Computing (TRUST'10). Berlin, Heidelberg: Springer-Verlag, 2010: 47–62. DOI: 10.1007/978-3-642-13869-0_4

[144] Trusted Computing Group. TCG Specification Trusted Network Connect – TNC IF-PEP: Protocol Binding for Radius Revision 0.7. [25 January 2011]. https://www.trustedcomputinggroup.org

[145] Trusted Computing Group. TCG Specification Trusted Network Connect – TNCIF-TNCCS: TLV Binding Revision 10. [25 January 2011]. https://www.trustedcomputinggroup.org

[146] Trusted Computing Group. TCG Specification Trusted Network Connect – TNC IF-IMV Revision 8. [25 January 2011]. https://www.trustedcomputinggroup.org

[147] Trusted Computing Group. TCG Specification Trusted Network Connect – TNC IF-M: TLV Binding Revision 30. [25 January 2011]. https://www.trustedcomputinggroup.org

[148] Trusted Computing Group. TCG Specification Trusted Network Connect – TNCIF-PTS Revision 1.0. [25 January 2011]. https://www.trustedcomputinggroup.org

[149] Trusted Computing Group. TCG Specification Trusted Network Connect – TNC IF-T: Protocol Binding for Tunnelled EAP Methods. Revision 10. [25 January 2011]. https://www.trustedcomputinggroup.org

[150] Trusted Computing Group. TNC Certified Products List. [25 January 2011]. http://www.trustedcomputinggroup.org/certification/tnc_certified_products_list

[151] libTNC Web site. [25 January 2011]. http://libtnc.sourceforge.net/

[152] Open1x Web site. [25 January 2011]. http://open1x.sourceforge.net/

[153] OpenSEA Web site. [25 January 2011]. http://www.openseaalliance.org/index.php?option=com_content&view=article&id=15&Itemid=30

[154] strongSwan Web site. [25 January 2011]. http://www.strongswan.org/

[155] Trust@FHH Web site. [25 January 2011]. http://trust.inform.fh-hannover.de/joomla/index.php/about

[156] Huawei Product. [25 January 2011]. http://www.huawei.com

[157] Hongpei L, Beijing TOPSEC Company. Overview of Trusted Network Architecture. [25 January 2011]. http://www.cd-topsec.com.cn/

[158] Anchtech, Trusted Network Connection Systems. [25 January 2011]. http://www.it.com.cn/f/solution/058/25/163036.htm

[159] Department of Commerce/NIST. Advanced Encryption Standard, FIPSPUB 197 [26 November 2001].

[160] Specification of SMS4. Block Ciphers for WLAN Products SMS4. [8 August 2017]. http://www.oscca.gov.cn/UpFile/200621016423197990.pdf

[161] Rivest RL, Shamir A, Adleman LM. A Method for Obtaining Digital Signatures and Public-Key Cryptosystems. Communications of the ACM, 1978, 21(2): 120–126. 10.1145/357980.358017

[162] Koblitz N. Elliptic Curve Cryptosystems. Mathematics of Computation, 1987, 48(177): 203–209. 10.1142/9789812703309_0006

[163] Miller VS. Use of Elliptic Curves in Cryptography. Lecture Notes in Computer Sciences: 218 on Advances in Cryptology- CRYPTO 85, 1985: 417–426. 10.1007/3-540-39799-X_31

[164] Public Key Cryptographic Algorithm SM2 Based on Elliptic Curves. [8 August 2017]. http://www.oscca.gov.cn/UpFile/2010122214822692.pdf

[165] American National Standard X9.62-2005. Public Key Cryptography for the Financial Services Industry. The Elliptic Curve Digital Signature Algorithm (ECDSA), 2005.

[166] Department of Commerce/NIST. Announcing the Secure Hash Standard. FIPSPUB 180-2, 2002.

[167] SM3 Cryptographic Hash Algorithm. [8 August 2017]. http://www.oscca.gov.cn/UpFile/20101222141857786.pdf

[168] Menezes S, Qu M, Vanstone S. Some New Key Agreement Protocols Providing Mutual Implicit Authentication. Second Workshop on Selected Areas in Cryptography (SAC 95), Heidelberg: Springer-Verlag, 1995: 22–32.

Index

DOI 10.1515/9783110477597-011

Advances in Computer Science

Volume 1
Color Image Watermarking,
Q. Su, 2016
ISBN 978-3-11-048757-2, e-ISBN (PDF) 978-3-11-048773-2,
e-ISBN (EPUB) 978-3-11-048763-3, Set-ISBN 978-3-11-048776-3

www.degruyter.com

Bei Fragen zur Produktsicherheit wenden Sie sich bitte an:
If you have any questions regarding product safety,
please contact:

Walter de Gruyter GmbH
Genthiner Straße 13
10785 Berlin
productsafety@degruyterbrill.com